Twenty-First-Century Popular Fiction

Edited by Bernice M. Murphy and Stephen Matterson

EDINBURGH
University Press

Edinburgh University Press is one of the leading university presses in the UK. We publish academic books and journals in our selected subject areas across the humanities and social sciences, combining cutting-edge scholarship with high editorial and production values to produce academic works of lasting importance. For more information visit our website: edinburghuniversitypress.com

Edinburgh University Press Ltd
The Tun – Holyrood Road, 12(2f) Jackson's Entry, Edinburgh EH8 8PJ

Typeset in in Goudy Old Style
by R. J. Footring Ltd, Derby, UK, and
printed and bound in Great Britain by
CPI Group (UK) Ltd, Croydon CR0 4YY

A CIP record for this book is available from the British Library

ISBN 978 1 4744 1484 5 (hardback)
ISBN 978 1 4744 1486 9 (webready PDF)
ISBN 978 1 4744 1485 2 (paperback)
ISBN 978 1 4744 1487 6 (epub)

Contents

Acknowledgements

The editors would like to thank their colleagues in the School of English, Trinity College, Dublin, and staff in the college library for their support and advice; a legal deposit copyright library is a stunning resource for studying popular fiction.

The enthusiasm and critical engagement of students undertaking the MPhil in Popular Literature since its inception in 2005 have also been invaluable. It has been a delight to work with Rebecca Mackenzie, Jackie Jones and Adela Rauchova at Edinburgh University Press, who were instrumental in the collection's inception and development.

We would like to thank DC Entertainment for permission to use the images from *The Multiversity* #1, © DC Comics.

Bernice Murphy would like to dedicate this book to her aunt, Brid McBride, whose love of reading has always been an inspiration.

Introduction: 'Changing the Story' – Popular Fiction Today

Bernice M. Murphy and Stephen Matterson

In the months following the 2008 death of literary icon David Foster Wallace, among the heartfelt tributes, critical reassessments and extracts from his work that circulated on the web was the archived syllabus for his 1994 college class 'Literary Analysis I: Prose Fiction'. Some observers were surprised by the fact that Wallace's reading list was entirely composed of works of popular fiction. The novels cited included works by suspense author Mary Higgins Clark (*Where Are the Children?*) and horror superstar Stephen King (*Carrie*), thrillers by Thomas Harris (*Black Sunday* and *The Silence of the Lambs*), a blockbuster by Jackie Collins (*Rock Star*), a Western (*Lonesome Dove* by Larry McMurtry) and a work of fantasy (*The Lion, the Witch and the Wardrobe* by C. S. Lewis). Wallace was unapologetic about the fact that the course focused on 'what's considered popular, or commercial fiction', and argued that 'if the course works, we'll end up being able to locate some rather sophisticated techniques and/or themes lurking below the surface of novels that, on a quick read on airplane or beach, look like nothing but entertainment'. Under the heading 'WARNING', he added:

> Don't let any potential lightweightish-looking [sic] qualities of these texts delude you into thinking that this will be a blow-off-type class. These 'popular' texts will end up being harder than more conventionally 'literary' works to unpack and read critically.[1]

Wallace's prescient defence of genre fiction is interesting for many reasons, and not least because it rightfully acknowledges that thoughtful academic engagement with popular fiction is just as challenging – and worthwhile – as the study of more conventionally 'literary' texts. It also anticipates a change that has taken place in academia more generally. Since the 1990s, and certainly since the turn of the century, the study of popular fiction has been transformed from a relatively niche topic into one of the most vibrant and rapidly expanding areas of enquiry within contemporary literary studies. Works by genre authors are now taught at secondary, undergraduate and advanced postgraduate level in schools and universities across the UK, Ireland, the US and much of the rest of the world. Furthermore, as critics such as Joshua Rothman and Lev Grossman have argued, the boundaries between the 'popular' and the 'literary' are rapidly eroding, and more and more 'serious' writers are using genre in ways that would have been largely unthinkable a generation ago. Colson Whitehead was awarded the 2017 Pulitzer Prize for Fiction for a work of alternative history, *The Underground Railroad*, which was also shortlisted for the 2017 Arthur C. Clarke award for science fiction. His previous novel, *Zone One* (2011), was a work of 'Zombie lit'. Gillian Flynn's *Gone Girl* (2012) was nominated in 2013 for a major UK literary prize, the Baileys Women's Prize for Fiction, while Stephen King has now published in the *New Yorker* on several occasions. As one critic has noted, 'There was a time when a writer who topped bestseller lists with terrifying stories of homicidal writers, sadistic fans and haunted pet cemeteries would not have fit inside a magazine that graces its covers with a monocled dandy.'[2] *Twenty-First-Century Popular Fiction* reflects the fact that scholars engaging with this kind of writing no longer need to justify its standing as an intellectually challenging and worthwhile field of academic enquiry: this may now be taken as a given.

This collection is therefore not intended to serve as an introduction to or an overview of the academic study of popular fiction, or as an exploration of its historical origins. A growing body of valuable work has already been done in these areas, and those looking for further reading in this area might begin with the recommendations cited at the end of this Introduction. As the title underlines, the aim of this collection is to provide an informed, accessible and authoritative snapshot of the current state of popular fiction. Any undertaking of this kind must be, by its very nature, selective, so our emphasis here is on the work of twenty contemporary authors who have made key contributions to both the individual genres or sub-genres they are most associated with, as well as the current state of popular fiction more generally. Each chapter undertakes a timely assessment (or reassessment, in the case of the more established authors) of the work of the author concerned, as well as their place within the genre or genres with which they are most associated. The wider cultural standing of each author and their work is also considered. Finally, you will find useful supplementary material at the end of each chapter, which is intended to stimulate further reading and research. This consists of an annotated run down of 'key works' within the author's oeuvre as well as a select list of further critical reading. While we hope that the scope and accessibility of the collection mean that it will be of interest to the more general reader with an interest in contemporary popular fiction, the book also represents a valuable pedagogical and research tool, with the essays serving as starting points for further reading and research.

To date, little academic work has been done on many of the authors considered in this collection. This is either because they have come to public prominence very recently (Flynn, Howey, Priest, Brooks and James), or because their work has, with a few notable exceptions, tended to be critically overlooked, or, until recently, critically neglected (Picoult, Morrison, Roberts and Gaiman). An important part of the collection's remit, then, is to provide valuable critical assessments of the work of authors who, in some cases, are very high profile but, at the same time, under-studied. Our contributors are all experts on the authors they have written on here (and in several cases have written books about the writer and/or genre under discussion).

The collection is not organised by genre or historical period, but rather in order of when the subjects of the chapters were born, beginning with the most senior, Larry McMurtry (born in 1938), and ending with Hugh Howey and Cherie Priest (both born in 1975). We have chosen this method of organisation for several reasons. The first is that it allows us to begin by considering recent publications by authors who have, by and large, already had very long and successful publishing careers. Although McMurtry is a good decade older than Baby Boomers King, Pratchett, Martin and Roberts, before the advent of the present century all five authors had already had an immense impact upon the evolution of the genres with which they are most associated. McMurtry is the acknowledged master of the Western, a genre which was, during the middle of the twentieth century, immensely popular in print, film and television, but which is now generally regarded to have become less and less popular – yet at the same time, as Stephen Matterson's essay suggests, which has worked its way into a wider range of other genres, including horror, fantasy, science fiction, steampunk and the superhero narrative.

Stephen King is the most famous living horror writer (a genre that has otherwise been in a state of mainstream decline since its commercial peak in the mid-late 1980s) and as he has aged one of the most interesting aspects of his work has been his characteristic willingness to revisit his own oeuvre, as discussed here by Rebecca Janicker in the context of his elegiac 2013 novel *Dr Sleep*, the sequel to the 1977 classic *The Shining*. Questions of legacy and authorial longevity also surface in Jim Shanahan's chapter on Terry Pratchett, the fantasy author whose Discworld series only grew ever more ambitious, intellectually rich, and loaded in poignant thematic and personal significance as he very publicly struggled with serious illness. Longevity and developing reputation also feature in the chapter on George R. R. Martin, who, as Gerard Hynes observes, was a respected writer of fantasy and science fiction long before 2011. In that year the debut of the HBO TV series *Game of Thrones*, based on the 'A Song of Ice and Fire' epic fantasy novels (1996–), made him one of the most famous genre writers in the world. However, neither commercial success nor longstanding dominance of a major genre guarantees wider critical notice. Indeed, as Jarlath Killeen's chapter on Nora Roberts observes, although she has been for many decades one of the most prolific, beloved and commercially significant genre authors of our time, as is the case with the popular romance more generally, her importance has often been sorely overlooked.

We also have chapters on newer and more recently emerged authors, such as Gillian Flynn, Stephenie Meyer, Suzanne Collins, Cherie Priest, Hugh Howey, Max Brooks, Tana French and Jo Nesbø – who have all made a major impact within their respective genres and sub-genres since 2000. Some of the authors here have also been selected because they provide an opportunity for the discussion of notable recent trends within popular fiction. For instance, *World War Z* (2006) author Max Brooks helped to establish the zombie novel as a mainstay of popular publishing in recent years (the walking dead had by and large been confined to the big screen before then). Hugh Howey is a respected science fiction author who has made savvy use of the internet as both a publishing and a marketing tool. Like that of E. L. James, Howey's journey to publishing success underlines the ways in which many emerging popular fiction authors have decided to bypass or modify traditional publishing models (at least initially). Kate Roddy's chapter on Grant Morrison underlines the fact that comic books/graphic novels have become one of the most significant growth areas within popular fiction publishing in recent years, while Cherie Priest is at the forefront of the current renaissance of the steampunk sub-genre. Similarly, China Miéville is one of the writers most associated with the intriguing emergent publishing category the 'New Weird'.

Media crossover of popular fiction has been a constant aspect of its very nature, from the nineteenth-century stage adaptations of the Sherlock Holmes stories through to the potent symbiotic relation between the Western novel and the Western film. But this crossover has become remarkable since the turn of the twenty-first century, with a series of transformations related to the writing, publication and consumption of popular fiction, all of which are rooted in the technological revolution of the internet age from the early 1990s. The emergence of affordable and accessible e-readers, the rapid mainstreaming of digital publishing, and the arrival of internet fan fiction have resulted in some of the most radical developments in popular reading habits since the advent of mass literacy, and these have taken place in just over a generation. As the chapters here on E. L. James and Hugh Howey in particular illustrate, today's emerging authors have the option to bypass traditional publishing gatekeepers and methods altogether: both writers initially self-published their work online with considerable success before being taken up by mainstream print publishers. But, as this collection shows, even authors whose careers began long before this era have been profoundly affected by these innovations. Furthermore, as the chapters here on Neil Gaiman and J. K. Rowling demonstrate, the shrewd use of social media platforms such as Twitter now provide popular authors with a means of maintaining a high public profile that both intersects with and yet transcends their written work and subsidiary properties.

Furthermore, the longstanding tendency for well received works of popular fiction to spread rapidly to extra-literary platforms is now more evident than ever. At the time of writing, seventeen of the authors discussed here have had at least one (and in quite a few cases *many*) of their works adapted for television, film or comic book format. Indeed, for some of our more recent authors in particular, the relationship between on-screen and off-screen properties has been so blurred as to be increasingly interchangeable: both Gillian Flynn and J. K. Rowling have written screenplays based on their own work (Flynn adapted *Gone Girl* and Rowling expanded the 'Potterverse' to the USA in the original screenplay *Fantastic Beasts and Where to Find Them*), while the TV adaptation of George R. R. Martin's series A Song of Ice and Fire has now actually overtaken the plot of the novels upon which it is based. E. L. James famously began her writing career penning online fan fiction based upon the work of another of our subjects (Stephenie Meyer); and as Kate Harvey's essay on Rowling notes, the Harry Potter author has used her own web domain, Pottermore, greatly to enlarge the ever-growing Potterverse and the author's name is becoming a brand (users of the site will note that below the title of the homepage are the words 'From J. K. Rowling').

These transformations and crossovers are also indicative of the increasing elasticity of genre in popular fiction. It is true that many of the authors discussed here are operating within or are tweaking long-established genres and also working within long-established literary traditions. The crime novel or thriller still holds steady as a major publication area, and our essays focus on four of the most significant post-2000 areas: Dan Brown's conspiracy thrillers, Gillian Flynn's Domestic Noir, Jo Nesbø's Nordic Noir and Tana French's take on the police procedural. All of these authors work within a defined field with a recognisable literary history, and this is true of other key writers. *Fifty Shades of Grey* may have been 2012's biggest publishing sensation, but James's immensely successful Fifty Shades trilogy owes as much to the themes and plot conventions established in classic novels such as Samuel Richardson's *Pamela* (1740) and John Cleland's *Fanny Hill* (1748) as it does to the 'bodice ripper' tradition of the 1970s and '80s. Similarly, while Gillian Flynn's *Gone Girl* – published in 2012 – did much to fuel the demand for female-focused psychological suspense novels that are now categorised as 'Domestic Noir', novels of this sort are certainly nothing new, and Flynn's interest in domestic peril, untrustworthy husbands and dangerous women has a long lineage that includes Charles Perrault's *Bluebeard* (1697), Charlotte Brönte's *Jane Eyre* (1847) and Daphne du Maurier's *Rebecca* (1938), to mention only a few of the most obvious precursors. Stephen King provides a shrewd and useful narrative of the horror genre in his 1981 study *Danse Macabre*, while the genre of the Western has been in a state of constant referral back to its lineage: Larry McMurtry is keenly aware of the legacy provided by major precursors such as Owen Wister, Zane Grey and Louis L'Amour.

But while acknowledging the powerful generic history of popular fiction, what is most striking is the reinvention and reformulation of forms as new anxieties appear. This reinvention may also take the form of hybrid genre; in fact, the increasing dominance of non-realist or fantasy writing is a key feature of this collection. Five of the authors here featured (and they may well be the most widely read of all) work specifically in non-realist modes – Gaiman, Pratchett, Martin, Miéville and Rowling – while several others extend realism to its limits. Fantasy or non-realism may well be a means of forging new connections between older genres: Stephen King's Dark Tower series is classed as fantasy but includes core elements of the Western, while steampunk, examined here in Cherie Priest's fiction, is a deft combining of fantasy, science fiction and the Western.

This new hybridity is a key feature of this collection, as is the shift that the authors may readily make between popular genres. Even the long-established authors discussed here who are usually associated with one specific genre are all involved with others. Stephen King's most prominent books of late have been his crime novels in the End of Watch series; he has also published works of science fiction and fantasy, and written for TV, film and comic books. Under her pen name J. D. Robb, Nora Roberts is the acclaimed author of numerous romantic suspense novels; Gillian Flynn's novels are usually characterised as Domestic Noir, but from the very beginning of her career her work has contained strong Gothic elements as well. Since the print conclusion of the Harry Potter series, J. K. Rowling has established herself as a writer of screenplays, crime novels (under the pen name Robert Galbraith) and, with *The Casual Vacancy* (2012), ventured into general fiction. Terry Pratchett is most associated with fantasy but has also written a great deal of science fiction, while George R. R. Martin began his career as an author of horror and science fiction. China Miéville writes fiction that encompasses fantasy, horror, science fiction and political theory, while the author of the Twilight series (2005–8), Stephenie Meyer, transformed longstanding supernatural horror tropes into paranormal romance. Her follow-up novel, *The Host* (2008), was a work of science fiction, while her most recent book, *The Chemist* (2016), is a romantic thriller. The shifting reader demographic for popular fiction (especially when translated to other media) may help account for these generic blendings, and it is notable that several of the most prominent authors discussed here are most associated with young adult (YA) fiction, which itself now has significant crossover with adult readership.

As noted above, this collection may be considered a snapshot of current popular fiction. As such, it touches on a key element in the history of popular fiction: the fact that it often proves to be ephemeral, in sharp contrast to 'literary' fiction. Doubtless, if we were to look back at this line-up in twenty years' time, there would be names that still burn bright, alongside those that had faded into relative obscurity or become a historical curio. Indeed, the ebbs and flows of literary history is an enduringly fascinating topic, and even more markedly so with popular fiction, which tends to accelerate changing tastes. Who would have predicted, for instance, that E. L. James's Fifty Shades series, which began as a work of *Twilight*-inspired fan fiction, would become one of the major publishing sensations of recent years, and rapidly be adapted for the screen? Or foreseen that Scandinavian thrillers would be one of the biggest trends in publishing and popular culture during the second decade of the twenty-first century, or that 'sparkly' vampires and love-sick werewolves would captivate millions of teenage girls (and their Twi-moms), or that by 2015 around 80 per cent of all YA fiction was in fact sold to adults?[3] Or that 'zombie-lit' would become one of the most notable new sub-genres in publishing from roughly 2006 onwards?

We have no way of knowing which of these authors will be forgotten in a generation's time, or recalled only as literary oddities. But we can certainly say that the genres which have remained popular for many decades, or centuries, will probably still do so, however blended they may become, and however they might be radically changed by new reading habits caused by technological advances and new processes of disintermediation.

A NOTE ON THE COVER

Gregory Crewdson's impeccably staged image *Untitled (Opheila)* is from his 2001 Twilight series. Why did we choose it? Well, first of all, it's an incredibly evocative and atmospheric image, simultaneously serene and sinister: a death dream made vividly actual, horror fantasy and dread in an interior domestic space. It also invokes a pictorial history, drawing as it does on John Everett Millais's depiction of Shakespeare's character in his 1852 *Ophelia*. The woman in the picture, like her literary predecessor, appears to have taken her own life. One of the things that struck us about the image was the suggestive presence of books: a brightly coloured paperback book sitting atop a more sombre looking volume on the coffee table, and a busy-looking bookshelf, again with colourful tomes, in the background. This is more than just a throwaway detail (there's no such thing in Crewdson's carefully staged scenarios): this woman is clearly a reader. Furthermore, as can clearly be seen when one looks at an enlargement of the photograph, one of the authors she has been reading is none other than Nora Roberts, whose red-jacketed novel *Inner Harbour* (1999) sits on the coffee table. Are we meant to believe, then, that this woman's romance reading habits have contributed to the state of mind which has led to her death? That like the original Ophelia, she has been sorely misled by her girlish imagination and belief in true love? Or can the presence of Roberts here be seen as a consoling reminder of the comfort and pleasure more usually associated with one of the most read but least critically acknowledged of popular genres?

For us, the image also evokes the sublimely immersive possibilities of reading – escapism, reverie and imagination – as well as the fact that popular fiction, as our essays demonstrate, so often serves as a vivid dramatisation of the anxieties and preoccupations of the society from which it emerges. We see in the works of the authors cited here certain key themes emerging again and again: domestic disquiet, conspiracy, battles between the younger and older generations, murder, secrecy and betrayal. But there is also love, laughter, furious invention, a consistent blurring of the boundaries between the everyday and the fantastical, bravery, bravura and wit. Indeed, the power of storytelling is actually a major plot point (as well as an implicit concern) of many of the works discussed here: as Tara Prescott notes, Neil Gaiman has, throughout his career, championed the imaginative and social possibilities conjured up by story. *Gone Girl* famously exploits our willingness to believe in certain types of media narratives (which are themselves influenced by tropes found in popular fiction). While comic book writer Grant Morrison has spent much of his career playfully yet pointedly subverting the storytelling conventions of his medium in a manner that evokes postmodernism's most meta possibilities, so too, albeit to a lesser extent, has Terry Pratchett, in his ever-inventive Discworld series, which, as Jim Shanahan notes, also teaches us how to be (mostly) human. Max Brooks's *World War Z* may take the form of a post-conflict report, but it is also a tale about the necessity to reconfigure old narratives and modes of living and create new ones, if one is to survive; this thread can also be found in the other dystopian texts considered here, the Wool series and The Hunger Games. As another Pratchett stalwart, the inimitable Granny Weatherwax, observes, 'Everything's got a story in it. Change the story, change the world.'[4]

NOTES

1 Harry Ransom Center, 'Teaching Materials from the David Foster Wallace Archive' <http://www.hrc.utexas.edu/press/releases/2010/dfw/teaching/> (last accessed 17 May 2017).
2. Carolyn Kellogg, 'Stephen King in *The New Yorker*', *Los Angeles Times*, 3 March 2015 <http://www.latimes.com/books/jacketcopy/la-et-jc-stephen-king-new-yorker-20150303-story.html> (last accessed 17 May 2017).
3. Natasha Gilmore, 'Nielsen Summit Shows the Data Behind the Children's Books Boom', *Publishers Weekly*, 17 September 2015 <http://www.publishersweekly.com/pw/by-topic/childrens/childrens-industry-news/article/68083-nielsen-summit-shows-the-data-behind-the-children-s-book-boom.html> (last accessed 17 May 2017).
4. Terry Pratchett, *A Hat Full of Sky* (London: Doubleday, 2004), p. 338.

FURTHER CRITICAL READING

Berberich, Christine (ed.), *The Bloomsbury Introduction to Popular Fiction* (London: Bloomsbury, 2014).

Bloom, Clive, *Bestsellers: Popular Fiction Since 1900* (Basingstoke: Palgrave Macmillan, 2008).

Gelder, Ken (ed.), *New Directions in Popular Fiction: Genre, Distribution, Reproduction* (Basingstoke: Palgrave Macmillan, 2016).

Gelder, Ken, *Popular Fiction: The Logistics and Practices of a Literary Field* (London: Routledge, 2004).

Glover, David and Scott McCracken (eds), *The Cambridge Companion to Popular Fiction* (Cambridge: Cambridge University Press, 2012).

Murphy, Bernice M., *Key Concepts in Contemporary Popular Fiction* (Edinburgh: Edinburgh University Press, 2017).

CHAPTER I

Larry McMurtry's Vanishing Breeds

Stephen Matterson

The Texan writer Larry McMurtry has achieved major success in numerous popular genres. His impressive list of publications over a period of almost sixty years include several memoirs, collections of essays on the West, on Hollywood, on history and on storytelling, imaginative renderings of historical Western figures, several significant post-Golden Age Western novels and highly successful non-Western fiction. He has been involved in film and television; he and Diana Ossana won an Academy Award and a Golden Globe for their screen adaptation of Annie Proulx's short story for the film *Brokeback Mountain*, and there have been notably successful and influential adaptations of McMurtry's own work. His 1961 Western novel *Horseman, Pass By*, was reworked to become the film *Hud*, which won three Academy Awards. His novel *The Last Picture Show* (1966) was successfully adapted to film in 1971, as was his novel *Terms of Endearment* a decade later; between them the films won a total of seven Academy Awards. McMurtry's 1985 Pulitzer Prize-winning novel *Lonesome Dove* was adapted as a high-profile CBS television mini-series, which was followed by adaptations of the other three novels in McMurtry's tetralogy, also presented as mini-series.

McMurtry was born in Archer City, Texas, in 1936, a small town with a population of less than 2,000. It forms the setting, under fictive names (usually 'Thalia'), for much of his fiction, notably *The Last Picture Show* and its 1987 sequel, *Texasville* (the film versions of both novels were made on location in Archer City). Many of McMurtry's forebears had been cowboys, and his father was a rancher who stubbornly held on to this occupation even though in the mid-twentieth century it was increasingly obsolescent, with many of his neighbours forsaking cattle for small-scale oil production.[1] McMurtry graduated with a BA from the University of North Texas in 1958, before taking his MA at Rice University in Houston. He won a significant fellowship, named after the novelist and environmentalist Wallace Stegner, to study creative writing at Stanford, where his classmates included the novelist Ken Kesey and the acclaimed editor Gordon Lish. He then taught for a spell at Rice, but gave this up as his early fiction earned both acclaim and attention from Hollywood. Although he has lived in various places, notably Washington, DC, and Virginia, Archer City remains McMurtry's home, and is where he famously located one of the largest second-hand book stores in the US, called Booked Up. Since the late 1950s McMurtry had been involved in collecting and then in selling books, opening the first Booked Up store in Washington, DC, in 1971, followed by three more branches in Texas and Arizona. Over many years McMurtry bought up the stock of dozens of failing second-hand bookstores, and finally consolidated the four Booked Up stores into the single one in Archer City; it is estimated that at one time the store held a stock of more than 450,000 books. However, the store was considerably downsized in 2012 and after an auction it now holds about half that stock.

McMurtry repeatedly represents book-selling as he does his father's cattle ranching, a stubbornly defiant yet knowingly forlorn holding on to something that is losing value in a changing culture. Indeed, 'lastness' and the question of how things end or are necessarily transformed in order to adapt is an enduring theme in his writing, both fiction and non-fiction. It is a theme especially amenable to the fictive series, allowing for the unfolding of events and characters over a considerable time, and McMurtry has developed several of these. Indeed, *The Last Picture Show* and *Texasville* were followed by three other novels centred on the character Duane Moore (the most recent being *Rhino Ranch*, published in 2009). His most important series is Lonesome Dove, whose four novels follow the intertwined and changing lives of a group of cattle drovers (although, confusingly, the novel sequence does not match the chronology of the tetralogy). His other series are the six Houston novels (1970–92, including *Terms of Endearment*, 1975) and the Berrybender novels (2002–4), historically situated during the opening of the West.

Several critics on McMurtry have drawn attention to the idea that he writes out of ambivalence towards his subjects. *The Last Picture Show*, for instance, is driven by a sense that Thalia, the moribund Texan small town, is a place stifling ambition and potential, narrow in outlook and sensibility. But this conflicts with the sense that it is also a home, an ultimately durable site and a landscape that holds value and expresses a community; this is what its central character, Sonny, eventually realises.[2] Similarly, *Horseman, Pass By* is fuelled by a combination of moral hostility towards all that Hud Bannon represents and a kind of grudging awareness of his embodiment of a raw historical actuality. Indeed, from early in his career McMurtry acknowledged that readers would find 'a certain inconsistency in my treatment of Texas past and present – a contradiction of attractions, one might call it'.[3] On a much broader level, McMurtry's Western novels show a strong ambivalence towards the traditions and conventions of the literary Western. At times he seems to write out of hostility towards the myths that have accreted around the West, a hostility that results in a series of non-fictional attempts to restore historical actuality to near-legendary figures such as Crazy Horse, Buffalo Bill, Annie Oakley and Sacagawea. But this drive to assert the actuality of the West is typically countered by his strong awareness of the values and importance of what the myths of West represented, and why they survive. This is a stance that leads him, perhaps ironically, to chide those Western historians who look for historical actuality but fail to take into account the persistence and importance of accreted cultural memory. In particular, he considers the hopelessness of the task faced by Western historians, often represented in his essays and reviews by Patricia Nelson Limerick:

> It has been Ms Limerick's task . . . to continually restore the contexts which the romanticizers just as continuously dissolve. She is, I'm afraid, the Historian as Sisyphus, endlessly rolling the rock of realism up Pike's Peak, only to watch it roll right back down into the pines of romance. Hers . . . is a noble but thankless task; rain though they may on the rodeo-parade model of Western history, it's still that parade that people line up to see.[4]

The Western as an elaborated performance that is distanced from the real does not, McMurtry indicates, invalidate it at all. In fact, it intensifies the need to explore it as performance, as storytelling; it requires us to look more closely at it and to consider why we tell and listen to these stories, how we access them, what they mean and how they themselves are constantly transformed. 'This is the West, sir. When the legend becomes fact, print the legend.' This famous quotation from John Ford's 1962 film *The Man Who Shot Liberty Valance* succinctly encapsulates this idea. We are not seeking the factual in the Western, but the legend, and we want those legends retold to us again and again.

However, McMurtry's attitude towards the Western is complicated by his own insistence on historical actuality, hence the ambivalence that is evident in his approach. He takes issue with the historians who aim to correct legends, yet he cannot wholeheartedly engage with the formulas of the Western without a degree of scepticism. This makes him a radically different writer from those who created the literary Western as it flourished in the twentieth century, from Owen Wister's *The Virginian* (1902) through to the stirring formulas developed over the next decade by Zane Grey, to McMurtry's immediate forebear Louis L'Amour. The output and sales of Grey and L'Amour alone are extraordinary. Grey wrote more than sixty Western novels and by an estimate made in 1969 is reputed to have sold over 40 million copies.[5] L'Amour was to publish over 100 novels from his first in 1950 until his death in 1988, and by 2008 there were over 300 million copies of his books in print.[6] Such figures for Grey and L'Amour alone testify to the astonishing popularity of the literary Western, yet they were only the two leading authors, and there have been dozens more, from the dime novelists to Max Brand and Jack Schaefer. Further, McMurtry sagely reminds us that the staples of the performative Western were not literary alone and, indeed, may not have been particularly literary at all, citing the appetite of the settled East for images and stories of the unsettled West.[7] This hunger was fed by the dime novel, by paintings, images and artefacts as much as by literary fiction. He recalls that for his own amusement he once compiled a list of those who were instrumental in inventing the West:

> I lost the list but remember that it began with Thomas Jefferson and ended with Andy Warhol, the latter for his *Double Elvis*, in which the King appears as a

gunfighter. In between came gunmakers, boot makers, saddlemakers, railroad magnates, painters, Indians, actors, directors, liars of many descriptions, but not, by golly, very many writers: only Ned Buntline, Zane Grey, Max Brand, and Louis L'Amour.[8]

As is characteristic of other popular forms, the literary Western exists as part of a more complex web of media, building on and interacting repeatedly with a multiplicity of generic paradigms. This is notably true of many of the twenty-first-century writers in this collection, but it has been a generic feature of the Western from very early on, with respect to the dime novel and the comic book. Film is the most obvious medium that interacts with the literary Western, and the relation between film and fiction is so close as to be almost mutually symbiotic.[9] There's actually a good example of this in McMurtry's own career. In 1972, following the celebrated film version of *The Last Picture Show*, McMurtry wrote a story and a screenplay for another film project by the director Peter Bogdanovich. That fell through, but a decade later McMurtry reworked the screenplay and it became the Pulitzer Prize-winning novel *Lonesome Dove*. As a further twist, *Lonesome Dove* was reformulated into a popular television mini-series. (And, as McMurtry was wryly to remark, the mini-series was far more popular than the critically acclaimed novel had been.[10])

While McMurtry's work is clearly embedded in the traditions of the literary Western, it is so only in a relatively specialised way, with his focus on the figure of the cowboy in transition. In broad terms, the Western combines the genre of romance, as an Americanised modernisation of much earlier tales of knights on horseback (the classic shoot-out is a modernised version of the duel), and the folk tale, with a particular emphasis on the outlaw and on adventure. The Western develops more specifically from the five James Fenimore Cooper 'Leatherstocking' novels published between 1823 and 1841 (themselves indebted to the romances of Walter Scott), with their self-reliant scout pioneer, Natty Bumppo, who appears in the series under various nicknames. However indirectly, Natty is the archetype for hundreds of Western heroes: independent, self-reliant, at home in the wilderness, averse to domestication, helping in the opening of the land for settlement but reluctant or unable to settle there himself; a wanderer, familiar with violence. This latter feature is certainly one of the Western's defining characteristics, and it is often claimed that as a genre it arose in specific opposition to the female domestic novel (although the relation between domesticity and the Western hero is often considerably more complex than simply antagonism).[11] The development of the dime novel saw the first major period of the Western, from around 1860, but it was in the early twentieth century that the literary Western began to flourish, thanks to Wister's *The Virginian* and subsequently to the many novels of Zane Grey, notably *Riders of the Purple Sage* (1912), *Light of the Western Stars* (1913) and *The Vanishing American* (1925). Grey very self-consciously modelled his novels on *The Virginian* and was the first Western writer to derive a 'formula' for the genre.

The Western had a second golden period from 1940s to the 1970s, which saw the publication of now classic texts such as *Shane* (1949) by Schaefer and *Hondo* (1953) by L'Amour. This period coincides of course with a series of classic Western movies, notably from the directors John Ford and Howard Hawks, among others, but also with the complete dominance of Western-themed shows in the three US network television schedules. Screened from the mid-1950s to the early 1970s, series such as *Gunsmoke, Rawhide, Bonanza, Wagon Train, The Big Valley* and *The High Chaparral* (and there were dozens of others) have been among the most popular television series ever produced.[12] Many of these shows had of course migrated from radio or were spin-offs from cinema productions.

As it developed to its heyday in the 1950s, the literary Western involved a series of conventions which effectively defined it as a genre and set it apart from fiction that just happened to be set on the frontier. Typically, these conventions include the land in transition, in the process of being claimed and settled: in its classic formulation, the setting is the territory that is not yet a federal state in the Union. Characteristically, law is absent or is in abeyance, and consequently questions of justice must be settled by individuals, hence an emphasis on violence and on self-reliance. In this respect the Western is obedient to the idea represented in Frederick Jackson Turner's famous 1893 'frontier thesis' lecture, where he argued that the struggle to claim and settle the shifting wilderness became a defining feature for the American character.

However the conflict in the classic literary Western may be represented, at its heart is a fundamental disagreement over the use and ownership of the land. The most obvious conflict in this respect is between settler and native. The natives' usage of land (which in the plains meant the hunting of buffalo over vast spaces) is represented as wastefully incompatible with the agricultural uses that the white settler will make of it in order to support civilisation. This incompatibility gives the settlers the right to turn land into productive private property. As Theodore Roosevelt pithily and uncompromisingly put it:

> the conquest and settlement by the whites of the Indian lands was necessary to the greatness of the race and to the well-being of civilized mankind . . . This great continent . . . could not have been kept as nothing but a game preserve for squalid savages.[13]

The literary Western's allegiance to manifest destiny is often considerably more complex, though. The natives are frequently represented as the land's true inhabitants (rather than 'owners'), with a consequent questioning of the values of so-called 'civilized mankind', sometimes accompanied by an elegiac sense of regret for those whom Zane Grey called the vanishing Americans. This was evident even in the Western's originating texts, where Natty Bumppo refutes any affinity with the encroaching white settlements (whose existence he nevertheless facilitates), claiming true allegiance only with his blood-brother Chingachgook, the last of the Mohicans.

More typically, the Western conflict over land is concerned with its usages among the settlers in the post-frontier but pre-state condition. The ranchers need an open range for their cattle to graze and roam freely, and to allow them to conduct the annual cattle drive without obstruction. The farmers want the land enclosed, marked out as individual property and enforced by barbed-wire fences. This is the determining conflict with regard to the future of the territory. The ranchers and the cowboys working for them are typically represented as lawless, living on the frontier only because of the freedom it provides, escaping from domesticity and responsibility. The 'real work' demanded of the cowboy is an expression of true manhood in a place, perhaps the last place, where masculinity may be freely performed. (Running away to the frontier or territory to avoid the confining woman is a well established and enduring trope in American writing, epitomised by the ending of the classic American text *The Adventures of Huckleberry Finn*.) The farmers are typically represented as those looking to settle, to bring the rules of law and property rights to the nascent state, committed to family and domesticity, and, it might be added, to capitalism's core belief in land as individual property. The land is fenced off to become agriculturally productive, or even to become feminised space as the garden. The settlers are firmly committed to federal statehood, the ranchers to the freedoms offered by the status of territory. While this conflict is elemental, the settlers must compromise their values in order to combat the violence that the ranchers will use. The classic representation is of course *Shane*, set in the Wyoming territory in 1889 (Wyoming became a state in 1890). The mysterious, just-passing-through stranger known only as Shane is a masterful but reluctant gunfighter who is persuaded to fight on behalf of the settlers and who helps to defeat the ranchers. But his violence also means he can have no place in the future life of the community whose existence he has facilitated. The novel ends with him riding out of the valley, passing through once more, going further West to become a stranger again, another avatar of Natty Bumppo off to a place where the frontier is not yet closed.

The basic parameters of the rancher–settler conflict can be shifted and redefined in various ways. The cowboy/ranchers may be represented sympathetically (and elegiacally) as upholders of American values of freedom and self-reliance, while the settlers are extending Eastern values to a place fundamentally unamenable to them. Conversely, the ranchers might be represented as epitomising the dangers of unbridled capitalism, or the dangers of anarchy and male violence, with the settlers representing lawfulness, good order, family life and civic duty. Or, as in Annie Proulx's Wyoming-based short-story collection *Close Range* (1999), the heirs to the ranchers are failing because of the globalisation of capital, industrial-scale farming, with the new breed of homesteader being well funded retirees or commercially driven craft-workers with no interest in cultivating the land. This latter mode of conflict is particularly close to McMurtry's ongoing representation of the rancher displaced by modernity.

Schaefer has *Shane* narrated by Bob, the eleven-year-old son of the settlers Joe and Marian Starrett. This is an important aspect of the novel, and of the Western form generally, as it is very much about male identity and choice. While Bob lacks the mature outlook or the vocabulary needed to articulate this, the reader sees that the external conflict between rancher and farmer is being played out internally in Bob, where it has turned into a conflict between the different models of manhood represented by his father and by Shane. Bob idolises Shane, and his narrative makes him into a god-like figure, as the closing lines indicate: 'He was the man who rode into our little valley out of the heart of the great glowing West and when his work was done rode back whence he had come and he was Shane.'[14] This moment of elegiac representation as the wounded Shane leaves Bob's world is intensified by Shane's parting words to the young boy, telling him his father Joe is the 'real man' and that Bob must grow up 'strong and straight'.[15]

McMurtry's *Horseman, Pass By* shares the premise of *Shane*, here showing a late-teen male narrator, Lonnie Bannon, torn between models of male identity; it is also very much about the land in transition, with a threat to the family's cattle herd. One model is represented by Lonnie's ranch-owning octogenarian grandfather, Homer Bannon, the other by his uncle, Scott 'Hud' Bannon, Homer's stepson, who is in his mid-thirties (Homer and Hud are not blood relations). The chief events of the novel unfold over an outbreak of foot-and-mouth disease on the Bannon ranch, in which the government's destruction of the entire herd is threatened, and focuses on the conflict between Homer and Hud over how to deal with this. Homer is a man of honour and honesty, aligned we might say with what Turner hailed as the frontier virtues. He also embodies the values of rootedness, family and community, with the ranch functioning as a kind of English estate, suggesting a version of landed aristocracy committed to continuity, stability and community. As Homer says in angry reaction to the suggestion that if his herd is destroyed, the land can be used for oil, 'I guess I'm a queer, contrary old bastard, but there'll be no holes punched in this land while I'm here'.[16] In sharp conflict with these values, Hud is a hard-drinking, self-centred and unscrupulous womaniser. His first instinct is deceitfully to cover up the fact of the disease, and his second is to use it as an excuse to sell the ranch land for oil production.

In spite of their shared premise, the differences between *Shane* and *Horseman, Pass By* are crucial in reflecting on McMurtry's interrogation of the Western. For one thing, *Horseman, Pass By* is set in the mid-1950s, and in modernity both Homer and Hud are anachronisms. In fact, McMurtry represents the death of Homer, and his funeral in the final chapter, as the end of an era, after which Lonnie will leave Thalia (the elegiac elements are also of course apparent in McMurtry's choice of title, from W. B. Yeats's self-penned epitaph in the poem 'Under Ben Bulben'). While the novel insists on the scene of modernity, foregrounding music from the radio, automobiles, the rodeo and twentieth-century technology, it becomes a more complex study of the cowboy than simply an intergenerational clash of values between Homer and Hud. Hud represents another version of the cowboy, the other aspects of the frontier character. He relishes the coarse freedoms that the 'frontier' offers, in terms of the lax rule of law, violence and sexual relations (Lonnie's troubling adolescent development is foregrounded so that Hud's easy-going promiscuity is seen as attractive). Indeed, Hud's adulterous sexual relations are potentially threatening to the small-town sense of community. Yet although he may be an anachronism, Hud's acquisitive materialism marks him out as the figure most likely to succeed in modernity; here McMurtry updates the classic Western question of land use and ownership to make it local and familial. In this respect his novel concludes much more ambivalently than *Shane*. Schaefer leaves Bob with his ideal of Shane intact, even though he is now committed to the settler world of his father. Lonnie runs away from the ranch, carrying with him both the elegy for his grandfather and a self-troubling confused admiration for Hud. In plot terms, Homer and Hud effectively cancel out one another in an ambiguous though inevitably violent version of the traditional gunfight, but they coexist in Lonnie's mind as an ongoing conflict, from which he must take flight. McMurtry's own ambivalence towards the Western form is being played out, an elegiac recognition of what was lost with the transition from the ranches, combined with a suspicion that what was lost contained a certain kind of irredeemable ugliness.[17]

McMurtry's work published over the last twenty years or so has increasingly scrutinised and elaborated on this ambivalence. At times he represents the Western as a series of repeated tales, and considers how it aligns with the oral tradition represented by the 1930s cultural critic Walter Benjamin. In fact, this is exactly how Louis L'Amour came to see himself: 'I think of myself in the oral tradition – as a troubadour, a village tale-teller, the man in the shadows of the campfire. That's the way I'd like to be remembered – as a storyteller. A good storyteller.'[18] Elsewhere McMurtry seeks to access the actuality behind the tales, notably in his studies of Crazy Horse, Buffalo Bill (William Cody) and Annie Oakley, among others. Yet even there his main focus is on how these figures consciously became part of the Western's repertoire. As he put it with respect to Buffalo Bill, 'Somehow Cody succeeded in taking a very few elements of Western life – Indians, buffalo, stagecoach, and his own superbly mounted self – and creating an illusion that has successfully stood for a reality that had been almost wholly different'.[19] A constant theme of McMurtry is the endurance of the Western itself as a popular form, both for its capacity to meet the particular appetites of its readers and for its flexible adaptability to other genres; a supposedly vanishing breed is actually an enduring one. As he has reflected:

> The death of the cowboy . . . has been one of my principal subjects, and yet I'm well aware that killing the *myth* of the cowboy is like trying to kill a snapping turtle: no matter what you do to it, the beast retains a sluggish life.[20]

McMurtry might be reluctant to endorse the more outlandish twenty-first-century genre stretches of the Western, now including zombies, vampires, weird fiction and steampunk. But he would certainly acknowledge that these transformations are made possible by the very basis of the Western, and of other popular forms, in its being rooted in our ongoing need for stories and for storytellers.

NOTES

1. McMurtry has written often of his immediate forebears, and particularly considers the Texan cowboy in his essay 'Take My Saddle from the Wall'.
2. See Womble, 'Windswept and Scattered', and Busby, *Larry McMurtry and the West*.
3. McMurtry, 'Take My Saddle from the Wall', p. 165.
4. McMurtry, 'Cookie Pioneers', in *Sacagawea's Nickname*, pp. 85–6.
5. Gruber, *Zane Grey*, p. 143. The Directory of Western Authors website claims that annually over a million copies of his novels are still sold. See <http://www.westernauthors.com/Part_V.htm> (last accessed 23 June 2016).
6. Blurb on Louis L'Amour, *Hondo*, 2008 reissue.
7. McMurtry, *The Colonel and Little Missie*, p. 21.
8. McMurtry, 'Inventing the West', p. 21.
9. David F. Matuszak's *The Cowboy's Trail Guide to Westerns* is a comprehensive overview of film Westerns, and he points out that 'The history of Western movies is the history of the motion picture industry' (p. 3), beginning in 1903 with *The Great Train Robbery*.
10. McMurtry, *Walter Benjamin at the Dairy Queen*, p. 145.

11. See, for instance, Jane Tompkins's *West of Everything*, where this is very forcibly argued.
12. Some other television series were not technically Westerns but used the core elements of the form: famously, in the mid-1960s, Gene Roddenberry pitched *Star Trek* as a version of *Wagon Train*. See Wills, 'Wagon Train to the Stars'. One 1992 episode of *Star Trek: The Next Generation* (titled 'A Fistful of Datas') is an affectionate tribute to Westerns. Similarly, the television series *The Wild Wild West* began in 1965 as a mix of the Western with the then burgeoning spy thriller: its creator, Michael Garrison, described it as 'James Bond on horseback' (Kesler, *The Wild Wild West*, p. 112). The series and the three subsequent films are now considered seminal to the development of steampunk.
13. Roosevelt, *The Winning of the West*, p. 90.
14. Schaefer, *Shane*, p. 274.
15. Ibid., p. 263.
16. McMurtry, *Horseman, Pass By*, pp. 105–6.
17. The film version of the novel worked to make Hud a more attractive anti-hero than he is in the novel (the very casting of Paul Newman in the title role almost ensured this). His raping of Halmea, the Bannon's African-American maid, is made much more ambivalent, and Halmea herself is represented as white, thereby avoiding some of the issues the novel raises.
18. Louis L'Amour, quoted at <http://www.louislamourcollection.com> (last accessed June 23 2016).
19. McMurtry, *The Colonel and Little Missie*, p. 138.
20. McMurtry, *Walter Benjamin at the Dairy Queen*, pp. 185–6; original emphasis.

KEY WORKS

Horseman, Pass By (1961). Version of the frontier Western set in 1950s Texas, questioning the modes of masculinity that the Western supposedly endorsed; memorably filmed as *Hud*.
Lonesome Dove (1985). Epic representation of a late-nineteenth-century cattle drive from South Texas to the Canadian border, encompassing key aspects of frontier fiction; winner of the 1986 Pulitzer Prize for fiction and the first of what would be a tetralogy of novels.
Walter Benjamin at the Dairy Queen (1999). Primarily concerned with McMurtry's life as a reader, writer and second-hand bookseller, these elegantly constructed connected essays also explore the nature and function of storytelling, taking as a basis Benjamin's classic 1936 essay 'The Storyteller'.
Sacagawea's Nickname: Essays on the American West (2001). Superbly reflective essays focusing consistently on what McMurtry calls the 'invention' of the West, starting from his observation that 'the *selling* of the West preceded the *settling* of it' (p. 21; original emphasis).
The Colonel and Little Missie (2005). A searching analysis of William Cody (Buffalo Bill) and Annie Oakley as American superstars, and a historically focused reflection on how the staple elements of the Western were formulated as performance.

FURTHER CRITICAL READING

Busby, Mark, *Larry McMurtry and the West: An Ambivalent Relationship* (1995). Title indicates the approach; informed and succinct.
Campbell, Neil, *The Rhizomatic West* (2008). Key recent study, theoretically informed reflection on the varied forces making up the literary Western.
Miller, Cynthia J. and A. Bowdoin Van Riper (eds), *Undead in the West* (2015). An invaluable collection of essays on the extension of the Western into the horror genre.
Reilly, John M., *Larry McMurtry* (2000). Useful though slightly dated, concentrates well on the fiction.

Slotkin, Richard, *Regeneration Through Violence* (1973). Classic, indispensible study of the frontier, followed by two further critical analyses, *The Fatal Environment: The Myth of the Frontier in the Age of Industrialization, 1800–1890* (1985) and *Gunfighter Nation: The Myth of the Frontier in Twentieth-Century America* (1992).

Tompkins, Jane, *West of Everything* (1992). Landmark reconsideration of the genre, representing the Western as a male counter-genre to the contemporary female-inflected domestic novel.

Varner, Paul (ed.), *New Wests and Post-Wests* (2013). Useful collection of essays on a wide range of topics, including a chapter on McMurtry by Todd Womble.

BIBLIOGRAPHY

Booked Up website <http://www.bookedupac.com/about.php> (last accessed 23 June 2016).

Busby, Mark, *Larry McMurtry and the West: An Ambivalent Relationship* (Denton: University of North Texas Press, 1995).

Campbell, Neil, *The Rhizomatic West: Representing the American West in a Transnational, Global, Media Age* (Lincoln: University of Nebraska Press, 2008).

Gruber, Frank, *Zane Grey: A Biography* (New York: Amereon, 1969).

Kesler, Susan E., *The Wild Wild West: The Series* (Downey, CA: Arnett Press, 1988).

L'Amour, Louis, *Hondo* (New York: Bantam Books, 2008).

McAuley, James, 'Larry McMurtry's Dying Breed: A Visit to Archer City', *The New Yorker*, 30 August 2011 <http://www.newyorker.com/books/page-turner/larry-mcmurtrys-dying-breed-a-visit-to-archer-city> (last accessed 23 June 2016).

McMurtry, Larry, 'Cookie Pioneers', in Larry McMurtry, *Sacagawea's Nickname: Essays on the American West* (New York: New York Review Books, 2001), pp. 85–6.

McMurtry, Larry, *Horseman, Pass By* (London: Phoenix Books, 2000).

McMurtry, Larry, 'Inventing the West', in Larry McMurtry, *Sacagawea's Nickname: Essays on the American West* (New York: New York Review Books, 2001), pp. 15–32.

McMurtry, Larry, 'Take My Saddle from the Wall: A Valediction', in Larry McMurtry, *In a Narrow Grave: Essays on Texas* (New York: Simon and Schuster, 1968), pp. 165–98.

McMurtry, Larry, *The Colonel and Little Missie: Buffalo Bill, Annie Oakley and the Beginnings of Superstardom in America* (New York: Simon and Schuster, 2005).

McMurtry, Larry, *Walter Benjamin at the Dairy Queen: Reflections at Sixty and Beyond* (New York: Simon and Schuster, 1999).

Matuszak, David F., *The Cowboy's Trail Guide to Westerns* (Redlands, CA: Pacific Sunset Publishing, 2003).

Miller, Cynthia J. and A. Bowdoin Van Riper (eds), *Undead in the West: Vampires, Zombies, Mummies, and Ghosts on the Cinematic Frontier* (Plymouth: Scarecrow Press, 2012).

More, Rosalie, 'Authors of Popular Western Fiction', The Directory of Western Authors <http://www.westernauthors.com/default.asp> (last accessed 23 June 2016).

Reilly, John M., *Larry McMurtry: A Critical Companion* (Westport, CT: Greenwood Press, 2000).

Roosevelt, Theodore, *The Winning of the West* (New York: G. Putnam and Sons, 1889).

Schaefer, Jack, *Shane: The Critical Edition*, ed. James C. Work (Lincoln: University of Nebraska Press, 1984).

Slotkin, Richard, *Regeneration Through Violence: The Mythology of the American Frontier, 1600–1860* (Middletown, CT: Wesleyan University Press, 1973).

Tompkins, Jane, *West of Everything: The Inner Life of Westerns* (New York: Oxford University Press, 1992).

Turner, Frederick Jackson, 'The Significance of the Frontier in American History', in Martin Ridge (ed.), *Frederick Jackson Turner* (Madison: State Historical Society of Wisconsin, 1993), pp. 26–47.

Varner, Paul (ed.), *New Wests and Post-Wests: Literature and Film of the American West* (Newcastle upon Tyne: Cambridge Scholars Publishing, 2013).

Wills, John, 'Wagon Train to the Stars: *Star Trek*, the Frontier and America', in Douglas Brode and Shea T. Brode (eds), *Gene Roddenberry's Star Trek: The Original Cast Adventures* (Lanham, MD: Rowman and Littlefield, 2015), pp. 1–12.

Womble, Todd, 'Windswept and Scattered: Place and Identity in Larry McMurtry's *The Last Picture Show*', in Paul Varner (ed.), *New Wests and Post-Wests*, pp. 91–112.

CHAPTER 2

'Time to Open the Door': Stephen King's Legacy

Rebecca Janicker

Stephen King has been a steady and extraordinarily prolific writer of novels, short-story collections and comics, as well screenplays for film and television, from the late 1960s right into the second decade of the twenty-first century. King was born in Portland, Maine, in 1947. About two years later his father walked out, never to return, leaving King and his elder brother to be raised by their mother.[1] Having spent much of his childhood moving around New England, King majored in English at the University of Maine, Orono, where he studied American literature as well as producing fiction of his own.[2] While at college, King met fellow student Tabitha Spruce. The couple married in 1971 and the first of their three children was born shortly after that. The young family lived in the same part of Maine and King initially struggled to support them, balancing a high school teaching post in English and part-time work with his nascent literary career.[3] After sporadic sales of short stories to various men's magazines, King's fortunes changed with the success of *Carrie* (1974), which sold in excess of a million copies in paperback.[4] King and his family have continued to make a home in Maine from that time and his native state has supplied the backdrop to many of his works over the decades.

With the popularity of *Carrie*, which became a major motion picture directed by Brian De Palma in 1976, King made a decisive shift from aspiring writer to bestselling author and has enjoyed this status ever since. Towards the close of the first decade of the twenty-first century, Clive Bloom acknowledged King to be 'the best-selling American author of all time'.[5] Periodically dominating the bestseller lists for decades, King has shown no signs of waning in recent years and titles from *Dreamcatcher* (2001)[6] to *Mr Mercedes* (2014)[7] and its sequel *Finders Keepers* (2015)[8] and *End of Watch* (2016)[9] have reached the number one spot. Further to this, King's name has regularly been used to promote television series and movies adapted (with varying degrees of fidelity) from his writings. However, such elevated levels of popularity can bring their own issues and King has often faced censure on the basis of his fame. His abundant output, high profile and mass-market appeal conspire, for some, to work against his gaining a reputation as a serious writer. In 2003, he was awarded the Medal for Distinguished Contribution to American Letters by the National Book Foundation. Observing that the majority of those previously honoured thus were 'literary' authors, Ken Gelder remarks that 'King was a different kind of recipient . . . a one-person "industry"'.[10] Despite some denigration, King is an author who has received both mass endorsement and a measure of critical acclaim.

One reason for King's uneasy authorial status is his association with genre fiction, most especially with horror. Often dismissed as puerile, exploitative and low-brow, the preserve of what might broadly be referred to as the horror genre has been stigmatised since the rise of Gothic fiction in the eighteenth century. In tracing the relationship between Gothic and horror, Clive Bloom notes that 'gothic is *the* genre against which critics attempted to separate serious fiction from such popular entertainment and escapism'.[11] Long aware of these debates, King has remained an unapologetic proponent, as well as producer, of horror and Gothic fictions for most of his life. As he remarks in *On Writing*, 'I was built with a love of the night and the unquiet coffin, that's all. If you disapprove, I can only shrug my shoulders. It's what I have.'[12] This affinity can be traced back to King's childhood, when his enthusiasm was kindled by the discovery of a box of paperback fiction in a relative's attic. Left by his absent father, this collection comprised works by such authors as Frank Belknap Long, Zealia Bishop and, most significantly, H. P. Lovecraft. King has called this incident his 'first encounter with serious fantasy-horror fiction'[13] and thus singled it out as one that would help shape his fascination with the horror genre.

Burgeoning from its eighteenth-century roots, twenty-first-century horror takes diverse forms yet remains close to its origins. Characterised by an atmosphere of mystery and antiquity, early British Gothic was concerned with themes of death and premature burial, sleep and dreams, ghostly presences and the resurgence of the past.[14] These dramas were typically played out against physically repugnant and psychologically unsettling locations such as crumbling monasteries and castles. Many of these conventions were transplanted to the New World, where, despite the lack of those ancient buildings and social institutions on which the first instances of the genre depended, American Gothic came to perpetuate the initial preoccupation with troubled spaces and the impact of the past upon the present. Novels like Mary Shelley's *Frankenstein* (1818), Robert Louis Stevenson's *Strange Case of Dr Jekyll and Mr Hyde* (1886) and Bram Stoker's *Dracula* (1897) gradually established monstrosity and unnatural life as horror staples, and the twentieth century brought the new threat of cosmic horror from the likes of Lovecraft. Gina Wisker suggests that horror is 'more likely to use violence, terror, and bodily harm'[15] than the Gothic and works like Clive Barker's *Books of Blood* (1981–5) exemplify the sub-genre of body horror. Splatter-punk authors combine horror with extreme sexuality, as in Poppy Z. Brite's *Lost Souls* (1992), while Anne Rice's ongoing Vampire Chronicles series also explores sexuality through Gothic devices. Classic Gothic and horror tropes all find new expression in the twenty-first century, from innovative takes on haunted house tales and zombie fiction in Mark Z. Danielewski's *House of Leaves* (2000) and Max Brooks's *World War Z: An Oral History of the Zombie War* (2006) to the vampires and werewolves of Stephenie Meyer's young adult series Twilight (2005–8), discussed elsewhere in this collection.

Drawing time after time on ingrained horror conventions, and renowned as an exceptionally fruitful and lucrative writer, King unarguably occupies a prestigious place in the field of horror. Together with his use of intriguing scenarios and evocative settings, King's thematic interest in the bond between past and present marks out his work as intrinsically Gothic in nature. At one time or another, and sometimes on more than one occasion, King has written tales concerning characters and creatures from the sweep of horror fiction, variously tackling such supernatural beings as ghosts, vampires, werewolves and zombies, plus the Gothic double in The Dark Half (1989) and extra-terrestrial and inter-dimensional threats in the likes of IT (1986). He has also explored more realistic sources of fear, including abusive parents, serial killers, assassins and terrorists, a pandemic in The Stand (originally published 1978, revised and re-released 1990) and a rabid dog in Cujo (1981), plus a mad scientist in Revival (2014). Much of his fiction, whether it is essentially supernatural, linked to the tropes of science fiction or more grounded in everyday experience, features fundamentally unsettling, often blatantly shocking, episodes of violence or moments of revulsion and terror.

In addition to his copious horror production, King has recurrently experimented with other types of writing, including historical fiction. For example, 11/22/63 (2011) utilises time travel but minimises the role of the supernatural by using that device principally to enable a sustained exploration of America's fascination with the 1950s and 1960s and the promise of the Kennedy administration. Now and then, novels like Dolores Claiborne (1993) and novellas like 'The Body' and 'Rita Hayworth and Shawshank Redemption', both from the collection Different Seasons (1982), serve to demonstrate a less fantastic focus on serious issues such as domestic abuse and the power of friendship. Following in the footsteps of Edgar Allan Poe, consummate master of horror and originator of the detective genre with 'The Murders in the Rue Morgue' (1841), King recently made his own foray into the latter field with his Finders Keepers trilogy, completed in 2016 with End of Watch.

Stephen King has long been a household name and, at the time of writing, he has published upwards of forty novels, including seven published under the pseudonym Richard Bachman, eight collections of short stories, three collections of novellas, plus eight books in the Dark Tower series. He has also published several ebooks and even a pop-up book. King has produced several collaborative works over the years, such as The Talisman (1984) and Black House (2001) with Peter Straub, and a novel marked for release in late 2017, Sleeping Beauties, sees him collaborate with his son, author Owen King. King's non-fiction works include Danse Macabre (1981), a significant commentary on the horror genre, and the semi-autobiographical On Writing: A Memoir of the Craft (2000). In his survey of bestselling fiction, Bloom remarks that certain authors come to be 'equivalent to a brand name (and their work a branded product)',[16] counting King among the ranks of such luminaries as Agatha Christie, Ian Fleming and Jackie Collins, whose names instantly evoke their own distinctive bodies of work. Certainly, King's name has become inextricably linked in popular culture with the art of storytelling in general and the horror genre in particular. In a

2014 piece on King, Jane Ciabattari notes the comparisons drawn between King and Charles Dickens – both prodigious and popular authors, yet both targeted for their celebrity – concluding that King, as with Dickens, seems now sufficiently 'embedded in the culture'[17] for his longevity to be assured.

Much of King's considerable cultural impact can surely be attributed to the stress his stories place on human interest. Although his name will forever conjure up horrific images of monsters and supernatural forces, from the vampires of 'Salem's Lot (1975) to the ghosts of Bag of Bones (1999) and the zombie hordes of Cell (2006), it may not be the horror content *per se* that achieves real resonance with the wider public. Many critics have discerned a firm sense of political motivation to King's work and his ability to tap into social concerns makes his fiction seem continually relevant to his extensive readership. Indeed, Tony Magistrale asserts that King's 'deepest terrors are sociopolitical in nature, reflecting our worst fears about vulnerable western institutions – our governmental bureaucracies, our school systems, our communities, our familial relationships'.[18] Early novels like Carrie and The Shining (1977) deal with familiar themes of high-school bullying, alcoholism and domestic abuse. The preoccupation with all-too-human sources of anxiety continues to find its way into King's twenty-first-century fiction, with contemporary issues of a disquieting nature, from over-reliance on technology in Cell to the recession-era financial hardships and threat of terrorist attack depicted in the 'Finders Keepers' trilogy.

Over the years, King's own extensive body of work has been augmented by the profusion of adaptations and this process has inevitably raised his profile even higher. From prominent early films like Carrie and Stanley Kubrick's version of The Shining (1980), through to sleeper hits like Frank Darabont's The Shawshank Redemption (1994) and Tod Williams's Cell (2016), movies with King's name attached have been a regular cinematic fixture. A film called The Dark Tower, based on King's series of the same name, was due for cinematic release in 2017, and Part One of the film adaptation of IT was planned for the big screen later that same year. His fiction has also frequently made its way onto the small screen. Several novels have been made into mini-series, including 'Salem's Lot, IT, The Stand and Bag of Bones, appearing in 1979 (CBS), 1990 (ABC), 1994 (ABC) and 2011 (A&E) respectively. In addition to these projects, King has written original screenplays for television mini-series, including Storm of the Century (ABC, 1999) and Rose Red (ABC, 2002). More recently, Under the Dome (2009) was adapted into a major television series, running for three seasons on CBS from 2013, while 11/22/63 premiered in February 2016 on the subscription streaming channel Hulu. A television adaptation of The Mist was due to premiere on SpikeTV in the summer of 2017. Besides King's literary output, then, the sheer media presence generated by his work means that his cultural impact is inescapable, even to those who might not read his fiction.

Given the extent of King's publications, it is perhaps inevitable that some works will fade into relative obscurity, for example novels such as Rose Madder (1995) or The Girl Who Loved Tom Gordon (1999), while others will go on to make a lasting impression. As King's first hardcover bestseller, and with its subsequent eminence as a Kubrick film, The Shining has loomed large on the popular cultural landscape for almost four decades. Famously unhappy with Kubrick's vision, which downplays the role of the supernatural and places little emphasis on character background, King revisited his landmark novel in 1997 by collaborating as screenwriter with director Mick Garris for an ABC mini-series adaptation notable for its fidelity to the source material. Since that time, mindful of the novel's enduring legacy, King has repeatedly pondered the fate of Danny Torrance, the young child at the heart of all three renderings of the tale, 'calculating [his] age, and wondering where he was'.[19] It seems that the reading public has been equally curious. When the long-awaited sequel, entitled *Doctor Sleep*, was published in 2013, it soon achieved hardcover bestseller status, as had *The Shining* so many years before.[20]

In the original novel, the main protagonist is a young writer, Jack Torrance, who is desperate to reconcile his responsibility to support his family with his personal ambition to achieve literary success. Out of this necessity, he relocates wife, Wendy, and son, Danny, to the luxurious Overlook Hotel in Colorado's Rocky Mountains so he can take on the post of winter caretaker. The Overlook is eventually revealed to be haunted, the malevolent supernatural forces which normally lie there dormant being triggered by Danny's psychic abilities: the 'shining' of the title. King's novel focuses closely on how Jack's character has been shaped by his past. Abused as a child by his violent father, the adult Jack has a history of alcoholism and seems doomed to replicate his own troubled childhood in his relationship with Danny. Jack's upbringing and fraught attempt to provide for his family after his drinking costs him a steady teaching job imbue the narrative with a sense of impending tragedy. Further, the forces haunting the Overlook progressively exploit Jack's weaknesses, with the intention of turning him against his son. These key themes of familial discord, the injurious effects of alcoholism and the seeming inexorability of fate, made disturbingly manifest by King's stock-in-trade of veiled menace and palpable monstrosity, all make their way readily into *Doctor Sleep*.

In many ways *The Shining* can be seen as a study in what King himself described in a 1980 interview as 'a family coming apart'.[21] Alcoholism plays a major part in bringing about Jack's reduced circumstances and estranging him from his family. Once Jack is at the Overlook, the hotel fatally exploits this vulnerability. Detailing the explosion that destroys the hotel, leaving Wendy and Danny as two of the three survivors, *Doctor Sleep* begins from the point at which *The Shining* concludes. The preliminary observation that the boy was unharmed, 'physically, at least',[22] points to the lasting nature of the damage inflicted upon the remaining members of the Torrance family. Working swiftly to delineate what happens to them in the first few years after Jack's demise, most of *Doctor Sleep* concerns events in Danny's later life. Now known as Dan, he spends much of his young adulthood in a drunken haze, drifting from one casual job and sexual liaison to another. Any hope of developing a steady existence seems set to be undermined by a combination of his memories of the Overlook and his alcoholism. This condition is both a dreaded legacy from his father and a temporary solution to the problems caused by his shining:

> He had promised both his mother and himself that he would never drink like his father, but when he finally began, as a freshman in high school, it had been such a huge relief that he had – at first – only wished he'd started sooner. Morning

hangovers were a thousand times better than nightmares all night long. All of which sort of led to a question: How much of his father's son *was* he?[23]

Dan's nadir comes when he awakens in a dingy apartment with only scant memories of the night before. Leaving Deenie, his latest conquest, asleep, and her abused child, Tommy, to fend for himself, he absconds with money from her wallet. After months of wandering, Dan eventually comes to settle in New Hampshire, in a small town called Frazier.

Among the many pressures on Dan's father, Jack, was his authorial ambition. This is a recurrent motif for King, who often employs writer protagonists, notably in *Misery* (1987), *The Dark Half*, 'Secret Window, Secret Garden' (1990) and *Bag of Bones*, or other types of artists, as with *Cell* and *Duma Key* (2008). King thus uses his own fiction to explore themes of overt relevance to himself, such as the nature of the creative process and its impact on the creator. Although Dan is a healthcare professional and not a part of this tradition, his drinking problem plainly links him, via his troubled father before him, to King. In *On Writing* King details the first time he got drunk, at age eighteen, and explains that his alcoholism persisted throughout 'the first twelve years or so'[24] of his marriage, later to be compounded by drug addiction. In wryly noting that *The Shining* 'just happens to be about an alcoholic writer and ex-schoolteacher'[25] King indicates the extent to which, consciously or otherwise, his fiction has provided an outlet for his own issues. Following an intervention by family and friends, King became sober. Given his prior inclination for writing about personal matters, it seems only natural that King would choose to explore this development in his fiction.

With his extraordinary writing longevity, King has found plenty of opportunities to augment his literary world and has often returned to the same fictional settings, most notably Derry and Castle Rock in his native Maine, as well as to some of the same characters. Having identified ways in which *The Shining* offers an insight into his own past, it is unsurprising that King recently came to the decision that Danny Torrance's story had been left unfinished. In particular, King found himself asking the question: 'What would have happened to Danny's troubled father if he had found Alcoholics Anonymous instead of trying to get by with what people in AA call "white-knuckle sobriety"?'[26] Jack's own story may have already been told, but King has more to say about alcoholism, family and community, and Dan becomes the vehicle for delving into these concerns. Like its predecessor, *Doctor Sleep* contains a supernatural threat, here, the vampire-like paranormals who form a group, self-named the True Knot, which feeds off the 'steam' produced by children who 'shine'. Yet, as in *The Shining*, King's focus is on the more commonplace scourges of domestic abuse and alcoholism.

It is made clear early on that Dan is desperate to acknowledge and address his drinking problem despite a clear sense that he feels as trapped by his circumstances as had his father before him. Waking up and then throwing up in the aforementioned apartment, Dan tells himself: '*No more. I swear it. No more booze, no more bars, no more fights*. Promising himself this for the hundredth time. Or the thousandth.'[27] Dale Bailey argues that Jack is 'doomed' to succumb to the Overlook's malign influence because he is 'driven by the biological and environmental curses he has inherited from his family'.[28] The stark statements that chase Dan's italicised thoughts, in revealing that he has made himself countless vows about confronting his condition, indicate the extent of his plight. Unlike his father, Dan was physically able to escape the forces that haunted the Overlook and even, years later, to begin his life anew. However, some time after settling in Frazier, still experiencing the dreams and visions that have haunted him since childhood, Dan comes to realise that 'the Overlook was still not done with him'.[29]

Both novels make use of the Gothic trope of haunting to convey the anxious relationships that their protagonists have with the past. This trope dramatises the hold of history and indicates the need to confront unpalatable truths:

> Haunting is arguably the clearest manifestation of Gothic's deep-seated fixation with the return of the repressed – its drive to expose forgotten, ostensibly vanquished, past events that cannot lie forever dormant.[30]

Mired in the Torrance family's history of alcoholism and beleaguered by his memories of the Overlook, Dan is haunted in more ways than one. Besides the weight of these burdens, he is perpetually disturbed by the more recent memory of the young woman, Deenie, and child, Tommy, whom he abandoned a few years ago. Dan cannot fail to be aware of the power of the past to influence the present and, even as he puts roots down in Frazier, this recollection proves to be an enduring source of shame.

As with King, who attended Alcoholics Anonymous as part of his own quest for sobriety, Dan starts to attend AA meetings. Originating from a chance encounter in 1935, when a businessman travelling through Ohio reached out to another alcoholic for support, AA grew to encompass thousands of locally based chapters that 'existed only to serve alcoholics who genuinely desired to get better'.[31] Alcoholics are encouraged to make a pledge to the twelve-step programme at their first meeting. In his history of therapy in America, Jonathan Engel isolates a number of factors responsible for AA's efficacy. Two of these seem to be especially pertinent here and what unites them is an emphasis on community. One factor is AA's requirement that alcoholics be 'confronted by other alcoholics'[32] and the other is the pledge to provide mutual support, which ties group members into a state of 'structured intimacy and accountability'.[33] Though basically devoted to the twelve steps, Dan's anguish over Deenie and her son is a barrier to his commitment. Attending the meetings, he is ever aware of the hold of the past:

> At the end of almost every AA meeting, someone read the Promises. One of these was *We will not regret the past nor wish to shut the door on it*. Dan thought he would *always* regret the past, but he had quit trying to shut the door. Why bother, when it would just come open again?[34]

However, in spite of this recognition, and in true Gothic style, Dan buries his secret deeply within himself, thinking 'not for the first time or the last: *I will never speak of this*'.[35]

Besides the 'poisonous effects of guilt and shame'[36] identified by Eve Kosofsky Sedgwick as a hallmark of the genre, other key Gothic conventions occur throughout *Doctor Sleep*. For example, the shining is one of those altered states of consciousness often portrayed in the Gothic. Dan has long struggled to cope with this ability, turning to drink to blot out the distressing and overwhelming revelations. Yet one day his talent yields a more positive outcome. During an AA meeting in which Dan broods over his old regrets, the shining brings his mind into contact with someone who has a powerful shining of their own. As time goes by, the link between the two intensifies and his new companion is revealed to be Abra Stone, a young girl living twenty miles from Frazier. Forging a new life through commitment to the AA community, while listening to others share their stories and reflecting on his relationship with his sponsor, Dan is led into taking the first tentative steps towards someone who is fully cognisant of the power that has so tormented him.

Gothic is inherently concerned with stirring up the past and such activities usually necessitate a confrontation. Hence Dan, after so many years of fearful secrecy, must eventually confront the past to face the future. When Abra's ability enables her to see the threat posed by the True Knot, it is Dan to whom she turns for help. Dan and Abra join forces, along with friends and family, including another AA member, to defeat these creatures. To do this, Dan must both revisit the former site of the Overlook and embrace the shining, thus facing up to the ghosts of his past to help safeguard the future. It is here that another Gothic convention, the concealed family relationship, comes into play, as Abra is revealed to be Dan's niece. As Jack Torrance's illegitimate daughter, Abra's mother is shown to be Dan's sister. This revelation recasts the strong bond between Dan and Abra in familial terms and once more causes the theme of heredity to come to the fore. The fact that Dan's alcoholism comes from his father has always been apparent, but it now transpires that the shining is also Jack's legacy and is instrumental in bringing his descendants together. As *Doctor Sleep* draws to a close, Dan attends an especially significant AA meeting: the fifteen-year anniversary of his sobriety. Likening his anxious state of mind to the fear he felt at tackling the True Knot at the site of his darkest childhood memories, Dan finally prepares to disclose the secret about Deenie and Tommy. He couches this admission in the parlance of a key AA promise, saying "'I regret plenty, but it's time to open the door, little as I want to'".[37] With this confession he finally brings his secret to light and moves towards finding some measure of peace.

As the sequel to *The Shining*, one of Stephen King's best-known and most pored-over novels, *Doctor Sleep* undoubtedly represents an important entry in his vast body of work. Replete with monstrous beings and underpinned by supernatural forces, it forcefully upholds King's tradition of horror. With its thematic emphasis on the return of the repressed, and its use of haunting, this novel can be construed as a twenty-first-century example of the Gothic genre. Further, it can also be understood as an entirely personal, yet resoundingly familiar, literary exploration of an issue which King first tackled, albeit less directly, in *The Shining* and to which, in the fullness of time, he would ultimately need to return.

With his outstanding levels of marketability and exalted status as a brand name, Stephen King is unquestionably a major figure in the field of horror. Making his mark in the early 1970s, generating a huge quantity of fiction and an extensive range of films and television programmes through the decades since, King has made the transition to twenty-first-century titan of fiction. Though famous for his power to chill, startle or outright terrify his readers, as evidenced by his ready command of a panoply of monsters throughout the years, King also has the ability to engage with serious thematic concerns. An author who commands a high degree of interest time and time again, King has long stimulated and entertained the reading public and looks set to continue doing so further into the twenty-first century.

NOTES

 1. Coddon, 'Stephen King: A Biography', p. 17.
 2. Ibid., pp. 19–20.
 3. Ibid., p. 21.
 4. Ibid., p. 22.
 5. Bloom, *Bestsellers*, p. 315.
 6. 'Hardcover Bestsellers/Fiction', *Publishers Weekly*, 2 April 2001, p. 76.
 7. 'Hardcover Bestsellers/Fiction', *Publishers Weekly*, 16 June 2014, p. 20.
 8. 'Hardcover Bestsellers/Fiction', *Publishers Weekly*, 15 June 2015, p. 17.
 9. 'Hardcover Bestsellers/Fiction', *Publishers Weekly*, 27 June 2016, p. 12.
10. Gelder, *Popular Fiction*, p. 159.
11. Bloom, 'Introduction: Death's Own Backyard', p. 2; original emphasis.
12. King, *On Writing*, p. 182.
13. King, *Danse Macabre*, p. 117.
14. Sedgwick, *The Coherence of Gothic Conventions*, pp. 8–9.
15. Wisker, *Horror Fiction*, p. 8.
16. Bloom, *Bestsellers*, p. 38.
17. Ciabattari, 'Is Stephen King a Great Writer?'.
18. Magistrale, *Landscape of Fear*, p. 2.
19. King, 'Author's Note', p. 483.
20. 'Hardcover Bestsellers/Fiction', *Publishers Weekly*, 7 October 2013, p. 16.
21. Quoted in King, 'Terror Ink', p. 105.
22. King, *Doctor Sleep*, p. 3.
23. Ibid., p. 173.
24. King, *On Writing*, p. 104.
25. Ibid., p. 100.
26. King, 'Author's Note', p. 483.
27. King, *Doctor Sleep*, p. 35.
28. Bailey, *American Nightmares*, p. 94.
29. King, *Doctor Sleep*, p. 75.
30. Janicker, *The Literary Haunted House*, p. 29.
31. Engel, *American Therapy*, p. 119.
32. Ibid., p. 122.
33. Ibid., p. 123.
34. King, *Doctor Sleep*, p. 81.
35. Ibid., p. 162.
36. Sedgwick, *The Coherence of Gothic Conventions*, pp. 8–9.
37. King, *Doctor Sleep*, p. 472.

KEY WORKS

Dreamcatcher (2001). Childhood friends reunite as adults to tackle a monstrous extra-terrestrial threat.

From a Buick 8 (2002). A group of state troopers harbours a vintage Buick Roadmaster with links to another dimension.

Cell (2006). Clayton Riddell faces a world irrevocably changed by a virus transmitted via cell phones.

Lisey's Story (2006). Lisey, widow of bestselling novelist Scott Landon, confronts the dark reality underpinning her husband's fiction.

Duma Key (2008). Recuperating from an accident, Edgar Freemantle finds that painting brings healing but also troubling visions.

Under the Dome (2009). Small-town pressures intensify when an invisible dome separates Chester's Mill from the outside world.

11/22/63 (2011). High-school teacher Jake Epping travels back to 1950s America in a bid to foil the Kennedy assassination.

Mr Mercedes (2014). The first in a trilogy of detective novels, the other two being *Finders Keepers* (2015) and *End of Watch* (2016), sees retired policeman Bill Hodges on the trail of the eponymous killer.

Revival (2014). Jamie Morton finds his life intertwined with that of Charles Jacobs, a one-time minister obsessed with life's deepest mysteries.

The Bazaar of Bad Dreams (2015). Many tales in this collection of short horror and mystery fictions culminate with a twist.

FURTHER CRITICAL READING

Magistrale, Tony (ed.), *The Films of Stephen King: From 'Carrie' to 'Secret Window'* (New York: Palgrave Macmillan, 2008). This collection draws together chapters on film adaptations of King's work, including John Carpenter's *Christine* (1983), Frank Darabont's *The Green Mile* (1999) and David Koepp's *Secret Window* (2004).

Sears, John, *Stephen King's Gothic* (Cardiff: University of Wales Press, 2011). From *Carrie* to *Duma Key*, Sears traces and examines Gothic tropes and preoccupations throughout King's oeuvre.

Simpson, Philip L. and Patrick McAleer (eds), *Stephen King's Contemporary Classics: Reflections on the Modern Master of Horror* (Lanham, MD: Rowman and Littlefield, 2014). Incorporating some of King's most recent publications, such as *11/22/63* and crime novel *Joyland* (2013), this collection takes King scholarship into the twenty-first century.

Strengell, Heidi, *Dissecting Stephen King: From the Gothic to Literary Naturalism* (Madison, WI: Popular Press/ University of Wisconsin Press, 2005). Investigating influences on King, including the Gothic, fairy tales and literary naturalism, Strengell uses numerous examples of his fiction to explore the monsters, archetypes and themes shaping his work.

BIBLIOGRAPHY

Bailey, Dale, *American Nightmares: The Haunted House Formula in American Popular Fiction* (Bowling Green, OH: Bowling Green State University Popular Press, 1999).

Bloom, Clive, *Bestsellers: Popular Fiction Since 1900*, 2nd edn (Basingstoke: Palgrave Macmillan, 2008).

Bloom, Clive, 'Introduction: Death's Own Backyard', in Clive Bloom (ed.), *Gothic Horror: A Reader's Guide from Poe to King and Beyond* (Basingstoke: Macmillan, 1998), pp. 1–22.

Ciabattari, Jane, 'Is Stephen King a Great Writer?', BBC: Culture, 31 October 2014 <http://bbc.com/culture/story/20141031-is-stephen-king-a-great-writer> (last accessed 22 January 2016).

Coddon, Karin, 'Stephen King: A Biography', in Karin Coddon (ed.), *Readings on Stephen King* (Farmington Hills, MI: Greenhaven Press, 2004), pp. 16–27.

Engel, Jonathan, *American Therapy: The Rise of Psychotherapy in the United States* (New York: Gotham Books, 2008).

Gelder, Ken, *Popular Fiction: The Logics and Practices of a Literary Field* (London: Routledge, 2004).

Janicker, Rebecca, *The Literary Haunted House: Lovecraft, Matheson, King and the Horror in Between* (Jefferson City, NC: McFarland, 2015).

King, Stephen, 'Author's Note', in Stephen King, *Doctor Sleep* (London: Hodder, 2013), pp. 483–5.

King, Stephen, *Danse Macabre* (London: Warner Books, 1993).

King, Stephen, *Doctor Sleep* (London: Hodder, 2013).

King, Stephen, *On Writing: A Memoir of the Craft* (London: Hodder and Stoughton, 2000).

King, Stephen, 'Terror Ink', in Tim Underwood and Chuck Miller (eds), *Bare Bones: Conversations on Terror with Stephen King* (New York: McGraw-Hill, 1988), pp. 93–124.

Magistrale, Tony, *Landscape of Fear: Stephen King's American Gothic* (Bowling Green, OH: Bowling Green State University Popular Press, 1988).

Sedgwick, Eve Kosofsky, *The Coherence of Gothic Conventions* (North Stratford, NH: AYER Company Publishers, 1999).

Wisker, Gina, *Horror Fiction: An Introduction* (New York: Continuum, 2005).

CHAPTER 3

Terry Pratchett: Mostly Human

Jim Shanahan

Terence David John Pratchett (1948–2015) was born in Beaconsfield, Buckinghamshire, England, and is most famous for the bestselling Discworld series of humorous fantasy novels that began with *The Colour of Magic* (1983) and numbers forty-one titles. His early novels *The Dark Side of the Sun* (1976) and *Strata* (1981) are often cited as influences on the style and tone of his Discworld universe. Discworld itself is, as the name suggests, a flat, disc-shaped world, slowly turning on the backs of four enormous elephants, which are themselves standing on the shell of Great A'Tuin, a 10,000-mile-long space turtle slowly making its way through the universe. Pratchett also collaborated with Neil Gaiman in writing the apocalypse spoof *Good Omens* (1990), and with the prolific Stephen Baxter on the Long Earth series of science fiction novels (2012–16).

Pratchett is also a major writer of fiction for young readers. His first published novel, *The Carpet People* (1971, revised 1992), his Bromeliad (or 'nome') Trilogy of *Truckers* (1988), *Diggers* (1990) and *Wings* (1990), and his Johnny Maxwell Trilogy comprising *Only You Can Save Mankind* (1992), *Johnny and the Dead* (1993) and *Johnny and the Bomb* (1996) are all aimed (insofar as Pratchett ever 'aimed' his books) at young people. More recently his non-Discworld novels *Nation* (2008) and *Dodger* (2012) were also written with a young adult readership in mind. Set in an alternative version of nineteenth-century Earth, *Nation* reflects the issues and outcomes that were staples of all Pratchett's fiction: the transition from a childlike to an adult view of the world; the power of story; the necessity of retaining that which is empowering about tradition but to triumph over superstition; the need to find better ways to order the world; the power of the individual to change that world; and an eschewal of conventional 'happy' endings in favour of endings that are both realistic and sustainable. Some of Pratchett's Discworld novels can also be categorised as young adult fiction: *The Amazing Maurice and His Educated Rodents* (2001) won the Carnegie Medal in 2001, and the Tiffany Aching series of novels in particular appeals to a younger readership. Pratchett's disdain for the very notion of 'age appropriate' material means that his children's fiction often deals with quite dark and what might be considered 'adult' issues. It is less writing *for* children and more, as Peter Hunt has observed, about the experience of childhood itself.[1] The Discworld has also generated a plethora of companion material on which Pratchett collaborated, produced to satisfy a loyal readership wishing to know more.

Pratchett worked as a journalist in the provincial press and subsequently as a press officer for a number of power stations before becoming a full-time writer after the success of the first Discworld novels. He received an OBE in 1998 and was knighted for his services to literature in 2009. In 2008 he was diagnosed with posterior cortical atrophy, a rare variant of Alzheimer's disease. Despite this 'embuggerance', as Pratchett termed it, his productivity was barely checked, although eventually he was forced to compose through dictation or voice recognition software. Pratchett became a fervent advocate for the right of terminally ill people to choose death by assisted suicide and continued to produce at least one book a year, with the final one, *The Shepherd's Crown*, a Discworld novel, appearing posthumously in September 2015.

Pratchett's popularity with the reading public has few contemporary rivals. At the time of his death in March 2015, it was claimed that his books had sold 85 million copies in thirty-eight languages.[2] His appeal goes beyond the traditional market for 'high' or 'swords and sorcery' fantasy. Regarding Pratchett merely as a writer of funny fantasy would be as reductive as describing Jonathan Swift as a humourist or a children's author. Swift, Voltaire, Charles Dickens, P. G. Wodehouse, G. K. Chesterton and Evelyn Waugh are as much Pratchett's literary antecedents as J. R. R. Tolkien, Robert E. Howard or H. P. Lovecraft. Just as Dickens's novels became less exuberant and more socially focused as time passed, Pratchett's novels become increasingly concerned with what it means to be a person, whether that 'person' is a witch, a golem, a vampire, a semi-reformed conman, a goblin or, indeed, a rat. 'People' and 'human' become conflated or interchangeable terms in Pratchett. You don't have to be human to be 'human', or people to be 'people'.

Unlike other fantasy writers such as Tolkien and George R. R. Martin, Pratchett has never taken the tropes of 'high' fantasy too seriously, but there is an underlying seriousness to his writing. Discworld has long since evolved from being a parody of a certain type of swords and sorcery fantasy writing (most obviously that of Fritz Leiber, Robert E. Howard and Anne McCaffrey) towards becoming a sophisticated critique of the values and attitudes of contemporary society. His Discworld, despite its fantastic nature, is essentially our world. For Pratchett, unlike Tolkien, C. S. Lewis or indeed, J. K. Rowling, there is no single incarnation of evil, no Sauron, White Queen or Voldemort to be defeated. His enemies are the baser elements within us all, and a wider culture encouraging uninformed prejudice and deliberate ignorance. These negative qualities are fairly evenly distributed among all species on Discworld and among all of humanity in our own world. If, as John Clute observes, tragic fantasy is uncommon,[3] laugh-out-loud fantasy is even rarer. There have been British exponents of humorous fantasy, notably F. Anstey and Edith Nesbit, and American writers such as Thorne Smith, Fletcher Pratt and L. Sprague de Camp, who were published in the pulp magazine *Unknown* (1939–43), but Pratchett's only peer as a humorous fantasy writer was his great friend Douglas Adams. Pratchett is not so much Tolkien with jokes as a more benevolent Tom Sharpe with wizards. He parodies but does not ridicule fantasy tropes.

In keeping with Pratchett's view that 'human' is a set of characteristics rather than a species, the Discworld universe is very much a human one, in the sense that gods are created and sustained by people's belief in them, and concepts such as death and time take human form. They are, after all, our concepts. Indeed, one of the central points of the entire Discworld series is that many of the things that are most important to people, such as money, or gods, or concepts such as law or justice, have no reality in themselves, but have existence only because we believe in them. As Death's apprentice, Mort, observes: 'THERE'S NO JUSTICE . . . THERE'S JUST US'.[4] On the whole, this is not a terribly comforting thought, but it can be an empowering one. It suggests that human agency is the great shaping factor, not just on the Discworld but in our world too.

Traditionally, the Discworld series is divided up into a number of sub-series that involve groups of characters clustered around key individuals: Rincewind and the wizards of Unseen University; Granny Weatherwax and the other witches of the kingdom of Lancre; the anthropomorphised figure of Death (one of Pratchett's most popular characters and a figure who makes an appearance in practically every Discworld novel); the hard-boiled copper Sam Vimes and the Ankh-Morpork City Watch; the reformed conman and show-off Moist von Lipwig; and the apprentice witch Tiffany Aching. Another popular character is the Librarian of Unseen University, who happens to be an orang-utan due to a magical accident. The Librarian features in most of the novels, either as a major figure or in a cameo role. He is an expert at travelling in 'L[ibrary]-space', a phenomenon created anywhere books are kept in close proximity to each other. Books are knowledge, and knowledge is power; power is energy, and energy is mass; and mass distorts time and space. The ability to travel in L-space becomes an important plot device in many Discworld novels.

Perhaps the most telling difference between Pratchett's Discworld and classic 'high' fantasy is Pratchett's sense of progress. High fantasy has a tendency towards the medieval and a return to a prelapsarian state of affairs, but the Discworld series is all about progress, about embracing change, and the benefits of new technology. While Pratchett wants people to see the universe in all its true magnificence, he also accepts that, in a practical sense, such an experience would be unbearable for anything other than a very short space of time. Our protection from such a fate is our humanity, which ensures that we are eventually bored even by the marvellous. Humans disrupt the smooth running of the universe, which is why they are despised by Pratchett's so-called Auditors of Reality, incorporeal but powerful manifestations who continually attempt to maintain universal order and who pop out of existence when they have a single individual thought. The real heroes on the Discworld are those who introduce beneficial change, whether that change is in the form of new ideas or new technology, and the villains are those who unthinkingly resist it.

Progress and modernisation occur at a terrific pace on the Discworld. Ankh-Morpork, the largest metropolis on the Disc, progressed from a medieval city-state to something resembling nineteenth-century London in just three decades or so (the events in the Discworld series seem to have occurred in real time). The city still has the trappings of medievalism in the form of trade guilds and in the (generally) benevolent dictatorship of Lord Havelock Vetinari. With the penultimate Discworld novel, *Raising Steam* (2013), the railway age arrived on the Disc. Technological progress is represented as generally positive, and species previously regarded with fear and contempt, such as goblins, have taken to the new technologies. If they have not entirely transformed public perception, many goblins, just like the mysterious golems and others, have at least carved out new roles for themselves in Discworld society. New technologies provide the conditions for tolerance, and the new open-mindedness with regard to what/who constitutes 'people' has in turn resulted in further technological improvements.

A core Discworld concept is that nothing existing or happening there is more bizarre than real life. Everything there has already been conceived of by us, and therefore is *real*, for a given value of real. In its structure and appearance the Discworld evokes Hindu creation myth and Anaximander's map of a flat Earth. Elements of our reality 'leak' into (or onto) the Discworld, albeit they become slightly different, reinforcing the sense of familiarity that most people feel when reading Pratchett's novels: part of the fun is seeing how the Discworld reflects and refracts our own experiences. Indeed, one of the striking things about the Discworld is how mundane and practical a world it is. Its unique configuration just doesn't matter on a day-to-day basis, and this is particularly true in the more recent novels. From a religious point of view, the Discworld's unique cosmic structure may be a slightly more comforting proposition than our situation; the turtle's seemingly purposeful journey through space at least suggests that it is going somewhere. There are gods on the Discworld, and they *do* exist, but acknowledging that they exist and actually *believing* in them are very different propositions. Gods are called into existence by us, and their power depends on how much we believe in them. In *Small Gods* (1992), Om, the Discworld god closest to the Christian God, has dwindled into the form of an old tortoise, because more people believe in the Church of Om than in Om himself. In contrast, Anoia, the goddess of Things That Get Stuck in Drawers, enjoys an upsurge of belief after being credited by Moist von Lipwig with helping him in *Going Postal* (2004). As a result, in *Making Money* (2007) she is tipped to become the Goddess of Lost Causes, a 'very profitable area'.[5] All of this may sound rather absurd, until one considers Catholic venerations such as those of St Anthony and St Jude.

Multiverse theory facilitates the existence of the Discworld. The idea that the multiverse is made up of an infinite number of parallel universes with their own particular laws of nature leads logically to the conclusion that anything that can be conceived of must exist somewhere.[6] Linked to this is the notion that everything that happens stays happened somewhere, and everything that could happen has happened or will happen somewhere. While the Discworld exists and operates on magical rather than scientific principles, the other important frameworking element of the Discworld is the fact that it runs on narrative imperative, a broad term that acknowledges the power of stories, or stories' desire to be told, or our expectations that stories will conform to certain conventions. It is here, perhaps, that Pratchett's fantasy world and our own reality come into closest contact, as a reminder that our world, or our reality, is largely constructed through story. We use stories to give meaning and shape to our lives. But this is not a deterministic straitjacket, since once we recognise the pattern of a story, we can change it. As Granny Weatherwax observes, 'Everything's got a story in it. Change the story, change the world.'[7] Closely allied to the power of story is the power of words (see below).

Good fantasy writing should make us look at our own world in a new way, to see it afresh, in all its wonder and, often, its absurdity. One of the most significant influences on Pratchett was his fellow Beaconsfieldian G. K. Chesterton, who argued that fantasy writing ought to concentrate on showing how fantastic ordinary things are when considered from a particular perspective.[8] This notion of the fantastic banal can have two different meanings. Over time, even the most fantastic things can lose the power to amaze. Conversely, anything, considered from a particular perspective, can seem fantastic. New things often seem fantastic until they become old things. Right from the beginning, Discworld novels addressed innovation. The alien concepts of tourism and insurance are introduced in the very first novels, *The Colour of Magic* and *The Light Fantastic* (1986), for example, and the Discworld versions of cinema and rock music are the subjects of *Moving Pictures* (1990) and *Soul Music* (1994) respectively. In Pratchett's twenty-first-century writing, the challenges of social and technological evolution become prominent themes. In *The Truth* (2000), a reactionary group of influential Ankh-Morporkians, opposed to Lord Vetinari's policy of welcoming non-human races who settle in the city, attempts to frame him for attempted murder in order to remove him from power. *The Truth* sees the introduction of printing with moveable type to Ankh-Morpork, something that upsets a number of vested interests, notably the engravers' guild. But since moveable type allows for words to be broken up and reconstituted as other words, it is perceived as dangerous by those for whom the integrity of words is important, such as the guardians of magic and religion. In replacing engraving, moveable type is replacing a medieval craft with modern technology. One by-product of this development is that newspapers, journalism and the circular concept of 'news' emerges: 'If it was in the paper, it *was* news. If it was news it went in the paper, and if it was in the paper, it was news. And it was the truth.'[9] Here is the power of the 'press', in both a literal and a metaphorical sense. Luckily for Vetinari, investigative journalism is another by-product of the printing press, and it results in him being freed from prison and restored to power. The new-fangled 'press' maintains an uneasy relationship with the executive and judicial powers – another indicator of modernity. Most importantly, the existence of a free press means that elites no longer control information. Of course, the emergence of responsible journalism also creates the space for the yellow press; while there is now such a thing as the 'public interest', it is not always what the public is interested in.

That moveable type would demand a new level of accountability from those in power is an example of an unintended consequence that is both the product of and the inspiration for modernisation. The main agent of modernisation in Pratchett's twenty-first-century novels is the reformed conman Moist von Lipwig, the central character in *Going Postal*, *Making Money* and *Raising Steam*. Behind Lipwig looms the Machiavellian figure of Vetinari, who recognises the need for modernisation but also has to balance progress with social stability and the interests of influential citizens. Technology and social progress go hand in hand, but there is often a price to pay, as Vetinari knows: 'Certain things become easier, but this makes them harder in other ways'.[10] Consequently, in *Making Money* the overarching theme of how we estimate worth is not just confined to the main plot's focus on the introduction of paper currency, but extends to how we value others. The golems in *Making Money* represent the ultimate Other, posing the question of how we value those who do not understand or subscribe to a liberal society's sense of freedom and individuality. The ability of a golem to work non-stop presents a severe threat to the Ankh-Morpork economy, and yet ultimately golems provide the basis for Ankh-Morpork's economic expansion. Such are the contradictions of modernity.

Although Pratchett had intended to write more Discworld stories,[11] it is difficult now not to read his final two novels, *Raising Steam* and *The Shepherd's Crown*, as valedictory texts. In *Raising Steam* the railway age finally arrives on the Disc, and with it, modernity. Pratchett's main concerns over the last twenty years of the Discworld series are to the fore here. Goblins, largely ignored before *Snuff* (2011), are perhaps the most reviled race on the Disc, but they take to the new technology in *Raising Steam* with gusto, just as they had embraced the clacks (a messaging system that serves as a kind of mechanical internet) in *Snuff*. Pratchett observes: 'The villains of the storybooks had found their place in society, at last. All it needed was technology.'[12] Innovation creates opportunity. The later Discworld novels stress that the city makes anything possible. While this is true in technological terms it is equally true societally. Nothing reflects the new multicultural Ankh-Morpork better than the composition of the City Watch, which by *Snuff* has a representative from almost every species. Enforcing the law without fear or favour becomes the test of a species' fitness to become 'human': 'if you could make it as a copper, then you could make it as a species'.[13]

In *Raising Steam*, steam power represents how change can be at once dangerous and beneficial. It needs to be treated with respect, and those who treat it lightly can, and do, come to a bad (or a superheated) end. *Raising Steam* reinforces a tendency that runs through almost all of Pratchett's writing, an essentially animistic view suggesting that everything is alive in some way or other. 'Differently alive' – a PC term coined by vampires, zombies and other undead figures on the Discworld for themselves – has both a humorous and a serious application typical of Pratchett. It applies to a whole range of things, from the First Syrian Bank, a planet that is alive in *The Dark Side of the Sun*, right up to Iron Girder, the Disc's first steam engine, as well as to the life given to concepts by the anthropomorphic representations created by believers, and the magic books that appear to be alive. Words give things life, and Pratchett's words give everything life of a sort. On the Discworld, if people believe something is alive, then it generally is. In *Raising Steam*, new technology must be embraced to make the world better but, equally, the enabling traditions that bind people together must be retained. The schism within dwarfdom between the conservative 'deep-downers' and those of a more progressive persuasion, simmering in Discworld novels since *The Fifth Elephant* (1999), comes to prominence in *Raising Steam*, and only the speedy construction of a railway between Ankh-Morpork and the distant and underdeveloped land of Überwald enables the Low King of the dwarfs to return home in time to quell a coup. The King could probably have been returned magically, or with the help of golems, but returning in time via the new technology of rail was a statement that the clock cannot be turned back. It is perhaps no coincidence that *Raising Steam* is the first Discworld novel to feature a detailed map of an extensive area of the Disc.[14] The railway not only changes formerly held perceptions of time and space, it also occupies space and forces us to fill in that space. Hitherto, Pratchett never felt constrained by existing maps: he introduced a new river in *Snuff*, and observed that the Chalk, a late addition to the geography of the Disc, was not in his original thinking but came into being because there was space for it.[15]

It is to the Chalk that we finally turn. Fittingly, Pratchett's final novel concentrates on the young witch Tiffany Aching, who draws her considerable power from the land that has been her ancestral home since time immemorial. For Pratchett it is a homecoming of a sort, the completion of a cycle, since the terrain and composition of the Chalk are very similar to where Pratchett lived out his life: the village of Broad Chalke, near Salisbury in Wiltshire. In *The Shepherd's Crown*, we witness the death of a seemingly indispensable character, Granny Weatherwax, a rock of stability and common sense; and the passing of the (very much unofficial) leadership of the witches on the Disc to Tiffany. It is a changing of the guard, a handing over of stewardship. Granny Weatherwax's death and the grand showdown with invading elves permit some characters who have slipped from view to make a reappearance.[16] One of the significant sub-plots mirrors that of *Equal Rites* (1987) in promoting gender equality; however, this time it features a young man who wishes to become a witch, hitherto an exclusively female profession. Again, the themes of modernity and redemption feature. In *The Shepherd's Crown*, Nightshade, the queen of the elves, is redeemed when she dies resisting her former subjects, having learnt to empathise with others through encountering suffering and hardship.

Despite the fact that modernisation is largely seen to be associated with the city, Pratchett's views on modernisation are actually clearest here in his last novel. The railway has come to the Chalk, and its rails are made of iron, a substance feared by elves, who seek to prevent progress by destroying the railway. Their defeat and the sealing off of the passage between worlds usher in a new era. Elves are arrogant and complacent, and that makes them stupid. They are cruel and evil not because they are intrinsically bad (although they *are* pretty bad) but because they lack empathy: they think only of themselves. Empathy is traditionally seen as the quality that marks us as human and separates us from animals, so elves, almost by definition therefore, cannot be human. They are incongruous figures in a 'human' world. But there is a warning for us here too: if you lose empathy you cease to be human. The elves are defeated by forces that they have not bothered to try to understand, but redemption, as Nightshade proves, is always possible. The fate of the individual always matters in Pratchett. If there can be good elves, then there can be good wizards, witches, trolls, vampires, werewolves, goblins, orcs; and humans. The existence of one good elf redeems the entire world. As usual, Pratchett's serious message is lightened with a comedic touch. The redundant but still potent king of the elves is given a men's shed by Tiffany to keep him amused and to cultivate new interests and memories. His new shed is balanced by Tiffany's rebuilding of her Granny Aching's shepherd's hut for herself.

At the heart of *The Shepherd's Crown* is this Pratchett notion of balance. Witches know magic is about balance, and so too is progress about balance. Witches use and maintain balance in their work, and sometimes that means *not* using magic. In an earlier Tiffany Aching novel, *I Shall Wear Midnight* (2010), Granny Weatherwax's broomstick remains the same broomstick, even though it has undergone many changes of handles and bristles. This is not just a rehashing of an old joke. The evolving broom represents not only the illusion of permanence, but also the continuity that is present in change. Granny, we are told by another witch, 'was no fool. She could see the future coming.'[17] There is no gainsaying the future, and the future is Tiffany Aching. As Tiffany grows in knowledge, wisdom and power, Granny Weatherwax can depart the scene: balance. Balance implies proportion, and the skill witches have of seeing what is really there. From her new/old hut on the Chalk, Tiffany could see the 'sun rise and set, and the moon dance through its guises – the magic of everyday that was no less magic for that'.[18] The transition from the flashy, pulp-magazine fantasy magic practised by the wizards, dragonriders and sourcerers (*sic*) of the early Discworld books to the 'magic of everyday' (or the fantastic banal) is the major story arc of the Discworld series, placing the witches and the craft they practise at the centre of the Discworld story. What began in *The Colour of Magic* with the inept wizard Rincewind acquiring a homicidal piece of wooden luggage made from the magical material sapient pearwood, ends, over three decades later, with a young woman, wise beyond her years and who just happens to be the most powerful witch on the Disc, patiently learning carpentry in order to build herself a simple wooden hut in which to live. Tiffany chooses to build her hut the hard way, but it is no less magical for that.

When the central concerns of Pratchett's writing are considered, it can be argued that he is not really a fantasy writer at all, since his stories are so deeply rooted in what it means to be a person. He is certainly a satirist, but he is also a consistently humane writer, even if his characters are not always strictly human. He is a religious, even a mystical writer in the broadest sense of the term. If not quite a *believer*, Pratchett believes in the unlimited potential and essential decency of people. But he might be happiest to be seen as a great celebrator of life in all its facets, including coping with change and death (and, of course, particularly Death). In Pratchett, 'humanity' is contagious, but unlike many contagions, it is worth catching. People are the great engine of the Discworld universe, propelling the Discworld along as surely as does Great A'Tuin. People are more powerful than gods, because you choose to be a person, and being a person means having to make choices, whereas gods have none: they are created by us, for us, to be the god of something we have nominated as important. Being truly human is also an ideal, and that means it is something that all can strive for, even if we generally fall short. Pratchett always allows for our essential humanity, and the best any of us can say about ourselves, and Pratchett's writing makes it clear that it *is* the best thing, is that we try to be 'mostly human', most of the time.[19]

NOTES

1. Hunt and Lenz, *Alternative Worlds in Fantasy Fiction*, p. 91.
2. <http://discworld.com/terry-pratchett> (last accessed 29 March 2016).
3. Clute, 'Fantasy', in Clute and Grant, *The Encyclopedia of Fantasy*, p. 339.
4. Pratchett, *Mort*, p. 270. When standing in for Death, Mort's speech is reported in the same way as the Discworld Death's is: in small capitals and no quotation marks. It's a Death thing.

5. Pratchett, *Making Money*, p. 305.
6. For an accessible summary of current physics thinking on the notion of multiple universes see <http://www.bbc.com/earth/story/20160318-why-there-might-be-many-more-universes-besides-our-own> (last accessed 24 March 2016); and for a philosophical argument for the existence of the multiverse (and Discworld) see Vacek, 'On the Possibility of the Discworld'.
7. Pratchett, *A Hat Full of Sky*, p. 338.
8. Pratchett, 'Notes from a Successful Fantasy Author: Keep It Real', in Pratchett, *A Slip of the Keyboard*, pp. 111–15, p. 111; Pratchett, 'Magic Kingdoms', ibid., pp. 149–55, p. 153.
9. Pratchett, *The Truth*, p. 133.
10. Ibid., p. 48.
11. Future ideas are outlined in Wilkins, 'Afterword', p. 336.
12. Pratchett, *Raising Steam*, p. 37.
13. Pratchett, *Snuff*, p. 117.
14. There was a detailed street map of a section of the city of Ankh-Morpork in *Night Watch* (2002), and a map of the countryside around Ankh-Morpork in *Snuff*, but nothing as extensive as the map in *Raising Steam*.
15. Pratchett, MA masterclass, conducted at Trinity College, University of Dublin, 9 March 2011.
16. For example, Eskarina Smith, the female wizard championed by Granny Weatherwax in one of the earliest Discworld novels, *Equal Rites* (1987), and Magrat Garlick, one-time New Age witch and general 'wet hen', now protective mother and queen of the pocket kingdom of Lancre, have cameos in *The Shepherd's Crown*.
17. Pratchett, *The Shepherd's Crown*, p. 183.
18. Ibid., p. 330.
19. The statement, 'mostly human, nearly normal', is used by Death's granddaughter, Susan Sto Helit, to describe herself. As the child of Death's adopted daughter and his human apprentice, Mort, Susan is fully human in a corporeal sense, but has somehow inherited some of her grandfather's non-human abilities. See Pratchett, *Thief of Time* (2001), p. 218.

KEY WORKS

Mort (1987). The first novel to present the Discworld as a coherent and consistent secondary world, and the first novel with Death as a central figure.

Wyrd Sisters (1988). Although loosely based on *Macbeth* and incorporating elements of other plays, this story sees a further move away from parody and introduces more sophisticated characterisation, most notably in the figure of Granny Weatherwax and the other witches of Lancre.

Guards! Guards! (1989). Introduces the character of Sam Vimes and the Ankh-Morpork City Watch, stalwarts of the Discworld series. This novel is a good starting point for new Pratchett readers.

Small Gods (1992). The most satirical and controversial of Pratchett's early novels, critiquing aspects of organised religion and religious fanaticism.

The Truth (2000). As the beginning of the technology series, this explores the nature of news, drawing on Pratchett's own experiences as a journalist.

The Amazing Maurice and His Educated Rodents (2001). This first Discworld book for children, imaginatively reworking 'The Pied Piper of Hamelin', directs many of Pratchett's themes towards younger readers.

Going Postal (2004). Introduces the reformed con-man Moist von Lipwig, who drives technological change in Ankh-Morpork in a number of subsequent novels.

Nation (2008). A young adult book (not in the Discworld series) considered by Pratchett to be his best work. Set in the wake (literally) of a natural disaster on a small Pacific island in an alternative nineteenth century, it plays with the notion of the world being turned upside down, and reinforces many of the ideas in the Discworld series.

Raising Steam (2013). The novel in which technological progress reaches its apotheosis on the Discworld, and fuses this progress with the political and social issues explored in the post-2000 novels.

The Shepherd's Crown (2015). Pratchett's final novel, in which the young witch Tiffany Aching finds her place in the world.

FURTHER CRITICAL READING

Butler, Andrew M., Edward James and Farah Mendlesohn (eds), *Terry Pratchett: Guilty of Literature*, 2nd edition (Baltimore, MD: Old Earth Books, 2004). The essay collection that set the agenda for Pratchett criticism.

Clute and Grant, *The Encyclopedia of Fantasy* (1999). Excellent contextual material for a consideration of Pratchett's work.

Held, Jacob M. and James B. South (eds), *Philosophy and Terry Pratchett* (London: Palgrave Macmillan, 2014). A collection of essays taking a philosophical approach to Pratchett's writing.

Hunt and Lenz, *Alternative Worlds in Fantasy Fiction* (2001). Considers the Discworld in relation to the worlds created by other major fantasy writers, such as Ursula Le Guin.

Pratchett, *A Slip of the Keyboard* (2015). The major source for Pratchett's own observations on his writing.

<http://www.lspace.org>. The most extensive website on Pratchett's life and work.

BIBLIOGRAPHY

Clute, John and John Grant (eds), *The Encyclopedia of Fantasy* (London: Orbit, 1999).

Hunt, Peter and Millicent Lenz, *Alternative Worlds in Fantasy Fiction* (London: Continuum, 2001).

Pratchett, Terry, *A Hat Full of Sky* (London: Doubleday, 2004).

Pratchett, Terry, *A Slip of the Keyboard: Collected Non-Fiction* (London: Corgi, 2015).

Pratchett, Terry, *Making Money* (2007; London: Corgi, 2008).

Pratchett, Terry, *Mort* (1987; London: Corgi, 1988).

Pratchett, Terry, *Raising Steam* (2013; London: Corgi, 2014).

Pratchett, Terry, *Snuff* (2011; London: Corgi, 2012).

Pratchett, Terry, *The Shepherd's Crown* (London: Doubleday, 2015).

Pratchett, Terry, *The Truth* (2000; London: Corgi, 2001).

Pratchett, Terry, *Thief of Time* (2001; London: Corgi, 2002).

Vacek, Martin, 'On the Possibility of the Discworld', in Jacob Held and James South (eds), *Philosophy and Terry Pratchett* (London: Palgrave Macmillan, 2014), pp. 269–86.

Wilkins, Rob, 'Afterword', in Pratchett, *The Shepherd's Crown*, pp. 335–8.

CHAPTER 4

From Westeros to HBO: George R. R. Martin and the Mainstreaming of Fantasy

Gerard Hynes

George R. R. Martin is the best-known contemporary writer of epic fantasy, a position he achieved in 2011 with the publication of the fifth volume of his A Song of Ice and Fire sequence, *A Dance with Dragons*, and the release of the HBO adaptation *Game of Thrones*. By April 2015, more than 60 million copies of his A Song of Ice and Fire books had been sold worldwide and the show was drawing in excess of six million viewers per episode.[1] He is a multiple winner of the Hugo, Nebula and World Fantasy awards and shares a level of public recognition comparable to J. K. Rowling or Terry Pratchett. This success took some time to achieve, however.

Born in Bayonne, New Jersey, in 1948, Martin became active in comic book fandom as a teenager. His earliest stories were published in fanzines such as *Ymir* and *Star-Studded Comics*.[2] While studying journalism at Northwestern University, he gained conscientious-objector status during the Vietnam War, using his anti-war science fiction story 'The Hero' (1970) as supporting evidence.[3] This story was his first professional sale, to *Galaxy* magazine, followed by sales to *Fantastic* and *Analogue*. Working in journalism, Martin was successful as a science fiction writer in the 1970s and as a horror writer in 1980s. His first novel, *Dying of the Light* (1977), examined the experience of death by individuals, cultures and whole planets. *Windhaven* (1981), co-written with Lisa Tuttle, explored the connection between class and technology on a windswept frontier planet. *Fevre Dream* (1982), set aboard an antebellum steamboat, recounted a struggle for power within the vampire community.

The Armageddon Rag (1983), a rock-music, fantasy murder mystery, was, however, a commercial failure and almost ended his writing career. Unable to sell his fifth book, Martin became a staff writer for the revived television series *The Twilight Zone* (1985–9) and writer-producer for the CBS series *Beauty and the Beast* (1987–90). At the same time, he began editing the shared-universe, mosaic-novel series Wild Cards (1987–95, 2002–). He returned to novel writing, this time to epic fantasy, in 1991, beginning work on a planned trilogy, which expanded to a six-book and, currently, seven-book series. A *Game of Thrones* was published in 1996, winning critical acclaim but limited commercial success. The series grew in popularity over the next decade, with A *Clash of Kings* (1998) reaching number 13 on the *New York Times* bestseller list in 1999 and A *Storm of Swords* (2000) number 12 in 2000. Both A *Feast for Crows* (2005) and A *Dance with Dragons* (2011) debuted at number 1, the latter bringing the earlier novels back onto the bestseller lists in its wake. At time of writing, the sixth book, *The Winds of Winter*, is still awaited.

Despite writing in a number of genres, Martin is known in popular culture almost entirely for his contribution to fantasy. Drawing from a number of taproot texts going back to the Epic of Gilgamesh, this genre emerged as a recognisable publishing category in the twentieth century in two stages: the pulp magazines of the 1920s through to the 1950s and the paperback boom following J. R. R. Tolkien's *The Lord of the Rings* (1954–5) in the 1960s. At the same time that science fiction was emerging as a genre in *Amazing Stories* (1926–) and *Astounding Stories* (1930–), pulp magazines such as *Weird Tales* (1923–54), *Unknown* (1939–43) and the slightly more upmarket digest *The Magazine of Fantasy and Science Fiction* (1949–) were publishing early fantasy. *Weird Tales* effectively established the careers of Robert E. Howard, H. P. Lovecraft and Ray Bradbury, while *Unknown* brought Fritz Leiber and L. Sprague de Camp to prominence. Meanwhile *Fantasy and Science Fiction* featured early work by Jack Vance, Shirley Jackson and Roger Zelazny.[4]

The success of *The Lord of the Rings* in paperback in the mid-1960s prompted Ballantine Books to commission the Ballantine Adult Fantasy imprint (1969–74), which marketed earlier writers such as William Morris, Lord Dunsany and Hope Mirrlees to Tolkien's readership. This retroactively created a fantasy tradition defined largely by proximity to Tolkien, partially overshadowing trends emerging in the magazines. Ballantine also commissioned the first new fantasy trilogy since Tolkien, Katherine Kurtz's The Chronicles of the Deryni (1970–3). The popularity of Terry Brooks's Shannara series (1977–) and Stephen R. Donaldson's Chronicles of Thomas Covenant (1977–2013) established the dominance of Tolkien-inspired medievalist fantasies in the following two decades.[5]

A Song of Ice and Fire can, therefore, be viewed as part of the 1990s growth of medievalist epic fantasy alongside the work of Robert Jordan, Terry Goodkind, Tad Williams and Robin Hobb.[6] Martin, however, has asserted that his medievalism is of greater historical verisimilitude, calling much medievalist fantasy 'Disneyland Middle Ages' and claiming: 'The middle ages or some version of the quasi middle ages was the preferred setting of a vast majority of the fantasy novels that I was reading by Tolkien imitators and other fantasists, yet they were getting it all wrong'.[7] Martin has himself been called the 'American Tolkien'[8] and has both expressed admiration for Tolkien and criticised his effect on the genre, in particular for his moral absolutism and sanitised political and military conflict.[9] Martin's ambiguous characters and emphasis on the lethal physicality of politics is precisely what has won him praise: 'It's men and women slugging it out in the muck for money and power and lust and love.'[10]

Just as the arrival of Terry Pratchett's satires signalled the fantasy genre had reached a level of maturity (where recognised tropes could be critiqued), Martin's work also challenges some of the conventions of post-Tolkien epic fantasy. He noticeably avoids archaism or elevated style, with even his kings' diction being notably un-Tolkienian:

> 'Why do you always have to be so headstrong?'
> 'Ah, fuck you, Ned,' the king said hoarsely. 'I killed the bastard, didn't I?'[11]

This is connected to an overall undermining of noble institutions. Martin's knights are murderers and rapists; they are swords wrapped in silk ribbons, in the words of Sandor Clegane.[12] The Night's Watch, an ancient order sworn to protect the realm from supernatural foes, is an under-resourced penal battalion. The handsome prince Joffrey Baratheon is a deranged psychopath.

Martin is careful to complicate easy distinctions between good and evil. Even the sympathetic Starks are introduced beheading a deserter. Good characters die squalidly and are punished for making morally laudable decisions. When Ned Stark attempts to spare the Lannister children he is beheaded for his efforts. Unlike the works of Tolkien or Jordan, there is no Dark Lord to embody the forces of evil. While there is a cataclysmic confrontation building – 'Winter is coming' – most characters are not paying attention to it, ignoring the supernatural Others who threaten to bring everlasting winter. When winter finally arrives in A Feast for Crows, Jaime Lannister sees soldiers heedlessly playing in the snow like children.[13]

The level of fantasy slowly builds as the series progresses. A Game of Thrones is bookended by the appearance of an ice-zombie and the return of dragons to the world but there is little magic in between. Dwarfs are humans with dwarfism, not a separate race. Elves are entirely absent. For the majority of characters, magic is not part of their lives, and the gradual eruption of the fantastic into their world mirrors the experience of the reader. This emphasis on 'realism', a problematic concept when discussing fantasy, has caused Martin to be grouped with other fantasy writers in a sub-genre titled 'grimdark'. The term derives from the dystopian, science fiction tabletop game Warhammer 40,000 (1987–): 'In the grim darkness of the far future, there is only war.' It is usually discussed in terms of grittiness, violence, anti-heroism and a cynical, ostensibly 'realistic' outlook. Depending on the commentator, the label means either praise for moral complexity and an unflinching examination of human brutality or censure for gratuitous violence.[14] Martin was by no means the first writer to write violent and morally ambiguous fantasy, as Robert E. Howard, Michael Moorcock, Mark Lawrence and Mary Gentle all preceded him. But his commercial success and perceived influence on a number of writers of dark and gritty fantasy, such as Joe Abercrombie (who tweets as @LordGrimdark), Richard K. Morgan, R. Scott Bakker and Luke Scull, stimulated discussion about the possible existence of a new movement in fantasy.[15]

Martin's most significant contribution to fantasy may, however, not be in terms of style and tone but in convincing mainstream audiences of the acceptability of the genre, and publishers and studios of its profitability, a process begun by Peter Jackson's film adaptations of The Lord of the Rings (2001–3). Houghton Mifflin Harcourt has recently added science fiction and fantasy to its Best American series and commissioned a fantasy and science fiction list.[16] In 2015 Simon and Schuster launched its own fantasy and science fiction imprint, Saga Press.[17] Though he is not solely responsible for fantasy's current health, Martin's popularity is not unrelated to these developments.

Although Martin had been a prominent fantasy author for over a decade, the HBO adaptation launched in 2011 made him a household name. Described by showrunner David Benioff as 'the Sopranos in Middle Earth', the prestige of the mob drama served to counterbalance and legitimise the fantasy elements.[18] Prejudice against fantasy can be seen in Ginia Bellafante's bewildered and hostile review of the first series in the *New York Times*, calling it 'boy fiction' and suggesting the show might be worth the effort 'if you are not averse to the Dungeons and Dragons aesthetic'.[19] Even more favourably disposed critics emphasised the politics and plotting while excusing the fantasy.[20] The series can, however, be partially credited with an increase in fantasy television, including the commissioning of *Outlander* (Starz, 2014–), *The Shannara Chronicles* (MTV, 2016–) and *The Magicians* (Viking, 2016–). The adaptations of Neil Gaiman's *American Gods* (Starz, 2017), Stephen King's *The Dark Tower* series (Sony, 2017) and Patrick Rothfuss's *The Kingkiller Chronicle* (Lionsgate, forthcoming) were also made possible by the financial success of *Game of Thrones*. Despite its critical and commercial success, the series immediately drew controversy for its graphic violence and explicit sex, or what Basil Glynn, in another context, calls 'The erotic spectacle of female bodies being sexually abused and the violent spectacle of male bodies being physically abused'.[21] Myles McNutt coined the term 'sexposition' to describe the numerous expository speeches delivered by or to naked individuals.[22] There has been, however, a noticeable gender divide in the show's nude scenes, and while it features an unusually large female cast it tends to use female extras as little more than titillating props.

More controversial than the presence of nudity has been the amount of sexual violence, including the transformation of consensual sex scenes, between Daenerys and Khal Drogo, and Jaime and Cersei Lannister, to rapes and the invention of sexual abuse not found in the books, including the torture of prostitutes by King Joffrey and the rape of Sansa Stark by Ramsay Bolton. Martin has defended the sexual violence in the show on the same grounds as he has defended his books: accuracy to medieval social norms, particularly during wartime. He has also contended that the fantasy elements must be grounded in history if the narrative is to remain credible.[23] This unfortunately suggests that a non-patriarchal society would be an inherently fantastical strain on audience credulity.

Even before the HBO series launched, Martin drew an impassioned fandom, with the Brotherhood Without Banners, the main fan group, existing since 2001.[24] The growing intervals between A Song of Ice and Fire books have, however, turned a certain percentage of fans into 'GRRuMblers', who make callous suggestions that Martin may follow the example of his friend Robert Jordan, who died twelve books into a fifteen-book series.[25] The impatience of these fans has inspired blogs, memes and parody songs, prompting Neil Gaiman to warn that 'George R. R. Martin is not your bitch'.[26] This level of emotional investment in Martin's work, whether positive or negative, may indicate an increasingly close and emotive relationship between audience and author generated by social media.

The HBO series has itself posed a dilemma for fans of the books in that the show has now passed the novels in a number of plotlines, while also departing from them on several points. This increasing divergence fundamentally alters the relationship between books and show. Previously, readers had enjoyed a position of privileged knowledge, safe from spoilers; now they must decide the extent to which the new material should influence their reading of *The Winds of Winter*. This level of trans-mediality, with Martin's Westeros existing in multiple canonicities in different media, complicates discussions of adaptation. As Zoë Shacklock argues, it may be necessary to rethink adaptation as 'content flow within a continuing narrative, rather than the re-iteration of a single original text', acknowledging the flexible nature of narrative, authorship and consumption in contemporary media.[27]

Martin's work since 2000 has been dominated by A Song of Ice and Fire. Three volumes, *A Storm of Swords*, *A Feast for Crows* and *A Dance with Dragons*, have appeared with *The Winds of Winter* and *A Dream of Spring* promised. The sequence is what Kari Maund calls a 'scripted series', with the individual books bound by an overarching plot and continuing characters.[28] The most notable feature of the series is what Joe Abercrombie calls its 'lethal unpredictability'.[29] Martin has gone to considerable lengths to challenge fantasy readers' expectations regarding character and narrative, infamously killing off the apparent protagonist, Ned Stark, before the end of the first volume.

Focalisation is deployed carefully throughout the series, with every chapter written in close third person limited. Having members of the Stark family as six of the original eight point-of-view characters encouraged the belief that they would be the protagonists of the series. While the Starks have remained central to events, this has guaranteed neither safety nor success. The introduction of new point-of-view characters in subsequent volumes has required that readers reassess their interpretation of characters, perhaps most effectively in the case of Jaime Lannister. Introduced as the 'Kingslayer', murderer of the last Targaryen king, he is quickly discovered to have an incestuous relationship with his sister, something he conceals by throwing the witness, a seven-year-old child, from a window.[30] Captured by the Starks and challenged by Catelyn Stark as a murderer and oathbreaker, he retorts that a knight's vows are incompatible and self-contradictory.[31] In *A Storm of Swords*, however, Jaime becomes a point-of-view character for the first time, and reveals that has been faithful to one woman his whole life, joined the Kingsguard to protect his sister, and killed King Aerys to save the population of King's Landing.[32] Traumatised by the loss of his sword hand, he strikes up an unlikely friendship with a female knight, Brienne of Tarth, and saves her from rape and murder.[33] Her stubborn idealism forces him to reconsider the possibility of chivalrous action, and so he names his new sword Oathkeeper, gives it to Brienne and sends her to deliver Sansa Stark to safety.[34] Although he still has a poisonous relationship with Cersei and resolves sieges by threatening slaughter, he spends much of the fourth and fifth books negotiating peace in the Riverlands. It is indicative of Martin's ability at characterisation that an incestuous child-murderer can become one of his most nuanced characters.

Martin also uses his characters' relationships with the in-universe equivalent of fantasy literature – chivalric romance – to make readers question the limitations of generic fantasy. Daenerys reflects on the stories of Westeros: 'Children's stories, ... too simple and fanciful to be true history. All the heroes were tall and handsome, and you could tell the traitors by their shifty eyes.'[35] Sansa Stark, by contrast, can be seen as a stand-in for the naive fantasy reader.[36] Early on, she constantly filters her experiences through chivalric and romantic songs. She thinks she loves prince Joffrey without knowing him, gets drunk on the pageantry of her first tournament, and believes the prince and queen must be good because they are beautiful. She is quickly brought up against the reality of life at court. Her prince kills her father, has his guards humiliate and beat her, and repeatedly threatens to rape her. Yet for a time she clings to romances, claiming that her brutalisers are 'no true knights' and attempting to make her life conform to the romance of Florian and Jonquil.[37] As the series progresses, however, Sansa becomes an increasingly critical reader of medievalist romances, pitying young girls for believing in knights.[38] By the end of A Feast for Crows, Sansa deploys fiction to her own advantage, taking on the persona of Alayne Stone, a disguise convincing enough that her chapter titles are henceforth 'Alayne' rather than 'Sansa'. In this case an experienced and disenchanted reading of fantasy/ romance is encouraged.

Martin also challenges fantasy's narrative tropes by raising reader expectations only to dash them. Where Tolkien argued that eucatastrophe, 'the sudden joyous turn', was essential to fantasy, Martin repeatedly offers dyscatastrophe, a sudden turn to the worse.[39] Three moments stand out. In A Storm of Swords, after deaths, defeats and betrayals, Martin allows readers to believe that the fortunes of the Starks will finally begin to improve. Robb Stark is mending his alliance with the Freys and extracting his army from the south to reclaim his ancestral seat. The penultimate chapter before the catastrophe ends with: 'We're going home.'[40] Instead, the Red Wedding becomes a massacre where Catelyn Stark must watch her son be betrayed and murdered by the Freys and Boltons before she herself is killed.[41]

Later in the same volume, Tyrion Lannister, one of Martin's most popular characters, is accused of regicide and demands trial by combat. His champion, Prince Oberyn Martell, seizes this opportunity to take revenge on the especially despicable Ser Gregor Clegane for the rape and murder of his sister, Elia Martell, and her children. Oberyn runs rings around Clegane, demanding a confession and repeating 'You raped her. You murdered her. You killed her children.' Just as it seems Oberyn has won, Clegane grabs him and, while confessing, crushes Oberyn's head.[42] That this also condemns Tyrion is almost incidental. Finally, near the end of A Dance with Dragons, it appears that Jon Snow has managed to unite the Wildlings and the Night's Watch against the supernatural White Walkers when a letter arrives, claiming that the Boltons have defeated Jon's ally Stannis Baratheon and are hunting for Jon's sister Arya Stark. Just as it seems Jon will lead a force south to punish Bolton and reclaim Winterfell, his companions in the Night's Watch turn on him and stab him to death.[43] Repeatedly Martin offers a potential eucatastrophe only to kill the characters who would carry it out.

As well as being praised for this unsentimental unpredictability when it comes to the survival of characters, Martin's skilful orchestration of multiple plots has received attention. A Dance with Dragons has eighteen point-of-view characters and at least as many interlocking main plotlines. This has led Lev Grossman to claim that Martin's 'skill as a crafter of narrative exceeds that of almost any literary novelist writing today'.[44] Martin's plots are unusually complicated, for epic fantasy or any other genre.

There are currently at least half a dozen contenders, with shifting alliances, for the Iron Throne, and major plotlines are occurring in at least ten distinct geographical regions. Despite Grossman's admiration, however, it could be argued that Martin's control of his sprawling narrative is under strain. Unable to resolve the plot of his fourth book without delaying it, he divided it geographically into A Feast for Crows and A Dance with Dragons.[45] Although A Dance with Dragons advanced the narrative beyond the end of A Feast for Crows, it ended immediately before a number of set-piece battles, which were moved to The Winds of Winter. Martin has himself frequently referred to 'the Meereenese knot' to describe the problem of reconnecting the multiple plots converging on Daenerys in Meereen to the plots occurring in Westeros.[46] The long gaps between novels, with five years between the third and fourth books, six between the fourth and fifth, both testify to the complexity of Martin's narrative and to the difficulties, shared with many epic fantasists before him, of controlling continuous prose narrative over several thousand pages.

While Martin has been praised for his characterisation and plotting, the level of sexual violence in his works has drawn considerable criticism.[47] Despite the controversy over sexual violence in the HBO series, there are in fact more rapes, both described and implied, in the books, with even point-of-view characters such as Daenerys and Cersei being victims.[48] Rape may be condemned in Westeros, with rapists officially hanged, castrated or condemned to life service on the Wall, but few rapists are punished for their crimes, and commanders mostly turn a blind eye to their troops' depredations.[49] Every army, save for Daenerys's eunuchs, engages in rape. Social class offers no protection, with queens and noblewomen victimised. Point-of-view characters, including Sansa, Brienne and Arya, are repeatedly threatened with rape by several male characters. The books also include child rape and male rape.[50] In short, Martin has created what Caroline Spector calls an 'environment of sexual oppression', an 'omnipresent threat' of sexual violence; yet this is rarely commented upon by characters.[51]

More controversial than the sheer quantity of sexual violence is its treatment. Martin has self-identified as a feminist, but although both male and female characters face physical abuse, overwhelmingly it is Martin's female characters who are sexually abused.[52] Rape is primarily used to illustrate the depravity of male characters; for example, Gregor Clegane's men describe in detail their rape of a thirteen year old girl,[53] while the victims of rape are rarely permitted to give their account. Cersei Lannister is one of the few female characters to do so, comparing herself to a sold horse ridden and beaten whenever her owner liked.[54] She also manages to take revenge on her rapist, Robert Baratheon, though this is hardly condoned as it sets off the series' main war. Her account also occurs in the same chapter in which she condemns one woman to death and sexually abuses another, undermining any reader sympathy.[55] Perhaps most troublingly, rape is so ubiquitous in Westeros as to become normalised: Palla's 'dress had been ripped in two' and 'she held it up with a clenched fist and walked as if every step were agony';[56] Lollys Stokeworth is raped by 'half a hundred shouting men' and Lord Hewett's unnamed daughter is raped in her hall in front of her sisters.[57] When Jaime Lannister has a rapist executed, the man is bewildered by the thought of punishment: 'I had her before, a hunnerd times . . . We all had her.'[58] Although rape is considered morally reprehensible by many of Martin's characters, it is largely accepted as a fact of life. Martin's world may reject the primness of much epic fantasy, but in the process has developed troubling new tropes around sexual violence, with unforeseeable long-term effects on the genre.

Ultimately, Martin's importance as a contemporary writer lies in his engagement with the tropes and norms of fantasy. He has produced innovative work which rewards knowledge of the genre's traditions while simultaneously critiquing them. He has grounded fantasy in the squalid practicalities of political conflict and refused to conform to the ethical and narratival conventions of the genre. The graphic sexual violence of his works counterbalances earlier euphemism and reticence but at the cost of a desensitised acceptance of it. His narrative is remarkably coherent in its sprawling complexity but he still shares other epic fantasy authors' difficulties controlling plot over narratives of unprecedented length. Perhaps most significantly, Martin has brought an often disreputable genre to an unprecedented mainstream audience.

NOTES

1. Alter, 'Game of Thrones Writer George R. R. Martin Posts Winds of Winter Novel Excerpt'.
2. Martin, Dreamsongs, pp. 9–19.
3. Ibid., p. 65.
4. Ashley, 'Magazines', 'Weird Tales', 'Unknown' and 'Magazine of Fantasy and Science Fiction'.
5. James, 'Tolkien, Lewis and the Explosion of Genre Fantasy', pp. 62–78.
6. See Mendlesohn and James, A Short History of Fantasy, pp. 145–50.
7. Hodgman, 'George R. R. Martin, Author of "Song of Ice and Fire" Series'.
8. Grossman, 'The American Tolkien'.
9. Gilmore, 'George R. R. Martin: The Rolling Stone Interview'.
10. Grossman, 'The American Tolkien'.
11. Martin, A Game of Thrones, p. 504.
12. Martin, A Storm of Swords, p. 494.
13. Martin, A Feast for Crows, p. 836.
14. Compare Joe Abercrombie, 'The Value of Grit', with Liz Bourke, 'The Dark Defiles by Richard Morgan'.
15. Grimdark has yet to receive any academic examination, though there has been much online discussion regarding its nature, influences and long-term survival. See for example Moher, 'Thinking Out Loud About Grimdark'.
16. Deahl, 'HMH Launches SF/F List Curated by "Best American" Series Editor'.
17. <http://sagapress.com> (last accessed 30 August 2017).
18. Katcha, 'Dungeon Master: David Benioff'.
19. Bellafante, 'A Fantasy World of Strange Feuding Kingdoms'.
20. For example, Goodman, 'Game of Thrones: Review'.
21. Glynn, 'The Conquests of Henry VIII', p. 161.
22. McNutt, 'Game of Thrones – You Win or You Die'.
23. Hibberd, 'George R. R. Martin Explains Why There's Violence Against Women on Game of Thrones'.
24. <http://brotherhoodwithoutbanners.com/> (last accessed 30 August 2017).
25. Miller, 'Just Write It!'
26. Gaiman, 'Entitlement Issues . . .'.
27. Shacklock, 'A Reader Lives a Thousand Lives Before He Dies', p. 263.

28. Maund, 'Reading the Fantasy Series', pp. 148–9.
29. Abercrombie, 'Introduction', p. 5.
30. Martin, *A Game of Thrones*, p. 81.
31. Martin, *A Clash of Kings*, pp. 578, 581.
32. Martin, *Storm of Swords*, pp. 26, 156, 158.
33. Ibid., pp. 345, 510.
34. Ibid., pp. 753, 828.
35. Ibid., p. 814.
36. Teitelbaum, 'Decapitating the Chivalric Hero'.
37. Martin, *A Storm of Swords*, pp. 21, 184.
38. Ibid., p. 222.
39. Flieger and Anderson (eds), *Tolkien on Fairy-Stories*, p. 75.
40. Martin, *A Storm of Swords*, p. 567.
41. Ibid., pp. 580–4.
42. Ibid., pp. 388–90.
43. Martin, *A Dance with Dragons*, pp. 907–13.
44. Grossman, 'George R. R. Martin's *Dance with Dragons*'.
45. Martin, *A Feast for Crows*, pp. 853–4.
46. For example, Martin, 'Talking About the Dance'.
47. See Spector, 'Power and Feminism in Westeros'.
48. Martin, *A Game of Thrones*, p. 228; *A Feast for Crows*, p. 598.
49. For example, Martin, *A Dance with Dragons*, p. 945.
50. Martin, *A Storm of Swords*, p. 441; *A Dance with Dragons*, p. 747.
51. Spector, 'Power and Feminism in Westeros', p. 185.
52. Salter, '*Game of Thrones*'s George R. R. Martin: "I'm a Feminist at Heart"'; Frankel, *Women in Game of Thrones*, p. 5.
53. Martin, *A Clash of Kings*, pp. 342–3.
54. Ibid., p. 620.
55. Martin, *A Feast for Crows*, pp. 598–604.
56. Martin, *A Clash of Kings*, p. 490.
57. Martin, *A Clash of Kings*, p. 439; *A Feast for Crows*, p. 547.
58. Martin, *A Feast for Crows*, p. 553.

KEY WORKS

'A Song for Lya' (1974). Science fiction novella, winning a Hugo Award, where the exploration of an alien parasite by two human telepaths mirrors an examination of love and relationships.

Dying of the Light (1977). A science fiction work examining death on the level of both individual and society.

'Sandkings' (1980). Science fiction story, winning both Hugo and Nebula Awards, where an alien species is manipulated for sadistic pleasure before it escapes and evolves.

Fevre Dream (1982). A vampire novel set aboard an antebellum steamboat, tracing a power struggle within the vampire community.

'The Pear-Shaped Man' (1988). A horror story, winning the Bram Stoker Award, about an unsettling obese man who invades his neighbour's life.

'The Skin Trade' (1988). Martin's contribution to urban fantasy, specifically werewolf noir.

A Game of Thrones (1996). The work that established Martin as a major writer of epic fantasy.

A Storm of Swords (2000). The most violent and dramatic volume in 'A Song of Ice and Fire', infamous for the Red Wedding.

A Dance with Dragons (2011). Martin's longest and most complicated work so far.

FURTHER CRITICAL READING

Battis, Jes and Susan Johnston (eds), *Mastering the Game of Thrones: Essays on George R. R. Martin's A Song of Ice and Fire* (Jefferson, NC: McFarland, 2015). Focuses on Martin's narrative style, representations of the body and adaptation.

Carroll, Shiloh, 'Rewriting the Fantasy Archetype: George R. R. Martin, Neomedievalist Fantasy, and the Quest for Realism', in Helen Young (ed.), *Fantasy and Science Fiction Medievalisms: From Isaac Asimov to Game of Thrones* (Amherst, NY: Cambria, 2015), pp. 59–76. Addresses Martin's claim to write a more realistic medievalism than most epic fantasists.

Frankel, *Women in Game of Thrones*. Focuses on depictions of women in the HBO series and accusations of misogyny therein, though also engages in dialogue with the books.

Klastrup, Lisbeth and Susana Tosca, '*Game of Thrones*: Transmedial Worlds, Fandom and Social Gaming', in Marie-Laure Ryan and Jan-Noël Thon (eds), *Storyworlds Across Media: Towards a Media-Conscious Narratology* (Lincoln: University of Nebraska Press, 2014), pp. 295–314. Puts Martin's work in the context of transmedial worldbuilding, emphasising the participation of fans through social media.

Lowder, James (ed.), *Beyond the Wall: Exploring George R. R. Martin's A Song of Ice and Fire* (Dallas: Benbella Books, 2012). Somewhat uneven collection with an emphasis on historicity, trauma and the status of fantasy.

BIBLIOGRAPHY

Abercrombie, Joe, 'Introduction', in Scott Lynch, *The Lies of Locke Lamora* (London: Gollancz, 2011), pp. 4–5.

Abercrombie, Joe, 'The Value of Grit', Joe Abercrombie website, 25 February 2013 <http://www.joeabercrombie.com/2013/02/25/the-value-of-grit/> (last accessed 28 March 2016).

Alter, Alexandra, '*Game of Thrones* Writer George R. R. Martin Posts *Winds of Winter* Novel Excerpt', *New York Times*, 2 April 2015 <http://www.nytimes.com/2015/04/03/business/media/winds-of-winter-excerpt-published-by-george-rr-martin-on-his-site.html?_r=0> (last accessed 28 March 2016).

Ashley, Mike, 'Magazines', 'Weird Tales', 'Unknown' and 'Magazine of Fantasy and Science Fiction', in John Clute and John Grant (eds), *The Encyclopedia of Fantasy* (1997) <http://sf-encyclopedia.uk/fe.php> (last accessed 28 March 2016).

Bellafante, Ginia, 'A Fantasy World of Strange Feuding Kingdoms', *New York Times*, 14 April 2011 <http://www.nytimes.com/2011/04/15/arts/television/game-of-thrones-begins-sunday-on-hbo-review.html> (last accessed 28 March 2016).

Bourke, Liz, '*The Dark Defiles* by Richard Morgan', *Strange Horizons*, 17 April 2015 <http://www.strangehorizons.com/reviews/2015/04/the_dark_defile.shtml> (last accessed 28 March 2016).

Deahl, Rachel, 'HMH Launches SF/F List Curated by "Best American" Series Editor', *Publishers Weekly*, 9 November 2015 <http://www.publishersweekly.com/pw/by-topic/industry-news/publisher-news/article/68624-hmh-launches-new-sf-f-list.html> (last accessed 28 March 2016).

Flieger, Verlyn and Douglas A. Anderson (eds), *Tolkien on Fairy-Stories* (London: HarperCollins, 2006).

Frankel, Valerie Estelle, *Women in Game of Thrones: Power, Conformity and Resistance* (Jefferson, NC: McFarland, 2014).

Gaiman, Neil, 'Entitlement Issues . . .', *Neil Gaiman's Journal*, 12 May 2009 <http://journal.neilgaiman.com/2009/05/entitlement-issues.html> (last accessed 28 March 2016).

Gilmore, Mikal, 'George R. R. Martin: The *Rolling Stone* Interview', *Rolling Stone*, 23 April 2014 <http://www.rollingstone.com/tv/news/george-r-r-martin-the-rolling-stone-interview-20140423?page=4> (last accessed 28 March 2016).

Glynn, Basil, 'The Conquests of Henry VIII: Masculinity, Sex and the National Past in *The Tudors*', in Beth Johnston, James Aston and Basil Glynn (eds), *Television, Sex and Society: Analyzing Contemporary Representations* (London: Continuum, 2012), pp. 157–74.

Goodman, Tim, '*Game of Thrones*: Review', *Hollywood Reporter*, 15 April 2011 <http://www.hollywoodreporter.com/review/game-thrones-review-174120> (last accessed 28 March 2016).

Grossman, Lev, 'The American Tolkien', *Time*, 13 November 2005, <http://content.time.com/time/magazine/article/0,9171,1129596,00.html> (last accessed 28 March 2016).

Grossman, Lev, 'George R. R. Martin's *Dance with Dragons*: A Masterpiece Worthy of Tolkien', *Time*, 7 July 2011 <http://content.time.com/time/arts/article/0,8599,2081774,00.html> (last accessed 28 March 2016).

Hibberd, James, 'George R. R. Martin Explains Why There's Violence Against Women on *Game of Thrones*', *Entertainment Weekly*, 3 June 2015 <http://www.ew.com/article/2015/06/03/george-rr-martin-thrones-violence-women> (last accessed 28 March 2016).

Hodgman, John, 'George R. R. Martin, Author of "A Song of Ice and Fire" Series: Interview on the Sound of Young America', *Bullseye with Jesse Thorn*, transcript by Sean Sampson, 19 September 2011 <http://www.maximumfun.org/sound-young-america/george-r-r-martin-author-song-ice-and-fire-series-interview-sound-young-america#transcript> (last accessed 28 March 2016).

James, Edward, 'Tolkien, Lewis and the Explosion of Genre Fantasy', in James and Mendlesohn (eds), *The Cambridge Companion to Fantasy Literature* (2012), pp. 62–78.

James, Edward and Farah Mendlesohn (eds), *The Cambridge Companion to Fantasy Literature* (Cambridge: Cambridge University Press, 2012).

Katcha, Boris, 'Dungeon Master: David Benioff', *New York Magazine*, 18 May 2008 <http://nymag.com/arts/books/features/47040/> (last accessed 28 March 2016).

McNutt, Myles, '*Game of Thrones* – You Win or You Die', *Cultural Learnings*, 29 May 2011 <http://cultural-learnings.com/2011/05/29/game-of-thrones-you-win-or-you-die/> (last accessed 28 March 2016).

Martin, George R. R., *A Clash of Kings* (1998; London: Voyager, 2003).

Martin, George R. R., *A Dance with Dragons* (London: Voyager, 2011).

Martin, George R. R., *A Feast for Crows* (London: Voyager, 2005).

Martin, George R. R., *A Game of Thrones* (1996; London: Voyager, 2003).

Martin, George R. R., *A Storm of Swords* (2000; London: Voyager, 2003).

Martin, George R. R., *Dreamsongs: GRRM. A Retrospective* (London: Gollancz, 2003).

Martin, George R. R., 'Talking About the Dance', *Not a Blog*, 19 May 2011 <http://grrm.livejournal.com/217066.html> (last accessed 28 March 2016).

Maund, Kari, 'Reading the Fantasy Series', in James and Mendlesohn (eds), *The Cambridge Companion to Fantasy Literature* (2012), pp. 147–53.

Mendlesohn, Farah and Edward James, *A Short History of Fantasy* (London: Middlesex University Press, 2009).

Miller, Laura, 'Just Write It! A Fantasy Author and His Impatient Fans', *New Yorker*, 11 April 2011 <http://www.newyorker.com/magazine/2011/04/11/just-write-it> (last accessed 28 March 2016).

Moher, Aidan, 'Thinking Out Loud About Grimdark', *A Dribble of Ink*, 27 February 2015 <https://medium.com/a-dribble-of-ink/let-s-unpack-grimdark-8aedb13a5e9f#.8m1b1ual7> (last accessed 28 March 2016).

Salter, Jessica, '*Game of Thrones*'s George R. R. Martin: "I'm a Feminist at Heart"', *Telegraph*, 1 April 2013 <http://www.telegraph.co.uk/women/womens-life/9959063/Game-of-Throness-George-RR-Martin-Im-a-feminist.html> (last accessed 28 March 2016).

Shacklock, Zoë, 'A Reader Lives a Thousand Lives Before He Dies: Transmedia Textuality and the Flows of Adaptation', in Jes Battis and Susan Johnston (eds), *Mastering the Game of*

Thrones: Essays on George R. R. Martin's A Song of Ice and Fire (Jefferson NC: McFarland, 2015), pp. 262–79.

Spector, Caroline, 'Power and Feminism in Westeros', in James Lowder (ed.), *Beyond the Wall: Exploring George R. R. Martin's A Song of Ice and Fire* (Dallas: BenBella Books, 2012), pp. 169–88.

Teitelbaum, Ilana, 'Decapitating the Chivalric Hero: On *Game of Thrones*', *Los Angeles Review of Books*, 30 March 2013 <https://lareviewofbooks.org/essay/decapitating-the-chivalric-hero-on-game-of-thrones> (last accessed 28 March 2016).

CHAPTER 5

Nora Roberts: The Power of Love

Jarlath Killeen

I t's official: Nora Roberts is cool. Moreover, since this quality was ascribed to her
by one of the coolest people alive, Stephen King, there is no disputing it. In 2007
King graded the coolness quotient of a number of high-profile celebrities (including
himself), for the pop culture bible *Entertainment Weekly*. He concluded that while
poor Tom Hanks is destined to remain forever square (though eminently likeable),
others, like Morgan Freeman, Bruce Springsteen, Elmore Leonard and (this came as
something of a surprise) Nora Roberts just have the elusive 'it factor': 'Gotta say it:
Nora Roberts is cool. I don't make the news, honey, I just report it. There's no rhyme
or reason to the coolness thing.'[1] King sounds slightly begrudging, as if he were com-
mitting a cultural crime by recognising the coolness of a writer working in perhaps
the least 'cool' genre of them all, the popular romance.

King's hesitancy is understandable given the precariousness of his own reputation
and that of the genre in which he made his name. After all, horror has had to struggle
to gain a modicum of literary respectability, and it has often done so by explicitly
defining itself against and opposed to the romance. In King's own *Misery* (1987), the
protagonist is a successful writer of historical romances yearning for acceptance by
the literary establishment, who tries to appease his high-culture critics by killing off
the heroine of his serial romances. Paul Sheldon is horrifically punished by being
imprisoned and tortured by what King appears to think is an only slightly exaggerated
version of the average romance reader.[2] Admitting Nora Roberts is 'cool', then, is
probably something of a concession for King. His most prominent academic defender,
Tony Magistrale, has explicitly contrasted King with Roberts to highlight King's
originality and the Roberts's formula dependence:

> it seems obvious that King's achievement is somehow different from and vastly
> more important than the canons of other enormously popular writers – such as
> Danielle Steel, John Grisham, and Nora Roberts . . . whose themes strike me

as highly repetitive and formulaic . . . [Roberts is] firmly wedded to most of the predictable conventions of the romance genre.[3]

The romance has been the obvious target for such popular and academic detraction for years now. That King acknowledges not only Roberts's cultural presence but her cultural authority in the contemporary moment (also in 2007, *Time* magazine declared her to be one of the 100 most influential people in the world)[4] is significant, and was capitalised on by Roberts's publishers, who cannily placed his words on the front cover of a number of her novels.

Nora Roberts is certainly a force to be reckoned with. To claim her as, perhaps, the most significant novelist alive today may not be an exaggeration, depending on how 'significant' is understood. In a breezy survey, Mary Ellen Snodgrass proclaimed Roberts as 'the world's best-selling novelist since 2000'.[5] At the time of writing (April 2017), Roberts had had 225 novels published since her first, *Irish Thoroughbred*, appeared in 1981, a mere 192 of which have appeared on the *New York Times* bestseller lists, with 58 of them going to the number 1 spot (though that august publication has so far deigned to review only one of them).[6] Indeed, so prolific and so popular is Roberts that her work has spent the equivalent of nineteen years on that bestseller list, and a Nora Roberts novel sells about once every three seconds. According to her website, 'There are enough Nora Roberts books in print to fill the seats of Wrigley Field *over* 9,900 times', so that 'If you place all Nora's books top to bottom, they would stretch across the United States from New York to Los Angeles 18 times'.[7] She writes an average of five novels a year and Roberts estimates that it takes her about forty-five days to produce a clean draft.[8] Anthony Trollope was once called a 'novel machine', given his formidable reputation for producing gigantic three-volume novels at an astonishing rate while maintaining his job in the postal service.[9] Trollope explained that he set himself the daily task of producing 250 words every quarter of an hour between 5.30 and 8.30 a.m., and that if he finished one novel before the end of his daily grind he would just turn the page and start a new one. Even measured against Trollopian standards, Roberts's productivity is astonishing (though her novels are nowhere near as long as those of Trollope).[10] She works for eight hours a day and casts herself as a hard-working professional whose profession just happens to be writing.

> I sit in front of the keyboard all day . . . I usually go up to my office by 9:00 and work for about 6–8 hours . . . I don't believe in waiting for inspiration. It's my job to sit down and figure out what to write.[11]

Roberts indicates here that while she is a romance writer, she is not a Romantic one, and holds no faith in the 'great author' theory; she just gets on with her job.

Remarkably, this enormous productivity has had, as far as the best informed in the romance community are concerned, no impact whatsoever on the quality of her work; she is considered not only one of the most prolific romance writers around but also one of the best. Pamela Regis, the most significant contemporary scholar of popular romance, affirms that 'Roberts is a master' of the form.[12] Unsurprisingly, the Romance Writers of America (RWA), a non-profit association dedicated to the promotion of romance, which has over 10,000 members, has bestowed many accolades upon her. Indeed, Roberts has won more RITA Awards than any other romance writer since their inception in 1982:[13] an astonishing nineteen to date, in multiple categories. She has been inducted into the RWA's Romance Hall of Fame in three categories (Contemporary Single Title Romance; Romantic Suspense; Long Contemporary Romance) and in 2008 the RWA's 'Lifetime Achievement Award', which she won in 1997, was renamed the 'Nora Roberts Lifetime Achievement Award', thus effectively canonising her as the most important popular romance writer . . . ever.[14]

Famously, Roberts turned to writing in desperation. The Maryland-born mother of two was stuck at home during a 1979 blizzard and, bored and exhausted from constantly entertaining her children, having embroidered and needlepointed her way to distraction, and confronted with 'a dwindling supply of chocolate', she began writing stories as an outlet for her frustration. Since she had been reading romances, this was the genre she turned to.[15] After a number of rejections, Roberts eventually found a publisher, Silhouette,[16] for *Irish Thoroughbred*, and she quickly became both adept at working in a variety of romance sub-genres and enormously popular with the romance readership. While Roberts is simultaneously one of the most popular and prolific writers in the world, she is certainly not as well known in academic and even journalistic circles as other household names like J. K. Rowling, John Grisham and Stephen King. To date, there have been no scholarly monographs focusing on her work, and just a scattering of academic and newspaper articles, though An Goris wrote a brilliant doctoral dissertation about Roberts and romance.[17] Although it is true to say that popular literature is now recognised as a significant field of literary study, and genres like science fiction and detective fiction are widely studied, this is still not true of the popular romance, which remains the ugly sister of the pop lit establishment. In 2013, romance accounted for sales of $1.08 billion, 13 per cent of all sales of adult fiction. But despite these enormous figures, which far outstrip those of its nearest rivals, inspirational literature and crime fiction,[18] the academy remains hesitant about the genre. Maryan Wherry notes that 'discussion or study of popular romance still begins with a defence of the genre or an argument asserting the value of studying the genre, calling for recognition and respect'.[19]

At one time, romance, like all genre fiction, was criticised because of the formulaic nature of its plots, but given the academic embrace of other structurally rigid genres, plot predictability is no longer the major reason why romance leads in sales but comes last in literary and academic respectability. Certainly, the romance plot *is* predictable and its ending preordained. Each romance has as its focus a love story concluding with a happy ending (what has come to be termed the 'Happily Ever After' or HEA), a formula pithily described by Sarah Wendell and Candy Tan: 'Boy meets girl. Holy crap, shit happens! Eventually, the boy gets the girl back. They live Happily Ever After.'[20] Romance scholars Janice Radway and Pamela Regis offer thorough and elaborate explanations of this formula, which has either thirteen (Radway) or eight (Regis) elements, depending on your perspective, each of which can be adapted, stretched and modified.[21] There is no requirement for each element to appear in every romance, although it is fair to say that, to be a romance, the love story *must* be central and there *must* be a HEA.[22] Scholars who grant literary complexity to the detective story, possibly the most rigidly formulaic of all genre fiction, can hardly gripe about the relatively elastic conventions of the romance.

A probable reason for the still-contested position of Popular Romance Studies is that the enormous impact of second-wave feminist critiques of the genre continues to be felt. In crucial interventions in the 1970s which shaped the academic appreciation of the genre for three decades, Ann Douglas characterised the romance as 'soft core' pornography for women,[23] while Germaine Greer pointed to the enormous female readership of romance as evidence of women 'cherishing the chains of their bondage'.[24] As is now apparent, these criticisms were based on a very superficial familiarity with the genre, and were typified by a tendency to take a small sample from a particular period as universally true. Greer, for example, mentions only a couple of novels by Georgette Heyer and Barbara Cartland (who wrote something like a novel a week at the height of her powers), both published in 1968, and extrapolates from them the politics of the genre. Given the enormous output of not only Cartland (well over 700 novels in total), but of romance writers more generally, it is frankly ludicrous to characterise even the 'queen of romance' on the basis of a couple of novels.[25] These early feminist criticisms were substantially revised by much more careful considerations of the romance by Janice Radway and Tania Modleski in the 1980s, though both still concluded that, for women, the genre was ultimately part of the problem rather than part of the solution.[26] Radway's study ends on the depressing note that 'it is tempting to suggest that romantic fiction must be an active agent in the maintenance of the ideological status quo because it ultimately reconciles women to patriarchal society'.[27] However, both of these brilliant scholars also based their conclusions on a very small sample of romance novels, and neither considered the work of Roberts at all (understandable, given that she had not yet reached world domination at that stage in her career).

These studies, and their second-wave feminist predecessors, were very influential, not least in romance writing circles themselves, and their conclusions seeped into the popular discourse concerning the genre. That romance is 'bad' (especially for women) is one of the things most students seem to 'know' before they ever start to read the romance in an academic setting,[28] and fans of the genre often still admit to hiding their passion to avoid the disdain of others. In ten years of teaching romance fiction to students from across the Anglophone world, I continue to encounter knee-jerk dismissal, and this from those who have chosen to study popular literature. Indeed, I have met only three students who were willing to admit in front of their peers that they were active readers of the romance (though others did confess to liking it in private conversations). Roberts herself (in a characteristically candid way) pours scorn on the contention that romance readers have internalised genre conventions, and find it difficult to differentiate between romantic fantasy and banal reality:

> Some critics claim that reading romance is bad for women, that it gives them unrealistic expectations. When I hear this statement, all I can think is those critics don't rate female intelligence very highly. Are we stupid? Are we so ridiculously impressionable that we must be protected because we can't separate fiction from reality?[29]

As well as combatting academic criticisms of the genre discursively, Roberts has directly addressed these in her fiction. In *Brazen Virtue* (1988), published four years after Radway's *Reading the Romance*, a phone sex operator is raped and killed by a psychopath who believes that any woman capable of fantasising about sex and violence must, by definition, desire brutal intercourse. In this novel Roberts challenges the argument that female fantasies translate into real-life desires, and suggests that anyone who thinks they do is deranged.

Roberts herself is perfectly capable of criticising the genre and changing it from the inside. She complained that the romances of the 1970s were over-populated by antiseptic and wan heroines needing rescue by older, wealthier men – a legacy of the Gothic romance, with female protagonists more liable to faint than fight back when pursued by darkly attractive villains:

> He was often a Greek tycoon; she was often orphaned and raised by aunts. She's on her way to a new job, working for the richest man in the free world. In the airport, she's rushing through with her battered suitcase. She runs into this man, and the suitcase falls open, revealing a pitiful wardrobe – it's all neat and well-mended but sad. And he calls her a clumsy fool, and helps her stuff her clothes back into the suitcase and storms off, and the next day she goes into the offices of the richest man in the free world and who should be there but the man she ran into at the airport.[30]

Irritated by these 'conventions', Roberts challenged them, and not just by swapping the passive virgin for a stereotypically 'sassy' or 'feisty' alternative: for the most part, Roberts's heroines are fully realised characters carefully situated in well researched and precisely constructed lives and careers. These heroines have (believably) been lion trainers (*Untamed*, 1983), arson investigators (*Blue Smoke*, 2005), antique dealers (*Hidden Riches*, 1994), academics and strippers (*Three Fates*, 2002), archaeologists (*Birthright*, 2003), bed-and-breakfast operators (*Born in Ice*, 1994), scientists (*Without a Trace*, 1990), DJs (*Night Shift*, 1991), along with a couple of dozen other occupations.[31]

Moreover, far from the heroine being the receptive and passive figure (as many casual scorners of the romance are still apt to assume), in a Roberts novel she is just as likely to be the romantic aggressor, or initially far less interested in a love affair than her male counterpart. For example, in *Blue Smoke*, one of Roberts's best novels, the hero, Bo Goodnight, falls for the heroine, Reena Hale, years before she is even aware of his existence, and his desperate, though appealing, adoration eventually wins her over. She is by far the more sexually assertive of the two, and their love scenes involve her biting, stripping and seducing him in ways that had traditionally been the preserve of the hero:

> Outside the gate, she pushed him back against a tree, clamped her lips on his . . . She nuzzled his ear, breathed into it. 'Why don't I take you to my place.' She took his hand, headed back to the sidewalk.[32]

In *Montana Sky* (1996), the tomboy heroine, Willa Mercy, is in many ways a 'masculine' figure, an excellent rancher, hunter and rodeo rider, and the plot endorses these masculine qualities, making them central to her attractiveness rather than requiring her to renounce them for more traditionally feminine pursuits.[33] As Goris explains, 'the narrative consistently validates many of Willa's more masculine traits and behaviours, which often serve to empower her in the Western and very masculine world in which she moves and in which the novel is set'; and this reversal of conventions is not unusual in a Roberts novel.[34]

Roberts has undoubtedly stretched genre conventions in many ways, and has experimented in a variety of sub-genres, including suspense and paranormal and futuristic romance, notably as J. D. Robb, the pen-name she adopted for her 'In Death' series, set in mid-twenty-first-century New York. She has also stretched the genre in terms of length, a crucial factor in terms of categorising romance novels. Yet this stretching and experimentation do not account for her enormous popularity, as she remains 'conservative' by comparison with many of her romance peers. Tellingly, Regis's chapter on Roberts in A Natural History of the Romance Novel is called 'One Man, One Woman' (a title which could be changed to 'One White Man, One White Woman'). Given the current popularity of sub-genres such as multicultural and erotic romance (including ménage and BDSM), Roberts can sometimes appear to be a traditional, steadying and comforting presence in the now heady and experimental world of the contemporary popular romance. Her sex scenes are raunchy and erotic when compared with the euphemisms and evasions of the romances of the 1950s and 1960s, and liberatory next to the rape-inflected bodice rippers of the 1970s, such as Kathleen Woodiwiss's now notorious The Flame and the Flower (1972) and Rosemary Rogers's Sweet Savage Love (1974). But they look positively vanilla beside the jet-packs and butt-plugs of E. L. James's 'Fifty Shades' trilogy (2011–12) or the Masters of the Shadowlands series by Cherise Sinclair; old-fashionedly heterosexual next to LGBT romances like Marie Sexton's Promises (2010) or Heidi Cullinan's Fever Pitch (2014); positively bygone in comparison with ménage novels by Megan Hart such as Tempted (2008); and very white beside the work of the likes of Milan Vohra. Roberts herself has positively ruled out erotic novels, explaining in 2009:

> I'm not going to write about stuff that you might read about in some erotica – you know, blood play . . . And I'm probably not going to do S&M. I'm not going to do any harsh sex that involves pain.[35]

Moreover, Roberts has so far decided against exploring the possibilities of the inspirational romances, exemplified by the novels of Francine Rivers, clearly because this sub-genre is mostly written by Christian conservatives, and Roberts admits to being a 'very lapsed' Catholic.[36] These comparisons are not made in order to disparage Roberts's work. The point here is that while Roberts certainly experiments with the genre, she is willing to work within genre limitations, and it is no surprise that she is particularly good at writing category romances, perhaps the most rigid of all romance subcategories.

Roberts is probably less interested, however, in testing genre boundaries than candidly examining the romantic landscape of contemporary women and suggesting ways in which her readers should negotiate it. Taking consideration of three of Roberts's post-2000 novels – the 2001 winner of the Romantic Suspense RITA *Carolina Moon* (2000), the *New York Times* number 1 bestseller *Angels Fall* (2006) and one of her most significant contributions to the genre *Blue Smoke* (2005) – her popularity could be accounted for by the skill with which she both acknowledges the deeply troubled nature of present-day romantic reality and, despite this problematic context, suggest reasons for continued romantic hope for her readers.[37]

Love and romance are certainly contested sites and conflicted experiences at present. The philosopher Harry Frankfurt points out that most of us have 'a nagging anxiety or unease' when it comes to love which makes us 'troubled, restless, and dissatisfied with ourselves', so that love is more often associated with pain than pleasure.[38] Roberts does not minimise the hurt and disquiet that are inextricable parts of contemporary romantic life; she consistently demytholigises marriage, the traditional goal of the romance plot, and depicts it as a wholly compromising experience for women. In *Carolina Moon*, one character muses on the difference between the excitement of courtship and the drudgery of marriage, reflecting that while the company of men is pleasant now and again,

> marrying one . . . was a different kettle . . . Marry one, and you spent your life picking up after him, watching him fart and scratch and God knows what while you sweated to make the paycheck stretch.[39]

The hero and heroine both come from profoundly dysfunctional homes, their parents having made very bad marriages. The novel's most stereotypically 'perfect' marriage, between the town mayor, Dwight, and his high school girlfriend Lissy, turns out to be the most deceptive, since Dwight is actually a killer and pervert who enjoys assaulting women. Dwight's Beaver Cleaver fantasy marriage actually triggers his psychosis:

> All my life I heard, Be a man, Dwight . . . [So] I got confidence, got myself in shape, and didn't I end up with the prettiest girl in Progress? I got respect. A beautiful wife, a son. I got position.[40]

Roberts suggests here that the cultural pressure to achieve a romantic ideal may be a causal factor in male violence and female suffering. Likewise, in *Angels Fall*, the villain's desire simultaneously to maintain a stereotypical masculinity and traditional marriage propels him to kill his mistress:

> I love my wife, my kids. Nothing's more important. But there are needs, that's all. Two, three times a year I took care of those needs. None of it ever touched my family. I'd say I was a better husband, better daddy, better man for taking care of them.[41]

Sustaining cultural myths of love and marriage seemingly requires women's corpses.

Given the number of 'bad' relationships in her novels, it seems probable that the commitment of the hero and heroine is not intended to represent a 'realistic' goal for the reader. Roberts recognises that romance can be dangerous – especially to her female characters, who often end up physically bruised and psychologically scarred because of love. As Eva Illouz explains in her examination of love in modernity, it is an 'ontological threat' to the integrity of the self. In modernity, individuals look to love relationships for reassurance about their own worth as individuals, so that 'ontological security and a sense of worth are now at stake in the romantic and erotic bond'.[42] This existential investment in love makes an individual's sense of self precarious, because modernity makes the maintenance and sustainability of long-term romantic relationships difficult, tracked by transience and fracture. To protect themselves against this (inevitable) misery, modern individuals erect existentially protective barriers. Consequently, as the sociologist Charles Taylor puts it, the self is simultaneously vulnerable and 'buffered', a buffering that makes sustainable commitment incredibly difficult to achieve.[43] For many theorists, the precariousness of love and the ontological threat that love poses are especially acute for women, because 'in modernity men have internalised and most forcefully practised the discourse of autonomy', and can therefore evade its effects more successfully than their romantic partners.[44]

While acknowledging and depicting the threat that love might represent, Roberts offers her readers hope of an alternative kind of love, one which is transformative and ultimately stabilises the self rather than endangers it, even though her protagonists must first go through a psychically violent period so that their buffered selves can be breached. In a Roberts romance the protagonists are jolted out of an essentially pseudo, sleepwalking existence into an encounter with their essential selves, a process which involves the body, the mind and (finally) the soul.[45] Given the buffered existence of the modern self, the violence of the love and desire (for the right person) in the romance is understandable, since an anaesthetised self needs to be fully awakened. In *Carolina Moon*, the erotic encounters between the heroine, Tory Bodeen, and hero, Cade Lavelle, are defined by intensely violent images. As they make love, Tory experiences a physical assault:

> the sudden demand stabbed into her, shocking the senses, scraping the nerves. She arched as heat balled in her belly, and the groan strangled in her throat . . . He dragged her up, hands rough, grip near to bruising, ripping another gasp from her.[46]

In *Blue Smoke*, Reena and Bo violently make love: 'the sound of her hips slapping against the wood of the door as he pounded into her was viciously arousing. It was violent and fast and amazing.'[47] In *Angels Fall*, lovemaking for Reece Gilmore and Brody becomes a kind of 'frenzy', as Brody's 'mouth tore from hers to feast at her throat while her fingers dug into the muscles of his back'.[48]

This assault on the body jolts the protagonists into greater awareness of themselves and the other, and transforms a profane experience into a sacred one transcending the physical. 'Jesus. Jesus Christ', Bo murmurs after lovemaking;[49] 'God, thank God', a post-coital Reece whispers;[50] 'God. God', moans Tory.[51] Oceanic feelings are aroused by the orgasmic pleasure experienced in communion with the soul mate, and signify the shift of the protagonists into a different order of existence characterised by plenitude and security. In *Angels Fall* the lovers lie 'replete' in pleasurable plenitude, but also 'dazzled, and grateful'.[52] The love between the hero and heroine is played out in moments of self-recognition and complete acceptance of the other. The lovers frequently look at and acknowledge each other during intercourse: 'Just look at me' Brody asks Reece;[53] 'Open your eyes, Tory, look at me . . . Say my name'.[54] Communion of the body leads to a communion of selves and souls; it is not surprising that meeting the 'right' person in a romance novel is both exhilarating *and* frightening. The physical and existential shock experienced by the protagonists is also why the psychic violence of the language brings these scenes dangerously close to sounding like descriptions of rape, especially since Roberts does not always insist that verbal expressions of consent are given and the protagonists more often than not appear to understand their needs through a kind of telepathy, probably better considered as an ontological communication.[55] The profoundly transformative nature of these relationships for the buffered self is frequently resisted, as the rational mind struggles to retain control. In a Roberts novel, the 'barrier' preventing the protagonists getting together is usually not an external force, but rather the protagonists' fear of opening themselves up fully to complete communion.

Roberts recognises the dangers of love and romance for the contemporary self, particularly for women, and offers not avoidance of these threats but acceptance that, despite them, love and romance are not going to go away, no matter how many ideological criticisms they confront. She also represents love as a pleasurable *as well as* a painful experience and, more significantly, that loving the (ontologically) 'right' person is potentially self-transforming. Following their near-death struggles, Tory and Cade embrace and are symbolically blessed: 'The sun shimmered in thin beams, and moss dripped with rain. Flowers, bright blossoms, floated silently down the river.'[56] At the end of *Angels Fall*, Reece and Brody take breakfast together as 'the morning bloomed bright with hints of summer that would stretch through fall'.[57] These are utopian conclusions, but they are achieved in a context where the majority of 'romantic' relationships are possibly doomed, and after an extraordinary psychic and existential struggle for the protagonists. Roberts's cultural coolness comes, perhaps, from her continuing ability to inject some desperately needed transformative hope into what can at times seem like a jaded and cynical romantic reality.

NOTES

1. King, 'Stephen King on Who's Cool (And Who's Not)'.
2. For King's relationship to romance, see Lant, 'The Rape of the Constant Reader'.
3. Tony Magistrale, 'Why Stephen King Still Matters', p. 354.
4. See <http://content.time.com/time/specials/2007/time100/article/0,28804,1595326_1595332_1616215,00.html> (last accessed 20 July 2016).
5. Snodgrass, *Reading Nora Roberts*, p. 1.
6. Schappell, '*Northern Lights*'. Schappell wasn't impressed, complaining that Roberts's 'plots are far more simplistic than those of big guns in the mystery genre'. She is, however, making a category mistake here – romantic suspense is not the same as detective fiction.
7. These statistics are taken from the 'Did You Know?' section of Roberts's official website <http://noraroberts.com/did-you-know/>; original emphasis (last accessed 20 July 2016).
8. Cadwallader, 'Nora Roberts'.
9. Kendrick, *The Novel-Machine*.

10. In *A Natural History of the Romance Novel*, Pamela Regis includes Trollope's *Framley Parsonage* (1861) as one of a number of precursors to the contemporary romance (pp. 93–8).
11. Roberts, 'Interview'.
12. Regis, *A Natural History of the Romance Novel*, pp. 183–4.
13. The RITA awards, named after Rita Clay Estrada, the first President of the RWA, 'promote excellence in the romance genre by recognizing outstanding published romance novels and novellas'. See <https://www.rwa.org/page/the-rita-award> (last accessed 20 July 2016).
14. See the awards pages of the website of the Romance Writers of America <https://www.rwa.org/p/cm/ld/fid=535> and <https://www.rwa.org/p/cm/ld/fid=543> (last accessed 20 July 2016).
15. See <http://noraroberts.com/bio/> (last accessed 20 July 2016).
16. Harlequin, through its Silhouette and Mills and Boon imprints, is the most important and largest publisher of romance fiction.
17. See Goris, 'From Romance to Roberts and Back Again'. Goris notes that 'Apart from this dissertation, there is no scholarly work that provides a comprehensive overview of Roberts' oeuvre, career or significance to contemporary popular culture. In scholarly terms Roberts' oeuvre is then, quite literally, unexplored terrain' (p. 13). See also Goris, 'Mind, Body, Love', and Regis, 'Complicating Romances and Their Readers'.
18. For industry statistics see the RWA website <https://www.rwa.org/p/cm/ld/fid=580> (last accessed 20 July 2016).
19. Wherry, 'More Than a Love Story', p. 66.
20. Wendell and Tan, *Beyond Heaving Bosoms*, p. 11. The 2009 Fireside edition detailed in the bibliography features a front-cover blurb by Roberts.
21. Radway, *Reading the Romance*, p. 134; Regis, *A Natural History*, p. 19.
22. Goris, 'From Romance to Roberts and Back Again', p. 27.
23. Douglas, 'Soft-Porn Culture', pp. 25–9.
24. Greer, *The Female Eunuch*, p. 202.
25. Though Cartland's open contempt for contemporary feminism and changing gender politics, and her idealisation of the regency period as characterised by romantic stability, problematise any revisionist re-reading of her oeuvre. See the advice she doles out in *Barbara Cartland's Etiquette Book*.
26. See Modleski, *Loving with a Vengeance*.
27. Radway, *Reading the Romance*, p. 217.
28. See Driscoll, 'Genre, Author, Text, Reader', pp. 12–13.
29. Roberts, 'The Romance of Writing', p. 200. For other responses to feminist criticism by romance writers, see Krentz (ed.), *Dangerous Men and Adventurous Women*.
30. Roberts, quoted in Collins, 'Real Romance'.
31. For a more extensive list see Goris, 'From Romance to Roberts and Back Again', pp. 249–50.
32. Roberts, *Blue Smoke*, p. 258.
33. Transformation of tomboys into prom queens is a typical trope of the Cinderella romance, which has had a huge influence on the romance plot. See Lee, 'Guilty Pleasures'.
34. Goris, 'From Romance to Roberts and Back Again', p. 384.
35. Quoted in Collins, 'Real Romance', n.p.
36. Ibid. For inspirational romance, see Neal, *Romancing God*.
37. It is important to recognise that, given her output, three novels can in no way be seen as representative of Roberts's oeuvre, and any conclusions reached here should be tested in a much more capacious study.
38. Quoted in Illouz, *Why Love Hurts*, p. 6.
39. Roberts, *Carolina Moon*, p. 95.
40. Ibid., p. 404.
41. Roberts, *Angels Fall*, p. 470.
42. Illouz, *Why Love Hurts*, p. 110.

43. Taylor, *A Secular Age*, pp. 37–42, 134–42, 300–7, 488–90.
44. Illouz, *Why Love Hurts*, p. 136.
45. Interestingly, commentators have focused on the mind–body relationship in romance, bypassing the importance of the soul (as in 'soul mate'). See the diverging opinions of Catherine Belsey in *Desire* and An Goris in 'Mind, Body, Love'.
46. Roberts, *Carolina Moon*, p. 209.
47. Roberts, *Blue Smoke*, p. 259.
48. Roberts, *Angels Fall*, p. 237.
49. Roberts, *Blue Smoke*, p. 259.
50. Roberts, *Angels Fall*, p. 239.
51. Roberts, *Carolina Moon*, p. 257.
52. Roberts, *Angels Fall*, p. 239.
53. Ibid., p. 238.
54. Roberts, *Carolina Moon*, p. 210.
55. The violence of these encounters has been the source of continued unease to many scholars of the romance. See Toscano, 'A Parody of Love'. My thinking on this issue has been shaped by discussions with my graduate students Meadhbh McGrath and Alexandra Dech.
56. Roberts, *Carolina Moon*, p. 409.
57. Roberts, *Angels Fall*, p. 480.

KEY WORKS

Many of Nora Roberts's novels have been published in multiple editions; the year of publication of the original editions only is here cited.

Irish Thoroughbred (1981). Roberts's first novel; conventional and very much of its time. A virginal Irish heroine falls in love with a rich, experienced and mysterious American horse-farm owner. The book is indicative of Roberts's ability to work skilfully within the conventions, and also begins what would be a sustained interest in Irish plots, characters and atmosphere.

Brazen Virtue (1988). Golden Medallion award winner for Best Romantic Suspense in 1989. A problematic novel, investigating the connection between (often violent) fantasy sex and pathology, it is possibly Roberts's response to feminist readings of the romance genre as 'soft core' misogynist pornography for the ideologically interpellated female reader.

Hidden Riches (1994). A RITA award winner for Romantic Suspense, set in the world of antiques and featuring one of Roberts's most complex and frustrating heroes in the (absurdly named) Jed Skimmerhorn, an out-of-control former police captain who both epitomises macho brutality and is a complex, wounded, weak and vulnerable man emotionally traumatised by his troubled childhood.

Montana Sky (1996). Roberts's very successful first attempt at developing multiple, equally significant courtship plots within one narrative, an experiment she has repeated a number of times (see especially *Three Fates*, 2002).

Carolina Moon (2000). Another award winner (best Romantic Suspense). A pacey and exciting thriller, punctuated with rather unnecessary disquisitions on organic farming delivered by the hero. It offers serious critiques of marriage, the nuclear family and male aggression, and features a shift into paranormal themes (the heroine has telepathic powers); these developed as major aspects of Roberts's subsequent work. A good example of her ability to cross generic boundaries, combining traditional romance, romantic suspense and the paranormal romance.

Remember When (2003). Part One is an efficient, if fairly standard, romantic suspense story set in the present day, by Nora Roberts. Part Two is by her alter ego J. D. Robb and is an entry in the 'In Death' series, set in a futuristic New York and featuring detective Eve Dallas. An interesting novel for comparing the different personae adopted by Roberts and Robb and their very different writing styles. Part One was awarded the RITA award for Romantic Suspense.

Blue Smoke (2005). A very powerful, sexually forward heroine (fire-fighter and arson investigator) is matched by a much more passive hero, resulting in the stretching of the romance genre. One of Roberts's best novels and a deserved Quill Foundation Book of the Year.

Angels Fall (2006). Women's ability to recover from male violence is one of Roberts's most persistent 'themes', and this novel is one of her best explorations of it. Won the Quill Foundation Book of the Year award.

FURTHER CRITICAL READING

Fletcher, Lisa, *Historical Romance Fiction: Heterosexuality and Performativity* (Aldershot: Ashgate, 2008). Attempts to move romance criticism beyond the focus on gender, which has dominated analysis, towards sexuality, examining the ways in which romantic love has been 'heterosexualised' in both the popular historical romance (Georgette Heyer) and literary fiction (John Fowles and A. S. Byatt). However, Fletcher arrives at conclusions very similar to those of Janice Radway two decades before, and examines a similarly restricted range of texts.

Frantz, Sarah S. G. and Eric Murphy Selinger (eds), *New Approaches to Popular Romance Fiction: Critical Essays* (Jefferson, NC: McFarland, 2012). Key resource for appreciating the full range of the best current scholarship on the popular romance and of contemporary approaches to the genre. The best section is 'Close Reading the Romance', where four exemplary essays subject a single romance text to the kind of analysis which an earlier generation of scholars thought either impossible or pointless.

Goris, An, 'From Romance to Roberts and Back Again: Genre, Authorship and the Construction of Textual Identity' (2011). So far, the only sustained critical treatment of Roberts; a sympathetic, wide-ranging, astute and deeply informed consideration of the genre as well as Roberts. Goris has read everything written by Roberts and Robb (a feat in itself).

Radway, Janice A., *Reading the Romance* (1984). Pioneering ethnographic investigation of a romance reading group. While Radway's conclusions have been seriously questioned by subsequent scholars, her work was crucial in shifting ideological and scholarly attitudes away from an almost instinctual disregard for the genre towards a much more nuanced appreciation and understanding.

Regis, Pamela, *A Natural History of the Romance Novel* (2003). The most substantial and influential of the new wave of Romance Studies. Regis exposes the limitations of the feminist criticism of the popular romance of the 1970s and 1980s and demonstrates how the genre evolves over time and is deeply indebted to canonical literature.

BIBLIOGRAPHY

Belsey, Catherine, *Desire: Love Stories in Western Culture* (Oxford: Blackwell, 1994).

Cadwallader, Carole, 'Nora Roberts: The Woman Who Rewrote the Rules of Romantic Fiction', *The Observer*, 20 November 2011 <http://www.theguardian.com/books/2011/nov/20/nora-roberts-interview-romance-fiction> (last accessed 20 July 2016).

Cartland, Barbara, *Barbara Cartland's Etiquette Book: A Guide to Good Behaviour from the Boudoir to the Boardroom* (London: Random House, 2010).

Collins, Lauren, 'Real Romance', *New Yorker*, 22 June 2009 <http://www.newyorker.com/magazine/2009/06/22/real-romance-2> (last accessed 20 July 2016).

Douglas, Ann, 'Soft-Porn Culture', *New Republic*, 30 August 1980, pp. 25–9.

Driscoll, Beth, 'Genre, Author, Text, Reader: Teaching Nora Roberts's *Spellbound*', *Journal of Popular Romance Studies*, 4:2 (2014), pp. 1–16 <http://jprstudies.org/wp-content/uploads/2014/10/GATR_Driscoll.pdf> (last accessed 20 July 2016).

Goris, An, 'From Romance to Roberts and Back Again: Genre, Authorship and the Construction of Textual Identity' (PhD dissertation, Katholieke Universiteit Leuven, 2011).

Goris, An, 'Mind, Body, Love: Nora Roberts and the Evolution of Popular Romance Studies', *Journal of Popular Romance Studies*, 3:1 (2012) <http://jprstudies.org/wp-;content/uploads/2012/10/JPRS3.1_Goris.pdf> (last accessed 20 July 2016).

Greer, Germaine, *The Female Eunuch* (London: Paladin, 1971).

Illouz, Eva, *Why Love Hurts: A Sociological Explanation* (Cambridge: Polity, 2012).

Kendrick, Walter, *The Novel-Machine: The Theory and Fiction of Anthony Trollope* (Baltimore, MD: Johns Hopkins University Press, 1980).

King, Stephen, 'Stephen King on Who's Cool (And Who's Not)', *Entertainment Weekly*, 9 November 2007<http://www.ew.com/article/2007/11/09/stephen-king-whos-cool-and-whos-not> (last accessed 20 July 2016).

Krentz, Jayne Ann (ed.), *Dangerous Men and Adventurous Women* (Philadelphia: University of Pennsylvania Press, 1992).

Lant, Kathleen Margaret, 'The Rape of the Constant Reader: Stephen King's Construction of the Female Reader and Violation of the Female Body in *Misery*', *Journal of Popular Culture*, 30 (1997), pp. 89–115.

Lee, Linda J., 'Guilty Pleasures: Reading Romance Novels as Reworked Fairy Tales', *Marvels and Tales*, 22:1 (2008), pp. 52–66.

Magistrale, Tony, 'Why Stephen King Still Matters', in Charles L. Crow (ed.), *A Companion to American Gothic* (Chichester: Wiley, 2014), pp. 353–64.

Modleski, Tania, *Loving with a Vengeance: Mass-Produced Fantasies for Women* (Hamden, CT: Archon, 1982).

Neal, Lynn S., *Romancing God: Evangelical Women and Inspirational Fiction* (Chapel Hill: University of North Carolina Press, 2006).

Radway, Janice A., *Reading the Romance: Women, Patriarchy, and Popular Literature* (Chapel Hill: University of North Carolina Press, 1984).

Regis, Pamela, *A Natural History of the Romance Novel* (Philadelphia: University of Pennsylvania Press, 2003).

Regis, Pamela, 'Complicating Romances and Their Readers: Barrier and Point of Ritual Death in Nora Roberts's Category Fiction', *Paradoxa: Studies in World Literary Genres*, 3:1–2 (1997), pp. 145–54.

Roberts, Nora, *Angels Fall* (London: Piatkus Press, 2006).

Roberts, Nora, *Blue Smoke* (London: Piatkus Press, 2005).

Roberts, Nora, *Carolina Moon* (London: Piatkus Press, 2000).

Roberts, Nora, 'Interview' <http://www.nora-roberts.co.uk/2008/07/16/nora-roberts-exclusive-interview> (last accessed 20 July 2016).

Roberts, Nora, 'The Romance of Writing', in Kay Mussel and Johanna Tunon (eds), *North American Romance Writers* (Lanham, MD: Scarecrow Press, 1999), pp. 191–203.

Schappell, Elissa, '*Northern Lights*: Living in Lunacy', *New York Times*, 10 October 2004, <http://www.nytimes.com/2004/10/10/books/review/10SCHAPPE.html> (last accessed 20 July 2016).

Snodgrass, Mary Ellen, *Reading Nora Roberts* (Santa Barbara: Greenwood Press, 2010).

Taylor, Charles, *A Secular Age* (Cambridge, MA: Belknap Press, 2007).

Toscano, Angela R., 'A Parody of Love: The Narrative Uses of Rape in Popular Romance', *Journal of Romance Studies*, 2:2 (2012) <http://jprstudies.org/wp-content/uploads/2012/04/JPRS2.2_Toscano_ParodyofLove.pdf> (last accessed 20 July 2016).

Wendell, Sarah and Candy Tan, *Beyond Heaving Bosoms: The Smart Bitches' Guide to Romance Novels* (New York: Fireside, 2009).

Wherry, Maryan, 'More than a Love Story: The Complexities of the Popular Romance', in Christine Berberich (ed.), *The Bloomsbury Introduction to Popular Fiction* (London: Bloomsbury, 2015), pp. 53–68.

CHAPTER 6

The King of Stories: Neil Gaiman's Twenty-First-Century Fiction

Tara Prescott

Neil Gaiman was born to Sheila and David Gaiman on 10 November 1960 in Porchester, England. His parents nourished their son's bookish ways, frequently dropping him off at the library, without suspecting that he would become one of the most beloved storytellers currently writing in English. While preparing for his bar mitzvah, young Gaiman immersed himself in biblical stories and 'wound up getting a fabulous course in obscure Jewish mythology'.[1] He was raised Jewish, attended Church of England schools, and his parents later studied Dianetics and Scientology.[2] This exposure to multiple belief systems informs some of Gaiman's works, including his first novel, *Good Omens* (1990), an apocalyptic comedy co-authored with Terry Pratchett. Gaiman's career as a writer started with short stories and essays for men's magazines, eventually leading to his first book, a biography of the pop band Duran Duran (1984). This was followed by a creative biography, *Don't Panic: The Official Hitchhiker's Guide to the Galaxy Companion* (1988; expanded and retitled version 1993). He met and married an American, Mary McGrath, and they had three children: Michael ('Mike', b. 1983), Holly (b. 1985) and Madeleine ('Maddy', b. 1994). After a long separation, Gaiman and McGrath divorced in 2008.

In 1987, Gaiman collaborated with artist Dave McKean on the graphic novel *Violent Cases*, the first of several works that caught the attention of American publishers. He next wrote the comic *Black Orchid* (1988, also illustrated by McKean), which offers a deeply psychological and artistic reading of an existing DC Comics heroine. The comic's success prompted Gaiman's editor to request more reimaginings of dormant DC characters. He duly selected the Sandman, a 1930s crime-fighter who wore a yellow gas mask. This character became Dream, the physical embodiment of dreams, and the heart of the ground-breaking *Sandman* comic, which ran from 1989 to 1996.

The Gaimans moved to the US in 1992, selecting a Victorian house in rural Wisconsin. Gaiman's British upbringing made him well suited to observe American culture from a fresh perspective, an aspect that fuelled his modern epic, *American*

Gods (2001). This novel is a brilliant and wholly unexpected departure from Gaiman's short-form work: a dense, richly plotted narrative filled with characters representing multiple literary, cultural and religious traditions. The novel's opening lines immediately signal its blunt, adult, playful tone: 'Shadow had done three years in prison. He was big enough and looked don't-fuck-with-me enough that his biggest problem was killing time.'[3] At first glance, the large taciturn ex-con would seem like a very different sort of protagonist from an author best known at that time for writing about superheroes, godlike figures and fantasy characters. Only his odd name alerts the reader to the fact that Shadow Moon – like nearly every character he meets – is not what he seems. As he drives across America on a quest he does not understand, Shadow stops at quintessentially American roadside attractions and encounters gods old and new.

American Gods is a love letter to America, *On the Road* meets the *Poetic Edda*, a gritty road-trip novel that manages to be both familiar in its realism and supernaturally infused. *American Gods* became a critical and commercial success, rocketing up the *New York Times* bestseller list and shifting Gaiman's reputation from that of respected comic-book writer to award-winning novelist (the acclaimed 2017 television series based on the novel has increased Gaiman's public profile even further).[4]

Gaiman worked on *American Gods* for several years, and while awaiting its publication he started another ground-breaking work that belied the expectations of its form: www.neilgaiman.com. An early adopter of social media, he continued to find new ways of interacting with his fans, joining Twitter in 2008 as @neilhimself, followed by nearly 2.55 million people at the time of writing. Gaiman's online omnipresence in speeches, readings, musical performances, guest blogs and tweets has helped to mainstream the genres he is most associated with: comics, fantasy and children's literature. Perhaps more than any other author, Gaiman reaches out through various online outlets to interact with his fans, engage with other artists and promote causes related to literacy, equality, freedom of speech and social justice. That he is known for his reimaginings of ancient storytelling forms makes Gaiman's embrace of newly emerging technology and social media even more striking.

Gaiman's prominence on Twitter and in fan communities surged after he met Dresden Dolls singer and performance artist Amanda Palmer. The two collaborated on Palmer's book *Who Killed Amanda Palmer* (2009) and became romantic partners, sharing their developing relationship with their respective fans online. The couple married in 2011 and had a son, Anthony ('Ash', b. 2015), to whom Gaiman dedicated his first collection of essays, *The View From the Cheap Seats* (2016).

Gaiman is celebrated for his prolific nature, willingness to cross genres and adopt new media, engagement with readers and social activism. He is a *New York Times* bestselling author who has won the Newbery Medal as well as the Hugos, Nebulas and Bram Stoker awards. The array of accolades is proof of what his fans have long known: that Gaiman is the muse of a new generation, as kind-hearted as his everyman protagonists and as lexically adept as even his most devilish trickster figures. Through his colourful fantasies and dark, Gothic nightmares, Gaiman resists entrenched hierarchies and blurs literary distinctions: between fiction and non-fiction, between books for adults and books for children, and especially between popular books that readers crave and literary works that critics honour. It is difficult to categorise his works because they are 'genre pieces that refuse to remain true to their genres'.[5] He resists labels, crossing boundaries with his work as much as his characters cross between the worlds of the lucid and the dreaming, the real and the imaginary, the modern and the ancient.

Gaiman has written creative non-fiction, comics, science fiction, Gothic horror, fantasy, poetry, children's books, young adult fiction, film and television and video game scripts, and online works (including blogging, journals and social media). Across genres, he is known for the ways he incorporates and adapts mythology, folklore and fairy tales. 'It's hard to say exactly where myths end and folk tales and religions begin. I like to think that myths are ways of making sense of the world', Gaiman notes.[6] Importantly, all of these 'ways of making sense of the world' are based in oral tradition. Therefore it is fitting that Gaiman has maintained a strong presence in radio, audiobooks, audio theatre, vlogging and more. Gaiman's stories have a captivating quality that makes them addictive to read and a pleasure to share with others.

In addition to his work with fantasy and myth, Gaiman is celebrated for his devotion to children's literature. While being interviewed about writing for children by his daughter Maddy, Gaiman stated:

> Writing for children is more fun, but writing for children is harder. Grownups are a bit more forgiving. You can pad books for grownups a bit. You can write bits that are just there because you kind of like them. Whereas for kids, I try very, very hard to make sure there aren't any words wasted.[7]

Gaiman's consummate respect for young readers appears throughout his stories as well as his personal life. He has especially been a champion for giving children credit for handling darker themes and stories that have been traditionally decried as 'too mature' for young audiences. He does not make the distinctions between literature that is fit for adults and literature that is meant for children; instead, he has written dense novels marked by fantasy and childlike whimsy and shorter, deceptively easy-to-read stories that incorporate adult themes of death, loss, pain and sexuality.

Gaiman's ability to write for all ages as well as his particular blend of popular and critical success came to a head in 2009 at the annual conference of the American Library Association. He was there to receive the Newbery Medal for *The Graveyard Book* (2008). Controversy around this prize was growing, as the top scholars and professionals in the field debated whether 'popular' works should win the Newbery, one of the most prestigious awards for children's literature.[8] In his acceptance speech, he directly addressed the debate:

> It was as if some people believed there was a divide between the books you were permitted to enjoy and the books that were good for you, and I was expected to choose sides. We were all expected to choose sides. And I didn't believe it, and I still don't. I was, and still am, on the side of books you love.[9]

Gaiman has continued to write the books people love, without regard for the types of stories children and adults 'should' read. A strong example of this is his shift into picture books. In 2013, he worked with illustrator Adam Rex to create *Chu's Day*, a picture book about a panda cub with a devastatingly explosive (and cute) sneeze.

He then wrote the sequels *Chu's First Day at School* (2014) and *Chu's Day at the Beach* (2015). Even in their most stripped-down form, his picture books still contain hallmarks of his distinctive style: Gothic settings, everyday magic, unexpected plot twists, autobiographical threads, tongue-in-cheek humour and a playful disregard for the boundaries between the everyday and the fantastic.

Gaiman has a history of writing within, and of championing, genres that have struggled to gain academic and literary respect, starting with comics, fantasy and young adult books and, more recently, picture books and online collaborations. He has readily experimented with alternative ways of delivering his work to his fans, including online publishing and distribution formats (BlackBerry, iTunes, Audible), digital storefronts (HumbleBundle), live video (Periscope) and social media (Twitter, Instagram, Facebook, blogging). He was also one of the first authors to adopt online platforms for interacting with fans and frequently attributes his success to his relationships with them. As he writes in *The View from the Cheap Seats*, 'Literature does not occur in a vacuum. It cannot be a monologue. It has to be a conversation, and new people, new readers, need to be brought into the conversation too.'[10]

In addition to honouring his readers as collaborators, Gaiman is also vocal about the writers who have inspired him. It is not difficult to find Gaiman's influences referenced in his stories, as in 'A Study in Emerald' (2003, written in the style of Arthur Conan Doyle's Sherlock Holmes stories), 'The Problem of Susan' (2004, in relation to the character from C. S. Lewis's 'Narnia' books) and, of course, 'The Man Who Forgot Ray Bradbury' (2011). His work is frequently compared to that of authors he admires, including H. P. Lovecraft, J. R. R. Tolkien, Harlan Ellison and G. K. Chesterton. Noting the literary establishment's habit of under-appreciating women authors, Gaiman has also acknowledged those who inspired him, including Enid Blyton, P. L. Travers, Ursula Le Guin, Diana Wynne Jones, Shirley Jackson, Angela Carter and Madeleine L'Engle.[11]

Gaiman's legacy will no doubt include the ways he has celebrated and reimagined people and genres that have that have long suffered from marginal status, championed literacy and other social causes, and utilised multiple forms of communication to interact with fans and effect change. In the 1990s, Gaiman quickly emerged as an author who crafts engaging female characters who were historically under-represented in the traditionally male genres of comics, science fiction and fantasy. According to its editor, Karen Berger, *Sandman* was the first modern comic to attract a large female readership. 'You look around a room where Neil is, and half of the fans are women, if not more', she notes.[12] *Sandman* permanently altered the trajectory of modern comics and the 'effect was akin to that of Tolkien on the fantasy novel – everything afterward is in some way influenced'.[13] The success of *Sandman* not only showed publishers that readers were hungry for complex, rich narratives that stretched the boundaries of form, but also that they wanted more characters who reflected their own diversity, which was much broader than the perceived audience of young white men. John Parker notes that *Sandman*

> defined the Vertigo aesthetic for at least a decade, inspiring not only numerous spin-offs, but arguably the imprint's entire tone and approach. Years after it

ended . . . Reprints of the original series still sell something like six figures every year.[14]

In addition to creating compelling female characters, Gaiman has also incorporated strong LGBTQ characters into his stories. Rather than being depicted as 'aberrant' characters whose stories function as cautionary tales, characters like Desire from *Sandman*, Wanda from *Sandman: A Game of You* and Sam from *American Gods* are multidimensional, engaging and empowering.

While telling the stories of people who are marginalised or who live on the periphery by choice, Gaiman also continues to write in support of underdog genres. He has consistently spoken out for the importance of storytelling and defending any book that inspires people to read, regardless of its perceived 'literary' merit. Gaiman notes:

> Fiction has two uses. Firstly, it's a gateway drug to reading . . . And reading is key. There were noises made briefly, a few years ago, about the idea that we were living in a post-literate world, in which the ability to make sense out of written words was somehow redundant, but those days are gone: words are more important than they ever were: we navigate the world with words, and as the world slips onto the web, we need to follow, to communicate and to comprehend what we are reading.[15]

From *Sandman* to the novel that won the Newbery Medal, *The Graveyard Book*, and Twitter collaborations, Gaiman's work, along with that of authors such as J. K. Rowling, has helped garner legitimacy and respect for the types of texts that readers love that have been historically derided as fringe works, light fantasy or 'stories for kids'.

The impact of his work continues to spread, appearing in multiple languages and formats throughout the world and across different media. He has written scripts for movies, including *Princess Mononoke* (1997) and *Beowulf* (2007), and his own novels have been adapted into films, such as *Stardust* (2007) and *Coraline* (2009). Fans are eagerly awaiting the film based on his 2006 short story 'How to Talk to Girls at Parties' and the television series based on *Sandman*. His wider cultural impact is evident in Gaiman's large and diverse fanbase, a mixture of cosplayers and comic geeks, parents and children, musicians and scientists, artists and bloggers. He has used his reach with fans to advocate for non-profit and social causes, including raising funds for the Comic Book Legal Defense Fund, the Reading Agency and the UN Refugee Agency (UNHCR), the last of which appointed him as a global Goodwill Ambassador in 2017. This is part of a belief not only in the celebration of stories, but also in the protection of the cultures and people who create them.

Throughout Gaiman's diverse body of work, there are consistent patterns that continue to delight readers. He frequently misleads with red herrings, subverts expectations or withholds just the right amount of information, such as writing stories like 'Snow, Glass, Apples' (1994) and *The Sleeper and the Spindle* (2013) about well known figures like Snow White and Sleeping Beauty but never explicitly naming them. In many ways his stories inhabit a shared universe, with themes and characters appearing in different permutations in different texts. These include the humorous cameos of the Queen of Melanesia, the Norse god Loki and a trio of women who appear at different times as goddesses, witches or the Greek Fates. He is interested in figures who cross borders, who either choose or are forced to leave their environments and are then thrust into new (and often threatening) worlds. In encountering these worlds, Gaiman's characters often gain a stronger understanding of themselves. Many of his protagonists are relatable, mild-mannered misfits and outsiders, just enough at odds with their homes and lives that they have an advantage when thrust into a challenging adventure.

Gaiman's pace of publication increased in the 2000s, and his breakout works of the twenty-first century point to established interests as well as trajectories for the future. Although he continues to be a powerful presence in comics, contributing to several different titles as a guest writer, his most recent work has shifted primarily to prose fiction and non-fiction. One pivotal text in terms of Gaiman's career and its challenges to established genre expectations is *The Graveyard Book* (2008). Inspired by Rudyard Kipling's beloved *Jungle Book* stories, *The Graveyard Book* follows the adventures of young orphan Nobody 'Bod' Owens, who escapes the scene of his parents' murder and toddles into a graveyard. There he is adopted and raised by ghosts and other shadowy figures. Gaiman uses the *Jungle Book* frame – a collection of individual stories to teach lessons – to explore important themes that are essential to young people on the verge of adulthood, including understanding morality, socialisation, equality, justice and the quest for self. Many of *The Graveyard Book*'s characters and stories have *Jungle Book* analogues, and part of the fun of the novel is seeing how beloved characters like Baloo the bear, Bagheera the black panther and even the Bandar-log monkeys appear in Gaiman's modern Gothic version. But *The Graveyard Book* is much more than simply a reimagined *Jungle Book*. It is 'a universe of borrowing, exaggeration, reflection, and reversal' that reveals 'more universal themes instead of morals'.[16] Just as Gaiman transformed early DC characters in *The Sandman*, placed the quest for the Holy Grail in an Oxfam shop in 'Chivalry' (1992) and transported the X-Men into Elizabethan England in *Marvel: 1602* (2003–4), in *The Graveyard Book* he challenges the reader's perceptions of a well known, canonical story, expanding the possibilities of the original tale. Like its source text (or texts, since the *Jungle Book* stories were released in two volumes), *The Graveyard Book* has appeared in multiple versions, the original one with illustrations by *Sandman* artist Dave McKean and including a graphic novel version by P. Craig Russell (2014). As fans wait for a rumoured film adaptation, Gaiman has continued to work on other representations of childhood, including one notably darker and meant for adults.

The Ocean at the End of the Lane (2013) is in some ways a companion piece to *The Graveyard Book*. It is the most autobiographical of Gaiman's novels to date, and the frame narrative focuses on a man who returns to the town where he grew up in order to attend a funeral, but who is soon absorbed by memories of life-changing events that happened when he was just a boy. The unnamed protagonist is a seven-year-old, lonely and afraid, who accidentally allows a monster from another realm to enter his world. His only respite is the family of neighbours down the lane, the Hempstocks, a trio of magical women who offer him solace and guidance in his fight to save his and his family's lives. At times bittersweet and surprisingly violent, *The Ocean at the*

End of the Lane offers readers glimpses into Gaiman's history while also prompting examinations of the role of memory and the loss of innocence that all adults endure.

This text captures several aspects of Gaiman's most recent work: it is semi-auto-biographical, a juvenile's story told with thoroughly adult and threatening scenes, a mixture of the mundane with the mythical. Gaiman clarifies, 'It's absolutely not autobiographical in the sense that it happened to me . . . the family in here isn't my family. But it's very, very close to my point of view.'[17] The genesis of the story is that Amanda Palmer was in Australia for four months working on an album and Gaiman set out to tell her a story that offered a glimpse into his childhood. In digging more into the history of the home where he grew up, Gaiman discovered that a suicide had taken place there. The little story that was to become *Ocean* began to take on a life of its own. *Ocean* focuses on the power of language and memory and the horror in the everyday. In many ways, the otherworldly threats that the boy faces are nowhere near as terrifying as the domestic violence and betrayal he experiences in his own home. Despite its fantasy elements, the book is also thoroughly grounded in reality, including that fact that, in real life, most stories do not have clear-cut happy endings. The book perfectly captures what it feels like to be a young person, to have that specific point of view. This is something that appears in many of Gaiman's books but, as he notes, it reaches a new level with *Ocean*:

> In this book, I wanted to hold onto something that I remembered as a kid, which was reading children's books by adults. And I would read these books and I would go, you have no idea what it's like to be a kid. How can you not remember? And promising myself that when I grow up I would write children's books and I would remember what it had been like to be a kid.[18]

Gaiman, like his *Sandman* character Dream, is the King of Stories, and has co-edited anthologies of other people's work as well as released collections of his own, including *Smoke and Mirrors* (1998), *Fragile Things* (2006), *M is For Magic* (2007), *Trigger Warning: Short Fictions and Disturbances* (2015), *The View From the Cheap Seats* (2016) and *Norse Mythology* (2017). As the title of *Trigger Warning* demonstrates, Gaiman is in tune with emerging controversies in American culture, and writing in real time to issues affecting his readers. The term 'trigger warning' is used both online and in college classrooms to prepare audiences (especially those who may be survivors of sexual assault) for violent material that may trigger traumatic memories. In his introduction to the collection, Gaiman acknowledges sympathy for traumatised readers but also the fact that life itself comes without warning: 'What we read as adults should be read, I think, with no warnings or alerts beyond, perhaps: enter at your own risk'.[19] He then humorously offers life advice in the form of pre-flight safety instructions: '*Secure your own mask before helping others*'.

Like his earlier collections, *Trigger Warning* offers an unexpected menagerie of poems, short prose pieces, short stories and miscellanea. It includes the short story collection *A Calendar of Tales* that was the product of fan collaboration on Twitter, a Sherlock Holmes tale (with decidedly Gaiman supernatural flair) 'The Case of Death and Honey'; a Doctor Who story, 'Nothing O'Clock', to join Gaiman's *Doctor*

Who episodes 'The Doctor's Wife' and 'Nightmare in Silver'; a new *American Gods* story, 'Black Dog', and his tribute to David Bowie, 'The Return of the Thin White Duke', which was widely shared online, with illustrations by Yoskitaka Amano, after Bowie's death on 10 January 2016. Many of the stories end with sudden twists that call the veracity of the entire narrative into question. They drive the reader to read and re-read them, collecting new breadcrumbs each time. *Trigger Warning* begins with a behind-the-scenes introduction in which Gaiman provides details and context for each of the works. It offers readers a chance to learn more not only about the stories but also about Gaiman's approach to writing itself:

> All too often short-story collections are viewed as vanity projects or are published by small presses, are not seen as real in the way that novels are real. Still, for me, short stories are the places where I get to fly, to experiment, to play . . . when I put stories together themes reoccur, reshape, and become clear. I learn what I've been writing about for the previous decade.[20]

In many ways, it is a step towards the release of his next major work, where Gaiman focuses more clearly on himself as the subject of his writing.

In 2016, Gaiman returned to his creative nonfiction roots, releasing his first collection of essays, *The View from the Cheap Seats*. Collecting over sixty works, *Cheap Seats* offers a treasure trove of Gaiman's sharp-witted observations that have been scattered across graduation speeches, YouTube clips and assorted publications. The collection's title comes from an essay about Gaiman's awkward experience at the 2010 Academy Awards, which occurred on the first anniversary of his father's death. A little flummoxed by the pageantry and his invisible status as a writer (invited by *Coraline* director Henry Selick), Gaiman accidentally treads on actress Rachel McAdams's gown and considers a rebellion from the lowly ranks of the first mezzanine. It is a reminder that the events of everyday life, even an extraordinary life like Gaiman's, are the stuff of fiction too, and that the world of creative non-fiction has a place alongside fantasies and poems, comics and novels. Perhaps Gaiman's most unusual recent turn is *Norse Mythology*, a collection that unexpectedly skyrocketed to the top of the bestseller lists immediately after its release in 2017. In this book, Gaiman takes fragments of Norse myths that have come down to us (partially from ancient texts like the *Prose Edda* and the *Poetic Edda*), fills in the gaps with research and reimagines them for a modern audience.[21]

In 'A Writer's Prayer', Gaiman writes, 'let me not be one of those who writes too much. / Who spreads himself too thinly with his words / . . . / like butter spread too thinly over toast'.[22] This poem shows his awareness of the danger in taking on too many projects, and though his literary and artistic output is astonishing, Gaiman has managed to avoid this fate. Rather than thinly buttered toast, his work is far more like the magical, nourishing slab of honeycomb drizzled with cream that the Hempstocks serve in *The Ocean at the End of the Lane*. And as Gaiman shifts from beloved cult figure to literary celebrity, he continues to create thoroughly original, entertaining stories that inject ancient magic into the rapidly evolving modern world.

He uses his work to call for compassion and empathy worldwide. As he writes in 'How Dare You: On America, and Writing About It':

On the one hand, there's you, and on the other hand, there's America. It's bigger than you are. So you try to make sense of it. You try to figure it out – something which it resists. It's big enough, and contains enough contradictions, that it is perfectly happy not to be figured out.[23]

Perhaps the strongest legacy Gaiman's fiction leaves is its ability to help readers empathise with others, and to gain strength while living in contradictory, challenging times.

NOTES

1. Available at <http://www.blastr.com/2015-12-23/exit-sandman-neil-gaiman-goes-depth-overture-one-2015s-best-comics> (last accessed 13 June 2016).
2. Campbell, *The Art of Neil Gaiman*, p. 22.
3. Gaiman, *American Gods*, p. 3.
4. During 'An Evening With Neil Gaiman' at the Segerstrom Center for the Arts in Costa Mesa, California, on 30 March 2017, Gaiman noted that the TV series *American Gods* was released at a particularly poignant moment in American culture, just in the wake of crackdowns on immigration after the election of President Donald Trump. He observed, 'We put something into the world we didn't think was contentious . . . now it's saying something much bigger and stronger'.
5. Available at <http://www.newyorker.com/magazine/2010/01/25/kid-goth> (last accessed 13 June 2016).
6. Available at <http://www.theguardian.com/books/2013/jun/14/neil-gaiman-top-10-mythical-characters> (last accessed 13 June 2016).
7. 'Maddy Gaiman Interviews Her Dad' <http://www.neilgaiman.com/Cool_Stuff > (last accessed 30 June 2016).
8. The President of the Association for Library Service to Children, Pat Scales, defends the historically 'less-popular-but-good-for-you' nature of the winners, stating, 'It is about literary quality. We don't expect every child to like every book' (quoted in Strauss, 'Critics Say Newbery-Winning Books Are Too Challenging for Young Readers'). John Beach, a professor of literacy education at St John's University, who has researched patterns in award-winning children's books, notes: 'The Newbery has probably done far more to turn kids off to reading than any other book award in children's publishing' (quoted in Strauss, ibid.).
9. Gaiman, 'The Newbery Medal Acceptance Speech', pp. 16–25.
10. Gaiman, *The View From the Cheap Seats*, p. 2.
11. On 4 April 2016 Neil Gaiman Tweeted a list of 'Women writers who inspired me . . .'. Quoted at <https://www.theguardian.com/books/booksblog/2016/apr/06/10-inspiring-female-writers-you-need-to-read> (last accessed 30 August 2017).
12. Available at <http://www.newyorker.com/magazine/2010/01/25/kid-goth> (last accessed 13 June 2016).
13. Wagner, Golden and Bissette, *Prince of Stories*, p. xii.
14. Available at <http://comicsalliance.com/tribute-gaiman-the-sandman/> (last accessed 13 June 2016).
15. Available at <https://www.theguardian.com/books/2013/oct/15/neil-gaiman-future-libraries-reading-daydreaming> (last accessed 13 June 2016).
16. McStotts, 'The Jungle, the Graveyard and the Feral Child', p. 68.
17. Available at <http://www.bbc.com/news/entertainment-arts-22904585> (last accessed 13 June 2016).

18. Available at <http://www.bbc.com/news/entertainment-arts-22904585> (last accessed 13 June 2016).
19. Gaiman, *Trigger Warning*, p. xii.
20. Ibid., p. xvi.
21. During 'An Evening With Neil Gaiman' held at the Segerstrom Center for the Arts, Costa Mesa, CA, on 30 March 2017, Gaiman also discussed *Norse Mythology*'s unusual tone. He joked that he wanted to capture the sound of 'stories told during long nights in mead halls with people who were a little bit drunk'.
22. Gaiman, 'A Writer's Prayer'.
23. Gaiman, *The View From the Cheap Seats*, p. 65.

KEY WORKS

Neverwhere (London: BBC Books, 1996). Richard Mayhew is an ordinary Londoner until the day he intervenes in the life of an injured girl on the street and ends up in London Below, a magical parallel London beneath the world he once knew.

American Gods (New York: William Morrow, 2001). Part road-trip novel, part modern mythological odyssey, *American Gods* follows the quest of ex-con Shadow Moon across America in order to fulfil his commitment to an enigmatic employer, Mr Wednesday, and avoid gods set on killing him.

Coraline (New York: HarperCollins, 2001). The novella's eponymous heroine, upset with her family's recent move and a lack of attention from her parents, starts to explore what at first seems to be an ordinary old house. Yet she finds a small door into another house, a parallel version of her own.

The Sandman: Overture (Burbank: DC Comics, 2015). Created over twenty years after the end of the original *Sandman* series, *Overture* is a prequel comic, focused on what led up to Morpheus's imprisonment at the start of the *Sandman* series. Gaiman was the writer, while J. H. Williams III did the artwork, Dave Stewart was the colourist and Todd Klein did the lettering.

Norse Mythology (New York: W. W. Norton, 2017). A collection of deceptively straightforward tales, occasionally punctuated with moments of Gaiman's hallmark humour, covering stories from the Norse pantheon that are both familiar (for instance those about Thor and his hammer Mjollnir, Odin and the gods of Asgard) and new (most notably 'Freya's Unusual Wedding', in which Loki tricks an ogre into marrying Thor-in-drag).

FURTHER CRITICAL READING

Burdge, Anthony S., Jessica Burke and Kristine Larson (eds), *The Mythological Dimensions of Neil Gaiman* (Crawfordville, FL: Kitsune Books, 2012). A collection of fifteen essays by fans and literary scholars on the relationships between Gaiman's texts and their mythological and folkloric sources and inspirations, with particular focus on titles that are often neglected in the criticism.

Campbell, Hayley, *The Art of Neil Gaiman*. Written by Gaiman's 'scary goddaughter' (the daughter of artist and Gaiman collaborator Eddie Campbell), this comprehensive collection offers short synopses, photographs, reproductions of Gaiman's handwritten drafts and notes, and an extensive bibliography of Gaiman's oeuvre.

Prescott, Tara (ed.), *Neil Gaiman in the 21st Century* (Jefferson, NC: McFarland, 2015). A collection of eighteen essays on the full range of Gaiman's work published since 2000. It includes an interview with J. H. Williams III, the artist who collaborated with Gaiman on *Sandman: Overture*.

Prescott, Tara and Aaron Drucker (eds), *Feminism in the Worlds of Neil Gaiman* (Jefferson,

NC: McFarland, 2012). Gaiman's character Death was the unexpected fan favourite from *Sandman*, but she is just one of several compelling female characters created by Neil Gaiman. This collection of essays examines Gaiman's works, including *Sandman, Black Orchid, Good Omens, Marvel 1602* and *Coraline*, using feminist criticism and gender studies.

BIBLIOGRAPHY

Campbell, Hayley, *The Art of Neil Gaiman* (New York: HarperCollins, 2014).
Gaiman, Neil, 'A Writer's Prayer', in *Telling Tales* (Audiobook, 2003).
Gaiman, Neil, *American Gods* (New York: Harper Torch, 2001).
Gaiman, Neil, 'The Newbery Medal Acceptance Speech', in *The Graveyard Book* (New York: HarperCollins, 2008), pp. 16–25.
Gaiman, Neil, *The View From the Cheap Seats* (New York: William Morrow, 2016).
Gaiman, Neil, *Trigger Warning* (New York: HarperCollins, 2015).
Gaiman, Neil, 'Why Our Future Depends on Libraries, Reading and Daydreaming', *The Guardian*, 15 October 2013 <https://www.theguardian.com/books/2013/oct/15/neil-gaiman-future-libraries-reading-daydreaming> (last accessed 20 June 2016).
Goodyear, Dana, 'Kid Goth: Neil Gaiman's Fantasies', *New Yorker*, 25 January 2010 <http://www.newyorker.com/magazine/2010/01/25/kid-goth> (last accessed 29 June 2016).
Higham, Nick, 'Meet the Author: Neil Gaiman on His Most Personal Novel Yet', BBC, 17 June 2013 <http://www.bbc.com/news/entertainment-arts-22904585> (last accessed 20 June 2016).
McStotts, Jennifer, 'The Jungle, the Graveyard and the Feral Child: Imitating and Transforming Kipling Beyond Pastiche', in Tara Prescott (ed.), *Neil Gaiman in the 21st Century* (Jefferson, NC: McFarland, 2015), pp. 65–82.
Parker, John R., 'Bring Us a Dream: What Sets Neil Gaiman's "The Sandman" Apart?', Comics Alliance, 30 November 2015 <http://comicsalliance.com/tribute-gaiman-the-sandman/> (last accessed 20 June 2016).
Sagers, Aaron, 'Exit Sandman: Neil Gaiman Goes In-depth With Overture, One of 2015's Best Comics', blastr, 23 December 2015 <http://www.blastr.com/2015-12-23/exit-sandman-neil-gaiman-goes-depth-overture-one-2015s-best-comics> (last accessed 20 June 2016).
Strauss, Valerie, 'Critics Say Newbery-Winning Books Are Too Challenging for Young Readers', *Washington Post*, 16 December 2008 <http://www.washingtonpost.com/wp-dyn/content/article/2008/12/15/AR2008121503293.html> (last accessed 20 June 2016).
Wagner, Hank, Christopher Golden and Stephen R. Bissette, *Prince of Stories: The Many Worlds of Neil Gaiman* (New York: St Martin's, 2008).

CHAPTER 7

Jo Nesbø: Murder in the *Folkhemmet*

Clare Clarke

The sales figures Norwegian author Jo Nesbø (pronounced Yoo Nesber) has achieved are dizzying: his eleven Harry Hole crime novels (plus thirteen other stand-alone works) have, at last count, sold twenty-three million copies worldwide (they have been translated into forty languages); his worldwide English-language sales have averaged 500,000 copies a year since 2005; five million copies of his works have been sold in Norway alone, a country with a population of only five million; one Nesbø novel is sold every twenty-three seconds in the UK.[1] As a measure of Nesbø's current cultural cachet, the author has recently been commissioned to retell Shakespeare's *Macbeth* as a modern Nordic Noir novel.[2] He is, then, assuredly the latest 'King' of Nordic Noir; a crown he inherited from Stieg Larsson, the author regularly credited for the recent surge of interest in Scandinavian crime fiction following the commercial success of *The Girl with the Dragon Tattoo* (2005).[3] Along with fellow Nordic Noir superstars Larsson, Karin Fossum, Camilla Läckberg and Henning Mankell, Nesbø has secured commercial and critical acclaim for this recent incarnation of the crime novel and a place for himself in the annals of the genre's history.

Nesbø's biography itself is the stuff of fiction. He came to writing late, aged thirty-seven, and went on to be Norway's wealthiest and most successful author. He started his working life as a professional footballer, playing for Molde, one of the Norwegian Premier League's top clubs. A serious knee injury cut his footballing career short at the age of just eighteen. He did three years' military service and then went to business school, where he trained in economics. Then followed a string of jobs, as a taxi driver, a fisherman, a freelance journalist and finally a stockbroker. As a hobby, he formed the rock band Di Derre ('Them There'); however, this sideline was to provide Nesbø's first taste of stardom:

> One night a young jazz bass player I knew listened to some of my songs. The next day we started a band, Di Derre. A year later we were touring. Two years

later we had a recording contract. Our second album became the best-selling album in Norway in years. Our concerts sold out in hours. And suddenly we were pop stars.[4]

Nesbø had not yet given up his day job as a financial analyst for the country's largest brokerage firm when he was commissioned to write a memoir about life as one of Norway's leading rock stars. He boarded a flight to Australia, determined to take a break from his job and the band, to work on his memoir and to recharge his batteries. Ironically, in attempting to flee both successful careers, Nesbø found a third. On the flight to Sydney, he began writing. Rather than a memoir, however, he decided to begin a crime novel about a burnt-out, jet-lagged Norwegian cop travelling to Australia to solve a crime. This novel, which was complete upon his return from Australia six months later, was *Flaggermusmannen* (literally, 'The Bat-Man') (1997), later published in the UK/US as *The Bat*. A further ten Harry Hole novels have followed to date, alongside four stand-alone novels, three 'Olav Johansen' thrillers, four children's books, numerous awards, at least a couple of movie adaptations and phenomenal global success.

Such is the slow-paced nature of academic publishing that few studies have yet appeared which deal in detail with Nesbø's success, or even with the success of Nordic Noir more broadly.[5] When asked to account for the success of Scandinavian crime fiction, Nesbø himself admits he's at a loss: 'I've been trying to come up with a smart answer, but I really don't know'.[6] This chapter seeks to answer that question by placing Nesbø's work in the context of the twentieth and twenty-first century's most influential Scandinavian crime writers, Maj Sjöwall, Per Wahlöö, Henning Mankell and Stieg Larsson. It examines the generic and thematic features shared by significant works of Nordic Noir, before looking in more detail at Nesbø's *The Snowman* (*Snømannen*, 2007), the book that would and secure his place as the current king of Nordic Noir.

Writing about the mystery novel in 1949, Raymond Chandler observed:

> its form has never been perfected, it has never become fixed. The academicians have never got their dead hands on it. It is still fluid, still too various for easy classification, still putting out shoots in all directions.[7]

Nearly seventy years later, the crime genre is still putting out shoots in all sorts of geographical and generic directions. Its fluidity and flexibility continue and this is perhaps why crime fiction still fascinates readers and dominates bestseller lists. One of the most popular recent offshoots emerged from Scandinavia in the middle of the twentieth century. Over a period of ten years, between 1965 and 1975, Maj Sjöwall and Per Wahlöö jointly authored a series of ten bleak police procedural novels about Inspector Martin Beck and his colleagues at the Stockholm National Homicide Department. These novels, focusing on the investigation of social issues such as prostitution, immigration, terrorism, even the assassination of a prime minister (foreshadowing the assassination of Swedish PM Olof Palme in 1986), inaugurated the paradigms of the genre now widely known as Nordic Noir.[8] At their heart were crimes occurring in a bleak and unwelcoming landscape, investigated by a lonely, compromised detective; the novels have a pared-down style. With this series, the duo relocated the crime novel in modern Sweden. If, as Chandler suggested, Dashiell Hammett's hardboiled fiction had taken the crime novel out of the English drawing room and dropped it into the American alley, Marxist journalists Sjöwall and Wahlöö wanted to use the genre to split apart the utopian image of the *Folkhemmet* – the People's Home – Sweden's post-war welfare state.[9] Charlotte Barslund succinctly sums up the exasperation that underpins this desire: 'There's a frustration in the Scandinavian countries that even the best social democracy in the world doesn't equal a crime-free society . . . Life should be good there, but it isn't.'[10]

In the 2000s and 2010s, Nordic Noir became a widespread cultural phenomenon as a literary and a multi-media event. Between 2008 and 2010, UK television station BBC4 screened double episodes of the Swedish television adaptation of *Wallander* (dir. various, 2005–10) on Saturday and Sunday evenings. This proved to be a winning formula, reigniting interest in Henning Mankell's nine Wallander novels, published between 1997 and 2013. It led also to the BBC's screening of numerous other Scandinavian crime serials – starting with Danish serial killer mystery *Forbrydelsen* [*The Killing*] (2007), shown in 2008. This was perfectly timed to capitalise upon the success of Larsson's *The Girl with the Dragon Tattoo* – the bestselling novel in the UK that year. The series soon developed a cult following, and became the subject of numerous newspaper articles and reviews. Steven Peacock notes that 'the curious apogee' of interest in the series was fans' obsessive need to acquire a knitted sweater in the style of one worn by detective Sarah Lund.[11] Up there with Lieutenant Columbo's raincoat and Sherlock Holmes's deerstalker hat in the history of detective fiction fashion, Sarah Lund's knitwear, made by a tiny company in the Faroe Islands, inspired unauthorised copies, with an ensuing lawsuit, and now has its own website – www.sarahlundsweater.com. A US version of *Forbrydelsen*, named *The Killing*, and relocated in Seattle, premiered in 2011 and ran until 2014. The Danish sequel, *Forbrydelsen II*, was screened in 2009, quickly followed by other Nordic crime exports: Danish political thriller *Borgen* (2010), Swedish/Danish police procedural *The Bridge* (2011–) and Swedish detective drama *Sebastian Bergman* (2012). BBC4's Nordic Noir success continued with Icelandic series *Trapped* (2016), which drew over a million viewers for its finale in March 2016.[12]

Alongside Nordic Noir on screen, the 2000s also witnessed an explosion of literary Nordic Noir, by authors such as Mankell, Arnaldur Indridason, Arne Dahl and Yrsa Sigurðardóttir, to name just a few. This work largely shares with Sjöwall and Wahlöö the bleak landscape, the broken or compromised detective, and a desire to interrogate the dark underbelly of the outwardly prosperous and socially democratic Scandinavian nations. It also shares with Sjöwall and Wahlöö the appropriation of early-twentieth-century American Noir's mood of 'alienation, pessimism, and uncertainty' – the detective is often vulnerable and is unclear whether he or she will be able to restore order in any meaningful way.[13] This is certainly true of the works that most scholars of the genre recognise as the keynote of Nordic Noir's twenty-first-century success, Larsson's 'Millennium' trilogy, beginning with the English-language publication of *The Girl with the Dragon Tattoo* in 2008.[14]

The novel had been posthumously published in its original Swedish in 2005; relaunched for an international audience in July–September 2008, it went on to be the bestselling novel in Europe that year. In 2009 it debuted at number 4 on the *New York Times* bestseller list, remaining near the top of that list for many months. As a crusading journalist, one of the world's foremost authorities on right-wing groups, Larsson shared with Sjöwall and Wahlöö a desire to interrogate utopian images of the Swedish state. The novel's original Swedish title, *Män Som Hatar Kvinnor* (Men Who Hate Women), and its superscriptions, such as '46% of the women in Sweden have been subjected to violence by a man', indicate its serious intent to illuminate the abuses of women perpetrated by various Swedish institutions, the family and the state itself.[15] Indeed, the reader must determine whether the central crime of this novel is the abuse and 'murder' of Harriet Vanger by her brother and father or the unflinchingly portrayed systematic sexual abuse of investigator Lisbeth Salander at the hands of her state-appointed guardian, Nils Bjurman.[16] The further two novels in the trilogy, *The Girl Who Played with Fire* (2009) and *The Girl Who Kicked the Hornet's Nest* (2010) continued the theme of abuses against women. The combination of serious social commentary and serial killer thrills proved popular, with Larsson's trilogy having sold 80 million copies worldwide by late 2015. In September 2015, Knopf published a fourth instalment to the 'Millennium' series, *The Girl in the Spider's Web*, written by David Lagercrantz. It sold over 200,000 copies in its first week and in early 2016 remained steadily near the top of the UK paperback fiction charts.

Following Larsson's success, publishers and readers clamoured to discover the next Nordic Noir talent. In the UK and US, Jo Nesbø was marketed as 'the new Stieg Larsson', despite having published his first novel eight years before the Swedish publication of *The Girl with the Dragon Tattoo*. Nesbø has expressed frustration that bookstores lured buyers by affixing to the covers of his novels stickers that said 'Read this if you like Stieg Larsson': 'The idea that Scandinavian crime writers have something in common is a myth. The biggest thing they have in common is that they are from Norway, Sweden or Denmark.'[17] Indeed, Nesbø's objection illustrates one of the difficulties of talking about Nordic Noir. As becomes clear here, and as with the crime fiction more broadly, the term 'Nordic Noir' is critically unstable; its borders are difficult to trace and define. Part of the problem, doubtless, as Nesbø expresses, is the lumping together of fiction from five nations, Sweden, Finland, Norway, Denmark and Iceland, each with a distinct history and identity, under one homogenising blanket term. Nesbø's Hole novels are set in Australia, Thailand and Norway's Oslo, as opposed to Larsson's Stockholm, Mankell's Ystad or Indridason's Reykjavik. One thing that Nesbø undoubtedly does share with Larsson is 'phenomenal, jaw-dropping sales'.[18] Nesbø's work also shares with that of Larsson, as well as with the work of Sjöwall and Wahlöö, crimes occurring in a bleak, unforgiving landscape, a compromised detective hero and a desire to interrogate the Scandinavian family and the Scandinavian state as sites of corruption. To these, though, Nesbø yokes features of the early- to mid-twentieth-century US Noir thriller and the late-twentieth-century serial killer thriller, in the style of Thomas Harris.

Nesbø's crime novels have a rather complex and confusing publication history. It is telling that the author's website and his Amazon page provide detailed information on the series' sequence, in order that readers may come to the novels in the correct order. His first two novels, *Flaggermusmannen*, published in Norway in 1997, and

Kakerlakkene [*Cockroaches*] (1998), are somewhat anomalous, in that neither is set in Norway. The first book introduces detective Harry Hole (pronounced Harry Hu-leh) and follows his journey to Australia to solve the murder of a young Norwegian woman. Nesbø's second novel also sees Hole dispatched abroad, this time to Thailand, to investigate the murder of the Norwegian ambassador. As such, the novels speak to the increasingly globalised nature of crime in the modern world, something to which Nesbø would return in later novels, which also see Harry working abroad.[19] It was only many years later, after Nesbø had gained a large and devoted international audience, following the publication of later Hole books, set in Norway, that these first two novels were translated and published worldwide. In fact, *Marekors* [*The Devil's Star*] (2003), Nesbø's fifth Hole novel, was his first to be published in the UK, in 2005. Speaking in 2010, Nesbø explained this decision: 'At the time Harry Hole started to be exported, it seemed a better idea to start with Harry where he belongs, in Oslo.'[20] The UK/US publication of *The Devil's Star* was followed by *The Redbreast* [*Rødstrupe*, 2000] in 2006, *Nemesis* [*Sorgenfri*, 2002] in 2008, *The Redeemer* [*Frelseren*, 2005] in 2009, *The Snowman* in 2010 [*Snømannen*, 2007], *The Leopard* in 2011 [*Panserhjerte*, 2009], *Phantom* [*Gjenferd*, 2011] and *The Bat* [*Flaggermusmannen*, 1997] in 2012, *Police* [*Politi*, 2013] and *Cockroaches* [*Kakerlakkene*, 1998] in 2013, and *The Thirst* [*Tørst*, 2017] in 2017.

The Redbreast, Nesbø's third novel and his fourth to be published in the UK, then, is the first in the so-called 'Oslo Sequence'; that is, it is the first Hole novel set in Norway. Employing character and structural tropes familiar to readers of crime fiction, the novel introduces Hole as Oslo's best detective, but a flawed character, described in *The Snowman* as 'unhealthy attitude to alcohol, difficult temperament, lone wolf, unreliable, doubtful morality'.[21] Elsewhere, his depression, alcoholism and opposition to authority are said to render him 'a danger to himself and those around him'.[22] Hole's name (which translates simply as 'hole') of course reinforces the idea of the character's vulnerability and moral emptiness; as Nesbø has put it, 'he's a kind of black hole, where everything is kind of pulled in, and nothing escapes'.[23] Inspired by his father's interest in World War II, Nesbø uses *The Redbreast* to interrogate the influence of right-wing ideology in post-war Norway. When a Nazi sympathiser is found murdered, Harry's investigation of neo-Nazi circles in Norway leads him to uncover uncomfortable truths about Norway's relationship with right-wing ideology. The novel's multiple strands – Hole's investigations, a neo-Nazi group, the killer and his motivations, and a series of events during WWII – function as 'counter-narratives' to 'canonical history'.[24] As such, then, it hearkens back strongly to the work of Sjöwall and Wahlöö in its desire to expose uncomfortable truths about Scandinavian national and political identity.

Andrew Pepper has noted the prevailing critical tendency 'to overlook connections between the Anglo-American crime fiction and other national crime fiction traditions, particularly continental Europe'.[25] Thus, Nordic Noir, for instance, is often evaluated only in relation to earlier Scandinavian crime fiction. Nesbø's work, however, demands to be viewed in relation to its engagement with Anglo-American traditions. *The Snowman* is self-consciously American from the outset as, through Harry, Nesbø wryly acknowledges his debt to one of the most popular late-twentieth-century American genres – the serial killer thriller. *The Snowman* opens with Harry Hole suspecting that the presence of a snowman at the scenes of thus-far unconnected murders of a number of women around Norway constitutes the signature of a serial killer. Hole's colleagues scoff at this assumption: 'he's morbidly obsessed with serial killers, Hole is'.[26] They read this laughable obsession, which has led Hole to 'cry wolf' at least three times, as evidence of his Americanisation. It is blamed on his attendance at an FBI course on serial killers in Chicago: 'He thinks this is the USA . . . We haven't had a single serial killer in Norway. Ever. Those guys only exist in the USA, but even there usually only in films.'[27]

Following the critical and commercial success of Thomas Harris's Hannibal Lecter books and film adaptations, particularly *Red Dragon* (1981) and *The Silence of the Lambs* (1988), the serial killer thriller became one of the most popular late-twentieth-century American genres. This trend emerges hand in hand with what Mark Seltzer has termed 'wound culture', a 'fascination with torn and open bodies and torn and opened persons, a collective gathering around shock, trauma and the wound'.[28] For Seltzer, this wound culture is the dominant public spectacle of modern American life. The trend encompasses not only a prurient interest in the torn-apart bodies of victims, but also 'opens to our gaze the wounded psyche of the killer whose aberrations are expressed in the wounds he inflicts on others'.[29] As Philip Jenkins pithily puts it, 'John Wayne symbolised an older, mythical America, while the modern nation produced John Wayne Gacy'.[30] If the serial killer has replaced the cowboy as the modern American (anti-)hero, the commercial success of serial killer fiction and film is the most obvious cultural reflection of this obsession. In *The Snowman*, Harry's assumptions are proved correct, of course: the Oslo police are indeed dealing with a serial killer. In resituating the serial killer narrative in Norway, Nesbø is wilfully hitching his wagon to one of the most popular recent forms of Anglophone crime fiction; as one reviewer of *The Snowman* notes, 'This isn't Norwegian. It's full-blooded American . . . These are the same mean streets they're taking us down, only now they're covered with snow.'[31]

The Snowman also shares with the work of Nesbø's hero, Jim Thompson, a distinctly Noir sensibility. For Lee Horsley, the iconic figures of Noir 'are more complex and ambiguous than the traditional detective, the cowboy, or the action hero'.[32] Indeed, in *The Snowman* the line between detective and criminal is nebulous. Harry is obsessive, self-loathing, damaged, driven to investigate crime not out of a desire for truth and justice but, as his lover Rakel puts it, by 'anger. And the desire for revenge.'[33] Harry's new partner, the young, beautiful and talented Katrine Bratt, fresh from the Sexual Investigation Unit in Bergen, enjoys hard rock and harder sex; she is every bit as obsessive and damaged as Hole himself. Her obsession with avenging the death of her father, corrupt Bergen police detective Gert Rafto, murdered by the Snowman, leads her to a successive obsession with Hole: '[I] chose you. To find the Snowman for me.'[34] Over the course of the narrative, Katrine fakes a letter from the Snowman to Harry, sexually entraps, ties up and beats a suspect, goes on the run, is herself suspected of and arrested for being the Snowman, and eventually ends the novel in a mental hospital, diagnosed with psychosis. The novel's detectives, then, are emphatically not uncomplicated avatars of justice and morality. Rather, they are deeply flawed individuals driven by obsession, lust and revenge, much like the corrupt Los Angeles police in James Ellroy's neo-Noir LA Quartet.

Nesbø's *The Snowman* also shares with much Noir and neo-Noir the idea of the family as the site of 'malcontent, evil, muted rage, long-bred resentments and jealousies', and crime.[35] The intimations of incest at the heart of the Sternwood mansion in Chandler's *The Big Sleep* (1939) are made explicit in neo-Noir works like Roman Polanski's film *Chinatown* (1974) and Ellroy's novel *The Black Dahlia* (1987). These works illustrate the ways in which Noir is often structured by what has been termed a 'Gothic causality', where the outwardly respectable family is threatened by the disclosure of unpalatable truths.[36] *The Snowman* is structured around similar questions of family and paternity.[37] Early in the novel, Harry listens to a radio programme presenting new research claiming that 15–20 per cent of Swedish children 'have a different father from the one they – and for that matter the postulated fathers – think. Twenty per cent! That's every fifth child. Living a lie.'[38] Hole's investigation soon leads him to uncover the dangerous power of this female infidelity. He finds that each of the killer's victims is a married mother who has had multiple affairs; each of their children is fathered by a man who is not her husband.

One such child is Rakel's son, Harry's cherished stepson, Oleg. Another is Rakel's new husband-to-be, the Snowman, Mathias. His narrative, beginning Part Five of the novel, constitutes a confessional on how he came to envisage his crimes. As a teenager, Mathias was mocked over a strange hereditary affliction – he was born without nipples: 'Mum had told him and Dad that her father, who died when Mum was small, didn't have any nipples, either'.[39] But, looking through family photo albums, Mathias sees a photo of his bare-chested grandfather, which proves that this is a lie. When Mathias catches his mother having sex with another man – a man without nipples – he realises the truth about his paternity. Immediately after this revelation, Mathias kills his mother, punishing her for her infidelity and her lies: 'my mother was a liar and a whore'.[40] From his biological father, Mathias has inherited a rare disease, scleroderma, which will lead to the gradual tightening of his skin, resulting in a painful death. As the Snowman, he re-enacts his mother's punishment, torturing and killing nine other mothers whose children are the products of extramarital affairs. Like Matthias's mother, these women are all *mères fatales*, and their infidelity means that their children are fathered by men who pass on terrible hereditary illnesses. The sins of the mother and the father are visited upon the children, all of whom, like Mathias, are sentenced to painful and untimely deaths.

In the final showdown between Hole and the Snowman, Mathias casts himself as the keeper of patriarchal authority and the denouncer of a corrupt and morally bankrupt society. He suggests that his killings cleanse society in the same way as the police should, but cannot: 'we're in the same business, Harry. Fighting disease. But the diseases you and I are fighting can't be eradicated. All our victories are temporary. So it's just the fight which is our life's work.'[41] The novel ends on a note of uncertainty, once again drawing attention to the equivalence between Harry and the Snowman. Mathias is alive in jail and Harry ensures that his shoelaces are taken away. He does this not out of compassion, as his colleagues suspect, but out of a desire to see Mathias suffer the lingering painful death to which his hereditary medical condition condemns him. Which is worse, Harry wonders, 'taking the life of a person who wants to live or taking death from a person who wants to die?'[42]

As an indicator of his popularity, Nesbø's Harry Hole is soon to make the transition from page to screen. For years, Nesbø turned down bids to option his Hole novels for Hollywood. 'I'd rather have 1000 different Harrys in the mind of my readers', he said, 'than one chosen by a director'.[43] Recently, though, he agreed to sell the rights for *The Snowman* (and all of the Hole novels) to Working Title, Joel and Ethan Coen's production company.[44] The film, starring Michael Fassbender as Hole, was due to premiere in autumn 2017. While Domestic Noir has arguably recently taken over from Nordic Noir as the most commercially and critically successful crime fiction genre, Nesbø and Harry Hole nonetheless look set to remain important parts of Anglophone popular culture.

NOTES

1. 'Good Year for Nesbø', *Norwegian American Weekly*, 3 February 2015 <http://www.na-weekly.com/news/good-year-for-Nesbø/> (last accessed 23 April 2016).
2. For the occasion of the 400th anniversary of William Shakespeare's death, in 2016 Hogarth Shakespeare commissioned a number of high-profile modern authors to produce modern retellings of Shakespeare's canonical works. Gillian Flynn was to write a new version of *Hamlet*, while Anne Tyler's take on *The Taming of the Shrew*, Margaret Atwood's rewriting of the *The Tempest* and Howard Jacobson's retelling of *The Merchant of Venice* all appeared in 2016. Nesbø chose to reimagine *Macbeth* as a modern Nordic Noir novel.
3. Forshaw, *Nordic Noir*, p. 81.
4. Nesbø, 'joNesbø.com: Autobiography'.
5. For book-length studies on Nordic Noir (some of which deal only with Sweden, however), see Forshaw, *Death in a Cold Climate*; Peacock, *Swedish Crime Fiction*; Nestigan and Arvas (eds), *Scandinavian Crime Fiction*. Two chapters in Louise Nilsson, David Damrosch and Theo D'Haen (eds), *Crime Fiction as World Literature* (London: Bloomsbury, 2017), also discuss Nordic Noir.
6. 'Crime Fiction Master Jo Nesbø Comes to Yorkshire', *Yorkshire Post*, 6 April 2015 <http://www.yorkshirepost.co.uk/news/crime-fiction-master-jo-Nesbø-comes-to-yorkshire-1-7192351> (last accessed 23 April 2016).
7. Chandler, Gardiner and Sorley Walker (eds), *Raymond Chandler Speaking*, p. 70.
8. It is important to note, however, that Sjöwall and Wahlöö were not the first Scandinavian writers of crime fiction. Indeed, Nils Nordberg has argued that 'Mordet på Maskinbygger Roolfsen' ('The Murder of Engineer Roolfsen'), an 1839 short story by Norwegian writer Maurits Hansen, must be acknowledged as the world's first detective fiction, as it predates Edgar Allan Poe's 'Murder in the Rue Morgue' (1841), the story generally taken to be the first work of detective fiction. See Nordberg, 'Murder in the Midnight Sun'.
9. The term *Folkhemmet* had been coined by Prime Minister Per Albin Hansson to describe the fair and egalitarian social welfare system (with education, health, pension rights, old age care and gender equality) established as a result of the country's affluence following neutrality in two world wars.
10. Quoted in Forshaw, *Death in a Cold Climate*, p. 101.
11. Peacock, *Swedish Crime Fiction*, p. 2.
12. Hughes, '*Trapped*, Unlikeliest TV Hit of the Year, Draws to a Close'.
13. Peacock, *Swedish Crime Fiction*, p. 3.
14. For a detailed history of Swedish crime fiction see Bergman, *Swedish Crime Fiction*, and Peacock, *Swedish Crime Fiction*. For a broader and brisker overview of Nordic Noir see Forshaw, *Death in a Cold Climate*. Larsson's *Girl with the Dragon Tattoo* is still the Nordic Noir work about which most academic criticism has been written. It is the subject of essays

by eminent critics Peter Messent and Stephen Knight in their respective recent books on the most significant works of crime fiction, *The Crime Fiction Handbook* and *Secrets of Crime Fiction Classics*.

15. Larsson, *The Girl with the Dragon Tattoo*, p. 113.

16. There has been some critical debate about whether Larsson's novels can be considered feminist while portraying graphic sexual violence against women. See King and Smith (eds), *Men Who Hate Women and Women Who Kick Their Asses*, and Åström, Gregorsdotter and Horeck (eds), *Rape in Stieg Larsson's Millennium Trilogy and Beyond*.

17. Hesse, 'Jo Nesbø'.

18. Forshaw, *Nordic Noir*, p. 82.

19. For more on global crime fiction see: Pepper, *Unwilling Executioner*; King, 'Crime Fiction as World Literature'.

20. Foster, 'PW Talks with Jo Nesbø'.

21. Nesbø, *The Snowman*, p. 198.

22. 'Harry Hole: Character Profile', joNesbø.co.uk <http://joNesbø.com/harry-hole/character-profile/> (last accessed 21 April 2016).

23. Nance, 'Q&A: Jo Nesbø on *Police*, Harry Hole'.

24. Meyhoff, 'Digging into the Secrets of the Past', p. 69. The novel's focus on the uncomfortable truth about Norway's right-wing extremists, of course, would come to international attention following the worst atrocity in modern Norwegian history – the murder of seventy-seven children by neo-Nazi Anders Behring Breivik in 2011.

25. Pepper, *Unwilling Executioner*, p. 8.

26. Nesbø, *The Snowman*, p. 82.

27. Ibid., pp. 82–3.

28. Seltzer, *Serial Killers*, p. 1.

29. Horsley, *Twentieth-Century Crime Fiction*, p. 118.

30. Jenkins, *A Decade of Nightmares* pp. 19, 69.

31. Curtis, 'Scandinavian Thriller Obsession'.

32. Horsley, *The Noir Thriller*, p. 10.

33. Nesbø, *The Snowman*, p. 33.

34. Ibid., p. 391.

35. Dickos, *Street with No Name*, p. 146.

36. Skenazy, 'Behind the Territory Ahead', p. 114.

37. Berit Åström's excellent essay '"Because My Mother Was a Liar and a Whore"' also focuses on issues of paternity in *The Snowman*, although it relates these issues not as I do, to Noir and genre, but rather to 'sociological research on misattributed paternity'.

38. Nesbø, *The Snowman*, p. 11.

39. Ibid., p. 367.

40. Ibid., p. 440.

41. Ibid., p. 490.

42. Ibid., p. 451.

43. Hesse, 'Jo Nesbø, The Next Stieg Larsson?'

44. Birnbaum, 'Crime Pays'.

KEY WORKS

Flaggermusmannen (1997); *The Bat* (2012). Nesbø's first Harry Hole novel.

Snømannen (2007); *The Snowman* (2010). The novel with which Nesbø became an international success.

Hodejegerne (2008); *Headhunters* (2008). A stand-alone comic crime novel, set in the high-stakes world of art theft. This was the first of Nesbø's works to make the transition from page to screen. In 2009, Swedish production company Yellow Bird (also responsible for Swedish-language film and television productions of Larsson's Millennium trilogy and Henning Mankell's Kurt Wallander novels) bought the rights to *Headhunters*. With a screenplay by Nesbø, the film was released in 2011 and went on to become the highest-grossing Norwegian movie of all time.

Gjenferd (2011); *Phantom* (2012). The ninth in the Hole series novel ends ambiguously with Harry Hole's death. This led many readers and critics to speculate that this novel was Nesbø's version of Arthur Conan Doyle's 'The Final Problem', where Doyle killed off his most famous creation, Sherlock Holmes. However, Harry returned to life in *Police* (2013) [*Politi*, 2013].

Tørst (2017); *The Thirst* (2017). After a four-year haitus, Nesbø returned to Hole with *The Thirst*, published in April 2017. In 2017, Harvill Secker also published a twentieth-anniversary edition of Nesbø's first Hole novel, *The Bat*.

FURTHER CRITICAL READING

Forshaw, *Death in a Cold Climate*.
Nestigen and Arvas (eds), *Scandinavian Crime Fiction*.
Peacock, *Swedish Crime Fiction*.

BIBLIOGRAPHY

Åström, Berit, '"Because My Mother Was a Liar and a Whore": Adulterous Mothers and Paternity Uncertainty in Jo Nesbø's *The Snowman*', in Vanessa Reimer and Sarah Sahagian (eds), *The Mother-Blame Game* (Toronto: Demeter Press, 2015), pp. 204–18.

Åström, Berit, Katarina Gregorsdotter and Tanya Horeck (eds), *Rape in Stieg Larsson's Millennium Trilogy and Beyond: Contemporary Scandinavian and Anglophone Crime Fiction* (Basingstoke: Palgrave, 2012).

Bergman, Kerstin, *Swedish Crime Fiction: The Making of Nordic Noir* (Milan: Mimesis Edizioni, 2014).

Birnbaum, Robert, 'Crime Pays: Jo Nesbø Talks About Killing Harry Hole and the Best Job in the World', *The Millions*, 17 February 2002 <http://www.themillions.com/2012/02/crime-pays-jo-Nesbø-talks-about-killing-harry-hole-and-the-best-job-in-the-world.html> (last accessed 12 June 2016).

Chandler, Raymond, Dorothy Gardiner and Kathrine Sorley Walker (eds), *Raymond Chandler Speaking* (Berkeley: University of California Press, 1997).

Curtis, Bryan, 'Scandinavian Thriller Obsession', *Newsweek*, 15 May 2011 <http://europe.newsweek.com/scandinavian-thriller-obsession-67569?rm=eu> (last accessed 2 May 2016).

Dickos, Andrew, *Street with No Name: A History of the Classic American Film Noir* (Lexington: University of Kentucky Press, 2002).

Forshaw, Barry, *Nordic Noir: The Pocket Essential Guide to Scandinavia Crime Fiction, Film, and TV* (Harpenden: Oldcastle Books, 2013).

Forshaw, Barry, *Death in a Cold Climate: A Guide to Scandinavian Crime Fiction* (Basingstoke: Palgrave Macmillan, 2012).

Foster, Jordan, 'PW Talks with Jo Nesbø: Norwegian Noir', *Publishers Weekly*, 25 January 2010 <http://www.publishersweekly.com/pw/by-topic/authors/interviews/article/41723-pw-talks-with-jo-Nesbø.html> (last accessed 26 April 2016).

Hesse, Monica, 'Jo Nesbø, The Next Stieg Larsson? The Norwegian Author Is No Fan of the Thought', *Washington Post*, 3 May 2011 <https://www.washingtonpost.com/lifestyle/style/jo-Nesbø-the-next-stieg-larsson-the-norwegian-author-is-no-fan-of-the-thought/2011/05/03/AFdj3GhF_story.html> (last accessed 12 June 2016).

Horsley, Lee, *The Noir Thriller* (London: Palgrave Macmillan, 2009).

Horsley, Lee, *Twentieth-Century Crime Fiction* (Oxford: Oxford University Press, 2005).

Hughes, Sarah, '*Trapped*, Unlikeliest TV Hit of the Year, Draws to a Close',*The Guardian*, 11 March 2016 <http://www.theguardian.com/tv-and-radio/2016/mar/11/trapped-unlikeliest-tv-hit-of-the-year-draws-to-a-close> (last accessed 21 April 2016).

Jenkins, Philip, *A Decade of Nightmares: The End of the Sixties and the Making of Eighties America* (Oxford: Oxford University Press, 2006).

King, Donna and Carrie Lee Smith (eds), *Men Who Hate Women and Women Who Kick Their Asses: Stieg Larsson's Millennium Trilogy in a Feminist Perspective* (Nashville, TN: Vanderbilt University Press, 2012).

King, Stewart, 'Crime Fiction as World Literature', *CLUES: A Journal of Detection*, 32:2 (autumn 2014), pp. 8–19.

Knight, Stephen, *Secrets of Crime Fiction Classics* (Jefferson, NC: McFarland, 2014).

Larsson, Stieg, *The Girl with the Dragon Tattoo* (London: MacLehose Press, 2008).

Messent, Peter, *The Crime Fiction Handbook* (Oxford: Wiley-Blackwell, 2012).

Meyhoff, Karsten Wind, 'Digging into the Secrets of the Past: Rewriting History in the Modern Scandinavian Police Procedural', in Andrew Nestigen and Paula Arvas (eds), *Scandinavian Crime Fiction* (Cardiff: University of Wales Press, 2011), pp. 62–77.

Nance, Kevin, 'Q&A: Jo Nesbø on *Police*, Harry Hole', *Chicago Tribune*, 20 October 2013 <http://articles.chicagotribune.com/2013-10-20/features/ct-prj-1020-jo-Nesbø-police-20131020_1_harry-hole-crime-fiction-printers-row-journal> (last accessed 26 April 2016).

Nesbø, Jo, 'joNesbø.com: Autobiography' <http://joNesbø.com/jo-Nesbø/biography/> (last accessed 24 April 2016).

Nesbø, Jo, *The Snowman* (London: Harvill Secker, 2010).

Nestigan, Andrew and Paula Arvas (eds), *Scandinavian Crime Fiction* (Cardiff: University of Wales Press, 2011).

Nordberg, Nils,'Murder in the Midnight Sun: Crime Fiction in Norway 1825–2005', *Crime Time* <http://www.crimetime.co.uk/mag/index.php/showarticle/2155> (last accessed 22 April 2016).

Peacock, Steven, *Swedish Crime Fiction: Novel, Film, Television* (Manchester: Manchester University Press, 2014).

Pepper, Andrew, *Unwilling Executioner: Crime Fiction and the State* (Oxford: Oxford University Press, 2016).

Seltzer, Mark, *Serial Killers: Death and Life in America's Wound Culture* (London: Routledge, 1998).

Skenazy, Paul, 'Behind the Territory Ahead', in David Fine (ed.), *Los Angeles in Fiction* (Albuquerque: University of New Mexico Press, 1995), pp. 103–37.

CHAPTER 8

'It's a Trap! Don't Turn the Page': Metafiction and the Multiverse in the Comics of Grant Morrison

Kate Roddy

Grant Morrison (b. 1960) is a Glasgow-born writer, playwright and occultist who rose to prominence with his work for mainstream comic book publishers DC and Marvel Comics in the late 1980s and early 1990s. He is celebrated as an innovative and influential writer of publisher-owned superhero properties such as Batman, Superman and the X-Men, and as a creator of independent postmodern comic titles such as *The Invisibles* (1994–2000) and *The Filth* (2002–3). Morrison credits his Cold War upbringing as a major influence on his work. His father was a working-class World War II veteran who became a pacifist and undertook spying activities for the Campaign for Nuclear Disarmament (CND).[1] He recounts that as a child he accompanied his father on highly illegal missions to take pictures of underground nuclear bases,[2] and he has written of the lasting impression that the hand-drawn CND manifestoes had upon his young mind, with their vistas of 'shattered, obliterated skeletons contorted against blazing horizons of nuked and blackened urban devastation'.[3] Morrison found relief from these apocalyptic nightmares within the pages of superhero comics. As he read, he discovered that comics were not merely an avenue for escapism into 'dramas spanning decades and galaxies',[4] but also a powerful symbol of mankind's better nature and the ultimate triumph of the imagination:

> In Superman and his fellow superheroes, modern human beings had brought into being ideas that were invulnerable from harm, immune to deconstruction, built to outsmart diabolical masterminds, made to confront pure Evil and, somehow, against the odds, to always win.[5]

It is the seriousness and sensitivity with which Morrison treats his superheroic subject that marks him out as a leader in the field. While near-contemporaries such as Alan Moore (famed for his 1986 deconstructionist epic *Watchmen*) ultimately dismiss the superhero as juvenile and culturally barren,[6] Morrison has continually sought to reclaim this figure as an emblem of hope and utopian aspiration. His work challenges the low cultural value generally ascribed to mainstream comics, as well as the idea that the superhero is a ridiculous or irrelevant cultural figure. He asserts:

> Superhero stories speak loudly and boldly to our greatest fears, deepest longings, and highest aspirations. They're not afraid to be hopeful, not embarrassed to be optimistic, and utterly fearless in the dark . . . At their best, they help us to confront and resolve even the deepest existential crises. We should listen to what they have to tell us.[7]

Morrison's importance derives not just from his affection for his subject matter, but also from his ability to bring what Marc Singer terms an 'auteurist sensibility' to an industry that demands that creators work in assembly-line conditions and operate within strict limitations concerning how the publisher's creative properties can be used.[8] Morrison's creativity, combined with his seeming mastery of superhero comics continuously published over a period of more than seventy-five years, enables him to craft fresh narratives in a genre often criticised for its repetitive and self-plagiarising nature. In addition to this, Morrison's career-long obsession with metafiction, non-linear narratives and the existence of higher realities adds complexity and depth to his work, hooking readers with narratives that go beyond the adventures of men in tights to bend the mind with far-out metaphysical concepts.

The term 'comic' covers many different genres and kinds of material culture. These include newspaper strips; political cartoons; children's picture books; European comic albums (e.g. the Tintin and Asterix series); mainstream comic books (e.g. those published by Marvel and DC); underground comix; and graphic novels. The distinction between a comic book and a graphic novel is contentious and frequently debated, with some arguing that the latter is merely a snobbish term used to confer respectability upon a much-maligned medium (Art Spiegelman, for instance, has dismissed graphic novels as simply 'well-dressed comic books').[9] Others, such as Jan Baetens and Hugo Frey, insist on the utility of the distinction.[10] Broadly defined, a graphic novel is a publication with high production values, bound as a volume and sold in high street bookshops, that is the work of auteur creators, and which contains matter that constitutes a distinct body of work (rather than serialised adventures). A comic book is a publication that usually results from an assembly-line creation process involving a large number of people (writers, pencillers, cover artists, inkers, colourists, letterers and editors), and which has relatively low production values (folded pages held together by staples in a format known in the industry as a 'floppy'). Comic books are serialised narratives released in regular instalments, and since the 'direct market' shift of the 1970s, they have mainly been available for purchase from specialised retailers, mainly comic book shops. Falling somewhere between 'graphic novel' and 'comic book' is the 'trade paperback' or 'TPB' (also sometimes 'trade hardback'), a collected edition of work originally published in instalments for the direct market and subsequently made more widely available. Some works generally termed 'graphic novels' are more properly TPBs; for example, Moore and Gibbon's *Watchmen* and Frank Miller's *The Dark Knight Returns* (1986) were both published serially before collection.

Morrison's career has undoubtedly benefited from the heightened cultural awareness and profitability of the graphic novel and TPB formats. During the so-called 'British invasion' of the mid- to late 1980s, a number of dynamic young creators, including Morrison, Moore and Neil Gaiman, were headhunted from the UK by a then DC Comics editor, Karen Berger, to work on new comic titles for what would later become Vertigo, a DC imprint aimed at producing innovative and non-Code-compliant works for an adult readership.[11] Morrison's breakout work for DC was the graphic novel *Arkham Asylum: A Serious House on Serious Earth* (1989), sales of which were boosted both by the medium's new-found respectability and the publicity generated for the Batman franchise by Tim Burton's film of the same year.[12] Although Morrison has written many different genres of comic, from the psychedelic sci-fi/fantasy of *The Invisibles* to polemical meditations on animal rights in *We3* (2004), he is most famous for his work on superheroes. Indeed, for reasons that have to do with both the history of the genre and the entrenched selling strategies of the 'big two', Marvel and DC, 'comics' and 'superheroes' are virtually synonymous.[13]

The American comic book industry came about in the late 1920s, when it was discovered that collections of newspaper comic strips sold well on the newsstands.[14] Enterprising publishers such as Malcolm Wheeler-Nicholson then took this a step further with the decision to publish original material. Siegel and Shuster's *Action Comics* #1 (1938) introduced Superman to the world and all the key elements of the superhero mythos: a bold, primary-coloured costume (modelled on that of a circus strongman), amazing powers, a secret identity and a mission to fight evil and help mankind. So began what came to be known by comics scholars and fans as the Golden Age, the period from 1938 to 1954, when comics underwent rapid expansion and some of the most enduring and recognisable characters were created, including Batman, The Flash, Captain Marvel, Namor the Sub-Mariner and Captain America.

In 1954 the comics industry was hit by a crisis in the form of a book titled *Seduction of the Innocent* by one Dr Fredric Wertham, a German-American psychiatrist who claimed that comics were violent, obscene and likely to cause homo-erotic and sadistic longings in the adolescent reader. Wertham's objections launched a US Congressional inquiry into the comic book industry and this increased scrutiny led to the industry having to adopt a strict censorship code, imposed through industry self-regulation under the Comics Code Authority (CCA). Comics publishers rallied after Wertham's attack and so began what came to be known as the Silver Age (c. 1956–70). Comics of this period were characterised by wackiness and a preoccupation with science and invention, as embodied by the Fantastic Four (a property of Marvel Comics, which began publishing in 1961). A key text of the age is *The Flash* #123 (1961), subtitled 'The Flash of Two Worlds'. In this story, the second-generation Flash, Barry Allen, encounters the Golden Age Flash, Jay Garrick. Allen immediately recognises Garrick because in the world of the former, the latter has appeared in 'fictional' comic book adventures. This landmark comic effectively brought into being what is now termed the 'DC multiverse' and staked out two of its separate fictional realities: Allen and the other Silver Age heroes occupied 'Earth-One'; the Golden Age Flash and his friends existed on 'Earth-Two'.[15] Thus, DC's characters (formerly past and present) came to occupy separate worlds which exist simultaneously and send each other metaphysical status reports in the form of superhero comic books. The existence of a multiverse and of differing levels of fictionality within the comics text are ideas that Morrison has foregrounded in his work since the beginning of his career, and are concepts central to an understanding of a recent major work, *The Multiversity* (2014–15).

The Bronze Age (c. 1970–85) was characterised by a turn towards social issues, including environmentalism, racism and drug use, and also saw the rise of brooding anti-heroes such as the Punisher and Wolverine. The age's preoccupation with inserting 'realism' into the lives of superheroes led into what is often referred to as the Dark Age of comics (c. 1986–95[?]), typified by the aforementioned *Watchmen* and *The Dark Knight Returns*. Grim and gritty in tone, these comics sought to deconstruct conventional notions of the superhero by portraying the 'heroes' as brooding and sociopathic, often crippled by addiction or sexual hang-ups.

There is little critical or fan agreement concerning what the current age of superhero comics should be called. Morrison, most optimistically, suggests 'Renaissance', seeing the current age as one where the positivity and invention of the Golden and Silver Ages can be combined with sophisticated storytelling.[16] Randy Duncan and Matthew J. Smith have christened the period stretching from the late 1980s to the present 'the Era of Reiteration', seeing the current comics scene as sunken in nostalgia and pandering to a 'small, highly-specialized' audience.[17] While there is some justice in Duncan and Smith's view of contemporary superhero comics as insular and fanboy centric, this is only one strand of the current publishing model. What defines the modern-day comics industry is the cross-media marketing of its properties. Significantly, in 2009 both DC and Marvel Comics became subsidiaries of larger entities within the entertainment industry (Marvel merging with Disney, DC with Warner Brothers). Thus, comic books are now only one facet of a sales model that includes film and TV tie-ins and the proliferation of 'merch': t-shirts, action figures and other collectables. In addition to the creation of new platforms to market their intellectual properties, mainstream publishers have also increased the accessibility of their comics: the existence of Comixology and similar platforms means that readers can download material rather than purchasing hard copies from specialised retailers.

Morrison's prominence within the genre is due to a number of qualities of his writing that make him supremely suited to the needs of mainstream comics publishing. The first such quality is his ability to craft sophisticated, postmodern narratives that transfer well from monthly floppies to trade paperbacks, and thus make his work doubly profitable for the publisher. Second is his ability to revitalise flagging titles and make new, definitive versions of existing characters and properties. For example, his *New X-Men* (2001–4) allowed the series to move away from the soap-opera sensibility it had developed under a previous long-serving writer, Chris Claremont, and added much-needed cool and narrative innovation. Third, and perhaps most importantly with regard to his tenure at DC, is his competency with long-term plotting and mastery of in-house continuity, qualities which enable him to function in the role of architect for flagship titles and the increasingly popular 'crossover events' (narratives distributed over a number of comics titles, usually dealing with some kind of crisis that has worldwide or even multiversal ramifications). These series are designed by the publishers to create a bump in sales by fuelling excitement within fandom via narratives that promise to profoundly change the landscape of the shared universe.

The Multiversity is a work that encapsulates Morrison's oeuvre, not merely reprising ideas that have been prominent in his work since the beginning of his career at DC, but taking many of them to extreme conclusions. These key Morrison preoccupations include metatextuality, the role of author, the role of reader and the past and future of the superhero genre. The work is an 'event' narrative that takes place across multiple universes. Like its large-scale continuity-altering predecessors, *Crisis on Infinite Earths* (1985–6) and *Final Crisis* (2008), it portrays the heroes of many different universes attempting to combat a great overarching threat that seeks to collapse the multiverse and kill all life within it. A brief summary of the work's complex plot is as follows: Nix Uotan, the last of a race of multiversal guardians called the Monitors, is living incognito on Earth-0 when he gets a distress signal from another world. Upon arrival at the source of the SOS, he finds a world in ruins, Earth-7 having been overrun by a group of seemingly invincible nightmare beings who call themselves 'the Gentry'.[18] Nix Uotan sacrifices himself to allow some of the Earth-7 characters to escape to the 'House of Heroes', a sanctuary in the 'bleedspace' within universes.[19] From this vantage point, heroes from across the fifty-two universes meet to try to conquer the Gentry, who are infiltrating the multiverse by means of a 'predatory story' in the form of a haunted text called 'Ultra Comics'.[20]

The Multiversity shows Morrison exerting an almost unprecedented degree of control over DC Comics' creative properties and continuity. While a lesser-known author might be allowed to add, in some minor capacity, to a comic book character's origin story or catalogue of adventures, here Morrison defines the parameters of the entire shared work of fiction. The grandness of the undertaking was indicated from the initial teaser for the series, a map of the DC multiverse showing the relative positions of the individual Earths within an 'orrery of worlds', followed by the sphere of gods (which includes heaven, hell and 'dream' – of *Sandman* fame), New Genesis (home of Jack Kirby's New Gods) and Apokolips (realm of DC's quondam 'big bad', Darkseid), and further still to limbo (where unread and out-of-continuity characters reside until they are needed again), then the Monitor Sphere, to the 'source wall' that delineates the limits of what is known, and the Overvoid beyond.[21] Most of these elements are not Morrison's inventions, but he is the first to visualise a united and coherent scheme for their relation to one another within the giant patchwork of so many years and hands.

The Multiversity takes from 'The Flash of Two Worlds' the concept that universes can communicate via comic books. The Earth-26 character Captain Carrot (whose alter ego, Rodney Rabbit, is himself a writer/artist for DC Comics) describes these texts as 'messages in bottles from neighbouring universes' and asserts, in a Borges-like comment, 'I always suspected that one world's reality is another's fiction'.[22] Morrison here returns to and complicates a concept that has been central to his comics since the early days for DC: that different levels of reality incorrectly perceive one another as 'fictional', or as having a lesser ontological status relative to themselves.

Morrison's scheme implies a radical flattening of hierarchies both within and beyond the text. Where comics readers might be inclined to think one version of the DC Comics universe is more canonical or 'real' than another (e.g. that Earth-0, where the most familiar in-continuity versions of Batman, Superman et al. reside, is more 'real', relatively speaking, than Earth-26, home of the anthropomorphic animal heroes Captain Carrot and the Zoo Crew), here they all appear on an equal ontological footing, united by the mission to save their shared habitat. Furthermore, the DC multiverse is shown to expand outwards to contain even the reader's own world, designated 'Earth-33' or 'Earth-Prime': '[a] mysterious world without superheroes [that] exerts a powerful and unknown influence on the progress and development of the multiverse'.[23]

Morrison's folding of 'our' world into the text is more than just a postmodern metatextual gesture: it is central to the way that the text's unique narrative structure functions. From Earth-33 comes 'Ultra Comics', both the title of a comic book which appears as the penultimate issue of *Multiversity* (and is previewed, dotted throughout the various universes in preceding issues) and the name of the book's central character. Ultra Comics is a living avatar of all comic books ever written. He narrates his own in-process creation to us, describing 'my body – made from cellulose pulp, salt water, and carbon . . . the staples of my spine'.[24] The source of Ultra's power is not a bite from a radioactive spider or alien parentage, but what the caption boxes describe as 'the ULTRAGEM! Imagination in solid crystal form'.[25] Ultra is what Morrison in his 'chaos magician' guise would describe as a 'sigil': a magical symbol powered by the will of the reader; or, as Ultra himself glosses, a 'circuit closing', for 'only TOGETHER can we bring the ULTRAGEM to LIFE . . . WE ARE ULTRA COMICS'.[26] 'Ultra Comics' therefore establishes a scenario where we, the readers, are working in tandem with the fictional hero to combat the invasion of 'a genuine threat from ANOTHER UNIVERSE'.[27]

Press-ganging readers into adopting an active role in what they might expect to be a prefabricated, inert narrative is a strategy that Morrison has honed over the course of his career. As I have argued elsewhere, Morrison's work has increasingly moved away from the linear, episodic narrative typically associated with superhero comics, which features a beginning where the character has essentially 'reset' following the conclusion of the last adventure (what Umberto Eco termed 'the oneiric climate'),[28] and moved towards fragmentary, non-linear narratives.[29] Many of Morrison's most celebrated works, such as *The Invisibles* and *Seven Soldiers of Victory* (2006–7), feature disruptions, repetitions and narrative gaps, requiring the reader to think in terms of repeating patterns and to order for themselves the units of meaning.

Morrison sees this narrative strategy as closely aligned with, and even dependent on, the unique qualities of the comic book as a medium. He describes the comic page as a 'magical' space, one which is very much under the reader's control: 'you can look at a panel, or a page as a whole, and you can go backwards, move around in the continuum of the comic'.[30] The base unit of the comic, the panel, is imagined by the author as a window to a moment in time and space, one which can connect to others in a linear sequence (reading across a page from left to right, top to bottom, as is conventional in Western comics), but also backwards, laterally, in fact in any direction and with any other individual panel of the sequence. *The Multiversity* frequently disorients the reader with panels that appear out of linear sequence, or strangely decontextualised. The issue 'Pax Americana' (pencilled by long-term Morrison collaborator Frank

Figure 8.1 *(above and opposite)* The Question investigates Nora O'Rourke's murder in 'Pax Americana'. From: *The Multiversity #1* © DC Comics

Quitely) is deliberately figured in small, rectangular panels, set in repeating patterns. This is done in a pastiche of Moore and Gibbon's *Watchmen*, which famously utilises three-by-three panel pages, arranged to evoke the sense of regular increments in time (a reminder of the doomsday clock's countdown to nuclear midnight).[31]

The unifying emblem of 'Pax Americana' is not of a forward-moving countdown, but a Mobius strip or infinity symbol (∞). The narrative continually moves between fixed points in time and space, looping forward and backwards on itself. The infinity sign appears not just as a visual symbol (engraved in President Harley's ring, for example)[32] but is embedded within the comic's dialogue and layouts, as in the conversation between Doctor Eden and his daughter Evie (AKA Nightshade). Reading the exchange between the two characters as they navigate a stairwell requires the reader to follow the panels in a figure of eight formation while the dialogue echoes the directional progress: 'everything goes into reverse . . . you twist everything'.[33] The ultimate synchronicity of verbal and visual narrative occurs over a two-page spread laid out in tiny four-by-four panel pages (one-upping Moore and Gibbons), reproduced here as Figure 8.1. The episode depicts three separate moments in time (the Question investigating Nora O'Rourke's murder; a farewell between Nora and the Peacemaker; and the moments just before her death) united by the same spatial canvas (the panels, when viewed from a satellite point of view, make up an image of the whole room). There are no cues for how the sequence should be ordered. The reader can choose to read horizontally or vertically; left page followed by right page; or as one continuous line; or to group the daytime panels as one narrative thread and the night time panels as another. Each panel is temporally unmoored, one card in a deck waiting to be shuffled and ordered by the reader.

The series continues to disorder space and time within the comic and, concomitantly, to challenge readers in their assumed role as passive consumers of the narrative. The beginning of 'Ultra Comics' shows us Ultra at the end of his adventure, 'from 24 hours and 38 pages in the future'.[34] He appears panicked and injured; a blood vessel has burst in his right eye. 'YOU! Yes, you!' he says, facing the fourth wall and pointing towards the reader. 'Don't GO. Don't leave me ALONE.'[35] The last panels of this sequence show Ultra being consumed by Geigerian eyes and tentacles. He still stares from the panel in horror: 'YOU! It was YOUR eye all along. THE OBLIVION MACHINE! We're in the oblivion machine! IT'S A TRAP! DON'T TURN THE PAGE!'[36]

The Multiversity therefore transforms the comic book from a harmless, inert piece of ephemera to a potentially 'infectious' and reader-implicating artefact. The narrative of 'Ultra Comics' is revealed to be a spring-trap that is activated by reading, and by choosing to continue with the narrative, the reader has helped the parasitic presence of the Gentry diffuse throughout the other comic book universes. In fact, several characters imply that we (the readers) *are* the Gentry: the Superman of Earth-23 traces the source of the infection to Earth-33 (Earth Prime, AKA the 'real' world): 'As far as I can SEE that's where ALL our troubles began'.[37]

The revelation that the comic's readers are the Gentry feeds into a meta-narrative that forms both a commentary upon and a critique of fan culture. The opening pages of the series show Nix Uotan engaging in a forum discussion on 'Ultra Comics' (*The*

Multiversity #1). The language he uses to describe the act of critiquing the text is sinister: a caption box (presumably relaying the words Nix has posted to the online forum) states: 'My review will be in the form of a live dissection', while Nix holds the comic's pages using surgical tongs and a scalpel, telling his chimp companion, Stubbs, 'I'm vivisecting a comic book'.[38] The implication is that a comic book is something vital and alive that can be tortured and harmed by entitled, careless readers. Near the end of the series, when the leader of the Gentry pulls away from the narrative with the pronouncement 'EMPTY IS MY HAND',[39] his fingers linger in the position where a reader would hold a comic, his abandonment of the multiverse perhaps suggesting fears of a similar disengagement by the readership.

Morrison has spoken about his fears for the future stability of comics: in particular, the rise of Internet piracy and a culture of criticism without commitment.[40] The opening and closing scenes of *The Multiversity* criticise these elements of fan culture, but they do so in a playful and metatextual way, encouraging the reader to take responsibility for how the narrative unfolds and to assist in crafting its ultimate meaning. Earth-23 Superman's last words in the comic are in fact a threat directed towards the denizens of Earth-33, that troublesome world without superheroes of its own which nonetheless has the god-like power to warp and even destroy the DC multiverse. He vows: 'And if they're OUT there, if they're somehow READING this – we're coming to GET them'.[41]

The Multiversity therefore showcases a broad selection of the qualities that have made Morrison such an important and influential figure within the superhero comics genre. First is his ability to serve as an architect, not only crafting individual stories on a small scale, but creating narratives that sketch out the boundaries of the shared fictional universe, reconciling over seventy-five years of publishing history in a scheme that is simultaneously ordered and creatively abundant. Unlike *Crisis on Infinite Earths*, DC's first attempt at streamlining continuity, *The Multiversity* does not seek to erase past iterations of the characters, but rather creates a space for all Batmen and Supermen (and even far-out and largely forgotten characters like Captain Carrot) to coexist peacefully. Second is his exploitation of the unique capabilities of the comic book medium: in collaboration with artists, Morrison creates narratives which demonstrate the multimodality of comics – the particular and innovative ways in which image and text combine to generate meaning – and the comic's ability to challenge readers and produce a subjective and unique reading experience. Third is the sophisticated nature of his storytelling, which is often self-reflexive and metatextual. Whereas most metatextual works merely draw attention to their own fictionality as a disruptive device, Morrison instead adopts it for the purposes of immersion. Of his early interest in the superhero genre, he says:

> I wanted to find out what it was like in there – where the sky was always blue, where everything was primary-coloured, where time was represented by boxes and you could cut between one moment and ten years over the space of a gutter.[42]

On this journey, he brings the reader along with him.

NOTES

1. Morrison, *Supergods*, p. xiii.
2. Patrick Meaney (dir.), *Grant Morrison: Talking with Gods*, Respect! Films, 2010.
3. Morrison, *Supergods*, p. xiv.
4. Ibid., p. xv.
5. Ibid.
6. Alan Moore, interviewed by Kelly, 'Alan Moore'.
7. Morrison, *Supergods*, p. xvii.
8. Singer, *Grant Morrison*, p. 3.
9. Spiegelman, 'Comix'.
10. Baetens and Frey, *The Graphic Novel*, pp. 1–23.
11. Singer, *Grant Morrison*, p. 53. Concern about comic books exerting a 'bad influence' on youth led to the industry voluntarily adopting a system of self-regulation, or Code-compliance, in 1954. After various erosions, the Code (discussed below) was finally abandoned in 2011.
12. Ibid., p. 64.
13. End-of-year figures from Diamond Comics Distributors for 2016 show Marvel Comics had the largest share of the current market (36.73 per cent retail market share and a 40.50 per cent unit market share); while DC Entertainment came second (29.47 per cent retail market share and a 29.04 per cent unit market share). See Michael Doran, 'December DC and Marvel Crossover Launches Help Year-End '16 Comic Book Sales Barely Increase Over '15', newsarama.com, 12 January 2017 <http://www.newsarama.com/32710-december-dc-marvel-crossover-launches-help-2016-comic-book-sales-barely-increase-over-2015.html> (last accessed 15 August 2017).
14. Wright, *The Classic Era of American Comics*, p. 3.
15. The DC multiverse has undergone several major reconfigurations, beginning with the event series *Crisis on Infinite Earths* (1985–6), where a supra-multiversal threat collapses the many worlds into one. This was an attempt by DC to streamline their continuity and make the comics more accessible to a younger readership.
16. Morrison, *Supergods*, p. 265.
17. Duncan and Smith, *The Power of Comics*, p. 24.
18. Grant Morrison, Ivan Reis, et al., *The Multiversity* #1, 'Cosmic Neighbourhood Watch' (New York: DC Comics, October 2014), in Morrison et al., *The Multiversity: The Deluxe Edition*, p. 8. All further page references relate to this collected edition.
19. Ibid., p. 21.
20. Grant Morrison, Ben Oliver, et al., *The Multiversity* #1, 'The Just' (New York: DC Comics, December 2014), p. 6.
21. The map was first released as advanced publicity for the series in mid-2014 – see for example <http://www.newsarama.com/21694-sdcc-2014-grant-morrison-maps-the-dc-multiverse-ahead-of-multiversity.html> (last accessed 15 August 2017). It was later reprinted as a two-page spread in Grant Morrison, Marcus To, et al., *The Multiversity* #1, 'The Multiversity Guidebook' (New York: DC Comics, March 2015), pp. 24–5.
22. Ibid.
23. Ibid., p. 51.
24. Grant Morrison, Doug Mahnke, et al., *The Multiversity* # 1, 'Ultra Comics' (New York: DC Comics, May 2015), p. 7.
25. Ibid., p. 10.
26. Ibid., p. 11.
27. Ibid., p. 5.
28. Eco, 'The Myth of the Superman', p. 17.
29. Roddy '"Screw Symbolism and Let's Go Home"'.

30. Grant Morrison, in Murray, 'More Space Combat!', p. 232.
31. The whole issue forms a response to *Watchmen*: the characters Blue Beetle, the Question, Captain Atom, Nightshade and the Peacemaker are the Charlton Comics properties (acquired by DC) that Moore originally wanted to use in his story, and later had to change to his own original ones that closely echo them (respectively, Nite Owl, Rorschach, Doctor Manhattan, Silk Spectre, the Comedian). 'Pax Americana' also features a presidential assassination, a sociopathic antihero trying to solve murders of his peers, and governmental attempts to control a disassociated being with god-like powers over time and space.
32. Grant Morrison, Frank Quitely, et al., *The Multiversity #1*, 'Pax Americana' (New York: DC Comics, January 2015), p. 1.
33. Ibid., p. 6.
34. Morrison, Mahnke, *et al.*, *The Multiversity #1*, 'Ultra Comics', p. 3.
35. Ibid., p. 2.
36. Ibid., p. 3.
37. Grant Morrison, Ivan Reis, et al., *The Multiversity #2*, 'Justice Incarnate' (New York: DC Comics, 2015), p. 47
38. Morrison, Reis, et al., *The Multiversity #1*, 'Cosmic Neighbourhood Watch', p. 3.
39. Morrison, Reis, et al., *The Multiversity #2*, 'Justice Incarnate', p. 45.
40. Grant Morrison, interview by Hiatt, 'Grant Morrison on the Death of Comics'.
41. Morrison, Reis, et al., *The Multiversity #2*, 'Justice Incarnate', p. 47.
42. Meaney (dir.), *Grant Morrison*.

KEY WORKS

Morrison, Grant and Chaz Truog, et al., *The Animal Man Omnibus* (New York: DC Comics, 2013). Originally published 1988–90. A loving homage to vanishing Silver Age characters. The series marks the beginning of Morrison's forays into metanarratives and experimental narratives, including a memorable final issue where Morrison himself enters the comic in a 2D 'fiction suit' to apologise to his traumatised protagonist.

Morrison, Grant and Dave McKean, *Arkham Asylum: A Serious House on Serious Earth*, 15th anniversary edition (New York: DC/Vertigo, 2004). Originally published 1989. Morrison's breakthrough work in US comics. McKean's unique collage-like visuals support Morrison's exploration of the depths of Batman's psychology in a story that draws from Christian and pagan mythos, Jungian archetypes and the surrealism of Lewis Carroll.

Morrison, Grant, et al., *The Invisibles Omnibus* (New York: DC/Vertigo, 2012). Originally published 1994–2000. Morrison's most well-known and long-running independent creation, the Invisibles are a cell of freedom fighters with psychedelic and reality-bending powers. Morrison describes the work as a whole as a 'hypersigil', an exercise in chaos magic designed to jump start the culture of the new millennium.

Morrison, Grant, Frank Quitely, Peter Doherty and Ellie De Ville, *Flex Mentallo, Man of Muscle Mystery: The Deluxe Edition* (New York: DC/Vertigo, 2012). Originally published 1996. A semi-autobiographical work about a self-hating musician and his relationship with the strong-man superhero he created in the self-drawn comics of his childhood.

Morrison, Grant, Frank Quitely, et al., *New X-Men Ultimate Collection*, 3 vols (New York: Marvel Comics, 2008). Originally published 2001–4. Morrison's innovative and sophisticated revamp of the X-Men franchise is supported by the finely detailed artwork of long-time collaborator Frank Quitely.

Morrison, Grant, et al., *Seven Soldiers of Victory*, 4 vols (New York: DC Comics, 2006–7). Originally published 2005–6. Seven lesser-known figures of the DC canon combat a time-travelling, culture-devouring race named the Sheeda. The comic's fragmentary, ambiguous narrative requires the input (and crossword-solving skills) of the conscientious reader.

Morrison, Grant, Frank Quitely and Jamie Grant, *Absolute All-Star Superman* (New York, DC Comics 2010). Originally published 2005–8. Freed from the constraints of continuity by the 'All-Star' imprint, Morrison reworks the Superman mythos to make it fresh and culturally relevant for contemporary generations. A dying superman struggles to complete twelve legendary labours before his apotheosis into a literal solar deity.

Morrison, Grant, et al., *Batman, Incorporated*, 2 vols (New York: DC Comics, 2012–13). Originally published 2010–13. Morrison plays with the concept of a superhero as commercial property, as Bruce Wayne goes public as the financial backer of the Batman, unveiling plans to franchise the Bat brand.

FURTHER CRITICAL READING

Bramlett, Frank, Adnan Mahmutovic, and Francesco-Alessio Ursini (eds), 'The Worlds of Grant Morrison', *ImageText*, 8:2 (2015) <http://www.english.ufl.edu/imagetext/archives/v8_2/> (last accessed 30 August 2017). A special issue of interdisciplinary comics journal *ImageText* devoted to essays on Morrison's work.

Callahan, Timothy, *Grant Morrison: The Early Years* (Edwardsville, IL: Sequart, 2007). A study of Morrison's early life and detailed discussion of his first major works.

Greene, Darragh and Kate Roddy (eds), *Grant Morrison and the Superhero Renaissance: Critical Essays* (Jefferson, NC: McFarland, 2015). A collection of essays centred on Morrison's concept of a contemporary cultural 'renaissance' in superhero comics.

Singer, *Grant Morrison*. An in-depth academic study of Morrison's work that examines the phases of his career and the development of his unique style.

BIBLIOGRAPHY

Baetens, Jan and Hugo Frey, *The Graphic Novel: An Introduction* (Cambridge: Cambridge University Press, 2015).

Duncan, Randy and Matthew J. Smith, *The Power of Comics: History, Form and Culture* (London: Continuum, 2009).

Eco, Umberto, 'The Myth of the Superman', *Diacritics*, 2:1 (1972), pp. 14–22.

Hiatt, Brian, 'Grant Morrison on the Death of Comics', *Rolling Stone*, 22 August 2011 <http://www.rollingstone.com/music/news/grant-morrison-on-the-death-of-comics-20110822> (last accessed 15 August 2017).

Kelly, Stuart, 'Alan Moore: "Why Shouldn't You Have a Bit of Fun While Dealing With the Deepest Issues of the Mind?"', *The Guardian*, 22 November 2013 <http://www.theguardian.com/books/2013/nov/22/alan-moore-comic-books-interview> (last accessed 15 August 2017).

Morrison, Grant, *Supergods: Our World in the Age of the Superhero* (London: Jonathan Cape, 2011).

Morrison, Grant, et al., *The Multiversity: The Deluxe Edition* (New York: DC Comics, 2015).

Murray, Chris, 'More Space Combat! An Interview with Grant Morrison', *Studies in Comics*, 4:2 (2013), pp. 219–34.

Roddy, Kate, '"Screw Symbolism and Let's Go Home": Morrison and Bathos', in Darragh Greene and Kate Roddy (eds), *Grant Morrison and the Superhero Renaissance* (Jefferson, NC: McFarland, 2015), pp. 43–63.

Singer, Marc, *Grant Morrison: Combining the Worlds of Contemporary Comics* (Jackson: University Press of Mississippi, 2012).

Spiegelman, Art, 'Comix: An Idiosyncratic Historical and Aesthetic Overview', *Print*, 42 (November/December 1988), p. 61.

Wright, Nicky, *The Classic Era of American Comics* (London: Prion, 2009).

CHAPTER 9

Panoptic and Synoptic Surveillance in Suzanne Collins's Hunger Games Series

Keith O'Sullivan

Suzanne Collins's The Hunger Games is a series of three young adult, dystopian novels, *The Hunger Games*, *Catching Fire* and *Mockingjay*, published by Scholastic between 2008 and 2010. Narrated from its sixteen-year-old protagonist's point of view, the trilogy follows the exploits of Katniss Everdeen, and her friend Peeta Mellark, as she battles against the might of the Capitol, a technologically advanced city in the post-apocalyptic nation of Panem. The Hunger Games has become a cultural phenomenon, with *The Hunger Games* and *Catching Fire* both listed as best sellers in the *New York Times* (the former for more than 200 consecutive weeks) and the trilogy itself as Amazon's top-selling series of 2012. Collins was also Amazon's bestselling Kindle author, surpassing J. K. Rowling's success with Harry Potter. The popularity of The Hunger Games led Collins to be included on *Time* magazine's list of the 100 most influential people of 2010. The trilogy was also adapted for film in four instalments (with *Mockingjay* filmed in two parts) between 2012 and 2015, receiving generally positive reviews from critics, and breaking a number of worldwide box-office records.

That the adaptation of The Hunger Games from book to film was a development that Collins embraced, to the extent that she co-wrote the screenplay for the first film, is unsurprising. Although she did not garner popular acclaim as a writer of fiction until her late thirties, Collins's professional writing career began in 1991, at the children's television network Nickelodeon. Her work there involved scriptwriting for a number of popular series, including *Clarissa Explains It All*, *Little Bear*, *Oswald* and *The Mystery Files of Shelby Woo*, while her first novel, *Fire Proof*, was published in 1999 as part of Nickelodeon's The Mystery Files of Shelby Woo series. Collins's early writing career was characterised by a focus on young adult audiences and child readerships.

Although not as well known as The Hunger Games, The Underland Chronicles, a series of five epic fantasy novels written by Collins and published between 2003 and 2007, introduces many of the dystopian themes that emerge in Collins's subsequent and more adult-oriented trilogy. Preceding The Hunger Games by only one year, and favourably received by critics, the series tells of the adventures of eleven-year-old Gregor in a subterranean 'Underland', beneath New York City, and his attempt to rescue his father, a prisoner of war, from giant rats called 'gnawers'. The Underland Chronicles is concerned with post-war, apocalyptic societies, state governance and surveillance, but it is not as dystopian as The Hunger Games, characterised as it is by its narrative of adventure for a younger readership.

While Collins drew on numerous sources, such as the Greek myth of Theseus and the Minotaur, Roman gladiatorial games, the Iraq War and reality television in writing her narrative, all three instalments of The Hunger Games series exemplify dystopian fiction as a genre. The etymological origins of *dystopia*, an antonym of *utopia*, are in the English transliteration of the Greek prefix *dus*, which nullifies the positive sense and increases the negative sense of a subsequent root, and *topos*, meaning place. In literature, dystopias are imagined places, typically environmentally degraded, where totalitarian elites repress the masses, often through state-sanctioned violence (which is sometimes presented as a spectacle), intrusive methods of surveillance, the conceal-ment or delimitation of information, and induced poverty.[1] The most influential example of dystopian fiction is George Orwell's *Nineteen Eighty-Four* (1949), which critiques omnipresent government surveillance, state propaganda and violence, and the criminalisation of independent thought.

Sharing many of the concerns of *Nineteen Eighty-Four*, The Hunger Games is set in Panem, an autocracy under the dictatorship of President Snow. Located somewhere in the ruins of North America in a future time, Panem consists of twelve districts (previously thirteen), whose inhabitants, for the most part, live in relative poverty, and the Capitol, whose citizens enjoy wealth provided for them by the usurpation of the resources of the districts. After crushing a rebellion that was staged seventy-four years before the events of *The Hunger Games*, during which the thirteenth district was effectively obliterated, the Capitol holds an annual event of remembrance that functions perversely as a spectacle of both forgiveness and repetitious punishment. In the event, titled the Hunger Games, two teenagers ('tributes') from each of the districts are selected randomly to participate in a gladiatorial *game* of survival in an expansive, enclosed arena (consisting of woods, a river and lake) until only one remains alive. In order to succeed, tributes must live off the land, avoid being killed by other competitors, and survive 'natural' disasters that are manipulated from a control centre by 'Gamemakers': in Collins's post-apocalyptic, secular world, Gamemakers are analogous to the capricious gods of Greek mythology.

Although the popularity of dystopian fiction for young adults, in general, is not a new phenomenon, the recent uptick in post-apocalyptic literature and film suggests, according to Christopher Schmidt, something 'more urgent and extreme'.[2] While the film adaptations of The Hunger Games subvert the socio-political critique of contemporary Western values implicit in Collins's dystopian fiction for the sake of playing up the romantic love triangle between Katniss, Peeta and Gale, both film and fiction depict a post-apocalyptic world that young readers can identify with. Suzanne Moore argues that what is truly striking about The Hunger Games, especially the film adaptations, is that they visually resemble the present, somewhere in the world: 'When Katniss stands in the rubble of her district razed to the ground, it could be parts of

Syria, Gaza, Iraq, and Afghanistan. Wild dogs pick over piles of corpses. Hospitals are deliberately bombed.'[3] The Hunger Games presents to its young adult readership a metaphorical rendering of the real world, complete with totalitarian authorities, displaced peoples, induced poverty, omnipresent surveillance, propagandist media and violent insurrections.

Notwithstanding its phenomenal popularity, the trilogy has received its share of unfavourable criticism, especially in relation to its literary quality. Collins's writing frequently lapses into error-ridden prose: misplaced modifiers abound, plural pronouns are sometimes attributed singular antecedents, punctuation is often syntactically confusing, and words are occasionally misused or misspelled. However, some of Collins's stylistic idiosyncrasies are the products of her background in writing for television, as is evident in the truncated sentences and the absence of verbs in the following extract from *The Hunger Games*:

> We're on a flat, open stretch of ground. A plain of hard-packed dirt. Behind the tributes across from me, I can see nothing, indicating either a steep downward slope or even a cliff. To my right lies a lake. To my left and back, sparse piney woods. This is where Haymitch would want me to go. Immediately.[4]

This extract, which functions more like stage or screen directions than narrative prose, is also indicative of the primarily visual quality of Collins's writing and goes some way to explaining her popularity to a contemporary young adult readership that is arguably comfortable with the terseness and multimodal (verbal and visual) nature of many current modes of communication (and, indeed, works of fiction, such as Stephenie Meyer's hugely popular young adult paranormal romance series Twilight). Issues of style aside, one of these modes of communication, social media, which include reality and celebrity television, plays a significant role in the political commentary the trilogy is engaged in. The fact that the Games are played out visually for the population of Panem implies a corollary with many readers' contemporary fascination with visual media, especially reality television. The trilogy suggests that such media have the potential to function as dominant apparatuses of power in relations between those with vested interests in the maintenance of the status quo and the masses. Employing social media as tools of spectacle and surveillance, a ruling elite, led by President Snow, films and televises the Games for the entertainment of the citizens of the Capitol and as a means of invoking fear in the inhabitants of the districts, with the intention of preventing another insurrection. The central role that media play in The Hunger Games, and in much dystopian, post-apocalyptic fiction, is a significant factor in the trilogy's appeal to contemporary readerships. Young adults, in particular, inhabit a world in which being connected to family, friends or acquaintances –'befriended' through social networks and accessible on smartphones, tablets or wearable technologies – also means relinquishing power to others: having one's movements tracked, communications cached and online activity commercialised.

While The Hunger Games displays a number of characteristics of dystopian fiction, one of the most significant is the metonym *bread and circuses* (from the Latin phrase *panem et circenses*, originated by Roman poet Juvenal). *Panem et circenses* is a phrase that suggests the superficial appeasement or distraction of the public from significant civic concerns by satisfying shallower or more immediate ones. In The Hunger Games, the citizens of the Capitol are kept apathetic to the plight of the inhabitants of the districts not just by their privileged lifestyles but also by the presentation of the Games as spectacle and entertainment; conversely, the inhabitants of districts are kept servile through fear of surveillance and punishment (as represented by the Games) and hope of reward (in the form of the provision of resources to the district of the winning tribute).

The clearest strategy that the Capitol uses to maintain the status quo and encourage social order is sovereign power. Michel Foucault, in Discipline and Punish (1977), argues that sovereign power has, throughout history, typically been associated with the spectacle of public torture and execution, and used to instil fear in those who witness its more brutal utilisations: sovereign power exercises control 'not only by making people aware that the slightest offence [. . . is] likely to be punished, but [also] by arousing feelings of terror by the spectacle of power letting its anger fall upon the guilty person'.[5] In The Hunger Games, the Capitol's elite initially relies on public whippings and summary executions to instil fear into the inhabitants of the generally submissive districts; however, as it slowly but systematically begins to lose control, undermined as it is by the actions of Katniss and Peeta, it increasingly resorts to spectacle.[6] Giving credence to Foucault's contention that 'from the point of view of the law that imposes it, public torture and execution must be spectacular',[7] the Capitol succumbs to such large-scale depravities as annihilating whole districts, the consequences of which it also televises.[8] Nevertheless, of all the spectacles the governing body of Panem uses to maintain its position, the Hunger Games themselves remain the most enduring, visual reminder of the state of power relations for the inhabitants of districts:

> Taking the kids from our districts, forcing them to kill one another while we watch – this is the Capitol's way of reminding us of how totally we are at their mercy. How little chance we would stand of surviving another rebellion. Whatever words they use, the real message is clear. 'Look how we take your children and sacrifice them and there's nothing you can do. If you lift a finger, we will destroy every last one of you. Just as we did District 13'.[9]

The Hunger Games series, however, also lends itself to being read (rewardingly) in light of another form of power identified by Foucault in Discipline and Punish, and which he explores through his social theory of panopticism: disciplinary power. While some may question the relevance of applying philosophical frameworks to young adult dystopian fiction, Sean Connors has argued that 'the dystopian genre, committed as it is to engaging in social critique, shares intellectual concerns similar to those embraced by social and cultural critics such as Foucault'.[10] Foucault developed panopticism as a philosophical response to English philosopher Jeremy Bentham's unrealised architectural panopticon, a circular building with individual cells for occupants and an observation tower at the centre from which an official, invisibly positioned, could surveil all within the building, and in so doing impose passive rather than active discipline. Because an occupant was only potentially subject to the gaze of the official (a gaze he or she could never be sure was fixed on him or her), Foucault argues that the occupant was, through feelings of paranoia, coerced into complying with the behavioural expectations of the official. Central to Foucault's panopticism is the idea that human populations can be systematically ordered and controlled, or disciplined, essentially, not just by brutal force but also through subtle manipulation. While panopticism is readily applicable to such institutions as prisons, it can also be a way of thinking about schools, workplaces and even hospitals. For Foucault, it is any

> location of bodies in space, of distribution of individuals in relation to one another, of hierarchical organization, of disposition of centres and channels of power, of definition of the instruments and modes of intervention of power . . . Whenever one is dealing with a multiplicity of individuals on whom a task or a particular form of behaviour must be imposed, the panoptic schema may be used.[11]

In The Hunger Games, the Capitol controls Panem predominately through the manipulation of geography: the thirteen districts are separated from one another by electrified fences and armed guards, making it difficult for the inhabitants of each to communicate with one other, let alone organise themselves into a collective that might challenge the status quo. The effectiveness of this strategy of distributing individuals in relation to one another is not lost on Katniss, who states, 'It's to the Capitol's advantage to have us divided among ourselves'.[12] The absence of technology within the districts, especially in the form of mobile phones and the Internet, further limits the possibility of communication between geographically delimited groups that might otherwise coalesce to challenge the power of the Capitol. While the absence of such technology may seem inconsistent with a trilogy written in the twenty-first century and set in a futuristic dystopia, as Jeremy Hsu has argued, The Hunger Games 'does not celebrate the progress of technology – an idea that historians of science and technology see as overly simplistic anyway. Instead, the books show how a society's technological choices reflect its political motivations and social priorities.'[13]

Along with geography, the districts are also organised hierarchically in relation to one another and the Capitol. District 2, in particular, is seen to benefit from its courting of the Capitol's favour. As reward for their acceptance, under subjugation, nonetheless, of the Hunger Games as an opportunity for the attainment of 'wealth' and 'glory', inhabitants of District 2 are rewarded with service as Peacekeepers: positions that essentially entail keeping other districts under the control of the Capitol's elite through threat of violence.[14] Within districts, too, there is hierarchical division. In District 12, that of Katniss and Peeta, there is a well-established divide between a merchant class, represented by the district's mayor and Peeta's family, and a working class, typified by the coalminers of the Seam and Katniss's family. The stratification of classes within districts as a result of social inequality benefits the Capitol by preventing social cohesion or common cause from developing. By dividing Panem into districts, and districts into social classes, the Capitol's elite is able to control and regulate the behaviour of manageable groups. However, perhaps the most insidious panoptic manifestation of disciplinary power in The Hunger Games is the extent to which districts are under the Capitol's surveillance. According to Foucault, in order to be exercised, disciplinary power has to be given the instrument of permanent, exhaustive, omnipresent surveillance, capable of making all visible, as long as it [. . . can] itself remain invisible. It [. . . has] to be a faceless gaze that [. . . transforms] the whole social body into a field of perception: thousands of eyes posted everywhere, mobile attentions ever on the alert, a long, hierarchized network.[15]

The range of surveillance practices detailed in The Hunger Games includes: paid informants, who report to the Capitol on breaches of state policy and regulations; scientifically engineered birds, called jabberjays, that can listen into conversations, memorise what they have heard and replicate speech when required; and cameras that record the everyday lives of the inhabitants of districts. Like the imagined occupants of Bentham's architectural panopticon as theorised by Foucault, who self-regulate their behaviour in light of the possibility that they may be under surveillance, the inhabitants of districts in The Hunger Games comply with hierarchically imposed rules and regulations because their daily lives are full of constant reminders that they are, in fact, held in the gaze of the Capitol. As Sean Connors writes:

the residents of the districts have fallen so completely under the control of the state that they are no longer able to resist its power. Instead, they self-monitor to ensure that they present themselves in a way that is consistent with what they assume the state expects of them.[16]

However, like Bentham's and Foucault's occupants of the panopticon, it is not essential that the inhabitants of districts know, with certainty, that they are being surveilled at any given moment, as the mere possibility of being the subject of the Capitol's gaze is enough to ensure compliance. Even a character as mentally strong as Katniss suffers the paranoia that can come with subjection to surveillance. In a conversation with President Snow, where he states his knowledge of her weekly illegal hunting forays outside the limits of District 12 with Gale, her eighteen-year-old best friend and hunting partner, Katniss displays unhealthy levels of introspection: 'Surely they haven't been tracking us in there. Or have they? Could we have been followed? That seems impossible. At least by a person. Cameras? That never crossed my mind until this moment.'[17]

Foucauldian panoptic readings of The Hunger Games aside, surveillance across the districts of Panem can also be read in light of other models of panopticism. While Jerome Dobson and Peter Fisher's first two models of panopticism broadly correspond to the Foucauldian and Orwellian 'Big Brother' conceptualisations of surveillance already discussed in this chapter, their third focuses on the role that geographical information systems (GIS) play in recording human movement. For Dobson and Fisher, the practice of tracking movement has the potential to enable one entity, a master, furtively to surveil and exercise control over the physical location of another individual, the slave.[18] In Collins's trilogy, it is in the arena of the Games itself that this form of surveillance is most acute: here, surveillance is implemented not only through cameras hidden in trees but also through the tracking of tributes' movements, which might be more accurately described as 'sousveillance'. At the start of the

Games, tributes are injected in the arm with a small metal tracking device that enables Gamemakers to trace their movements, locate them at will and manipulate the space around them. However, this heightened level of surveillance, which enables the entire population of Panem to view tributes twenty-four hours a day, represents a reversal or deconstruction of the panoptical polarity to such an extent that the arena may also be justifiably viewed in terms of Thomas Mathiesen's 'synopticon': a post-panoptic space categorised by the surveillance of the few by the many.[19]

While works of dystopian fiction do not always offer explicit solutions to the issues they raise, or consolation to readers who are left to face the *real* uncertainties of their own analogous world, The Hunger Games suggests that individuals, especially young adults as represented by Katniss, do have the potential to effect change on both personal and societal levels, particularly in relation to those who wield power through the panoptic and synoptic gaze of social media. Consequently, The Hunger Games' advocacy of adolescent agency makes evident the limitations of a Foucauldian reading of Collins's narrative. In fact, Foucault's theorisation of panopticism itself has been the subject of criticism, although, as Bart Simon has argued, that does not mean that a 'post-panoptic' condition is necessarily 'anti-' or 'post-' Foucauldian.[20] The most significant criticism of Foucauldian panopticism, in light of the narrative's advocacy of individual agency, is Majid Yar's contention that 'the concept of panoptic power may be somewhat overly dependent upon a monological understanding of "the gaze" as a pathological specular authority'.[21] Yar suggests that panoptic logic relies too much upon the subject actively investing panoptic gazes with authority, and that these gazes may, in fact, be more susceptible to the possibility of subversion and resistance than has been commonly acknowledged. One of the most memorable examples of the subversion of the panoptic and synoptic gaze of the Capitol in Collins's trilogy centres on the television interview Katniss gives before her second Games. In a provocative challenge to President Snow's demand that Katniss wears a wedding gown (a symbol of the future that she has jeopardised by challenging the status quo), her stylist for the Games, Cinna, modifies her dress so that when she spins on stage at the conclusion of the interview it catches fire and transforms into the plumage of a mockingjay. The mockingjay is a species of bird that resulted from the unforeseen mating of the scientifically engineered jabberjays and mockingbirds; however, unlike jabberjays, which were designed to eavesdrop on the conversations of rebels and repeat what they heard, mockingjays only mimic the songs of people they like, before sharing these songs with other mockingjays; consequently, they are powerful symbols of resistance. Cinna's action exploits the spectacle of Katniss as 'girl on fire' to garner the attention and favour of the citizens of the Capitol, while simultaneously politicising her as a symbol of revolution for the inhabitants of the districts.[22]

Connors has argued that the jabberjay itself is a compelling example of 'how characters in Collins's trilogy use tactics to manipulate power imbalances in the service of accomplishing their own ends'.[23] Employing Michel de Certeau's *The Practice of Everyday Life* (1984) as a modifier of Foucauldian panopticism, Connors contends that Katniss and other characters manage to circumvent the disciplinary mechanisms of the Capitol, despite having to act under its ceaseless gaze. What Connors finds significant is the distinction de Certeau makes between 'strategies', the actions of those who hold power, and 'tactics', the responses of those who are surveilled.[24] De Certeau suggests that although the individuals may be subject to panoptic – or synoptic – gazes, they are not necessarily rendered powerless: operating under surveillance, those who occupy weak spaces may resist disciplinary power by manipulating 'the mechanisms of discipline and conform to them if only in order to evade them'.[25] In The Hunger Games, the jabberjay's ability to replicate human voices and repeat dialogue constitutes, according to Connors, a strategy used by the Capitol to spy on the inhabitants of districts; however, Connors also maintains that the simple but effective response of the rebel fighters of telling the birds lies, which they in turn bring back to the Capitol, is a tactic that allows the rebels to exploit the situation to their advantage.[26]

While Katniss employs numerous tactics to circumvent the panoptic and synoptic gaze of the Capitol, one of the more effective tactics she uses is seduction. In 'On Postmodern Uses of Sex', Zygmunt Bauman proposes seduction as one of the most significant post-panoptic principles of social order; however, as Mathew Toll has argued, seduction does not render panoptical mechanisms redundant: because the surveillance of individuals is often 'used in the social manipulation of their desires . . . Mechanisms of seduction . . . coexist with panoptical apparatus'.[27] Unlike the inhabitants of District 2, who are seduced by the wealth of the Capitol into seeing the Games not as the apparatus of social order but rather as an opportunity for betterment (albeit in a consumerist sense), Katniss comes to identify seduction as a tactic of resistance. Although the Capitol's synoptic gaze initially bewilders her, as her physical appearance is remade for television cameras and her every move is documented, Katniss very quickly comes to realise that she can seduce the Capitol by shaping her behaviour to appeal to its whims and fashions. She presents herself in interviews, broadcast to the Capitol, in terms of the advice her mentor for the Games, Haymitch, has given her:

> '[Tell them that . . .] you can't believe a little girl from District Twelve has done this well. The whole thing's been more than you ever could have dreamed of. Talk about Cinna's clothes. How nice the people are. How the city amazes you. If you won't talk about yourself, at least compliment the audience. Just keep turning it back around, all right. Gush.'[28]

Most significantly, Katniss also plays the role of one half of star-crossed lovers, with the other half played by Peeta. Seducing the Capitol with a Romeo and Juliet story, she embraces the panoptic and synoptic gaze of its citizens to ensure that she and Peeta are sponsored to compete in the Games, thereby increasing their chances of survival. At the end of the seventy-fourth Hunger Games, when it is announced that only one tribute can win, Katniss again takes full advantage of her visibility to the Capitol. Along with Peeta, the other remaining tribute, she threatens to eat poisonous nightlock berries, which would result in their deaths. Knowing that it would rather have two victors than none, and that she and Peeta are its darlings, Katniss turns the Capitol's gaze back on itself. It is an act of rebellion that not only results in them both being declared winners of the Games but also disrupts disciplinary power and destabilises power relations. Like many of Katniss's acts of rebellion throughout

Collins's series, her final act of the seventy-fourth Games is one of tactical manipulation rather than violent insurrection.

Katniss suffers trauma from her ordeals, and has to perform multiple identities throughout The Hunger Games, to the extent that she has to try 'to remember who [. . . she is] and who [. . . she is] not'.[29] However, she never loses her core identity as a volunteer tribute and freedom fighter. As Connors suggests, 'it is no coincidence that [. . . Katniss], like the jabberjay, experiences a metamorphosis over the course of the series that results in her transforming into the Mockingjay, a symbol of the Rebellion'.[30] Throughout the series, Katniss continuously employs subversive, seductive tactics to respond to the panoptic and synoptic gazes of President Snow and the Capitol.

The Hunger Games ends with an epilogue set fifteen years after the rebels' victory over the Capitol, President Snow and Alma Coin (the duplicitous president of District 13 and one-time rebel leader of the uprising). Here readers learn that Katniss, who is with Peeta, and who is also the mother of two children, has settled in a meadow in District 12, far removed from the panoptical and synoptical pressures of her earlier life. The epilogue is, perhaps, overly, and maybe inadvertently, imbued with nostalgia for Arcadian simplicity, which has the potential to transform 'the past into a utopian homestead' and facilitate a critique of modernity as a departure from a time of 'authenticity'.[31] However, Katniss's tactical seduction of the disciplinary mechanisms of the Capitol suggests that power relations are never fixed and that change can be effected from within socio-political systems. It is an empowering and provocative ending for a work of twenty-first-century young adult popular fiction.

NOTES

1. Connors, '"I Was Watching You, Mockingjay"', p. 85.
2. Schmidt, 'Why Are Dystopian Films on the Rise Again?'
3. Moore, 'The Hunger Games'.
4. Collins, The Hunger Games, p. 148.
5. Foucault, Discipline and Punish, p. 58.
6. Collins, The Hunger Games, p. 202; Collins, Catching Fire, p. 63.
7. Foucault, Discipline and Punish, p. 58.
8. Collins, Catching Fire, p. 391; Collins, Mockingjay, p. 99.
9. Collins, The Hunger Games, pp. 18–19.
10. Connors, '"I Was Watching You, Mockingjay"', p. 88.
11. Foucault, Discipline and Punish, p. 205.
12. Collins, The Hunger Games, p. 14.
13. Hsu, '"Hunger Games" Exposes Myth of Technological Advancement'.
14. Collins, Mockingjay, p. 193.
15. Foucault, Discipline and Punish, p. 214.
16. Connors, '"I Try to Remember Who I am and Who I Am Not"', p. 151.
17. Collins, Catching Fire, p. 24.
18. Dobson and Fisher, 'The Panopticon's Changing Geography', pp. 307–23.
19. Mathiesen, 'The Viewer Society'.
20. Simon, 'The Return of Panopticism', p. 2.
21. Yar, 'Panoptic Power and the Pathologisation of Vision', p. 255.
22. Collins, Catching Fire, pp. 23, 207.
23. Connors, '"I Was Watching You, Mockingjay"', p. 97.

24. De Certeau, *The Practice of Everyday Life*, pp. 29–42.
25. Ibid., p. xiv.
26. Connors, '"I Was Watching You, Mockingjay"', p. 97.
27. Toll, 'Seduction and Panopticism'.
28. Collins, *The Hunger Games*, p. 118.
29. Ibid., p. 371.
30. Connors, '"I Was Watching You, Mockingjay"', p. 98.
31. Anttenon, *Tradition Through Modernity*, p. 59.

KEY WORKS

The Hunger Games (2008). Sixteen-year-old Katniss Everdeen, with Peeta Mellark, volunteers to participate in the seventy-fourth Hunger Games in place of her younger sister.

Catching Fire (2009). Katniss, accompanied by Peeta, is forced to compete with past victors of the Hunger Games in a special seventy-fifth edition, known as the Quarter Quell. Set six months after the conclusion of *The Hunger Games*, Katniss's success and defiance of the Capitol in the seventy-fourth Games have inspired rebellion in the districts.

Mockingjay (2010). The final instalment of the trilogy centres on the districts' rebellion against the Capitol and Katniss's mission to return to the Capitol and kill President Snow, with the help of a group of rebels known as the Star Squad. The book ends with an epilogue set fifteen years after these events.

FURTHER CRITICAL READING

Connors, Sean P. (ed.), *The Politics of Panem: Challenging Genres* (Rotterdam: Sense Publishers, 2014).

Dunn, George A. and Nicolas Michaud (eds), *The Hunger Games and Philosophy: A Critique of Pure Treason* (Hoboken, NJ: Wiley, 2012).

Evans Garriot, Deidre Anne, Whitney Elaine Jones and Julie Elizabeth Tyler (eds), *Space and Place in The Hunger Games: New Readings of the Novels* (Jefferson, NC: McFarland, 2014).

Henthorne, Tom, *Approaching the Hunger Games Trilogy: A Literary and Cultural Analysis* (Jefferson, NC: McFarland, 2012).

Pharr, Mary F., Leisa A. Clark, Donald E. Palumbo and C. W. Sullivan III (eds), *Of Bread, Blood and the Hunger Games: Critical Essays on the Suzanne Collins Trilogy* (Critical Explorations in Science Fiction and Fantasy No. 35) (Jefferson, NC: McFarland, 2012).

Wright, Katheryn, *The New Heroines: Female Embodiment and Technology in 21st-Century Popular Culture* (Santa Barbara: Praeger, 2016).

BIBLIOGRAPHY

Anttenon, Pertti J., *Tradition Through Modernity: Postmodernism and the Nation-State in Folklore Scholarship* (Helsinki: Finnish Literature Society, 2005).

Bauman, Zygmunt, 'On Postmodern Uses of Sex', *Theory, Culture and Society*, 15:3–4 (1998), pp. 19–33.

Collins, Suzanne, *Catching Fire* (New York: Scholastic, 2009).

Collins, Suzanne, *Fire Proof: The Mystery Files of Shelby Woo, No. 11* (New York: Aladdin, 1999).

Collins, Suzanne, *Gregor and the Code of the Claw* (New York: Scholastic, 2007).

Collins, Suzanne, *Gregor and the Curse of the Warmbloods* (New York: Scholastic, 2005).

Collins, Suzanne, *Gregor and the Marks of Secret* (New York: Scholastic, 2006).

Collins, Suzanne, *Gregor and the Prophecy of Bane* (New York: Scholastic, 2004).

Collins, Suzanne, *Gregor the Overlander* (New York: Scholastic, 2003).

Collins, Suzanne, *The Hunger Games* (New York: Scholastic, 2008).

Collins, Suzanne, *Mockingjay* (New York: Scholastic, 2010).

Connors, Sean P., '"I Try to Remember Who I am and Who I Am Not": The Subjugation of Women and Nature in The Hunger Games', in Sean P. Connors (ed.), *The Politics of Panem: Challenging Genres* (Rotterdam: Sense Publishers, 2014), pp. 137–56.

Connors, Sean P., '"I Was Watching You, Mockingjay": Surveillance, Tactics, and the Limits of Panopticism', in Sean P. Connors (ed.), *The Politics of Panem: Challenging Genres* (Rotterdam: Sense Publishers, 2014), pp. 85–102.

De Certeau, Michel, *The Practice of Everyday Life* (Berkeley: University of California Press, 1984).

Dobson, Jerome E. and Peter F. Fisher, 'The Panopticon's Changing Geography', *Geographical Review*, 97:3 (2007), pp. 307–23.

Foucault, Michel, *Discipline and Punish: The Birth of the Prison*, trans. A. Sheridan (1977; New York: Vintage Books, 1995).

Hsu, Jeremy, '"Hunger Games" Exposes Myth of Technological Advancement', Live Science, 23 March 2012 <http://www.livescience.com/19252-hunger-games-technologies-progress.html> (last accessed 1 May 2016).

Mann, Steve, Jason Nolan and Barry Wellman, 'Sousveillance: Inventing and Using Wearable Computing Devices or Data Collection in Surveillance Environments', *Surveillance and Society*, 1:3 (2002), pp. 331–55.

Mathiesen, Thomas, 'The Viewer Society: Michel Foucault's "Panopticon": Revisited', *Theoretical Criminology: An International Journal*, 1:2 (2003), pp. 215–32.

Meyer, Stephenie, *Breaking Dawn* (New York: Little, Brown and Company, 2008).

Meyer, Stephenie, *Eclipse* (New York: Little, Brown and Company, 2007).

Meyer, Stephenie, *New Moon* (New York: Little, Brown and Company, 2006).

Meyer, Stephenie, *Twilight* (New York: Little, Brown and Company, 2005).

Moore, Suzanne, 'The Hunger Games: Mockingjay's Bombed-Out Dystopia Is All Too Familiar: It Could Be Syria, Gaza or Iraq', *The Guardian*, 19 November 2014 <http://www.theguardian.com/commentisfree/2014/nov/19/the-hunger-games-mockingjays-bombed-out-dystopia-is-all-too-familiar-it-could-be-syria-gaza-or-iraq> (last accessed 1 May 2016).

Orwell, George, *Nineteen Eighty-Four* (1949; London: Penguin, 2013).

Schmidt, Christopher, 'Why Are Dystopian Films on the Rise Again?', *JSTOR Daily*, 19 November 2014 <http://daily.jstor.org/why-are-dystopian-films-on-the-rise-again/> (last accessed 1 May 2016).

Simon, Bart, 'The Return of Panopticism: Supervision, Subjection and the New Surveillance', *Surveillance and Society*, 3:1 (2005), pp. 1–20.

Toll, Mathew, 'Seduction and Panopticism', 19 January 2010 <http://dostoevskiansmiles.blogspot.ie/2010/01/seduction-and-panopticonism.html> (last accessed 1 May 2016).

Yar, Majid, 'Panoptic Power and the Pathologisation of Vision: Critical Reflections on the Foucauldian Thesis', *Surveillance and Society*, 1:3 (2003), pp. 254–71.

Zuboff, Shoshana, *In the Age of the Smart Machine: In the Future of Work and Power* (New York: Basic Books, 1988), pp. 315–61.

CHAPTER 10

E. L. James and the Fifty Shades Phenomenon

Dara Downey

Under the pen name E. L. James, English writer Erika Mitchell has written the bestselling Fifty Shades series of novels, of which there are currently four. James was born in London in 1963, to a Chilean mother and a Scottish father. Her father worked as a BBC cameraman, and after spending her childhood in Buckinghamshire and studying history at the University of Kent, she went on to become a studio manager at the National Film and Television School. During this time, she met her husband, Niall Leonard; the couple now live near Ealing, London, with their two sons. Leonard is a screenwriter, while James worked as a television producer until she found success through writing.[1]

James claims that the Fifty Shades phenomenon was the direct result of her watching the first *Twilight* film in 2008. With no previous writing experience, she began to write two novels, between January and April 2009. Discovering fan fiction in August of that year prompted her to write what would become the first two Fifty Shades books for FanFiction.net, under the pseudonym Snowqueens [sic] Icedragon.[2] The first book was originally called *Master of the Universe*, and was published in instalments, with James responding to and integrating fan comments and edits as she went along.[3] Featuring characters named Edward Cullen and Bella Swan, this was straightforward *Twilight* fan fiction, but with the supernatural elements omitted, and was extremely popular.[4] However, following complaints regarding the book's explicit, 'mature' content, which violated the site's terms of service, James moved it to her own website, 50Shades.com, and in 2011 took down the online text when an extended, reworked version was published by an Australian virtual publisher, the Writer's Coffee Shop.[5] Public interest was such that revised editions of the Fifty Shades books were published by Vintage in 2012.[6]

By June 2015, over 125 million copies of the first book, *Fifty Shades of Grey*, had been sold worldwide, and the following three books have proven equally popular.[7] In 2012, James was named *Publishers Weekly*'s Publishing Person of the Year, won the

National Book Award for popular-fiction book of the year, and was named one of the world's top 100 most influential people by *Time* magazine, while *Fifty Shades of Grey* was voted Book of the Year by the public in the National Book Awards.[8] However, it is not merely this remarkable success that makes James an influential figure among twenty-first-century popular-fiction writers. The Fifty Shades phenomenon, which currently spans four books, two film adaptations (in 2015 and 2017, with a third due in 2018) and a vast body of written commentary, merchandise, parodies and further fan fiction, has significantly augmented mainstream awareness of and interest in fan fiction more generally, women's erotica and the BDSM (Bondage and Discipline, Dominance and Submission, and Sadism and Masochism) community – though not always in positive ways.

To help understand the books' reception, it is useful to situate them within their wider generic context, though doing so is by no means an easy task, since they could easily be positioned within any one of a number of generic categories. James herself has been quoted as stating that 'the inspiration for the book was Beauty and the Beast, *Pretty Woman* and Mr Rochester in *Jane Eyre*'.[9] Certainly, an awareness of the classic fairy tale, now-canonical eighteenth- and nineteenth-century novels for and by women, and contemporary film are central to an understanding of the novels, as explored below. Nevertheless, the Fifty Shades books can be and often are also aligned with pornography, popular romance and erotica, and fan fiction.

As discussed below, outraged contemporary commentators and admiring fans alike have frequently, and somewhat uncritically, labelled Fifty Shades as pornography, and are somewhat justified in doing so, considering the history of the genre. Michael Gamer acknowledges that there was little distinctly pornographic material, as we would now recognise it, produced in eighteenth-century Britain, apart from John Cleland's *Fanny Hill* (1748).[10] During the nineteenth century, a far clearer category of fiction designed exclusively to titillate the reader emerged, and many of the best-known examples featured, like the Fifty Shades books, scenes in which pleasure and pain are intermingled. Well-known examples include John Benjamin Brookes's *The Lustful Turk* (1828) and Leopold von Sacher-Masoch's *Venus in Furs* (1870), both of which, like *Fanny Hill*, focus on previously inexperienced women being initiated into the singular sexual fantasy lives of demanding men. In the twentieth century, the term 'pornography' was popularly associated with exploitative, misogynistic films and magazines, generally displaying low production values. However, a number of prominent women writers also employed the genre as a means of critiquing gender dynamics, including Anne Desclos, who wrote *The Story of O* (1954) under the pen name Pauline Réage, and Catherine Millet, whose *The Sexual Life of Catherine M* (2001) was met with a rather lukewarm reception.[11] The possibilities opened up by the digital age for women writing within the genre were realised by the award-winning 'Belle de Jour' blog, penned anonymously by Brooke Magnanti. The blog was published as *The Intimate Adventures of a London Call Girl* in 2005, and adapted for television as *Secret Diary of a Call Girl* (2007–11). Magnanti's was identity revealed in 2009. Like *Master of the Universe*, the original online version can no longer be accessed easily.

As this implies, non-traditional paths to publishing have recently been embraced by women seeking to bypass stereotyped female sexual passivity, a trend pre-empted by the history of romance novels and soft-core erotica aimed at women readers. The Fifty Shades franchise is perhaps closest in form to the popular, Gothic, historical romances or 'bodice rippers' that came to prominence in the 1960s, 1970s and 1980s, of the kind written by Kathleen E. Woodiwiss, Joan Aiken and Victoria Holt, or indeed by the fictional Paul Sheldon in Stephen King's *Misery* (1987). As Janice Radway demonstrates in *Reading the Romance* (1984), from the 1930s onward, the market for such fiction was dominated by the Mills and Boon imprint, which was merged with Harlequin Romance in the 1970s. Clive Bloom notes the success of Mills and Boon, both in transforming books into desirable commodities and in encouraging readers to send in their own manuscripts for publication.[12] He describes these books as 'relaxing melodramas of personal destiny in which a heroine overcomes obstacles of esteem, social position and income to get her man'.[13] While many of the works produced by both companies featured rather less physical lovemaking than is to be found in Fifty Shades, towards the end of the century titles became more 'racy' in content. Quoting from Mills and Boon publicity, Bloom asserts that '[t]he *Temptation* series', for example, 'was a "line of sensually charged romantic fantasies" concentrated on the theme of female "destiny", American in viewpoint, containing a "high level of sexual tension" and written from the heroine's point of view'.[14] From here, Bloom argues, erotica or pornography ostensibly aimed at women emerged in the 1990s, but was largely unsuccessful in attracting an actual female readership; apparently over 90 per cent of Virgin's Black Lace imprint books sold to men, and the market declined rapidly.[15]

Arguably, the Fifty Shades phenomenon cannily exploits this gap in the market, even as it has fuelled demand for more sexually explicit romance fiction. What is more, just as Mills and Boon and Harlequin readers were encouraged to become writers, as indicated above, Fifty Shades began life as a work of fan fiction. Indeed, as Abigail de Kosnik points out, the books 'effectuated fan fiction's breakthrough into the general public's consciousness, drawing attention, notoriety, and controversy to the fan fiction genre by virtue of its extraordinary fame'.[16] Fan fiction is writing that appropriates characters and settings from pre-existing texts and reimagines them in scenarios that do not occur in the original, and that often subvert relationships and hierarchies as they are conceived in the 'canon' material.[17] Beginning in the 1960s with *Star Trek* aficionados taking the television series' plots and characters into their own hands in publications written and published by fans for fans, the genre flourished with the advent of the Internet.[18] However, such fiction is rarely published commercially as the Fifty Shades books ultimately were; James's works are, as a result, '[p]ositioned somewhere between the commercial and fan realms', creating a hybrid form that sits uneasily with 'conventional' reading audiences and the fan fiction community alike.[19]

Specifically, of course, Fifty Shades is *Twilight* fan fiction. More generally, it exploits the sexual tensions of the vampire-romance genre, which had evolved in the latter decades of the century from Anne Rice's philosophical Southern immortals, through the adolescent turmoil of Joss Whedon's Buffy and Angel in the eponymous television shows, finally taking explicit shape in the 'abstinence porn' of Stephenie Meyer's Twilight saga. As explored below, these texts, in which a virginal girl is swept up in a love affair with an older, dangerous man, are in many ways the latest incarnations of a storyline that functions as a sort of origin myth for modern, Western, heterosexual, middle-class gender relations, one that is evident in both 'canonical' and 'popular' romance fiction.

Unsurprisingly, then, itself a product of numerous other texts, *Fifty Shades of Grey* and its sequels have spawned a bewildering array of paratexts and paratextual materials. On the most basic level, the books have, like many popular-culture phenomena, inspired a wide range of commercial products, including keyrings mimicking one that the heroine Ana buys for Christian, a board game and fan art sold on platforms such as Etsy, which Bethan Jones sees as an extension of fan fiction itself.[20] More broadly, companies selling everything from obvious items like sex toys and luxury hotel stays to more obscure products, like the Twining's English breakfast tea preferred by Ana, have apparently benefited substantially from the exposure granted by the books' popularity.[21] Indeed, the London fire brigade has reported that, since 2013, the numbers of 999 emergency calls involving people stuck in handcuffs or chastity belts, or unable to remove genital rings and so on, have spiked significantly, a trend that they attribute to the success of the books and subsequent film versions.[22] What is particularly noteworthy, however, is the legacy of the books themselves as material objects. In 2016 a charity shop in Wales reported that it had received so many donations of copies of the four novels, which they have had difficulty selling on, that staff members have built a fortress in their offices from the books; the shop is now asking people to refrain from bringing any more.[23] The hard-copy volumes effectively function as waste matter in this scenario, a literal embodiment of the redundancies that are often part of print culture.

More positively, the Fifty Shades phenomenon has allowed more writers of fan fiction to profit from their work. As Kies points out, '[i]n 2013, Amazon launched Kindle Worlds, a platform for the sale of fan fiction of certain media properties specifically licensed for this purpose; the profits of sales would be shared by Amazon, the fan fiction writer, and the media partner'.[24] Nonetheless, the series' less than illustrious reputation has also had negative repercussions for fan communities. As Richard McCulloch admits, 'almost every person [he has] talked to about' his work on Fifty Shades 'has reacted with derisory laughter, bemusement, or utter confusion'.[25] These reactions are both due to a sense that the books are badly written, and from a generalised conviction that they are at once embarrassingly kinky, disappointingly bland in their portrayal of BDSM, and deeply misogynistic.[26] Bethan Jones notes that these issues, especially when combined with 'the poor quality of the prose', mean that, among bloggers, charitable organisations and mainstream media alike, the books are 'used as evidence that all fanfic is bad, not that James is simply a poor writer'.[27] Jones quotes from the US webpage for the National Center on Sexual Exploitation, 'an interfaith effort to counter pornography', which declares that:

> Our pornified culture is already affected by violent acts in mainstream porn and now, with the help of *Fifty Shades of Grey*, this violence is being further legitimized and broadly accepted by women. Now men don't have to entice women to engage in the violent acts that they regularly consume through pornography because *Fifty Shades of Grey* is doing it for them.[28]

Such views are in no way confined to religious groups. One online review asserts, '[t]his is not female fantasy, this is male fantasy. Point of fact, [it] borders on rape fantasy and the idea that anyone would derive enjoyment from watching this is abhorrent.'[29] As Richard McCulloch puts it, the fears expressed in these responses imply 'that dangerous fantasy might lay the foundations for a dangerous reality'.[30] Joseph Bristow argues that such thinking 'constructs gender differences in bleakly dualistic terms, making men into active abusers and women passive victims' who are easily influenced, mindlessly aping the actions and behaviours that they read about or watch.[31] Unsurprisingly, as Jones asserts, '[m]any BDSM bloggers' have expressed 'concerns about BDSM being conflated with abuse in the series'.[32]

Moreover, while criticisms of this nature may be partially justified by the problematic contents of the books, as outlined below, they also serve to downplay the extent to which the books and film attempt to give voice to female sexual desire, which has long been suppressed and even considered to be non-existent in Western culture. As pornography for men has become more visible and ubiquitous than ever, 'there is a dearth of films that foreground female erotics, pleasure and desire through a female gaze'.[33] Fifty Shades undeniably attempts to address this lack, and the rise in erotica for women in bookshops is testament to the series' success in making that desire more publicly acceptable.[34] The covers of Sylvia Day's popular Crossfire novels, beginning with *Bared to You* (2012), for example, explicitly mimic the iconography of James's books, featuring monochrome close-ups of expensive items of male attire, while a Google search for 'what to read after *Fifty Shades*' brings up innumerable sites and posts. Similarly, news that the film was in the early stages of casting prompted a spate of lovingly constructed fan trailers.[35] Not all of the responses have been so admiring, though, and endless parodies of both the film and the books clutter the Internet, including a blog called 'Fifty Shades of Tedious Fuckery' that provides detailed, mocking dissections of the books.[36]

All of this raises the question of what it is about the series that arouses so much anger and disdain. It is largely because it offers us a story so familiar as to be clichéd, but in terms so blatant and schematic that it excavates and renders explicit many of the problems that underpin stereotypical stories of heterosexual gender relations in modern Western culture. In essence, the four Fifty Shades novels chart the fraught relationship between the heroine, Anastasia Steele, a middle-class college graduate, and Christian Grey, a slightly older man who runs an enormous corporation and enjoys an active BDSM lifestyle. Predictably, Christian likes to be the 'dominant' in these relationships, and has gone through a string of brunette 'submissives', but has failed to form a lasting connection with any of them, due to childhood trauma and initiation into the 'scene' by an older woman when he was a teenager. Ana interviews Christian for a college newspaper and catches his eye while finding herself attracted to him in return, but as their relationship develops, she is reluctant to embrace the more bizarre or painful aspects of her lover's predilections, though the more straightforward or 'vanilla' sex scenes are regular and protracted. She also finds him difficult to read, and is frustrated by his controlling attitude, particularly when it comes to food and alcohol, his persistent and irrational jealousy, and his refusal to allow her to touch him (hence the need for chains and cable ties).

In *Fifty Shades of Grey* (2011), Ana eventually agrees to allow Christian to 'punish' her for disobedience (he dislikes when she rolls her eyes, bites her lip or contravenes his orders, all of which she does repeatedly – occasionally, rather confusingly, in order to goad him into initiating intercourse) by beating her with a belt. The experience is far less pleasant than she anticipates and appalled and hurt, she leaves him. The next two books, *Fifty Shades Darker* (2012) and *Fifty Shades Freed* (2012), are devoted to their reconciliation, the return of one of his former submissives, Leila, who becomes briefly homicidal, and the threat posed by Ana's boss, Jack Hyde, a sexual predator who also becomes homicidal (and who has rather grander ambitions than his female counterpart) after Christian buys the company where he works, and has him fired (it also transpires that they had been in foster care together when the two men were minors). The combined intensity of a kidnap situation, plus Ana's unplanned pregnancy, succeeds in finally breaking down the barriers between the couple, and the closing pages are devoted to their marital bliss, which unites idyllic parenthood with the odd playful spanking session, though Christian has given up wanting Ana to be his official submissive and is now far more open and patient. The fourth novel, simply titled *Grey* (2015), is essentially the first of the four novels here narrated from Christian's, rather than Ana's, perspective (both are first-person narratives), which James claims to have written in response to popular demand.[37] *Grey* offers readers insights into Christian's attraction to Ana, his traumatic memories of a drug-addicted mother who died in front of him, and the reasons behind his control issues. Stephenie Meyer has insinuated that the publication of *Grey* effectively ensured that her own *Midnight Sun*, a retelling of *Twilight* from Edward's perspective, would never be completed.[38] Sections of the book were released in 2008, after which Meyer ceased writing the proposed volume. *Grey* therefore functions as fan fiction that not merely mimics but actively supersedes its own original.

Nonetheless, this final novel never fully succeeds in rendering Christian a sympathetic character, or in exorcising the spectre of male violence against vulnerable, inexperienced women, not least because sex scenes in which Christian is entirely in charge literally dominate most of the series. Nonetheless, the series as a whole is neither straightforward erotica or unusually sexist in its gender dynamics. As Richard McCulloch argues, 'at least two very different versions of *Fifty Shades of Grey* can be convincingly inferred from its marketing – female-targeted erotica (selling Christian) on the one hand, and romantic melodrama (selling Ana) on the other'.[39] Consequently, he asserts, the text could just as easily have been characterised as 'a romance, coming-of-age tale, melodrama, fantasy, or a fairy tale', and indeed it fits these categories more comfortably than it does that of pornography or erotica, despite critical attempts to label it as such.[40] The basic plot certainly echoes familiar tropes from the fairy-tale tradition. However, while James herself mentioned 'Beauty and the Beast' as an inspiration, it is somewhat closer to a mixture of 'Cinderella' (the hyper-rich Christian showers Ana, who at the beginning of the trilogy works in a hardware store, with jewellery, clothes, computers and cars, before ultimately buying her a mansion) and 'Bluebeard', as Ana's relentless desire to probe into Christian's dark past continually exposes her to danger from his barely contained rages (though this is eventually sublimated into the figures of Leila and the transparently named Hyde).

As Jones points out, critics have also identified consonances between Fifty Shades and Charlotte Brontë's *Jane Eyre* (1847), in that in both, 'a somewhat innocent young heroine encounters a wealthy, powerful, dangerous, older, secretive man, uncovers his secrets, provides him with an emotional rescue, and forms a companionate union with him in the end'.[41] Indeed, Leila watches Ana as she sleeps, in a sequence that clearly evokes Bertha Mason's stalking of Brontë's eponymous heroine. It is here that it becomes possible to identify the recurrence in Western culture of plots in which an innocent young woman becomes involved with and ultimately rehabilitates a rich but dangerous, sexually experienced older man, and the extent to which the Fifty Shades books offer little more than a recent, popular and particularly unsubtle version of that plot.[42] As Nancy Armstrong points out, 'readers remain thoroughly enchanted by narratives in which a woman's virtue alone overcomes sexual aggression and transforms male desire into middle-class love, the stuff that modern families are made of'.[43] Moreover, as she argues, such novels potentially played a major role in defining the binaristic gendered separation of the political from the domestic realm.[44] In other words, domestic fiction, of which the Fifty Shades books are a recognisable, even overt extension and reincarnation, defines and shapes our understanding of sex and sexuality, rather than (or at least, as well as) vice versa.

Armstrong's model is based primarily on Samuel Richardson's lengthy epistolary novel *Pamela; or Virtue Rewarded* (1740–1), which bears some striking resemblances to the Fifty Shades books. Pamela is pretty servant girl who falls prey to her young master's inappropriate and inexorable advances. The indefatigable Mr B– tries stealth, violence, kidnapping, bribery and even a 'sham marriage' in his efforts to have his way with her, but she resists staunchly, successfully repulsing him by means of a settled strategy of repeatedly asserting the value of her virtue, fainting, hysterics, an abortive suicide attempt, and endless letter and diary writing, which seems to bother Mr B– the most. When her resistance eventually wears him down, a double transformation occurs, one central to *Pamela, Jane Eyre* and numerous other eighteenth- and nineteenth-century novels for and about women. The rake has been reformed, while the 'pert' rebel has grown passive, in preparation for heterosexual marriage, and this is made possible, the novel implies, through Pamela's refusal to give way to the rights and privileges that Mr B–, as a wealthy man, has come to expect (we later learn that he had previously seduced another young woman, with whom he has a child).

As Armstrong asserts, 'Richardson's story of relentless sexual pursuit and the triumph of female virtue proved infinitely reproducible', and this is amply evidenced by the many similarities between it, the romances explored by Radway and the Fifty Shades books.[45] Both before and after marriage, Mr B– presents Pamela with contracts, the first offering her money in exchange for sexual favours, which she refuses and responds to, point by point, and a second prescribing her proper behaviour as a wife, which she accepts without question. Ana and Christian also negotiate the terms of their relationship in writing. Early on in *Fifty Shades of Grey*, he emails her a contract that he gives to all his submissives, and demands that she sign it before they commence BDSM activities. Like Pamela, Ana first considers and then annotates the contract, redefining its terms, particularly in relation to food, exercise, masturbation and potentially painful sex acts, allowing herself more freedom than Christian would like.[46]

However, while Pamela is firm in her rejection of her master's profligacy, Ana is both repulsed and attracted by the more demeaning elements of Christian's behaviour and desires, an ambivalence central to the novel but also potentially troubling to many contemporary readers. After reading the contract, Ana thinks,

> He's my master! I'm to be dealt with as he pleases! *Holy shit!*
> I shudder at the thought of being flogged or whipped. Spanking probably wouldn't be so bad; humiliating, though. And tied up? Well, he did tie my hands together. That was . . . well, it was hot, really hot, so perhaps that won't be so bad. He won't loan me to another Dominant – damn right he won't. That would be totally unacceptable. *Why am I even thinking about this?*[47]

While *Pamela* and subsequent romance narratives present us with a relatively clear-cut moral universe, where the things that the male love interest wants are to be denied to him at all costs, Fifty Shades occupies rather murkier territory, as the above quotation implies. The drama of the novels revolves around Ana's discomfort with the BDSM 'play' that Christian sees as his 'safe zone', in that dominance allows him to enact fantasies of the control that was missing in his childhood experiences of neglect and grief. At the same time, his controlling behaviour extends beyond the 'Red Room of Pain', as Ana (in a nod to both *Jane Eyre* and Edgar Allan Poe's 1842 story 'The Masque of the Red Death') dubs his 'playroom'. Furthermore, the few moments in all four books in which he really hurts her during sexual activity are in direct response to her disobeying his multiple rules. In other words, this is not mere play – he truly wants to punish her. In a further twist, as the quotation above suggests, Ana does in fact find some of these activities arousing. The books are therefore a complex tangle, in which theatrical violence becomes real violence, violence is explained away as psychological self-care, and that self-care itself becomes both the obstacle hindering the central relationship and the very source of the attraction in the first place.

In this regard, the series is the direct inheritor of the twentieth-century 'romance' novels for and about women discussed by Tania Modleski and Janice Radway. As Modleski asserts, in Mills and Boon and Harlequin romances, 'the heroines engage in a continual deciphering of the motives for the hero's behaviour', because 'he is mocking, cynical, contemptuous, often hostile, and even somewhat brutal'.[48] The result is an uncomfortable convergence of sex and violence, of the hero's desire for the heroine and his desire to humiliate and hurt her.[49] The heroine is invariably portrayed as feeling and even occasionally expressing anger at the hero's less than attractive treatment of her, but, as in *Pamela*, the workings of the marriage plot and the narration itself serve to repress her, depicting her as cute and feisty rather than rebellious, even while she represses herself, swallowing her rage at the hero.[50] The books, by rewarding Ana with love, marriage and financial security for both placating Christian and playing into his hands, certainly seem to advocate such behaviour, and continue the long tradition in Western culture of placing the onus for taming men's sexual desire and economic privilege firmly on the shoulders of the women who love them. Much like Armstrong, while Modleski acknowledges the deeply problematic nature of such narrative and gender dynamics, she also argues that 'the contradictions in women's lives are more responsible for the existence of Harlequins than Harlequins are for the contradictions'.[51]

Although such assertions are difficult to prove, the very adaptability of this basic plot structure and the overwhelming popularity of the Fifty Shades franchise as a cultural phenomenon imply that, while we may like to imagine that gender politics have evolved, the Cinderella/Bluebeard dyad still has much to tell us about ourselves. As Twilight fan fiction that eschews the supernatural framing of the original, Fifty Shades literalises the idea that a violent monster is an ideal life partner. Indeed, the Twilight saga comes close to doing this via the continual references to Emily Brontë's Gothic novel *Wuthering Heights* (1847) as a model for Edward and Bella's relationship. Fifty Shades refigures this recent manifestation of the plot that has haunted our culture by reinstating the realism that characterised the 'classic' novels, such as Thomas Hardy's *Tess of the d'Urbervilles* (1892), which Ana reads obsessively. In doing so, James's books highlight the extent to which contemporary fantasies of heterosexual love and marriage demand as much critical interrogation as texts deemed more 'literary'; and, indeed, that examining recent books that are considered poorly written and ideologically problematic alongside those accepted as cultural mainstays is both illuminating and urgent.

NOTES

1. Brennan, 'E. L. James'.
2. Johnson, 'Who is E. L. James?'.
3. Jason Boog, 'The Lost History of *Fifty Shades of Grey*'.
4. See Jones, 'Fifty Shades of Exploitation'; Kies, 'A Red Room of Her Own', p. 35.
5. Jones, 'Fifty Shades of Exploitation'. See also Skurnick, '*Fifty Shades of Grey*, a Self-Published Ebook, Is the Future of Publishing'. At time of writing, the original text of *Master of the Universe* could be found at <https://ohfifty.com/downloads/MOTU_w_Outtakes_Snowqueens_Icedragon_COMPLETE.pdf>.
6. Jones, 'Fifty Shades of Exploitation'; and Boog, 'The Lost History of *Fifty Shades of Grey*'.
7. Flood, '*Fifty Shades of Grey* Sequel Breaks Sales Records'; and Meredith, '*Fifty Shades of Grey* Becomes the Bestselling Book of All Time'.
8. Flood, 'E. L. James Wins "Publishing Person of the Year" For Making Erotic Fiction "Hot"'; Flood, 'E. L. James Comes Out on Top at National Book Awards'; Luscombe, '*Time* 100: The List – E. L. James'; Flood, '*Fifty Shades of Grey* Voted Most Popular Book of 2012'.
9. Leigh, 'M&S Meets S&M'.
10. Gamer, 'Genres for the Prosecution', p. 1045.
11. Berens, 'The Double Life of Catherine M.'
12. Bloom, *Bestsellers*, pp. 124–8.
13. Ibid., p. 127.
14. Ibid.
15. Ibid., p.128.
16. De Kosnik, 'Fifty Shades and the Archive of Women's Culture', p. 117.
17. Ibid.
18. See Verba, *Boldly Writing*, pp. 1ff.
19. Kies, 'A Red Room of Her Own', p. 35. See also Gray, *Show Sold Separately*, p. 143.
20. Jones, 'Fifty Shades of Exploitation'.
21. Stampler, 'These 13 Companies Are Benefitting Most from *Fifty Shades of Grey*'.

22. Anon., 'Fifty Shades of Grey 999 Call Spike Expected by London Fire Brigade'.
23. Lutkin, 'Stop Donating Your Copies of Fifty Shades of Grey'; Saner, 'Fifty Shades of Grey'.
24. Kies, 'A Red Room of Her Own', p. 36.
25. McCulloch, 'Tied Up In Knots', p. 14.
26. Ibid., p. 4.
27. Jones, '"My Inner Goddess Is Smoldering and Not in a Good Way"', p. 24; Jones, 'Fifty Shades of Exploitation'.
28. National Center on Sexual Exploitation (n.d.), '#FiftyShadesisAbuse', available at <http://endsexualexploitation.org/fiftyshadesgrey/>, quoted in Jones, '"My Inner Goddess Is Smoldering and Not in a Good Way"', p. 27.
29. Salisbury, 'Fifty Shades of Grey Review'. See also McDermott, 'Triggered by Reviewing Fifty Shades of Grey'.
30. McCulloch, 'Tied Up In Knots', p. 11. See also Jones, '"My Inner Goddess Is Smoldering and Not in a Good Way"', pp. 26–7.
31. Bristow, Sexuality, pp. 157–8. See also Al-Mahadin, 'Is Christian a Sadist?', p. 567.
32. Jones, '"My Inner Goddess Is Smoldering and Not in a Good Way"', p. 22.
33. K, 'Gazing Grey and the Shading of Female Sexuality', p. 48.
34. See Roiphe, 'Working Women's Fantasies'.
35. See, for example, one featuring Alexis Bledel and Matt Bomer from 2012 <https://www.youtube.com/watch?v=swSA_GiBogo> (last accessed 30 March 2016).
36. Available at <http://redlemonade.blogspot.ie/p/fifty-shades-of-tedious-fuckery.html> (last accessed 29 June 2016).
37. Anon., 'E. L. James Whips Out New Grey'.
38 Renfro, 'Fifty Shades of Grey Is the Reason Fans Will Never Get the Twilight Spinoff They've Been Waiting Years For'.
39. McCulloch, 'Tied Up In Knots', p. 7.
40. Ibid., p. 5.
41. Larabee, 'Editorial', p. 223.
42. See McCulloch, 'Tied Up In Knots', p. 7.
43. Armstrong, Desire and Domestic Fiction, pp. 6–7.
44. Ibid., p. 10.
45. Ibid., p. 29.
46. James, Fifty Shades of Grey, pp. 165–75, 203–5.
47. Ibid., p. 174.
48. Modleski, Loving With a Vengeance, pp. 34, 36.
49. Ibid., p. 42.
50. Ibid., p. 47.
51. Ibid., p. 57. See also ibid., p. 44.

KEY WORKS

Fifty Shades of Grey (London: Arrow Books, 2012). The first book in the series.
Fifty Shades Darker (London: Arrow Books, 2012). Christian and Ana reconcile after a breakup.
Fifty Shades Freed (London: Arrow Books, 2012). Some dangerous situations ultimately lead to Ana and Christian's marriage, and his acceptance of 'vanilla' sex and romantic love.
Grey: Fifty Shades as Told By Christian (London: Arrow Books, 2015). Self-explanatory.

FURTHER CRITICAL READING

Hunter, I. Q., 'Pre-reading and Failing to Read Fifty Shades of Grey', Sexualities, 16:8 (2013), pp. 969–73. Includes sections on dismissive attitudes towards texts portraying women as desiring subjects.

Kendrick, Walter, *The Secret Museum: Pornography in Modern Culture* (New York: Viking, 1987). An exploration of the development of pornography.
Livingstone, Sonia, 'On the Continuing Problems of Media Effects Research', in J. Curran and M. Gurevitch (eds), *Mass Media and Society* (London: Edward Arnold, 1996), pp. 305–24. Discusses assumptions regarding the idea of popular culture influencing its audience.
Radway, Janice, *Reading the Romance: Women, Patriarchy, and Popular Literature* (Chapel Hill: University of North Carolina Press, 1991). A seminal study of plot dynamics and reading practices relating to popular romance fiction.

BIBLIOGRAPHY

Al-Mahadin, Salam, 'Is Christian a Sadist? *Fifty Shades of Grey* in Popular Imagination', *Feminist Media Studies*, 13:3 (2013), pp. 566–70.
Anon., 'E.L. James Whips Out New *Grey*', *Times Live*, 5 June 2015 <http://www.timeslive.co.za/thetimes/2015/06/05/EL-James-whips-out-new-Grey> (last accessed 9 June 2016).
Anon., '*Fifty Shades of Grey* 999 Call Spike Expected by London Fire Brigade', BBC News, 12 February 2015 <http://www.bbc.com/news/uk-england-london-31428072> (last accessed 30 March 2016).
Armstrong, Nancy, *Desire and Domestic Fiction: A Political History of the Novel* (New York: Oxford University Press, 1989).
Berens, Jessica, 'The Double Life of Catherine M.', *The Guardian*, 19 May 2002 <http://www.theguardian.com/books/2002/may/19/biography.features> (last accessed 29 March 2016).
Bloom, Clive, *Bestsellers: Popular Fiction Since 1900*, 2nd edition (Basingstoke: Palgrave Macmillan, 2008).
Boog, Jason, 'The Lost History of *Fifty Shades of Grey*', *GalleyCat*, 21 November 2012 <http://www.adweek.com/galleycat/fifty-shades-of-grey-wayback-machine/50128?red=as> (last accessed 28 March 2016).
Brennan, Zoe, 'E. L. James: The Shy Housewife Behind *Fifty Shades of Grey*', *The Telegraph*, 7 July 2012 <http://www.telegraph.co.uk/culture/books/9381428/EL-James-The-shy-housewife-behind-Fifty-Shades-of-Grey.html> (last accessed 28 March 2016).
Bristow, Joseph, *Sexuality* (London: Routledge, 1997).
De Kosnik, Abigail, '*Fifty Shades* and the Archive of Women's Culture', *Cinema Journal*, 54:3 (spring 2015), pp. 116–25.
Catastrope, Kitty, 'Fifty Shades of Tedious Fuckery' <http://redlemonade.blogspot.ie/p/fifty-shades-of-tedious-fuckery.html> (last accessed 30 March 2016).
Flood, Alison, 'E. L. James Comes Out on Top at National Book Awards', *The Guardian*, 5 December 2012 <http://www.theguardian.com/books/2012/dec/05/el-james-national-books-award> (last accessed 31 March 2016).
Flood, Alison, 'E. L. James Wins "Publishing Person of the Year" For Making Erotic Fiction "Hot"', *The Guardian*, 3 December 2012 <http://www.theguardian.com/books/2012/dec/03/el-james-publishing-person-of-the-year> (last accessed 31 March 2016).
Flood, Alison, '*Fifty Shades of Grey* Sequel Breaks Sales Records', *The Guardian*, 23 June 2015 <http://www.theguardian.com/books/2015/jun/23/fifty-shades-of-grey-sequel-breaks-sales-records> (last accessed 31 March 2016).
Flood, Alison, '*Fifty Shades of Grey* Voted Most Popular Book of 2012', *The Guardian*, 26 December 2012 <http://www.theguardian.com/books/2012/dec/26/fifty-shades-grey-most-popular-book> (last accessed 28 March 2016).
Gamer, Michael, 'Genres for the Prosecution: Pornography and the Gothic', *PMLA* 114:5 (October 1999), pp. 1043–54.
Gray, Jonathan, *Show Sold Separately: Promos, Spoilers, and Other Media Paratexts* (New York: New York University Press, 2010).

Johnson, Steve, 'Who is E. L. James?' *Chicago Tribune*, 3 May 2012 <http://articles.chicagotribune.com/2012-05-03/entertainment/ct-ent-0502-50-shades-of-grey-20120501_1_fan-fiction-book-signing-event-fans-bond> (last accessed 28 March 2016).

Jones, Bethan, 'Fifty Shades of Exploitation: Fan Labor and *Fifty Shades of Grey*', *Transformative Works and Cultures*, 15 (2014), n.p. <http://journal.transformativeworks.org/index.php/twc/article/view/501/422> (last accessed 31 March 2016).

Jones, Bethan, '"My Inner Goddess Is Smoldering and Not in a Good Way": An Anti-Fannish Account of Consuming *Fifty Shades*', *Intensities: The Journal of Cult Media*, 8 (January 2016), pp. 20–33.

K, Kavyta, 'Gazing Grey and the Shading of Female Sexuality', *Intensities: The Journal of Cult Media*, 8 (January 2016), pp. 47–58.

Kies, Bridget, 'A Red Room of Her Own: Dominants, Submissives, Fans, and Producers of *Fifty Shades of Grey*', *Intensities: The Journal of Cult Media*, 8 (January 2016), pp. 34–43.

Larabee, Ann, 'Editorial: *50 Shades of Grey* and the Moral Reading', *Journal of Popular Culture*, 48:2 (2015), pp. 223–4.

Leigh, Wendy, 'M&S Meets S&M', *The Sun*, 30 April 2012 <http://www.thesun.co.uk/sol/homepage/features/4287077/MS-meets-SM-Married-mum-Erika-James-who-wrote-erotic-bestseller-Fifty-Shades-Of-Grey.html> (last accessed 28 March 2016).

Luscombe, Belinda, '*Time* 100: The List – E. L. James', *Time*, 18 April 2012 <http://content.time.com/time/specials/packages/article/0,28804,2111975_2111976_2112140,00.html> (last accessed 31 March 2016).

Lutkin, Aimée, 'Stop Donating Your Copies of *Fifty Shades of Grey*', *Jezebel*, 24 March 2016 <http://jezebel.com/stop-donating-your-copies-of-50-shades-of-grey-1766976983?rev=1458868972493&utm_campaign=socialfow_jezebel_twitter&utm_source=jezebel_twitter&utm_medium=socialflow> (last accessed 31 March 2016).

McCulloch, Richard,. 'Tied Up In Knots: Irony, Ambiguity, and the "Difficult" Pleasures of *Fifty Shades of Grey*', *Intensities: The Journal of Cult Media*, 8 (January 2016), pp. 1–19.

McDermott, Roe, 'Triggered by Reviewing Fifty Shades of Grey', *Hot Press*, 16 February 2015 <http://www.hotpress.com/features/reports/Triggered-by-Reviewing-Fifty-Shades-of-Grey/13561614.html> (last accessed 31 March 2016).

Meredith, Charlotte, '*Fifty Shades of Grey* Becomes the Bestselling Book of All Time', *The Express*, 1 August 2012 <http://www.express.co.uk/news/uk/336759/Fifty-Shades-of-Grey-becomes-the-bestselling-book-of-all-time> (last accessed 31 March 2016).

Modleski, Tania, *Loving With a Vengeance: Mass-Produced Fantasies for Women* (New York: Methuen, 1982).

Renfro, Kim, '*Fifty Shades of Grey* Is the Reason Fans Will Never Get the *Twilight* Spinoff They've Been Waiting Years For', *Business Insider UK*, 9 October 2015 <http://uk.businessinsider.com/midnight-sun-interrupted-by-fifty-shades-of-grey-spinoff-2015-10?r=US&IR=T> (last accessed 14 April 2017).

Richardson, Samuel, *Pamela; or, Virtue Rewarded*, intro. Margaret A. Doody (London: Penguin, 2003).

Roiphe, Katie, 'Working Women's Fantasies', *Newsweek*, 16 April 2012 http://europe.newsweek.com/working-womens-fantasies-63915?rm=eu (last accessed 28 March 2016).

Salisbury, Brian, '*Fifty Shades of Grey* Review: An Abhorrent and Misogynistic Rape Fantasy', *Flickchart*, 13 February 2015 <http://www.flickchart.com/blog/fifty-shades-of-grey-review-an-abhorrent-misogynistic-rape-fantasy/> (last accessed 31 March 2016).

Saner, Emine, '*Fifty Shades of Grey*: The Book You Literally Can't Give Away', *The Guardian*, 23 March 2016 <http://www.theguardian.com/books/shortcuts/2016/mar/23/fifty-shades-grey-book-you-literally-cant-give-away> (last accessed 30 March 2016).

Skurnick, Lizzie, '*Fifty Shades of Grey*, a Self-Published Ebook, Is the Future of Publishing', *Daily Beast*, 17 March 2012 <http://www.thedailybeast.com/

articles/2012/03/17/50-shades-of-grey-a-self-published-e-book-is-the-future-of-ublishing.
html#url=/articles/2012/03/17/50-shades-of-grey-a-self-published-e-book-is-the-future-of-
publishing.html> (last accessed 28 March 2016).
Stampler, Laura, 'These 13 Companies Are Benefitting Most from *Fifty Shades of Grey*', 26 June
2012 <http://www.businessinsider.com/50-shades-of-grey-is-making-these-companies-rich-
2012-6?op=1&IR=T> (last accessed 30 March 2016).
Verba, Joan Marie, *Boldly Writing: A Trekker Fan and Zine History, 1967–1987*, 2nd edition
(Minnetonka, MN: FTL Publications, 2003) <http://www.ftlpublications.com/bwebook.
pdf> (last accessed 29 March 2016).

CHAPTER 11

Fact, Fiction, Fabrication: The Popular Appeal of Dan Brown's Global Bestsellers

Ian Kinane

In a survey conducted by *The Telegraph* on the bestselling authors of the early twenty-first century, Dan Brown was outsold only by J. K. Rowling and Roger Hargreaves (the creator of the Mr Men series). While Rowling's net profits from the Harry Potter series over the period 2000–9 was in excess of £200 million, Dan Brown's best-known and most controversial thriller, *The Da Vinci Code* (2003), outsold *Harry Potter and the Deathly Hallows* by over half a million units.[1] This is a remarkable accomplishment for a man who, prior to *The Da Vinci Code*'s release, had embarked on a doomed career as a singer-songwriter; co-authored a couple of uninspired, humorous self-help books with his wife under the pseudonym 'Danielle Brown', including *187 Men to Avoid: A Survival Guide for the Romantically Frustrated Woman* (1995) and *The Bald Book* (1998); and received very little critical or commercial attention following the release of his first three works of genre fiction, *Digital Fortress* (1998), *Angels and Demons* (2000) and *Deception Point* (2001).

Today, however, Brown has sold more than 200 million books worldwide and his work has been translated into fifty-six languages.[2] During the first decade of the twenty-first century, *The Da Vinci Code* alone was estimated to have sold more than eighty-one million copies worldwide.[3] Due to its phenomenal success, sales of Brown's previous three novels increased rapidly, and in 2004 all four of his completed novels appeared at the same time on the *New York Times* bestsellers list. *The Da Vinci Code*'s sequel, *The Lost Symbol*, released in 2009, sold two million copies in North America and the UK in the first week.[4] While not nearly as successful as its two immediate predecessors, Brown's most recent offering, *Inferno* (2013), also reached number 1 in US and UK bestseller lists in its first week, selling 1.4 million copies in the US market alone.[5] Brown's presence within twenty-first-century popular fiction, then, cannot be overstated. In 2005, at the height of Brown's notoriety, Michele Orecklin, an arts and entertainment editor at *Time* magazine, credited him with 'nothing less than keeping the publishing industry afloat' in the early 2000s.[6] As we shall see, Brown's success and popular appeal as a writer owe just as much to the tradition and impact of genre fiction in general, and to the inestimable sway and socio-political effects of the thriller form more specifically, as it does to the controversial nature of his subject matter.

Brown has stated that it was while holidaying in Tahiti with his wife that he came across Sidney Sheldon's 1991 novel *The Doomsday Conspiracy*, and that it was this reading experience that inspired him to become a writer of thriller fiction.[7] The thriller genre is often overlooked in critical discourse for its association with popular fiction or 'low' literary cultural forms, but the cultural impact of Brown's runaway success illustrates the political potential of genre fiction, as well as the economic and social impact of the thriller as one of contemporary culture's most dominant forms. Jerry Palmer, in his notable study of the genre, points out that thrillers are not just products of commerce: they 'are first and foremost the incarnation of an ideology', which posits a 'competitive individualism' as central to their formula, and presents society as 'devoid of conflict' in all manner.[8] Palmer also cites the thriller's malleability or its openness as a significant factor in its success, noting that thrillers 'can accommodate more or less any set of political beliefs'[9] – a not insignificant comment given that Dan Brown has been lambasted for seeming to endorse in his fiction a heretical set of religious politics. That the thriller is regarded by many of its proponents as a medium for the wholesale formulation and expression of blanket fears of the dominant political apparatuses (government conspiracies and Church cover-ups, for example) goes far towards an explanation of the genre's cultural status. The true success of the genre's potential as a political vehicle, which Brown has tapped into through his use of probing and controversial conspiracy narratives, is to introduce into the mainstream a discursive examination of 'the relationship between the legal order, considered a norm believed in by those living under it, and infractions against it'.[10] While the content and subject matter of these narratives (often impossibly elaborate conspiracies) warrant disbelief, the texts themselves frame an interrogation of the historicisation of political and religious meta-narratives, and the processes by which governmental and religious apparatuses reify their own dominance within society. Brown's success and notoriety lie not in the quality of his writing, but in the wider cultural *response* to his subject matter by the Church and other political commentators. In other words, the controversial claims of political and religious conspiracy raised in *The Da Vinci Code* only partially account for its immense success; ironically, it is the reaction of powerful religious figures in the media to these claims that elevates Brown's fiction and reifies within popular discourse the debate about political, religious and historical authority and the processes of historicising truth.

In March 2005, a full two years after the publication of *The Da Vinci Code*, Cardinal Tarcisio Bertone denounced Brown's bestseller as 'a sack full of lies against the Church and against the real history of Christianity'.[11] That religious leaders felt compelled to respond at all to Brown's conspiracy theories only seemed to ratify the book's claims, thereby sanctioning the belief raised in Brown's fiction that the Church was concealing something. Brown's book was denounced as political and religious bait, but the Church's ire drew unwanted attention to the very means by which the dominant Christian narrative – the 'real history of Christianity' – has been historicised as political and ideological 'fact'. Though Lisa Rogak concedes that '[s]ex combined with religion in any form was always a safe bet for generating controversy',[12] Brown's subsequent legal issues concerning the copyright to many of his more outlandish claims (notably his principal one, that Jesus and Mary Magdalene had a child) suggest that, in addition to a general scepticism about the author's continued excavation of other religious and historical mythologies in subsequent books, public interest and concern have mostly centred on whether Brown's claims, and the claims of his sources, are to be regarded sceptically. The clash between Brown's fictional bestseller and the doctrine of the Catholic Church has foregrounded cultural debates about the historicisation (and thus legitimisation) of several of our most prominent Christian myths, and the means by which history has been recorded as a fabric of literary texts encoded with cultural, political and ideological meaning.

In 2006, Michael Baigent and Richard Leigh, authors (with Henry Lincoln) of the 1982 international bestseller *The Holy Blood and the Holy Grail*, sued Brown's publisher, Random House, for plagiarism and copyright infringement, resulting in a much-publicised trial. Baigent and Leigh's book alleges, much like *The Da Vinci Code*, that Jesus married Mary Magdalene and fathered a child, and that Christ's descendants emigrated to what is now France and intermarried with nobility. The book further alleges that a secret society, the Priory of Sion, functions to protect the royal Merovingian bloodline of Christ, which survives to this day. The book was almost universally denounced by historians and scholars, who claimed that it presented as fact pseudo-historical material which derived from a wilful misinterpretation of historical documents. In spite of the authors' legal defeat, sales of *The Holy Blood and the Holy Grail* increased rapidly, no doubt bolstered by the publicity surrounding the trial. The content of both works has since resulted in a wealth of literary and quasi-historical imitations, journal articles and newspaper editorials, official denouncements from the Church and increased notoriety for all parties. The controversy surrounding *The Da Vinci Code* was not, in fact, entirely concerned with its veracity but with what Benjamin Kelly states is the 'authority within imagined communities as well as defining such communities against outsiders'.[13] Here, an important issue is underlined: the legal controversy surrounding Brown's claims aroused popular interest suggests that as much importance is given in the cultural imagination to fictionalised mythologies as to those that are commonly considered historical truths. Christian commentator David Couchman has suggested that Dan Brown's success, and the success of *The Da Vinci Code* in particular, as a fictional mythology, can be attributed to three principal factors: the controversial nature of the subject matter; the substantial push in marketing and advertising by his publishers; and the fact that Brown's content resonates within the contemporary cultural imagination.[14] In this respect, it is worth considering the specifics of Brown's content and trying to account for the popular appeal of his fiction.

On the level of superficial intrigue, Brown's books comprise several different types of codes and clue-puzzle mysteries, designed not only to complicate and advance the plot but also to compound the general air of mystery, secrecy and obfuscation in which Brown specialises. While the depth of knowledge and information required actually to solve most (or any) of these clue-puzzles is most likely beyond the capacity of the average reader, Brown's deliberate and sometimes awkward feeding of facts ensures that the reader is not lost in erudition for too long. Ken Gelder has noted that the 'entwining of entertainment and information is a key feature of much popular fiction'.[15] Brown's novels, then, represent the somewhat egalitarian and practical application of academia for the lay reader, with each of them presenting an academic treatise or thesis statement of sorts (for example, in *The Da Vinci Code*, that the true history of Christianity is not what we imagine it to be), and offering largely fantastic but nevertheless compelling 'evidence' to support this thesis.

Robert Langdon, effectively the reader's instructor in the *Da Vinci Code* (as well as the other entries in the Langdon series, *Angels and Demons*, *The Lost Symbol*, *Inferno* and *Origin*), is also an oddly egalitarian figure, both a blandly flavoured 'everyman' and an intellectual übermensch. As such, while in accordance with the conventions of thriller fiction, he is a (reasonably) ordinary man thrown into multiple extraordinary situations, his ordinariness and his ostensible classlessness are a dissimulation of sorts on Brown's part. As professor of the fictional discipline of 'symbology' at Harvard University, a widely published expert in his field, and in possession of a rare eidetic memory, Langdon can hardly be described as 'ordinary' nor entirely 'out of place' within the remit of what he is called upon to do in each novel. Jerry Palmer has stated that the notion of class has all but been erased from the thriller genre, and that 'the wrongs that are avenged and the threats that are averted [within thriller fiction] are universal', restoring a 'natural, therefore universal order'.[16] Langdon, however, is not as untroublingly classless as Brown would like us to believe – however much the author repeatedly insists on other characters addressing Langdon as 'Mister', and not in his official (superior) capacity as 'Professor'. The erudite world Langdon inhabits *is* politically class-based; what is threatened by the various conspiracies in Brown's fictional worlds (which, it should be stated, Langdon ultimately protects by not going public with any of the information he uncovers) are the interests and secrets of the upper echelons of religious and political powers, and their associated fears that ancient knowledge and/or political and religious secrets will be revealed to the masses. Brown successfully dissimulates the issues of class within his novels by encouraging the reader to believe in the classlessness of Langdon's intellectualism; it is under Langdon's aegis, and the ostensible altruism of his academic tutelage, that the reader is introduced to the history of symbolic language as well as all manner of erudite knowledge, and Langdon's position as an educator enables Brown effectively to feed the reader information. In this way, Langdon (and, thus, Brown) sets the pace for the reader's discovery of the shocking secrets within the texts through what appears to be the *mutual* discovery (by both the character and the reader in tandem) of crucial points of information for the advancement of the story. Langdon's intellectual superiority is rendered unthreatening precisely because it enables and rewards the reader's advancement towards the next clue in the text's mystery.

Much of Brown's work is also concerned more overtly with the historical and cultural clash of science and religion – probably the most dominant and consistent theme in his fiction. The world Robert Langdon inhabits is one in which science is continually beset by religious fundamentalism, and where scientific prescience is regarded with suspicion and fear by people of faith. Brown's presentation of the age-old conflict between science and religion plays right into what Rodney Clapp terms the 'zeitgeist of truthiness',[17] or the recent tendency within Western society to prioritise institutional transparency. Recent scandals within the Catholic Church have only galvanised the movement towards secularism that has largely defined the post-Renaissance period. Brown successfully taps into the mounting suspicion of religion in general, and the Catholic Church more specifically, by positing controversial (albeit contrived) theories as to what the Church might be hiding. Indeed, the Catholic Church does not come off well in Brown's fiction: between the Vatican's secret pay-deals with Opus Dei and other cover-ups in *The Da Vinci Code*, to the brazen hypocrisy of the Camerlengo and his struggle for power in *Angels and Demons*, the Catholic Church is painted as a viable target for anti-religious critics. In response to his religious detractors, Brown has stated that his writing is 'in no way anti-Christian or anti-Catholic' and that his books 'look at the Catechism and the history of Christianity through a slightly different lens'[18] – a claim that is hard to believe, given that Brown at times both sanctifies and discredits Catholicism, toying with the reader's notions of faith in much the same way that his novels lambast the authority of the Church for doing so. Though it is the hypocritical Camerlengo who is ultimately behind the death of the Pope and the Illuminati conspiracy in *Angels and Demons*, it is no coincidence that Brown gives this arch-conservative villain a damning and portentous speech about the prescience of scientific innovation, during which he declares that, in the ancient war between science and religion, science has won, not by providing answers to the bigger questions, but by 'so radically altering our society that the truths we once saw as signposts now seem inapplicable'.[19] Here, the Camerlengo rails against cultural reliance on scientific proofs above religious faith. In his quest to restore faith in the Church, the Camerlengo steals a canister of antimatter – a highly charged substance composed of unstable anti-particles – from the European Organisation for Nuclear Research (CERN), and secretes it away beneath Vatican City. When, just before the antimatter combusts, the Camerlengo retrieves the bomb and detonates it high above Vatican City, he claims that God himself has spoken to him, telling him the location of the bomb and how to save the Church from destruction. Unaware of the Camerlengo's involvement in this conspiracy, the public interpret this as an act of divine intervention, and immediately fall to their knees in reverence for the Camerlengo and for the Church, their faith in miracles and religion seemingly restored.

That the Camerlengo utilises cutting-edge scientific technology to meet his aims only further complicates and makes more ambiguous Brown's position on the debate between science and religion. Brown does not venerate science at the expense of religion; in fact, his fiction makes it abundantly clear that the issue of science versus religion is an unresolved one for the author. Certainly, part of the popular appeal of his novels is that while Brown facilitates a discourse between the prescience of science and the history of religion, he refrains from explicitly siding with either. Brown's novels frequently espouse the belief that science and religion are actually working towards the same goal, that is, proving the existence of God. Indeed, we are told that Leonardo Vetra, the theo-physicist murdered on the Camerlengo's orders at the beginning of *Angels and Demons*, has practically proven the existence of God through his work on particle physics, using the Large Hadron Collider at CERN.

In addition to riding the wave of anti-religious populism of the post-2000 era, another reason for the potency of Brown's appeal is his novels' destabilisation of establishment ideology through the use of conspiracy theories and the 'interplay between narrative history and fiction'.[20] Brown's books are not only full of (most likely unintentional) historical inaccuracies, but they also attempt to expose or bring to light certain information on individual historical figures or religious and cultural groups in a manner designed to engender the reader's distrust of historical institutions, and to solicit support for his own rewriting of history. This ranges from the wholesale ideological ransacking and exposé of 'secret' societies such as the Freemasons, the Illuminati and the Knights Templar, to the undercutting of certain historical figures' reputations. Brown plays on public distrust of governmental organisations through established and popular conspiracy theories, such as the Kryptos, a cryptographic sculpture located at the headquarters of the CIA in Langley, Virginia, and which remains today one of the world's most famously unsolved codes, as well as the purported inclusion of Masonic symbolism in the animated films of Walt Disney.[21]

Matthew Schneider-Mayerson has noted that post-9/11, the fear of further terror attacks and the resulting 'war on terror' 'generated an environment that encouraged conspiracism and thereby created a market for [Brown's] conspiracy-suffused writings'.[22] Brown's fiction successfully captures not only the widespread feelings of mistrust of government and religious powers, particularly in America, but highlights through Langdon's consistent refusal to divulge the many conspiracies he uncovers a troubling 'antidemocratic impulse' that reinforces political and class hierarchies, and consolidates the general public's '[ignorance] of the forces that move history'.[23] It is, perhaps, for this reason that, in addition to underlining the spurious means by which history becomes ideologically narrativised, a recurring archetype used within Brown's novels is the anonymous antagonist, usually a zealot or political/religious acolyte ostensibly working alongside Langdon, but who is secretly working against him (the Camerlengo in *Angels and Demons*; Sir Leigh Teabing in *The Da Vinci Code*). Much like the public fear of terror threats from without, Brown's use of this trope reflects the concomitant fear of an internal conspiracy,[24] or the fear that someone from *within* government or religious institutions is, unbeknown to us, shaping and controlling global forces in an attempt to hold sway over the public.

Indeed, the sheer number of conspiracy theories surrounding the events of 9/11 suggests that this idea has taken a firm hold within the mainstream cultural imaginary. Public fear of the threat from within not only reifies governments' monopolies on violence and anti-terrorist activities, but it also betrays a deep longing on our part for a 'consistent master historical narrative',[25] and a desire for transparency, through which the general public may comprehend and democratically assume a role in the historical *polis*. Furthermore, Brown's fiction is scathing of the role of the mass media in adversely serving the interests of conspiracy theorists and fear-mongers. If, as Brown notes, the media are 'the right arm of anarchy'[26] and '[t]errorism is a political weapon',[27] the novels, then, particularly *Angels and Demons*, are decidedly critical of the means by which the ruling class capitalises on media-inspired public fear as a political tool. It is through the media, Brown posits, that the political ruling class reinforces its agenda: by courting anarchic ideation and playing on the public's fear, governments become justified in forcibly reasserting themselves – à la George W. Bush and the war on terror. While the reader is inclined to reject the view propounded by the irksome and cynical journalist Gunther Glick in *Angels and Demons*, that '[v]iewers didn't want truth anymore; they wanted entertainment',[28] Langdon's refusal to take to the media with the numerous religious and political conspiracies he has been privy to suggests that, while Brown certainly courts anti-establishment feeling, and while his novels operate as vehicles for a certain disestablishment rhetoric, Langdon is a purveyor of conservatism, whose actions are somewhat conversely aligned with the ideologies of Brown's novels as thriller fictions. While Langdon is certainly the hero of Brown's novels, it is highly questionable as to whether, with his Harvard-educated background and his concealment of important public information, he is a champion of the commoner. One may wonder whether Brown is, in fact, covering himself here, in much the same way, for example, that Langdon's equivocation over some of the novels' more seditious historical claims somewhat inoculates the hero (and, by extension, Brown himself) from criticism. That is, while it is Sir Leigh Teabing in *The Da Vinci Code* who speaks to the more inflammatory ideas about the Church's history, Langdon's non-committal, 'academic' refusal to take a side allows him (and, again, Brown) to remain seemingly ideologically neutral for most of the novel.

Brown's work does not shy away from addressing complex questions of moral and ethical philosophy, and he successfully incorporates within his bestsellers material that would otherwise not be out of place in works of religious and scientific philosophy. His work can broadly be divided into two main categories: those books that deal with philosophical questions concerning humanity's origins, injustices in recorded history or considerations of spiritual and/or religious knowledge or wisdom that humanity is perceived to have forgotten and/or lost (*Angels and Demons*, *The Da Vinci Code*); and those that address pressing issues regarding the limits of human advancement and/or achievement, the prescience of science, and the moral and ethical implications of humanity's actions for the future of the species (*The Lost Symbol*, *Inferno*). It is not coincidental that the conflict between science and religion is framed temporally, as a clash between traditional and progressive methodologies, for his books stage precisely the debate between the burden of humanity's past and our present responsibility to future generations. Brown's work, in Jason Cowley's words, is filled with a deep 'eschatological anxiety'[29] that is reflective of the turbulence of contemporary times, and the modern fear of either fully embracing or discarding entirely either religion or science. Brown's fiction toes the line between the 'magic' of scientific advancements that have yet to come to pass (or are currently coming to pass) and humanity's unwillingness to jettison spiritual and religious thought: Leonard Vetra's discovery of antimatter in *Angels and Demons*; Katherine Solomon's research into noetic sciences and the measurement of the human soul in *The Lost Symbol*; and Bertrand Zobrist's discovery of a vector virus that causes selective infertility in humans in *Inferno*. These all represent both tremendous advancements for humanity, as well as the need for a discourse concerning the moral and ethical limits of these advancements. That Brown frequently calls to our attention the interrelation between spirituality/mysticism and physics is one his novels' enduring successes: his books have introduced into mainstream discourse widespread contemporary moral and ethical concerns. Also, that the subject matter of *Inferno* is concerned with the ethics of population control and eugenics is not a coincidence; he frequently addresses the population apocalypse theory[30] and the principles of Thomas Malthus's population control theory,[31] as well as the ethics of trans-humanism,[32] while nevertheless taking good care to avoid advocating or adopting a personal position on the issue.

Furthermore, that Brown describes *denial* as a 'global pandemic'[33] suggests that, while his books (*Inferno* in particular) certainly censure those who fail to act or speak out against injustice and wrongdoing in times of moral crisis (deliberately overlooking Robert Langdon's failings in this regard), one also cannot avoid the implicit critique his work as a whole levels against the history of human thought: that, much like the very conspiracy theories expounded by Brown's popular fiction, '[w]ide acceptance of an idea is not proof of its validity'.[34] The overarching theme of Brown's work, then, and certainly that which is lent credence by the public response to his controversial claims, may arguably be the indictment of humankind's passive acceptance of religious, political and historical meta-narratives, and the political ramifications of denying historical and religious alterity. The world of Brown's novels is, not unlike our own, one in which conspiracy has become a necessary vehicle for the maintenance of political and religious ideologies. To the extent that, as Langdon notes, '*every* faith in the world is based on fabrication',[35] so too does Brown's fiction serve to foster a healthy scepticism towards cultural and religious histories, which are in themselves ideological confabulations. It is not without great knowingness and a wryness of humour that Brown refers to the Bible as 'the ultimate bestseller of all time',[36] a comment which underlines the popularity and economic viability of religious meta-narratives, and the ways in which a particular ideology has been marketed to, and, moreover, has been collectively sanctioned by, mass culture.

NOTES

1. MacArthur, 'Bestselling Authors of the Decade'.
2. Information from author's webpage at <http://www.danbrown.com/#author-section> (last accessed 12 January 2016).
3. Marcus, 'Brown Is Back with the Code for a Runaway Bestseller'.
4. 'With *The Lost Symbol*, Dan Brown Takes Down Bill Clinton's Book Record', *New York Daily News*, 22 September 2009 <http://www.nydailynews.com/entertainment/music-arts/lost-symbol-dan-brown-takes-bill-clinton-book-record-article-1.406903> (last accessed 12 January 2016).
5. 'Dan Brown', 'The World's Highest Paid Celebrities 2015', *Forbes* <http://www.forbes.com/profile/dan-brown/> (last accessed 12 January 2016).
6. Orecklin, 'Dan Brown'.
7. Lattman, 'The Da Vinci Code Trial'.
8. Palmer, *Thrillers*, p. 66.
9. Ibid., p. 67.
10. Ibid., p. 151.
11. See Plumer, *The Catholic Church and American Culture*, p. 231.
12. Rogak, *Dan Brown*, p. 78.
13. Kelly, 'Deviant Ancient Histories', p. 375.
14. Couchman, 'Dan Brown', p. 71.
15. Gelder, *Popular Fiction*, p. 62.
16. Palmer, *Thrillers*, p. 121.
17. Clapp, 'Dan Brown's Truthiness', p. 22.

18. Quoted in Rogak, *Dan Brown*, p. 111.
19. Brown, *Angels and Demons*, p. 420.
20. Mexal, 'Realism, Narrative History, and the Production of the Bestseller', p. 1087.
21. Brown, *The Da Vinci Code*, p. 350.
22. Schneider-Mayerson, 'The Dan Brown Phenomenon', p. 194.
23. Ibid., pp. 196, 199.
24. Ibid., p. 197.
25. Mexal, 'Realism, Narrative History, and the Production of the Bestseller', p. 1092.
26. Brown, *Angels and Demons*, p. 236.
27. Ibid., p. 201.
28. Ibid., p. 219.
29. Cowley, 'The Author of the Bestselling *The Da Vinci Code* Has Tapped into Our Post-9/11 Anxieties and Fear of Fundamentalism', p. 19.
30. Brown, *Inferno*, p. 239.
31. Ibid., p. 199.
32. Ibid., p. 608
33. Ibid., p. 619.
34. Brown, *The Lost Symbol*, p. 117.
35. Brown, *The Da Vinci Code*, p. 451.
36. Ibid., p. 225.

KEY WORKS

Digital Fortress (1998). Brown's first novel, a techno-thriller examining the role of government surveillance and the ethical implications of spying on private citizens. When cryptographer Susan Fletcher uncovers a code that the NSA supercomputer, Digital Fortress, cannot break, she is quickly thrown into a chase to stop a large-scale government conspiracy. Apart from the prescience of its theme (surveillance and the eradication of public privacy), the novel met with lacklustre reviews.

Angels and Demons (2000). When a sample of highly unstable antimatter is stolen from CERN and planted beneath Vatican City, Harvard symbologist Robert Langdon is called upon to solve a series of clues that leads him on a treasure-hunt through the art history of ancient Rome, where he uncovers a conspiracy that threatens to bring down the Catholic Church. The first of Brown's novels to feature protagonist Robert Langdon. Although this book is Brown's best thriller, it was not as well received as *The Da Vinci Code*.

Deception Point (2001). A stand-alone techno-thriller novel featuring heroine Rachel Sexton, a White House intelligence analyst who uncovers a political conspiracy to take control of the presidency by faking the discovery of extra-terrestrial life that has apparently fallen to earth in a meteorite. The book was met with very little critical or commercial notice upon its release, and it is unsurprising that, following the success of *The Da Vinci Code*, Brown has focused on Robert Langdon's exploits instead.

The Da Vinci Code (2003). Brown's runaway bestseller, in which protagonist Robert Langdon must decipher a series of complex clues hidden in the artworks of Leonard Da Vinci, is one of the most profitable single volumes of popular literature of all time. The book is best known for its elaborate conspiracy theories concerning the Catholic Church's history, and the suggestion that Jesus Christ and Mary Magdalene sired a child. A fantastical and thrilling fiction to be taken with much, much more than a pinch of salt.

The Lost Symbol (2009). The sequel to *The Da Vinci Code*. Langdon is on the hunt for the titular lost symbol, hidden within the deep recesses of Masonic history in Washington, DC, which will enable its possessor to learn the ancient secrets of mysticism, which are protected by only a few chosen guardians. Brown relies on well known conspiracy theories in American historical lore, but the subject matter pushes the limits of credibility beyond that which his other works manage to sustain more successfully.

Inferno (2013). Langdon must decipher codes from Dante Alighieri's poem *The Divine Comedy* in order to prevent an act of biological terrorism. Brown's most recent novel and (at the time of writing) the least financially successful entry in the Robert Langdon series. Brown's use of his trademark style (clue-puzzles, ancient art history and symbolism) reaches its limits here, as the necessity for the villain's use of complex codes, riddles and wordplay seems largely contrived and somewhat unjustified.

FURTHER CRITICAL READING

Kelly, 'Deviant Ancient Histories'. A sociological study of the controversial polemics of *The Da Vinci Code* and an examination of Brown's fiction as a postmodernist sub-genre of history writing.

Maddux, '*The Da Vinci Code* and the Regressive Gender Politics of Celebrating Women'. An important counterargument to claims that Brown is a feminist writer; Maddux illustrates the ways in which Brown's celebration of women is restricted to the private sphere, and shows how his female characters reinforce gender binaries.

Mexal, 'Realism, Narrative History, and the Production of the Bestseller'. An erudite discussion of the ways in which the media's response to *The Da Vinci Code* created a new form of cultural and ecumenical discourse, and how the cultural mechanics of the bestseller has altered since the Church's engagement with Brown's themes.

Schneider-Mayerson, 'The Dan Brown Phenomenon'. An excellent critical analysis of post-9/11 American paranoia, and the ways in which this cultural environment both fostered and was exploited by Brown in his fiction.

Wright and Paul, *Decoding Da Vinci*. An impressive discussion of the ways Brown locates his fiction between ancient Christian mythology and contemporary neo-gnosticism, and how these intersecting discourses have given rise to fantastical conspiracy narratives such as *The Da Vinci Code*.

BIBLIOGRAPHY

Brown, Dan, *Angels and Demons* (London: Corgi Books, 2000).
Brown, Dan, *Deception Point* (London: Corgi Books, 2001).
Brown, Dan, *Digital Fortress* (London: Corgi Books, 1998).
Brown, Dan, *Inferno* (London: Corgi Books, 2013).
Brown, Dan, *The Da Vinci Code* (London: Corgi Books, 2003).
Brown, Dan, *The Lost Symbol* (London: Corgi Books, 2009).
Clapp, Rodney, 'Dan Brown's Truthiness: The Appeal of *The Da Vinci Code*', *Christian Century*, 123:10 (2006), pp. 22–5.
Couchman, David, 'Dan Brown: What Can the Church Learn from the Pied Piper of Post-modernity?', *Evangel*, 24:3 (2006), pp. 71–5.
Cowley, Jason, 'The Author of the Bestselling *The Da Vinci Code* Has Tapped into Our Post-9/11 Anxieties and Fear of Fundamentalism', *New Statesman*, 13 December 2004, pp. 18–20.
Gelder, Ken, *Popular Fiction: The Logics and Practices of a Literary Field* (New York: Routledge, 2004).
Kelly, Benjamin, 'Deviant Ancient Histories: Dan Brown, Erich von Däniken and the Sociology of Historical Polemic', *Rethinking History*, 12:3 (2008), pp. 361–82.
Lattman, Peter, '*The Da Vinci Code* Trial: Dan Brown's Witness Statement Is a Great Read', *Wall Street Journal*, 14 March 2006, <http://blogs.wsj.com/law/2006/03/14/the-da-vinci-code-authors-witness-statement-is-a-great-read/> (last accessed 13 January 2016).

MacArthur, Brian, 'Bestselling Authors of the Decade', *The Telegraph*, 22 December 2009 <http://www.telegraph.co.uk/culture/books/6866648/Bestselling-authors-of-the-decade. html> (last accessed 12 January 2016).

Maddux, Kristy, '*The Da Vinci Code* and the Regressive Gender Politics of Celebrating Women', *Critical Studies in Media Communication*, 25:3 (2008), pp. 225–48.

Marcus, Caroline, 'Brown Is Back with the Code for a Runaway Bestseller', *Sydney Morning Herald*, 13 September 2009 <http://www.smh.com.au/news/entertainment/books/brown-is-back-with-the-code-for-a-runaway-bestseller/2009/09/12/1252519678923.html> (last accessed 12 January 2016).

Mexal, Stephen J., 'Realism, Narrative History, and the Production of the Bestseller: *The Da Vinci Code* and the Virtual Public Sphere', *Journal of Popular Culture*, 44:5 (2011), pp. 1085–101.

Orecklin, Michele, 'Dan Brown', *Time*, 18 April 2005 <http://content.time.com/time/specials/ packages/article/0,28804,1972656_1972696_1973088,00.html> (last accessed 12 January 2016).

Palmer, Jerry, *Thrillers: Genesis and Structure of a Popular Genre* (London: Edward Arnold, 1978).

Patterson, James (ed.), *Thriller* (Ontario: MIRA Books, 2006).

Plumer, Eric, *The Catholic Church and American Culture: Why the Claims of Dan Brown Strike a Chord* (Chicago: University of Scranton Press, 2009).

Rogak, Lisa, *Dan Brown: The Man Behind* The Da Vinci Code (London: Robson Books, 2005).

Schneider-Mayerson, Matthew, 'The Dan Brown Phenomenon: Conspiracism in Post-9/11 Popular Fiction', *Radical History Review*, 14 (2011), pp. 194–201.

Wright, N. T. and Ian Paul, *Decoding Da Vinci: The Challenge of Historic Christianity to Conspiracy and Fantasy* (Cambridge: Grove Books, 2006).

CHAPTER 12

'I Need to Disillusion You': J. K. Rowling and Twenty-First-Century Young Adult Fantasy

Kate Harvey

The three years that separated the publications of *Harry Potter and the Goblet of Fire* (2000) and *Harry Potter and the Order of the Phoenix* (2003), the fourth and fifth novels in J. K. Rowling's Harry Potter series, represent a turning point in the popular fantasy sequence. *Goblet of Fire* broke sales records in the UK and US and prompted unprecedented media coverage of children across the Anglophone world dressing up and attending midnight release parties, feats that would be repeated with the release of the subsequent three novels.[1] At 636 pages, the novel is over twice as long as its predecessor, *Harry Potter and the Prisoner of Azkaban* (1999), and ends with villain Voldemort returned to full power and poised to bring down the wizarding world, signalling two features that would set the second half of the series apart: their length and their darker tone. Another key difference between *Goblet of Fire* and the three novels that preceded it is the amount of space devoted to events outside of Hogwarts school and the commentary they provide on social and political issues in contemporary Britain.

Between 2000 and 2003, the context in which the novels were published changed as a result of the activities of fans, lawyers, scholars and Rowling herself. This is the period in which online fan communities blossomed, and the Harry Potter fandom was among the most prominent of these. Fan sites not only discussed the existing novels but also kept fans up to date on the latest news about the film adaptations and the progress of the elusive fifth novel, as well as providing venues for the publication of fan fiction and fan art. Warner Bros acquired the film rights to the series in 1999 and film adaptations of the first three novels were released in 2001, 2002 and 2003. There were also two highly publicised legal battles surrounding the series, one involving Nancy Stouffer, an author who brought an ultimately unsuccessful plagiarism lawsuit against Rowling, and the other an attempt by Warner Bros to suppress online fan content which, it claimed, constituted copyright infringement.[2] During this same period, scholarly interest in 'the Potter phenomenon' was also at its height, with the first wave of academic work on the novels rushed to publication.[3]

By the time *Goblet of Fire* was published, Rowling's own success story had reached legendary status: the single mother on benefits, who was struck by inspiration while sitting on a stalled train and wrote it all down in an Edinburgh café in her spare time before landing a contract with one of the biggest children's publishers in the country (Bloomsbury) and being skyrocketed to fame and fortune. (In fact, Rowling had the idea for Potter before she married, had children and divorced.)[4] Commentators have been eager to draw parallels between her own rags-to-riches story and the Cinderella-like arc of Harry in *Harry Potter and the Philosopher's Stone* (1997),[5] while her sudden celebrity likely influenced the critique of contemporary media and celebrity cultures that is apparent throughout the series, most prominently in the character of tabloid journalist Rita Skeeter in *Goblet of Fire*. To date, Rowling has published seven Harry Potter novels, as well as three spin-offs for UK charities,[6] a two-part sequel for the stage,[7] as well as the screenplay for *Fantastic Beasts and Where to Find Them* (2016), the first in a new series of prequel films. In 2012 she launched Pottermore, 'a digital entertainment and e-commerce company'[8] for which Rowling has written short stories and additional background material relating to the 'Potterverse'. Rowling has also written four novels for adults: *The Casual Vacancy* (2012), which was published under her own name, and *The Cuckoo's Calling* (2013), *The Silkworm* (2014) and *Career of Evil* (2015), a crime series published under the pseudonym Robert Galbraith. Rowling's authorship of *The Cuckoo's Calling* was leaked in July 2013 and the media furore that followed this revelation demonstrates the continuing cultural impact of Harry Potter, an association that will likely hang over all of Rowling's future work. It is also virtually impossible to find a review of *The Casual Vacancy* that does not compare it to the Potter novels. After the identity of 'Robert Galbraith' was revealed, sales of *The Cuckoo's Calling* skyrocketed and literary critics went back over the novel to look for evidence linking it to Potter; *The Guardian*'s Mark Lawson observed, 'reading the book now is rather like watching a Derren Brown trick on freeze-frame replay, wondering if there are clues to how the wool was being pulled'.[9]

Much of the early publicity for the Harry Potter series revolved around its supposed impact upon children's literacy. The same narrative was repeated in news outlets around the world: Rowling had turned a generation of television- and video game-obsessed children into avid readers. As Elizabeth Teare puts it, the Potter phenomenon allowed children's book publishers:

> to retake the high ground and redirect the story they tell about themselves . . . Account after account in the press features a parent describing the change in her child (most often it is a mother and son), who has learned to love reading by reading these books: 'they took my non-reader and turned him into a reader'.[10]

Harry Potter was figured as a triumph for the printed word in the electronic age and the saviour of traditional literacy. However, this narrative does not take into account the fact that the initial success of the series was largely attributable to the activities of online fan communities,[11] nor the transmedial nature of the series as a whole. It was adapted into an equally successful and influential series of films (2001–11), which themselves were responsible for kick-starting the millennial trend for film adaptations of popular young adult fantasy series, including *Twilight* (2008–12), *The Hunger*

Games (2012–15), *Divergent* (2014–16) and *The Maze Runner* (2014–). Among other innovations, the Potter films established the now-common practice of splitting the final instalment of such series into two films. The films in turn have been adapted into eleven video games: one for each of the eight films, two 'Lego Harry Potter' games and a 'Quidditch World Cup' game. In addition to the official Pottermore site, mentioned above, several of the online fan sites that were established at the height of the books' popularity remain active at the time of writing, one of which, 'MuggleNet', has run a biweekly podcast (MuggleCast) devoted to Harry Potter since 2005.[12] Contrary to earlier claims that Potter prompted a generation of children to abandon their electronics for books, the iterations of the Potterverse in digital media have in fact been instrumental in ensuring the longevity of their printed counterparts.

Harry Potter was a catalyst for what has been termed 'crossover fiction', in other words fiction that is equally popular with children and adults (although the term most commonly refers to children's books that have 'crossed over' into the adult market). The Potter novels were by no means the first children's books to be read by adults; indeed, children's fantasy 'classics' like C. S. Lewis's *The Chronicles of Narnia* (1949–54) and J. R. R. Tolkien's *The Lord of the Rings* (1954–5) have arguably come to be known as such because of their popularity with adult as well as child readers. However, the term 'crossover fiction' was born in the early twenty-first century in response to the seemingly unprecedented popularity of series like Harry Potter and Philip Pullman's *His Dark Materials* (1995–2000) among adult readers. Rachel Falconer notes:

> The question as to why children's literature became so popular amongst adults was aired periodically throughout the decade on national radio and television, in newspapers, book clubs, and specialist academic journals . . . As these articles demonstrate, crossover novels emerged into the public arena amid a cacophonous mixture of outrage, disgust, defensiveness, and conspiratorial solidarity. The hostility to cross-reading expressed by these and other journalists suggests a broader anxiety about the blurring of boundaries between child or youth culture and adult culture in the millennial years.[13]

The success of the Potter series revived questions as to whether literary merit and commercial success are mutually exclusive, and whether books written for young audiences are by definition lesser than their adult counterparts. In January 2000, the *New York Times* controversially created a 'Children's Bestseller List', in direct response to the dominance of the first three Potter novels at the top of its longstanding weekly Bestseller List.[14] This decision was controversial for two reasons. First, it seemed to confirm 'a long-standing prejudice, the notion that even a highly regarded and phenomenally successful children's book could not be measured against critically acclaimed books for adults'.[15] Second, it seemed wilfully to ignore the swathes of adult readers who were buying the books for themselves. Rowling's British publisher, Bloomsbury, was not so ignorant, releasing editions of each of the books with 'adult' covers, which featured black-and-white photography instead of colour illustration, beginning in 1998. Although the 'adult' editions accounted for a small proportion of the series' sales, their existence nevertheless demonstrates an early awareness of its crossover audience.

Since 1997, Harry Potter has become the standard by which modern children's and young adult fantasy is measured. However, the Potter novels are also noteworthy for their blending of popular genres of children's literature; critics have noted similarities with boarding school stories, mythic romances, folklore, adventure novels, and pulp and detective fiction.[16] The first three novels in particular conform structurally and thematically to many of the conventions of children's fantasy, including an orphaned, adopted or otherwise parentless child protagonist, plots based around quests and/or overcoming monsters, a wise old mentor who dies before the hero can complete his task, a superlatively evil villain whom only the protagonist is capable of destroying, the fulfilment of a prophecy, and a variety of magical objects that may be helpful or harmful. Additionally, Catherine Butler observes that 'children's fantasies now usually ensure that encounters with the fantastic precipitate significant emotional growth, if not life-defining change, in their protagonists', and that this shift coincides with the increasing dominance of sequels and series since Harry Potter.[17] Indeed, Harry ages from ten to seventeen over the course of the series, with the last three novels emphasising his emotional maturation. In this respect, these millennial novels are arguably better read as an early example of the trend for young adult dystopian literature that began as the Potter series drew to a close than as classic children's fantasy. Like later popular dystopian series such as Suzanne Collins's The Hunger Games (2008–10) and Veronica Roth's Divergent (2011–13), the last three Potter novels focus on a teenage 'Chosen One' as a rallying point for rebellion against an unjust authoritarian regime, with the protagonist's adolescent struggles mirroring the increasingly dystopian society in which he lives.

In the third chapter of Order of the Phoenix, as Harry prepares to leave home and join the eponymous secret society dedicated to fighting Voldemort and his followers, Mad-Eye Moody says to Harry, 'Come here, boy . . . I need to Disillusion you'.[18] He is referring to a spell that will make Harry invisible, but the statement also alerts the reader to the tone the remainder of the series will take: Harry, and the reader, are about to enter the world of young adult literature, in which the protagonist is increasingly isolated and frustrated, in which adult authority is challenged and adult role models dethroned, in which the institutions holding together society are discovered to be hollow and fractious, and in which the distinction between 'good' and 'bad' becomes irreparably blurred. An ambiguous moral compass prevails in the later books, as ideas that were once taken for granted are contested and Harry learns that 'the world isn't split into good people and Death Eaters',[19] as his morally ambiguous godfather Sirius Black tells him. This is exemplified by Harry's growing distrust of and resistance against the ostensibly 'good' Ministry of Magic and its representatives. The fallibility of the Ministry is apparent as early in the series as the second instalment, Harry Potter and the Chamber of Secrets (1998), when Harry's friend Hagrid is wrongfully imprisoned and his mentor, Professor Dumbledore, is temporarily suspended as headmaster. However, these clear miscarriages of justice are attributed to the machinations of a single man, Lucius Malfoy. The overall integrity of the wizard government is not questioned until Goblet of Fire, in which both Harry and the reader are treated to glimpses into the inner workings of the Ministry. Ministry officials are revealed to be corrupt (Ludo Bagman), prejudiced (Amos Diggory), officious (Percy Weasley) and tyrannical in their pursuit of justice (Barty Crouch). This paves the way for the Ministry's denial of Voldemort's return to power in *Order of the Phoenix*, its subsequent ineptitude in dealing with the threat he poses in *Harry Potter and the Half-Blood Prince* (2005) and the ease with which Voldemort gains control of the Ministry in *Harry Potter and the Deathly Hallows* (2007). In *Goblet of Fire*, Harry is introduced to the Imperius Curse, which is demonstrated to students against the Ministry's wishes. The curse, which gives a wizard 'total control' over another person,[20] becomes a metaphor for the blind obedience expected by various adult authority figures in the novels, and Harry is shown to be particularly adept at resisting it. This foreshadows his rebellion in *Order of the Phoenix* against Dolores Umbridge, the Ministry's representative at Hogwarts, and his refusal to be 'used' as the Ministry's 'mascot' in *Half-Blood Prince*.[21] The Ministry as an institution, which stands as a symbol of arbitrarily imposed adult authority, is increasingly problematised as the series goes on, and as Harry and the implied reader age. As Falconer notes:

> Because young adult fiction has sought to articulate questions about rapid transitions, identity crises and epiphanies, it is proving to be a ready medium in which to capture the felt, everyday experience of a world on the cusp of fundamental change.[22]

In the last three Potter novels, the protagonist's physical and emotional states as an adolescent on the cusp of adulthood are mirrored by the changes taking place in his world. In *Order of the Phoenix*, Harry is frustrated at being treated like a 'child' by the adults around him, their denial of his capabilities is mirrored in the Ministry of Magic's denial of Voldemort's return to power. In *Half-Blood Prince*, with Voldemort's rise now common knowledge, there is widespread fear and uncertainty in the wizarding world, mirroring Harry's own uncertainty about his future after learning of a prophecy designating him the one destined to defeat Voldemort. And in *Deathly Hallows*, Harry comes of age the day before the Ministry falls under Voldemort's control.

Order of the Phoenix opens with a fifteen-year-old Harry noticeably more emotionally volatile than in the previous instalments. In the first chapter he is described as 'restless', 'frustrated and angry', and experiencing 'hopelessness' and a continual 'trapped feeling' as he indulges in resentment of his friends and Dumbledore for withholding information from him.[23] When he finally sees his friends Ron and Hermione, he lashes out at them in the first of many angry outbursts he has over the course of the novel, which reach their peak in the penultimate chapter, when he shouts at Dumbledore that mantra of adolescent frustration, 'YOU DON'T KNOW HOW I FEEL!'[24] The opening chapters seem designed to convey the message that Harry is not a little boy anymore, but an angst-ridden teen who is tired of being infantilised and condescended to. This sets the stage for his increasing isolation and martyrdom throughout the novel, as the authorities refuse to believe him, the press seek to discredit him and the adult members of the Order insist that he is 'too young' to join the fight.[25]

By the beginning of *Half-Blood Prince*, Harry's emotions have stabilised somewhat. Instead, he spends a considerable amount of time contemplating the implications of the prophecy in relation to his own identity. Meeting his friend Neville on the train, he ponders an alternative reality where Neville is the Chosen One and Harry is free to choose his own destiny:

> Neville had no idea how close he had come to having Harry's destiny. [. . .] Had Voldemort chosen Neville, it would be Neville sitting opposite Harry bearing the lightning-shaped scar and the weight of the prophecy . . . or would it? Would Neville's mother have died to save him, as Lily had died for Harry? Surely she would . . . but what if she had been unable to stand between her son and Voldemort? Would there, then, have been no 'Chosen One' at all? An empty seat where Neville now sat and a scarless Harry who would have been kissed goodbye by his own mother, not Ron's?[26]

Existential questions of identity are of course a staple of young adult fiction, with the protagonist on the cusp of adulthood unsure of what the future holds and faced with a choice between a future that has been laid out for him by adults and one he chooses for himself. Harry's special relationship with Voldemort is a frequent source of existential anxiety for Harry. At moments of heightened emotion he is able to see what Voldemort sees and feel what he feels, a connection which threatens his sense of self. This is made explicit in the film adaptation of *Order of the Phoenix*, when he confides his fears to Sirius and asks, 'What if I'm becoming more like him? . . . What if I become bad?'[27] At the end of the film, when Voldemort tries to possess Harry, Harry sees a vision of himself with Voldemort's head, and Dumbledore urges him to fight it by reminding him, 'It isn't how you are like him, it's how you are not'.[28] Throughout the series Rowling highlights the importance of individual choice over ability, heritage or destiny in shaping identity: Harry can choose not to be like Voldemort, just as Voldemort chose to fulfil the terms of the prophecy by singling Harry out.

His parents' legacy forms a crucial part of Harry's sense of self throughout the series. Additionally, the orphaned Harry is presented with several surrogate adult role models, both positive and negative, including Dumbledore, Voldemort, Sirius Black and Professors Lupin and Snape. Over the last three novels Harry is presented with evidence that each potential male role model may not be as unequivocally good or bad as he had been led to believe, and must come to recognise them as flawed, complicated human beings in order to develop into his own person (this never happens with his mother or any of the adult women in his life). In *Order of the Phoenix* he is shown 'Snape's worst memory',[29] in which he witnesses his father and Sirius as teenagers bullying Snape. This forces him to reassess his preconceptions about all three men:

> He had been so sure his parents were wonderful people that he never had the slightest difficulty in disbelieving the aspersions Snape cast on his father's character. Hadn't people like Hagrid and Sirius *told* Harry how wonderful his father had been? (*Yeah, well, look what Sirius was like himself*, said a nagging voice inside Harry's head . . . *he was as bad, wasn't he?*).[30]

When Lupin tries to placate Harry by telling him that his father and godfather were 'only fifteen' at the time, Harry responds 'heatedly' that he is also fifteen.[31] Lupin is another apparently infallible role model who eventually reveals character flaws. In

Deathly Hallows, it becomes apparent that he is using Harry's mission as an excuse to abandon his pregnant wife. He appeals to Harry's sense of filial obligation, saying, 'I'm sure James would have wanted me to stick with you', but Harry turns this back on him, saying, 'I'm pretty sure my father would have wanted to know why you aren't sticking with your own kid, actually'.[32] This is the first instance in the series of Harry addressing an adult authority figure on equal terms and, crucially, it is also the first time he calls Lupin by his first name, 'Remus', rather than his former title, 'Professor Lupin'.

The most important dethroning of Harry's former idols occurs in *Deathly Hallows* with the revelations about Dumbledore's history via a sensationalised posthumous biography entitled *The Life and Lies of Albus Dumbledore*. Over the course of the novel, he receives conflicting information about Dumbledore's past from a variety of sources, including rumours that he was complicit in his mother's abuse of his younger sister, that he kept her under house arrest and may have been responsible for her death and, perhaps most damning, that he had once had a close relationship with the dark wizard Grindelwald and subscribed to the latter's views on subjugating Muggles '*FOR THE GREATER GOOD*'.[33] These revelations cause Harry to re-evaluate his image of Dumbledore as a benevolent mentor and to debate whether to continue on the mission Dumbledore set for him. By the time he discovers the most significant piece of information that Dumbledore has withheld from him – that he had been essentially raising Harry to sacrifice himself, Christ-like, 'for the greater good' – a now thoroughly disillusioned Harry is not at all surprised: 'Dumbledore's betrayal was almost nothing. Of course there had been a bigger plan; Harry had simply been too foolish to see it, he realised that now. He had never questioned his own assumption that Dumbledore wanted him alive.'[34] Having been brought to an understanding of the adults in his life as complex and often morally dubious people, Harry finally has the answer to the question of who he is and what he is supposed to do, and this is figured as his final step into adulthood. After Harry has 'died', Dumbledore greets him in the afterlife with, 'You wonderful boy. You brave, brave man.'[35]

Speaking of *The Life and Lies of Albus Dumbledore*, Ron's Auntie Muriel says, 'I can't wait to read it, I must remember to place an order at Flourish and Blotts!',[36] no doubt alluding to the record numbers of pre-orders placed for the later Potter novels. This points to another factor that sets the last three novels apart from their predecessors: their self-conscious relationship with fan culture, as well as their awareness of the transmedial nature of readers' experience of the 'Potterverse' across a variety of official and unofficial media. The last three novels address a knowing reader, and dispense with the unwieldy expository passages that open the previous four. In the two to three years leading up to the publication of each of the last three volumes, online fan communities were rife with speculation about what would happen in them, from small details like who the new Defence Against the Dark Arts teacher would be to bigger questions like why Voldemort had targeted Harry as a baby. Feeding into this atmosphere of speculation and prediction, Rowling and her publishers allowed details of the upcoming novels to be released at regular intervals, including their titles, cover art for both the US and UK editions, short excerpts, and hints about new characters, deaths and romantic pairings. This in turn inevitably shaped the way the books' first readers would read them. For example, because the information that a major character would die in *Order of the Phoenix* was widely publicised prior to the release, readers could be expected to anticipate this and search for clues as they read as to who it would be. Over the course of the novel Rowling gives knowing readers a series of red herrings, teasing the deaths of Dudley Dursley, Ron, Hagrid, Mr Weasley and Professor McGonagall before Sirius finally dies. Before the release of *Half-Blood Prince*, potential readers were once again given the information that a major character would die. This time, however, it is apparent early on that Dumbledore is being targeted, through a series of failed assassination attempts, which the knowing reader could be expected to mistake for another red herring. In this way, Rowling plays with her fans' expectations, made possible by her savvy navigation of fan cultures.

Like the books, the Potter films are addressed to a dual audience of knowing and unknowing viewers. For film viewers who have read the books, there is heavy foreshadowing of events to come, as well as allusions to scenes and characters which were omitted from the films. Likewise, the novels released after the film adaptations were in production are noticeably more cinematic than their predecessors in terms of their structure and imagery. The convergence of film and book in the latter half of the series points to what seems to be a basic assumption of the more recent additions to the 'Potterverse': that popular series fiction transcends distinctions between media. The play *Harry Potter and the Cursed Child* and the film *Fantastic Beasts and Where to Find Them* were both published in book form – as a rehearsal script and a screenplay, respectively. *Cursed Child* begins with a scene that Potter fans are expected to recognise, a version of the epilogue of *Deathly Hallows*, in which a now grown Harry and his friends prepare to send their children to Hogwarts. *Fantastic Beasts*, set in New York in the 1920s, contains references to the American wizard school Ilvermorny, whose history curious fans can read about on the Pottermore website along with a guide to Prohibition-era America.[37] Whatever their narrative content, it is now a given that future instalments in the 'Potterverse' will continue to reward fans' negotiation of multiple media platforms. The Harry Potter series not only created a new generation of young readers but was also a catalyst for a fundamental change in the relationship between reader and text. In this respect, Rowling's work has set the tone for how popular series fiction is produced and consumed in the twenty-first century.

NOTES

1. 'Potter Is "Fastest-Selling Book Ever"', BBC News website, 22 June 2003 <http://news.bbc.co.uk/2/hi/entertainment/3005862.stm> (last accessed 15 February 2017); 'Harry Potter Finale Sales Hit 11m', BBC News website, 23 July 2007 <http://news.bbc.co.uk/2/hi/entertainment/6912529.stm> (last accessed 15 February 2017).
2. For further discussion of these cases, see the 'Introduction' to Whited, *The Ivory Tower and Harry Potter*.
3. See for example Whited, *The Ivory Tower and Harry Potter*; Anatol, *Reading Harry Potter*; Heilman, *Critical Perspectives on Harry Potter*.
4. 'J. K. Rowling' <http://www.jkrowling.com/about> (last accessed 11 February 2017).
5. See for example Park, 'Class and Socioeconomic Identity in Harry Potter's England'.
6. *Fantastic Beasts and Where to Find Them* and *Quidditch Through the Ages* for Comic Relief in 2001 and *The Tales of Beedle the Bard* in 2007 for Lumos.

7. *Harry Potter and the Cursed Child* (2016).
8. 'Pottermore' <http://www.pottermore.com> (last accessed 13 February 2017).
9. Lawson, '*The Cuckoo's Calling* by Robert Galbraith'.
10. Teare, 'Harry Potter and the Technology of Magic', pp. 331–2.
11. Borah, 'Apprentice Wizards Welcome', p. 351.
12. 'MuggleCast' <http://mugglecast.com> (last accessed 13 February 2017).
13. Falconer, *The Crossover Novel*, pp. 2–3.
14. Smith, '*The Times* Plans a Children's Best-Seller List'.
15. Whited, *The Ivory Tower and Harry Potter*, p. 6.
16. Alton, 'Playing the Genre Game', *passim*.
17. Butler, 'Modern Children's Fantasy', p. 225.
18. Rowling, *Harry Potter and the Order of the Phoenix*, p. 53.
19. Ibid., p. 271.
20. Rowling, *Harry Potter and the Goblet of Fire*, p. 188.
21. Rowling, *Harry Potter and the Half-Blood Prince*, p. 325.
22. Falconer, 'Young Adult Fiction and the Crossover Phenomenon', p. 89.
23. Rowling, *Harry Potter and the Order of the Phoenix*, pp. 12–14.
24. Ibid., p. 727.
25. Ibid., p. 83.
26. Rowling, *Half-Blood Prince*, pp. 133–4.
27. *Harry Potter and the Order of the Phoenix* (film).
28. Ibid. This film was released within a week of *Deathly Hallows*, when the full extent of Harry's connection with Voldemort is finally revealed, and it is likely that these aspects were emphasised deliberately in anticipation of the fact that many viewers would have already read *Deathly Hallows* and recognise the foreshadowing.
29. Rowling, *Harry Potter and the Order of the Phoenix*, p. 550.
30. Ibid., pp. 575–6.
31. Ibid., p. 590.
32. Rowling, *Harry Potter and the Deathly Hallows*, p. 175.
33. Ibid., p. 291.
34. Ibid., p. 555.
35. Ibid., p. 566.
36. Ibid., p. 128.
37. See <https://www.pottermore.com/writing-by-jk-rowling/ilvermorny> and <https://www.pottermore.com/features/pottermore-guide-to-the-twenties-crime-and-punishment> (both last accessed 15 February 2017).

KEY WORKS

Harry Potter novels: *Harry Potter and the Philosopher's Stone* (1997); *Harry Potter and the Chamber of Secrets* (1998); *Harry Potter and the Prisoner of Azkaban* (1999); *Harry Potter and the Goblet of Fire* (2000); *Harry Potter and the Order of the Phoenix* (2003); *Harry Potter and the Half-Blood Prince* (2005); *Harry Potter and the Deathly Hallows* (2007). Rowling's breakout fantasy series follows the adventures of an orphan who discovers he is a wizard at age eleven. Each novel sees Harry through another year studying magic at Hogwarts School of Witchcraft and Wizardry, and typically involves Harry saving the school and/or the wizarding world from some threat. The series as a whole is concerned with Harry's coming of age as a wizard and eventual confrontation with Voldemort, an evil wizard who murdered his parents.

The Casual Vacancy (2012). Rowling's first novel for adults is a social satire revolving around the fallout following the sudden death of a controversial parish councillor in a small town figured as a microcosm for contemporary England.

Cormoran Strike novels (as Robert Galbraith): *The Cuckoo's Calling* (2013); *The Silkworm* (2014); *Career of Evil* (2015). Initially published pseudonymously, this crime series features a memorable crime-solving team in disabled ex-SIB investigator Cormoran Strike and his clever temp-turned-assistant Robin Ellacott.

Fantastic Beasts and Where to Find Them, film, directed by David Yates, Warner Bros (2016). Rowling wrote the screenplay for this Harry Potter prequel, in which magical zoologist Newt Scamander attempts to round up his magical creatures, who have escaped in New York City; meanwhile, the city is threatened by an unknown magical force.

FURTHER CRITICAL READING

Anatol (ed.), *Reading Harry Potter Again*. An updated edition of Anatol's earlier *Reading Harry Potter* (2003), with all of the essays revised to take the end of the series into account. The essays on the socio-cultural impact of the series will be of particular interest to readers of this volume.

Falconer, *The Crossover Novel*. Falconer's study of 'crossover' fiction in the late 1990s and early 2000s includes a chapter on the later Potter novels, examining their appeal to adult readers.

Heilman (ed.), *Critical Perspectives on Harry Potter*. The second edition of one of the first academic studies of the Harry Potter series includes socio-political readings, essays on genre and analyses of the early film and video game adaptations.

BIBLIOGRAPHY

Alton, Anne Hiebert, 'Playing the Genre Game: Generic Fusions of the Harry Potter Series', in Elizabeth E. Heilman (ed.), *Critical Perspectives on Harry Potter*, 2nd edition (London: Routledge, 2009), pp. 199–223.

Anatol, Giselle Liza (ed.), *Reading Harry Potter: Critical Essays* (Westport, CT: Praeger, 2003).

Anatol, Giselle Liza (ed.), *Reading Harry Potter Again: New Critical Essays* (Santa Barbara: ABC-CLIO, 2009).

Borah, Rebecca Sunderland, 'Apprentice Wizards Welcome: Fan Communities and the Culture of Harry Potter', in Whited (ed.), *The Ivory Tower and Harry Potter*, pp. 343–64.

Butler, Catherine, 'Modern Children's Fantasy', in Edward James and Farah Mendlesohn (eds), *The Cambridge Companion to Fantasy Literature* (Cambridge: Cambridge University Press, 2012), pp. 224–35.

Falconer, Rachel, *The Crossover Novel: Contemporary Children's Fiction and Its Adult Readership* (Abingdon: Routledge, 2009).

Falconer, Rachel, 'Young Adult Fiction and the Crossover Phenomenon', in David Rudd (ed.), *The Routledge Companion to Children's Literature* (Abingdon: Routledge, 2010), pp. 87–99.

Galbraith, Robert, *Career of Evil* (London: Sphere, 2015).

Galbraith, Robert, *The Cuckoo's Calling* (London: Sphere, 2013).

Galbraith, Robert, *The Silkworm* (London: Sphere, 2014).

Heilman, Elizabeth E. (ed.), *Critical Perspectives on Harry Potter*, 2nd edition (London: Routledge, 2009).

Lawson, Mark, '*The Cuckoo's Calling* by Robert Galbraith: Review', *The Guardian*, 18 July 2013 <https://www.theguardian.com/books/2013/jul/18/cuckoos-calling-robert-galbraith-jk-rowling-review> (last accessed 15 February 2017).

Park, Julia, 'Class and Socioeconomic Identity in Harry Potter's England', in Anatol (ed.), *Reading Harry Potter*, pp. 179–89.

Rowling, J. K., *Fantastic Beasts and Where to Find Them* (London: Bloomsbury, 2001).

Rowling, J. K., *Fantastic Beasts and Where to Find Them: The Official Screenplay* (London: Little, Brown, 2016).

Rowling, J. K., *Harry Potter and the Chamber of Secrets* (London: Bloomsbury, 1998).

Rowling, J. K., *Harry Potter and the Deathly Hallows* (London: Bloomsbury, 2007).

Rowling, J. K., *Harry Potter and the Goblet of Fire* (London: Bloomsbury, 2000).

Rowling, J. K., *Harry Potter and the Half-Blood Prince* (London: Bloomsbury, 2005).

Rowling, J. K., *Harry Potter and the Order of the Phoenix* (London: Bloomsbury, 2003).

Rowling, J. K., *Harry Potter and the Philosopher's Stone* (London: Bloomsbury, 1997).

Rowling, J. K., *Harry Potter and the Prisoner of Azkaban* (London: Bloomsbury, 1999).

Rowling, J. K., *Quidditch Through the Ages* (London: Bloomsbury, 2001).

Rowling, J. K., *The Casual Vacancy* (London: Sphere, 2012).

Rowling, J. K., *The Tales of Beedle the Bard* (London: Bloomsbury, 2008).

Rowling, J. K., John Tiffany and Jack Thorpe, *Harry Potter and the Cursed Child* (London: Little, Brown, 2016).

Smith, Dintia, 'The Times Plans a Children's Best-Seller List', *New York Times*, 24 June 2000 <http://www.nytimes.com/2000/06/24/books/the-times-plans-a-children-s-best-seller-list.html> (last accessed 13 February 2017).

Teare, Elizabeth, 'Harry Potter and the Technology of Magic', in Whited (ed.), *The Ivory Tower and Harry Potter*, pp. 329–42.

Whited, Lana A. (ed.), *The Ivory Tower and Harry Potter: Perspectives on a Literary Phenomenon* (Columbia: University of Missouri Press, 2002).

CHAPTER 13

Jodi Picoult: Good Grief

Clare Hayes-Brady

J odi Picoult is the American author of twenty-four novels, of which four have been turned into television movies and one into a major Hollywood feature. A Princeton graduate, she published her first novel, *Songs of the Humpback Whale*, in 1992, and the longest gap between publications since then has been two years. While she wrote six novels before 2000, the bulk of her work, and certainly her best-known writing, has all appeared in the twenty-first century. Picoult commands impressive loyalty from her fan base of mostly young women, and is someone who also attracts generally reluctant readers. Picoult has divided readers and critics. While her novels regularly appear in the *New York Times* bestseller lists and her writing inspires devotion from her readers, her target readership is not necessarily 'highbrow'. A 2009 article in *Newsweek* noted that

> a woman in rhinestone-studded glasses confesses that she never read a book more than once, until she read *My Sister's Keeper*, Picoult's 11th novel, three times. 'I'm not really a big reader,' Natalie Delpratt, a 19-year-old student says, echoing the woman in the glasses. 'But I'm addicted to Jodi Picoult'.[1]

Picoult's work may be formulaic and carefully contrived, and occasionally risks mawkishness, but the critical suspicion and even hostility expressed towards her work fails to deter her avid readers, and her sustained popularity is indisputable. Writing in the *Financial Times* in 2009, Vanessa Friedman noted that:

> [Picoult] is often dismissed by reviewers, such as Michiko Kakutani of the *New York Times*, for being too facile in her treatment of serious topics; because she has yet to be nominated for an American book award and, for 20 years, was 'ignored' by the creative writing department of Princeton University . . . because she has to fight the idea that she is too prolific to be taken seriously (she has written a book a year for the past 16 years and has the next one in the bag and one already mapped out for 2011).[2]

Picoult herself, in a 2013 *New York Times* interview with Andrew Goldman, echoes this, saying she has 'heard the word "formulaic" come up when people criticize my books'.[3]

Stephen King identified Picoult in 2009 as 'somebody who's a terrific writer who's been very, very successful', aligning her with J. K. Rowling (while remarking that *Twilight* creator Stephenie Meyer 'can't write worth a darn').[4] While some critics dismiss Picoult's work as conventional, pot-boiling, superficial and saccharine, there are elements that set her apart her from the likes of Meyer. Picoult is keenly aware of her own populist appeal, and of the fact that her popularity is of the grass-roots rather than the award-committee kind, yet she is a thoughtful, talented and consistent writer, engaging in lucid prose with complex issues of contemporary relevance. Although her work may be consumed quickly and readily, it typically engages with profound issues of love, death, ethics and honesty. One of the major attractions of her fiction lies in its invitation to discuss socially relevant, often ethically thorny questions, and its provision of serious food for thought, thereby performing a very particular cultural task.

Picoult's writing is specifically marketed to women, especially mothers, and this styling as an author of 'women's fiction' comes with a set of assumptions and value judgements that often tend to be negative. Indeed, Picoult herself has famously spoken about the relative lack of critical attention paid to her work specifically and 'women's fiction' in general by the literary establishment. In 2010, Picoult and Jennifer Weiner (another *New York Times* bestselling author) highlighted what they saw as a gender-based double standard operating in the critical appraisal of literature. In a discussion with the *Huffington Post* over the heated debate that followed this criticism, referred to as the 'Franzen Feud' or 'Franzenfreude', Weiner argued that 'it's a very old and deep-seated double standard that holds that when a man writes about family and feelings, it's literature with a capital L, but when a woman considers the same topics, it's romance, or a beach book – in short . . . unworthy of a serious critic's attention'.[5] In the same interview, Picoult rather more diplomatically suggested that the *New York Times* reviews 'overall tend to overlook popular fiction whether you're a man, woman, white, black, purple or pink . . . but it's not universal'.[6] These comments ignited a lively debate among online commentators and communities that shows no sign of abating, with fairly consistent discussion around the need for and value of such restrictive labelling. Alison Flood has noted that '"women's fiction" is still considered a subcategory'.[7] Marketing on Amazon requires a book to be categorised according to defined options, as Randy Susan Meyers points out:

> you must pick a category from a list of wide ranging possibilities that include 10 sub-genres of women's fiction and zero that are labelled men's fiction. The message is clear. Men are the norm. Women are a sub-category.[8]

In a June 2016 blog post for the *New York Times*, Weiner wrote of her belief that 'there were books that mattered and books that did not'; she worried that her successful debut novel was one of the latter, and went on to argue that internalised sexism plays a part in women writers' own tendency towards self-deprecation.[9] While this debate is clearly far from over, it is clear that the term 'women's writing' is distinctly non-monolithic, and contains multitudes of subgroups. Elaine Showalter suggests, for instance, that what she calls American 'Chick Lit' has developed along lines 'more problem based and more politically aware than its British sister'.[10] While Showalter's use of the term 'Chick Lit' may be misapplied, given that the term is historically associated with the relationship struggles of women, the tone sits well with the substantial ethical themes of Picoult's writing, which include murder, genetic engineering and the many permutations and inequalities of the American justice system. In fact, Picoult rejects the application of the term 'Chick Lit' to her work, while acknowledging its power as a marketing tool.[11] Her work might instead be further refined with reference to the category described by Sonya Andermahr as 'women's grief fiction'.[12] Andermahr focuses on 'the family melodrama as an instance of popular, "middlebrow" women's fiction, which addresses and sometimes exploits women's vulnerability as mothers and their anxieties around mothering'.[13] Andermahr's essay focuses on Kim Edwards's *The Memory Keeper's Daughter* (2005), another book-club favourite popular with Jodi Picoult's target demographic.

Certainly, Picoult's work tends to fall into this category. Not all of her writing is explicitly concerned with motherhood, but her most popular and successful novels deal explicitly with questions of family. For instance, 1998's *The Pact*, Picoult's fifth novel, garnered widespread commercial acclaim, although it was critically overlooked. It describes the fallout from the death of a teenaged girl at the hands of her boyfriend, who claims they had made a murder-suicide pact. The couple are the children of neighbouring families and best friends, and the novel focuses on the reactions of the two families, both to their own and to each other's grief. Megan Harlan's review for the *New York Times* dismissed it as 'formulaic', noting that Picoult develops an interesting premise, the various ways in which parents may unconsciously exert pressure on their children, but that '[u]nfortunately, she burrows no deeper into this promising story than the legal-page-turner formula allows'.[14]

Harlan's review represents the common critical response to Picoult:, faint praise indicating the tepid response. Like Picoult's other works, *The Pact* does not feature in scholarly journals or discussions of major literary works, but neither does it attract any real opprobrium. The worst that can be said about the book is indeed that it feels formulaic. It is worth noting, however, that Picoult's writing is smooth and readable, even relatively early in her career, and that the novel is well structured, and at times compelling. The competing viewpoints and shifting temporal streams that make up the work are deftly interwoven, and Picoult's use of epigraphs at the beginning of each section places the novel in conscious conversation with a range of intertexts, all strategies also associated with literary fiction. *The Pact* may not be considered a masterpiece by contemporary critical standards, but it is not immediately clear why this is the case. By contrast, Christos Tsiolkas's novel *The Slap* (2008), a decade later, which is similarly structured on a multivocal frame and deals, similarly, with the boundaries of family and parenthood, was acclaimed. *The Slap* resonated with some of the same readership as Picoult's novels, and like much of Picoult's work it was adapted for television, but Tsolkias's novel received a much higher degree of critical discussion and acclaim. It is also featured much more commonly in scholarly journals, while maintaining a similar marketability to the 'formulaic' work of Picoult and her peers. While it is unlikely that the difference between the two novels comes down to pure marketplace sexism, their similarities are striking, and it seems clear that it is at least partly the 'women's fiction' label which has been applied to Picoult's work that divides them. Arguably, though, it is the soupçon of moral didacticism characteristic of Picoult's melodramas, rather than the fact that Picoult is a woman, that led to this and her other novels being critically overlooked. While the novel succeeds in portraying both adolescent depression and parental oblivion at different stages, one is unavoidably conscious that the reader's emotions and sympathies are being manipulated to achieve a particular response – a common characteristic of popular fiction. It is perhaps the nakedness of this strategy that discomfits critics and scholars and distances Picoult from mainstream literary 'respectability'.

The Pact is typical of Picoult's pre-2000 works, presenting a sophisticated plot structure focused largely on the nature of family and the impossibility of knowing another person intimately or accurately. More importantly, though, the novel perpetuates a thread that marks Picoult's work to date, and is still a centrepiece to her writing: the focus on storytelling and self-making. The Pact is subtitled A Love Story and, like other Picoult works, is explicitly and persistently concerned with the stories we construct for and about ourselves. In this respect, the multivocality that has become a Picoult hallmark reflects a deep meta-narrative engagement with the concepts of self-building and witnessing that are foundational to American forms of identity. Stretching from 1992's Songs of the Humpback Whale right through to 2016's Small Great Things (which entered the New York Times bestseller list at number 3), Picoult relies on the disjunctions between individual accounts to enrich and deepen her narratives, exploiting memory and perception to create the tensions upon which the stories rest. Indeed, 2013's The Storyteller addresses memory, heritage and forgiveness in the context of the Holocaust, and is explicitly concerned with the ways in which we represent ourselves, and with the redemptive power of storytelling. In this novel, a shy and mildly disfigured Jewish baker named Sage befriends an elderly German man named Josef, who later claims to be a former Nazi prison guard named Reiner Hartman, and who seeks from her both absolution and punishment. The novel is structured around a twin set of stories, his recollections to her and a fictional but heavily symbolised account of a vampire that is unattributed until late in the narrative. As is evident here, Picoult's writing, while it takes aim at hot-button issues often loosely based on true events, is essentially concerned not with what happens, but with how we *represent* what happens.

In The Pact, the movement between voices and times allows Picoult to drip-feed the major moments of narrative significance to the reader, while contextualising these developments amidst moments of crisis, major and minor, in the personal histories of the characters. The three sections in The Pact are entitled 'The Boy Next Door', 'The Girl Next Door' and 'The Truth', positioning Chris and Emily, and their families, immediately in a relationship of contingency; they exist and act relative to one another, rather than in their own right only. The first two sections open with quotations (Christopher Marlowe and Thomas Otway, followed by George Byron and Daniel Webster), moving from the topics of love and suffering in Chris's case to lies and confession in Emily's. The third section's prefatory quotations are about love (Khalil Gibran) and truth (Alfred Tennyson), linking the two previous sections and aligning the very idea of love with dishonesty. *The Pact* has its 'present day' in the aftermath of Emily's death, and is bookended by Chris's trial for her murder. The novel's subtitle is therefore telling: love is connected with story in a range of ways, from the traditional concept of a love story, particularly a tragic one, which might be considered the primary narrative layer of *The Pact*, to the direct connection of love with fiction or deceit, and finally also to the practice of self-narration and identity construction. Chris's eventual acquittal effectively silences Emily at several levels: structurally, by situating her death prior to the novel's opening; authorially, by denying her a direct first-person narration segment in the narrative (her diary is represented in other narrative voices); and socially, by concluding with Chris's acquittal, which reflects the witnessing and ratification of Chris's self-narrative, and by extension his memory of Emily's self-narrative. *The Pact*, then, consolidates Picoult's abiding interest in narrative, memory and testimony.

The novel for which Picoult is probably best known is *My Sister's Keeper* (2004), which further develops themes that dominated *The Pact*, chiefly family, memory and self-determination. *My Sister's Keeper* is the only Picoult novel to date that has been adapted into a widely released feature film, although several others, including *The Pact*, have been turned into television movies. The novel takes as its central ethical question the position of a so-called 'saviour sibling', a child conceived with the assistance of genetic design in order to donate umbilical cord blood to her sister, who suffers from an acute form of cancer. The Fitzgerald family conceive their youngest daughter Anna to be a specific genetic match and as the condition of their older daughter, Kate, continues to decline, Anna's bone marrow and blood are also used in her treatment. The novel opens with Anna's decision to sue her parents for medical emancipation to avoid donating a kidney to her sister, who is now in renal failure and in danger of death. Like *The Pact*, the novel dramatises a range of different voices. Interestingly, in this case, the primary silenced voice is not Anna's, but that of Kate, the sister in need of a kidney. Unlike *The Pact*'s Emily, though, Kate claims a voice in the end; she narrates the final chapter and epilogue directly. The novel shares a number of features with *The Pact*, including the use of literary epigraphs at the beginning of each section (this time beginning with American poets, including Carl Sandburg and Edna St Vincent Millay, and moving towards Shakespeare and Milton as the plot becomes more dramatic). Also, like *The Pact*, it is structured by the court case that will decide the family's fate.

The ethical question at the heart of *My Sister's Keeper* is that of breeding children for medical purposes, thereby posing related questions about cloning and bodily autonomy. Rather than engaging in abstract ethical discussion of this issue, the novel focuses on an ostentatiously ordinary family: a fire-fighter father, a stay-at-home mother whose past as a lawyer allows her to be simultaneously victim, perpetrator and prosecutor, and three children who have relatively normal relationships, all magnified and refracted through Kate's medical condition, upon which every element of their lives is focused. Consequently, the couple's eldest son is a delinquent, their marriage is under severe strain and both sisters are wholly subject to the medical demands placed on their bodies. Kate's imminent death hangs over the family, lending urgency and pathos to the otherwise ordinary developments of her adolescence – makeup, boyfriends, friendships and so forth. Like many of Picoult's works, *My Sister's Keeper* broaches a complex abstract question in a resolutely relatable setting, one of the keys to her continued success. This question at heart revolves, again, around language, power and choice. Anna sues for the right to make her own medical decisions, but the language used around her surgical operations is particularly interesting. Her involvement in her sister's treatment is described routinely as a form of 'donation', including by Anna herself, though the novel explores how these 'donations' are at best coerced and at worst forced.

Similar questions of language and choice arise in a much more critically successful book published a year later. A dystopian novel dealing with cloning, Kazuo Ishiguro's *Never Let Me Go* (2005) invites a post-humanist reading of British welfare and medical systems, as well as the ethics of cultivating the supply of healthy donor organs in living hosts who are not regarded as human. In this respect, the novel obviously differs from Picoult's more obviously realist family drama, but the central questions of both novels are fundamentally very similar. Like Anna, the characters in Ishiguro's novel are referred to as 'donors', the term suggesting an entirely illusory element of choice or agency in their participation in medical procedures. The style of the two novels is, however, markedly different, with Ishiguro adopting a tone of metaphysical observation (Ishiguro said that the novel originated as a thought experiment about radically curtailed lifespan, rather than an investigation into the nature and meaning of humanity) that contrasts sharply with Picoult's domestic drama, although both novels make use of first-person narrative throughout (Ishiguro uses a single narrative viewpoint while Picoult opts for her trademark polyphony). *Never Let Me Go*, which was also turned into a successful feature film and shortlisted for the Booker prize in the year of its publication, was met with ecstatic reviews, and praised for its sensitive, personalised treatment of a difficult issue. In the *New York Times* Sarah Kerr highlighted the 'feat of imaginative sympathy' that distinguished his creation of the novel's narrator, Kathy, although Kerr also acknowledged that the novel 'feels a bit too distant to move us to outright heartbreak'.[15] By contrast, almost precisely a year previously, *My Sister's Keeper*, despite dealing with a similar ethical quagmire, merited mention only in the paper's 'Books in Brief' section, in a short review with a decidedly scornful tone, where the novel was described using terms such as 'preposterous', 'limp cliché' and 'soap opera'.[16] Thematic and structural similarities notwithstanding, it is clear that Picoult's fiction does not command the same consideration as Ishiguro's. This is not to suggest that *My Sister's Keeper* should be read as a precursor or a peer to *Never Let Me Go*; they are decidedly different novels in both aim and execution, but their proximity in publication date as well as their shared conceit underscore the gulf between the very different critical receptions the authors were granted in the same publication. Once again, it is hard to avoid the sense that the 'women's fiction' label, especially when contrasted in this instance with Ishiguro's immense critical reputation as an acclaimed writer of 'literary' fiction, is a double-edged sword for Picoult: on the one hand, endearing her to the overwhelmingly female army of loyal book-buyers who make up her fan base, while at the same time excluding her from the level of critical consideration given to works of literary fiction dealing with broadly the same themes and preoccupations.

My *Sister's Keeper* is Picoult's best-known work to date, a mid-career peak that incorporates the elements that most endear her to readers. While Anna is the undoubted protagonist of the novel, by presenting multiple competing perspectives Picoult forces the reader to acknowledge the complexity and murkiness of the novel's central ethical issue. Anna is established as a resourceful and sympathetic protagonist, forcing a cathexis on the part of the reader that is then challenged by the problematic central plot device.[17] This contrived investment of emotional energy in a character, characteristic of Picoult's writing in general, can at times be a little clumsy. For example, in My *Sister's Keeper* we hear from Anna that her identity is so bound up in her sister's illness as to be inextricable, and that she fears oblivion or obscurity if her sister should die, which leads to the rather jarring pronouncement that 'if your parents have you for a reason, then that reason better exist. Because once it's gone, so are you.'[18] This judgement does not accord with Anna's treatment by her parents (particularly her father), who love her as an independent child rather than simply as a donor, but it speaks to Anna's fear and confusion over her role and power, drawing the reader into a sympathetic reading of her subsequent actions. Indeed, Michelle Jarman highlights the long cultural history of the idea of the child whose wellbeing is secondary to that of a disabled sibling, which 'becomes a driving reality within Picoult's fictional landscape [and] writes a script for mother-blame through a dysfunctional family that traces much of its imbalance back to Sara [the mother]'.[19] In this respect, the reader's sympathetic connection with Anna is founded on a problematic narrative trope: 'although Picoult provides ample justification for Sara's single-minded devotion to Kate', this makes Sara creates a somewhat implausible villain. For example, she says at one point (when her husband gives Anna a locket as a reward for yet another invasive medical procedure) that 'the thought of rewarding someone for their suffering, frankly, never entered my mind. We've all been doing it for so long.'[20] Sara's steamrolling dismissal of Anna's role in Kate's treatment, alongside her failure properly to parent her eldest son (a teenage arsonist whose self-aware acting out is too blatant to be believable) and her willingness not only to oppose Anna's request for emancipation but (implausibly) to act as her own attorney, make her quite unsympathetic, despite her position as the mother of a terminally ill child. Arguably, Picoult rather overcompensates here in order to secure the reader's investment in Anna.

My *Sister's Keeper* opens with a brief, unattributed prologue, after which we are immediately presented with Anna's voice, which sympathetically highlights both her youth and the conflict between her desire to make her own choices and her wish to help her sister. In the book's second chapter, a self-consciously 'unsympathetic' (which is to say, slightly but unconvincingly gruff) male character, Campbell, the lawyer who will take on Anna's case on a pro bono basis, describes his meeting with her in tones of reluctant but grudging admiration. The juxtaposition of Campbell's affected surliness with Anna's passionate confusion highlights the relative innocence of Anna's desire for self-government. Jarman notes that many of Picoult's novels rely on this 'pairing of sentimentalism and courtroom drama' that 'speaks to the tensions and connections between public life and domestic values' lying at the heart of her writing.[21] Another hallmark of Picoult's domestico-legal novels is the (usually courtroom-based) plot reversal. Here, Anna, who has resisted taking the stand, reveals that it was Kate who asked her to press the case for parental emancipation in the first place, as she did not want the transplant, echoing Chris's insistence in *The Pact* that Emily's death was at her own request.

Picoult's continued reliance on this formula – the bewildered innocent insisting that they have acted out of love, the hard-nosed but secretly sympathetic investigator and the dramatic revelation of a hitherto concealed truth – can lead the reader to feel simultaneously sympathetic to and resentful of the protagonist (and the author) for the transparency of the strategy, though, as Jarman notes, this is a feature of the courtroom drama, which 'demands a surprising secret to fuel the plot twist at the end of the story'.[22] The risk of irritation at the open manipulation of our sympathies aside, however, there is no denying that Picoult's formula is highly effective. Having encouraged (or coerced) the reader's cathexis with the protagonist, Picoult problematises the protagonist's position at ethical, moral and emotional levels, asking questions about legal responsibility, justice, memory and power. The formula then relies on one further crisis point, to allow for the kind of cathartic ending for which Picoult is famous. The major revelation reconfigures the narrative landscape so that the reader is again faced with an uncertain moral and ethical position, but that uncertainty is usually sublimated rather than resolved, often either by a death, or by the ratification of the protagonist's actions by an outside force, for instance a jury, as in *The Pact*. In *My Sister's Keeper*, the twist is engineered at the beginning of the narrative: we are conditioned by the prologue and the progression of the plot to expect Kate's death. Instead, Anna, having won her legal freedom (the outcome into which the reader's complex cathexis has been directed), is killed in a car accident, thus allowing Kate to receive her kidney after all, and live to fight another day. This ending, contrived and evasive though some have found it, allows us to experience the simultaneous catharsis of both Anna's freedom and her sister's salvation, underscored by the pathos of Anna's unexpected death. The novel's moral didacticism is heavily to the fore here: we generally cannot know either the day or the hour of a living person's death, and by spending all their lives focused on Kate's impending demise the Fitzgeralds have lost the opportunity to develop a healthy relationship with the daughter they will actually lose.

Picoult shows every sign of sticking to her basic narrative blueprint. In *The Storyteller*, Sage discovers the full truth about her elderly German customer, that he was a Nazi prison guard who sought her out to make amends for the suffering he had caused her grandmother, who is still alive. Then she and the hard-nosed FBI agent she is falling in love with arrange that he will confess his crimes. The double plot twist comes when Sage agrees to kill 'Josef' (whom she believes to be cruel concentration camp guard Reiner Hartman), as he has requested, only to realise that the old man is in fact Reiner/Josef's less brutal brother Franz, who has been impersonating Reiner-masquerading-as-Josef all along. *The Storyteller*'s moral messages are fairly heavy-handed: people are not what they seem, we ought not to judge those we do not know, and holding on to grief leads to a life of concealment. Indeed, Picoult's endings often veer into domestic melodrama, and their cathartic power can seem as forced as the cathexes that set them up. Nevertheless, her continued commercial success and obvious favour with readers again positions Picoult as a writer who shrewdly adheres to a successful formula. Her latest novel, 2016's *Small Great Things*, is a timely engagement with racial tension in the US, and has been well received, with the *Washington Post* calling it 'the most important novel Jodi Picoult has ever written'.[23] Like her previous works, it deftly engages with a thorny and divisive issue, and takes on complex current affairs with a light touch. However, the political and social immediacy of racial tension in the contemporary US may in future set this novel apart and see Picoult recognised as a more serious chronicler of her time. While she may perhaps be gaining a tentative foothold in the realms of 'literary' fiction rather than being categorised as a writer of 'women's fiction' only, on balance it seems more probable that Picoult's books will continue to garner scant critical attention and healthy sales figures. It is hard to imagine that the author will be any more bothered by this in the future than she seems now. As Picoult comments, 'I have learned to trust that the marketing departments know what they're doing. When 60 percent of book buyers are women, you can't fault a publisher for targeting that audience.'[24]

She remains a cultural force to be reckoned with; while her work may sometimes appear formula-driven and at times, for some readers and reviewers, overly manipulative, it is often incisive and always smoothly executed, balancing the 'combination of moral dilemma and character development'[25] to fulfil an obvious cultural need. While the literary marketplace adjusts to digitisation, both of material and of marketing, the purchasing power and cultural heft of consumers who read 'women's fiction' simultaneously continues to grow, and the market share of 'women's fiction' grows across platforms. Though her work may seem problematically formulaic to certain reviewers, Picoult is a standout talent who draws on a long literary heritage and engages with topics of keen contemporary relevance. She is a writer of twenty-first-century popular fiction whom we dismiss at our peril.

NOTES

1. Yabroff, 'Does Jodi Picoult Hurt Literature?'.
2. Friedman, 'Lunch with the FT: Jodi Picoult'.
3. Goldman, 'Interview with Jodi Picoult'.
4. Flood, 'Twilight Author Stephenie Meyer "Can't Write Worth a Darn", Says Stephen King'.
5. See Pinter, 'Jodi Picoult and Jennifer Weiner Speak Out On Franzen Feud'.
6. Ibid.
7. Flood, 'Women's Fiction Is a Sign of a Sexist Book Industry'.
8. Meyers, '"Women's Fiction?"'.
9. Weiner, 'The Snobs and Me'.
10. Showalter, *A Jury Of Her Peers*, p. 526.
11. Goldman, 'Interview with Jodi Picoult'.
12. Andermahr, 'Mourning, Melancholia and Melodrama in Contemporary Women's Grief Fiction'.
13. Ibid., p. 27.
14. Harlan, 'Review of *The Pact*'.
15. Kerr, '*Never Let Me Go*'.
16. Blum, 'Books in Brief: Fiction and Poetry'.
17. The term 'cathexis' here is meant in its simplest form, without the libidinal implications of Freudian psychoanalysis. The term should be taken to refer simply to the investment of energy and/or sympathy in a person or object.

18. Picoult, My Sister's Keeper, p. 8.
19. Jarman, 'Disability on Trial', p. 218.
20. Picoult, My Sister's Keeper, p. 231.
21. Jarman, 'Disability on Trial', p. 211.
22. Ibid., p. 210.
23. Brown, '"Small Great Things" Is the Most Important Novel Jodi Picoult Has Ever Written'.
24. Goldman, 'Interview with Jodi Picoult'.
25. Hart, Walker and Gregg, 'Communication Ethics and My Sister's Keeper', p. 123.

KEY WORKS

The Pact (1998). Picoult's fifth novel deals with a teenage girl's death at the hands of her boyfriend and the ramifications of the event for the two closely connected families. The first of Picoult's novels to be adapted as a television movie.

My Sister's Keeper (2004). Picoult's breakout success and best-known work, adapted as a successful Hollywood movie. It addresses the issue of medical consent and the idea of 'designer babies'. Anna Fitzgerald has been conceived to help her older sister Kate, who suffers from leukaemia. Kate's legal case taken out her against her parents divides the family and reckons with the gap between technology and ethical decision making.

The Storyteller (2013). While set in the present in the US, this novel emerges from World War II and eastern European folk mythology. Like many of Picoult's novels, it is directly concerned with narrative, with its main impetus coming from the stories told by an elderly German to the novel's lonely protagonist, and from the story he recalls within the story. Questions of self-revelation, deceit, atonement and historiography occupy the narrative.

Small Great Things (2016). Deals with race in the contemporary US. Ruth is a black labour and delivery nurse who regards herself as colour-blind and unaffected by racism. When she is blamed for the death of a baby she was forbidden to care for due to the racism of a patient, it forces her, and her white lawyer, to come to grips with their unacknowledged struggles with race. Mirrors Picoult's earlier works in its multivocal narrative and its use of legal and courtroom settings to interrogate current social and political issues.

FURTHER CRITICAL READING

Since Picoult's work has not yet received major critical attention, much of the suggested reading consists of articles or books concerned with women's writing more generally.

Andermahr, 'Mourning, Melancholia and Melodrama in Contemporary Women's Grief Fiction'.
Apostoli, Laura, *Exploring the Boundaries: Jodi Picoult's Literary Investigations into Bioethics and Biolaw* (Rome: Carocci editori, 2014).
Homestead, 'Did a Woman Write "The Great American Novel"?'
Jarman, 'Disability on Trial'.
Miller, 'Why Can't a Woman Write the Great American Novel?'
Prose, 'Scent of a Woman's Ink'.
Showalter, *A Jury of Her Peers*.

BIBLIOGRAPHY

Andermahr, Sonya, 'Mourning, Melancholia and Melodrama in Contemporary Women's Grief Fiction: Kim Edwards's *The Memory Keeper's Daughter*', *Hecate*, 37:1 (2011), pp. 27–45.
Blum, Meredith, 'Books in Brief: Fiction and Poetry', *New York Times*, 18 April 2004.

Brown, Eleanor, '"Small Great Things" Is the Most Important Novel Jodi Picoult Has Ever Written', *Washington Post*, 13 October 2016 <https://www.washingtonpost.com/entertainment/books/small-great-things-is-the-most-important-novel-jodi-picoult-has-ever-written/2016/10/12/f18eofdc-7eb4-11e6-8d13-d7c704ef9fd9_story.html> (last accessed 30 March 2017).

Flood, Alison, 'Women's Fiction Is a Sign of a Sexist Book Industry', *The Guardian*, 16 May 2014 <http://www.theguardian.com/books/booksblog/2014/may/16/women-fiction-sign-sexist-book-industry > (last accessed 30 March 2017).

Flood, Alison, 'Twilight Author Stephenie Meyer "Can't Write Worth a Darn", Says Stephen King', *The Guardian*, 5 February 2009 <https://www.theguardian.com/books/2009/feb/05/stephenking-fiction> (last accessed 19 April 2017).

Friedman, Vanessa, 'Lunch with the FT: Jodi Picoult', *Financial Times*, 2 May 2009, https://www.ft.com/content/68c84c5e-35dc-11de-a997-00144feabdco (last accessed 30 March 2017).

Goldman, Andrew, 'Interview with Jodi Picoult', *New York Times Magazine*, 8 February 2013 <http://www.nytimes.com/2013/02/10/magazine/jodi-picoult-does-not-write-chick-lit.html> (last accessed 30 March 2017).

Harlan, Megan, 'Review of *The Pact*', *New York Times*, 2 August 1998, BR16.

Hart, Joy L., Kandi L. Walker and Jennifer L. Gregg, 'Communication Ethics and *My Sister's Keeper*', *Communication Teacher*, 21:4 (2007), pp. 123–7.

Homestead, Melissa J., 'Did a Woman Write "The Great American Novel"? Judging Women's Fiction in the Nineteenth Century and Today', *Tulsa Studies in Women's Literature*, 29:2 (fall 2010), pp. 447–57.

Ishiguro, Kazuo, *Never Let Me Go* (2005; London: Faber and Faber, 2006).

Jarman, Michelle, 'Disability on Trial: Complex Realities Staged for Courtroom Drama: The Case of Jodi Picoult', *Journal of Literary and Cultural Disability Studies*, 6:2 (2012), pp. 209–25.

Kerr, Sarah, '*Never Let Me Go*: When They Were Orphans', *New York Times*, 17 April 2005, BR.

Meyers, Randy Susan, '"Women's Fiction?" "Men's Fiction?" "Human Fiction?" What Does It Mean?', *Huffpost*, The Blog, 13 July 2014 <http://www.huffingtonpost.com/randy-susan-meyers/post_7494_b_5263728.html?&> (last accessed 30 March 2017).

Miller, Laura, 'Why Can't a Woman Write the Great American Novel?', *Salon*, 24 February 2009 <http://www.salon.com/2009/02/24/elaine_showalter> (last accessed 30 March 2017).

Picoult, Jodi., *My Sister's Keeper* (2004; London: Hodder and Stoughton, 2013).

Picoult, Jodi., *The Pact* (1998; London: Hodder and Stoughton, 2013).

Picoult, Jodi, *The Storyteller* (2013; London: Hodder and Stoughton, 2013).

Pinter, Jason, 'Jodi Picoult and Jennifer Weiner Speak Out On Franzen Feud: HuffPost Exclusive', *Huffpost*, The Blog, 25 May 2011 <http://www.blogher.com/frame.php?url=http%3A%2F%2Fwww.huffingtonpost.com%2Fjason-pinter%2Fjodi-picoult-jennifer-weiner-franzen_b_693143.html&_back=http%3A%2F%2Fwww.blogher.com%2Fwriting-about-womens-writing-popular-fiction-and-franzenfreude> (last accessed 30 March 2017).

Prose, Francine, 'Scent of a Woman's Ink', *Harper's Magazine*, June 1998 <http://harpers.org/archive/1998/06/scent-of-a-womans-ink> (last accessed 30 March 2017).

Showalter, Elaine, *A Jury of Her Peers* (London: Virago Press, 2009).

Tsiolkas, Christos, *The Slap* (2008; London: Penguin Books, 2010).

Weiner, Jennifer, 'The Snobs and Me', *New York Times*, 10 June 2016 <http://www.nytimes.com/2016/06/11/opinion/the-snobs-and-me.html> (last accessed 30 March 2017).

Yabroff, Jenni, 'Does Jodi Picoult Hurt Literature?', *Newsweek*, 11 April 2009 http://europe.newsweek.com/does-jodi-picoult-hurt-literature-77445?rm=eu (last accessed 30 March 2017).

CHAPTER 14

'We Will Have a Happy Marriage If It Kills Him': Gillian Flynn and the Rise of Domestic Noir

Bernice M. Murphy

The summer of 2012 was the summer of *Gone Girl*. Published in June, the novel had by December sold 1.8 million copies. By the end of 2013, sales had hit six million and the novel was well into its fortieth printing.[1] While the numbers were impressive, the novel's wider cultural impact was just as striking. *Gone Girl* quickly became a major cultural talking point on both sides of the Atlantic. Gillian Flynn's sardonic depiction of the spite that festers beneath the façade of a seemingly idyllic marriage had hit the big time.[2] Indeed, it soon became clear that her third novel was garnering a level of critical interest rarely granted to works of popular fiction.[3] Some reviewers were quick to claim that this was no 'ordinary' genre novel. Outlining the novel's basic premise, Janet Maslin of the *New York Times* cautioned: 'Perhaps these sound like standard-issue crime story machinations. They're not. They're only the opening moves for the game Ms. Flynn has in mind, which is a two-sided contest in which Nick and Amy tell contrasting stories.'[4] She concluded by declaring, '"Gone Girl" is Ms. Flynn's dazzling breakthrough'.[5]

Maslin was not alone in praising Flynn. The novel's unusually broad reach was confirmed in 2013 when it appeared on the long list for one of the UK's most prestigious literary awards, the Women's Prize for Fiction (now known as the Baileys Women's Prize for Fiction). Though Flynn didn't make the shortlist, the fact that a thriller writer was in the running at all was considered newsworthy. Much of *Gone Girl*'s commercial success and critical prominence is related to Flynn's creation of the most controversial female character in twenty-first-century popular fiction so far. In an audacious mid-narrative twist, Amy Elliott Dunne – the 'Gone Girl' of the title – reveals herself to be a scheming, rage-suffused manipulator. The sweet-natured woman in peril whose fraught diary entries constituted much of the first half of the novel – 'Diary Amy' – is a fabrication crafted by 'Actual Amy' so as to create a cunning simulacrum of the news media's 'ideal' victim – white, middle class, attractive and pregnant.[6]

While Flynn and her publishers had been hoping to build upon the solid sales and positive critical responses garnered by her previous books, *Sharp Objects* (2006) and *Dark Places* (2009), no one expected her slippery new novel to capture the public imagination in this way.[7] *Gone Girl* was, as Flynn later put it, 'lightning in a bottle'.[8] Having until recently been an entertainment journalist, she was now, unexpectedly, a literary celebrity herself. Born in 1971, Flynn is the daughter of two community college professors. She has often credited her film professor father with introducing her to horror movies, with *Psycho* (1960) apparently a childhood favourite.[9] After studying at the University of Kansas, she undertook a Masters in journalism at Northwestern University, and eventually landed a job as a film and TV critic at *Entertainment Weekly*. It is little wonder, then, that her work has consistently displayed an insider's understanding of (and suspicion towards) the media.[10] When she was made redundant from *EW*, Flynn decided to write full time and began work on *Gone Girl*.[11]

Flynn was raised in Kansas City, Missouri, and the Midwestern setting of her novels lends them a distinctive sense of place. As Paul Harris has observed of *Gone Girl*'s locale:

> This is the same region that gave us Truman Capote's exploration of random, empty Kansas murders in his masterful *In Cold Blood*. This is a place founded on the old grass prairies, whose Native American inhabitants were butchered and displaced, and whose soil was ripped up. The Midwest is the Indian Creek Massacre and the 'dust bowl' as much as it is *Little House on the Prairie*.[12]

Flynn herself has stated of the region: 'To me it's great, underexploited literary terrain that's fun to roam around in. It has a strangely exotic feel to it because it's so underwritten and underused in literature.'[13]

Flynn's childhood was, by her own account, a perfectly happy one. However, as she later recounted, she was 'not a nice little girl'. When detailing various youthful indiscretions in an online piece, she segued into a commentary that gets to the heart of her remarkably consistent thematic concerns:

> Men speak fondly of these bursts of childhood aggression, their disastrous immature sexuality. They have a vocabulary for sex and violence that women just don't . . . and we still don't discuss our own violence. We devour the news about Susan Smyth or Andrea Yates – women who drowned their own children – but we demand these stories be rendered palatable. We want somber asides on postpartum depression or a story about the Man Who Made Her Do It. But there's an ignored resonance. I think women like to read about murderous mothers and lost little girls because it's our only mainstream outlet to even begin discussing female violence on a personal level. Female violence is a specific brand of ferocity. It's invasive . . . and the mental violence is positively gory.[14]

Flynn's fiction has so far has revolved around this conviction that women have the same right to be portrayed as unsympathetic, morally complex and unabashedly villainous characters as their male counterparts.[15] Amy in *Gone Girl* arguably even represents a highly meta twenty-first-century take on the traditional '*femme fatale* archetype.[16] When asked if this recurrent depiction of 'women who reliably outdo the men in their capacity for moral depravity' is compatible with her self-proclaimed feminism, Flynn responded:

> Is it really only girl power, and you-go-girl, and empower yourself, and be the best you can be? For me, it's also the ability to have women who are bad characters . . . the one thing that really frustrates me is this idea that women are innately good, innately nurturing. In literature, they can be dismissably [sic] bad – trampy, vampy, bitchy types – but there's still a big pushback against the idea that women can be just pragmatically evil, bad and selfish.[17]

All three of Flynn's novels to date (as well as her 2015 novella *The Grownup*, which was originally anthologised in 2014 as a short story under the title 'What Do You Do?') focus upon the difference between the façade unhappy women present to the outside world and the murkiest aspects of their inner selves. In the years since *Gone Girl*'s publication, Flynn's work has frequently been credited with helping to establish one of the hottest new categories in publishing: 'Domestic Noir'. While the term 'Domestic Noir' had previously been used to refer to female-centric Noir movies of the 1940s and 1950s,[18] in 2013 British author Julia Crouch used it to describe a new wave of female-written and female-focused thrillers:

> In a nutshell, Domestic Noir takes place primarily in homes and workplaces, concerns itself largely (but not exclusively) with the female experience, is based around relationships and takes a broadly feminist view that the domestic sphere is a challenging and sometimes dangerous prospect for its inhabitants.[19]

The term was soon being applied to novels written by a wide range of authors from both sides of the Atlantic, among them the likes of Megan Abbott, Laura Lippman, S. J. Watson, A. S. A. Harrison, Julia Heaberlin and Paula Hawkins; Hawkins' novel *The Girl on the Train* was one of the biggest sellers of 2015 and, like *Gone Girl*, was soon adapted for the screen.

Although female-focused psychological suspense thrillers remain one of the hottest tickets in contemporary publishing, they are certainly not a new phenomenon. Editor Sarah Weinman has persuasively argued that the work of Flynn and others currently writing in this vein was anticipated by the writing of a 'misplaced generation' of female crime writers publishing between the 1940s and the mid-1970s.[20] The case has also been made that many much older novels could also retrospectively be described as 'Domestic Noir', among them the likes of Charlotte Brontë's *Jane Eyre* (1847)[21] and Daphne du Maurier's *Rebecca* (1938).[22] Whatever one's take on the specific evolution and composition of the sub-genre, it is clear that in Flynn's work, as in other novels categorised in this way by readers and publishers, it is always the most intimate relationships, be they marital, romantic or familial, that represent the greatest source of threat.

This is certainly the case in Flynn's debut, *Sharp Objects*. The protagonist, damaged thirty-something Camille Preaker, is an underperforming and hard-drinking crime reporter. Following the murder of one young girl and the disappearance of another in her unlamented hometown, Wind Gap, Missouri, Camille is reluctantly sent back there on assignment. As the novel begins, Camille is working on a news story about a child neglect case that is, for her, revealingly, banal, 'a limp sort of evil'.[23] From the beginning then, the potential toxicity of family relationships – and in particular of the mother–child relationship – is highlighted. We are also made aware that it is Camille's job, as a member of the media, to write up these cases for public consumption. Although Camille is supposed to possess a degree of professional detachment, she cannot help but fall back into the well-worn grooves of her dysfunctional upbringing. When the mutilated body of the missing girl is found, it becomes clear to Camille that the death was caused by someone close to the victim. The painful demise of Camille's sister Marian many years before also hangs over the narrative. Although Marian is said to have died of natural causes, Camille is haunted by this tragic loss.

Camille's strained relationship with her mother, Adora, a glamorous forty-something described as looking like 'a girl's very best doll, the kind you don't play with', lies at the dark heart of the novel.[24] As the owner of the town hog-processing plant, Adora is the biggest employer in the locality. She gave birth to Camille when she was a teenager and their relationship has always been difficult. Indeed, in an early clue as to the horrific nature of Adora's twisted proclivities, her maternal instincts seem to kick in only when her children are sick. Camille is well aware that her parent's theatrical displays of empathy are inherently self-centred. 'Every tragedy that happens in the world happens to my mother, and this more than anything about her turns my stomach.'[25]

Ultimately, this detail becomes a vital clue towards understanding Camille's troubled past and unhappy present. She eventually realises that Adora slowly murdered sweet-natured, biddable Marian, because she revelled in the self-imposed martyrdom of 'caring' for the daughter she had made unwell in the first place. It is no wonder then that, for Camille, psychological distress must be painfully inscribed on the physical self. She has engaged in compulsive self-harming since early adolescence, carving words of totemic personal significance into her own flesh. Her scars, hidden beneath long sleeves and high necklines, represent an early example of the recurrent idea that pretty façades always conceal dark secrets in Flynn.

Camille is also the first example of a staple Flynn character type: the profoundly unhappy protagonist whose contempt for others (often other women) is surpassed only by her self-loathing. This undercurrent of compulsive bitchiness becomes particularly acute once Camille reluctantly reconnects with the vapid girls she went to high school with, all of whom are now gossipy, pill-popping wives and mothers. Adora has her own pack of wine-guzzling, well-to-do frenemies. The fact that the women of Wind Gap are perpetually trapped in 'Mean Girl' personas established decades before is underlined by the other key relationship in the novel, that between Camille and her much younger half-sister Amma. Thirteen-year-old Amma is the ringleader of a group of louche, hyper-sexualised young girls. As the sisters get to know one another better, Camille is shocked yet fascinated by her sibling's capacity for deception and tendency to make unsettling statements, such as 'When you die, you become perfect'.[26] The best Camille can ultimately do for Amma (who, it ultimately transpires, has been brutally murdering the young rivals for her mother's toxic affections), is provide legal accountability as well as a degree of understanding born of the fact that they were both raised in the same noxious environment. As Camille knows only too well, 'A child weaned on poison considers harm a comfort'.[27] Tellingly, Camille's only genuine sources of emotional support are her editor, Curry, and his wife, Eileen, a kindly older couple, who give her the love and emotional support her blood relations could never provide. Family ties in Flynn are always more likely to strangle than support.

In Flynn's second novel, *Dark Places*, horrific crimes once more take place in a small-town setting. Libby Day is the physically and emotionally disfigured survivor of the brutal murders, twenty-four years before, of her mother and two sisters. The person convicted of those murders was her older brother Ben, who has, in the years since, attracted a devoted fan club convinced that Libby's damning courtroom testimony was false. Libby matter-of-factly proclaims, 'I was not a lovable child, and I'd grown into a deeply unlovable adult'.[28] Financial desperation obliges Libby to accept payment for attending a meeting of an amateur crime investigation group known as The Kill Club, and for the first time in decades to reassess her perceptions of the crime that destroyed her family. Libby is a caustic moocher who instinctively sizes up everyone she meets to see how she can benefit from their pity. Forever defined in the eyes of those around her by that terrible night back in the mid-1980s, she is, literally, yesterday's news. This sense of arrested development extends even to her out-of-kilter physicality: she has both a 'stunted, childish body' and incongruously large breasts.[29] Now in her early thirties, Libby has never had a real job or a lasting relationship, and has burned ties with the one living relative who cares for her.

Dark Places alternates Libby's present-day first-person perspective with chapters that flash back to the days before the murders took place. The main focus in these chapters is her mother, Patty, and Ben, who was then an insecure teenager embroiled in a stormy relationship with Diondra, his demanding girlfriend. It is in relation to Ben's story that Flynn's take on one of the most notorious media frenzies of the decade – the so-called 'Satanic Panic' that flourished in certain pockets of the rural US[30] – can be clearly detected.[31] However, as past and present begin to collide, and a new perspective on the murders emerges, it gradually becomes clear that in *Dark Places*, as in *Sharp Objects*, the real explanation is much more complicated than initial reports suggested.

Flynn's work so far has consistently displayed an acute awareness of tensions related to social class. This is most apparent here in her nuanced depiction of Patty, a loving and hardworking single mother up to her neck in economic quicksand. As well as casting a new light upon the real causes of the massacre, Flynn's poignant evocation of Patty's dire lack of options significantly illuminates the present. Libby's compulsive petty thievery takes on enhanced significance once we become privy to the Day family's hand-to-mouth existence back in the 1980s. In addition, rich-girl Diondra's cruel mocking of Ben's desperate economic situation provides an early indication of her monstrous self-interest. As the novel's violent denouement underlines, teenage girls – and adult women still trapped in teenage behaviours – should always to be carefully watched in Flynn's work. However, *Dark Places* does end with a measure of hope – Libby has finally discovered the truth about what really happened to her family, and although this discovery places her in yet more danger, the novel's tentatively hopeful conclusion also suggests that she will finally be able to begin moving beyond her horrific past.

Gone Girl begins as a kind of suburban-set Bluebeard narrative for the twenty-first century: an innocent wife is terrorised by a violent and deceptive husband. However, it is also, crucially, a desolate story of mutual marital unhappiness revolving, for Amy at least, around one key question: 'Can you imagine, finally showing your true self to your spouse, your soul mate, and having him *not like you?*'[32] *Gone Girl* contains many familiar ingredients. We once more have: a protagonist (Nick) who must reluctantly return to a Missouri hometown; a focus on the relationship between the 'real' self and the façade presented to the world; and an uncompromising exploration of the female capacity for violence. Furthermore, in *Gone Girl* Flynn again casts a critical eye over the media's preoccupation with a certain kind of 'perfect' victim (i.e. white, pretty, female and middle class). This time, however, we also have two protagonists who have previously made their living as journalists, telling us competing versions of the story. The main difference between *Gone Girl* and Flynn's earlier novels is that, for the first time, a male character, Nick Dunne, also takes centre stage.[33]

Amy Elliott Dunne represents the most compelling result so far of Flynn's contention that a truly equitable representation of women means acknowledging that they are just as capable of villainy as men. Amy's revenge plot involves such an insane degree of subterfuge, fine detail and long-term planning that it arguably situates her within the 'evil genius' pop culture pantheon more commonly occupied by male characters such as Hannibal Lecter and Moriarty. Always convinced that she could commit the perfect murder if she put her mind to it, the discovery that Nick has been cheating on her inspires Amy to finally put such a plan in to action – the twist in the tale being the fact that the murder is her own.[34] As she tells us at the start of the revelatory 'Part Two' of the novel (subtitled 'Boy Meets Girl'),[35] 'I wrote her very carefully, Diary Amy. She is designed to appeal to the cops, to appeal to the public should portions be released. They have to read this diary like it's some sort of Gothic Tragedy.'[36]

At the core of Actual Amy's anger lies the fact that she has always felt the need to present herself to the world as 'perfect'. Despite her delight at being the centre of her parents' universe, the inspiration for their bestselling series of 'Amazing Amy' children's books, she is bitterly jealous of the stillborn sisters who preceded her:

[they] get to be perfect without even trying, without even facing one moment of existence, while I am stuck here on earth, and every day I must try, and every day is a chance to be less than perfect. It's an exhausting way to live.[37]

Amy's only respite comes in the form of her relationship with Nick. For a few years, she feels content, certain that she is embodying the best possible version of herself.[38] She dubs this persona 'the Cool Girl':

That night at the Brooklyn party, I was playing the girl who was in style, the girl a man like Nick wants: the Cool Girl. Men always say that as the defining compliment, don't they? She's a cool girl. Being the Cool girl means that I am a hot, brilliant, funny woman who adores football, poker, dirty jokes, and burping, who plays video games, drinks cheap beer, loves threesomes and anal sex, and jams hot dogs and hamburgers into her mouth while somehow maintaining a size 2, because Cool Girls are above all hot. Hot and understanding . . . Men actually think this girl exists. Maybe they're fooled because so many women are willing to pretend to be this girl . . . There are variations to the window dressing, but believe me, he wants Cool Girl, who is basically the girl who likes every fucking thing he likes and doesn't ever complain.[39]

This now infamous passage rapidly inspired a slew of blog posts and opinion pieces, and even entered the cultural lexicon alongside other loaded descriptors for a certain 'type' of young woman, such as 'Manic Pixie Dream Girl'. What some commentators failed to appreciate was the 'Cool Girl' speech's specific context within Flynn's novel. It is a tirade spewed out by a character whose devastation and bitterness means that it simply cannot be taken at face value. Amy's pitiless, hyperbolic contempt for the young women she sees as adopting a certain kind of man-pleasing persona (and for the men, who, like Nick, are dumb enough to fall for it) is a furious critique of *her own* capitulation to societal expectations, and a scathing takedown of her cheating husband. It is certainly *not* intended to be read as an objective piece of cultural commentary on the part of either Amy or Flynn. Indeed, Amy is a probable sociopath who even admits that she has been self-consciously mimicking 'normal' human interaction for decades.[40] It is no wonder then that she would suspect other people – and particularly other women – of behaving exactly as she does. Although she has grown up with every kind of financial and educational opportunity, she has always been an inherently dissatisfied individual who, like Camille and Libby before her, cannot help but be the product of her upbringing. However, unlike her fictional predecessors, Amy has not been damaged by trauma or abuse, but rather their apparent opposite: the cloying worship of parents, who, as she self-servingly puts it, 'made me this way and then deserted me'.[41] Crucially, Amy's desire for annihilation is directed as much towards herself as it is towards her husband. For all her anger towards Nick, she cannot contemplate life beyond their failed marriage and the devastating blow to her self-image this failure will cause. She believes that her carefully orchestrated death will both provide the final evidence needed to secure Nick's conviction, and finally make her 'perfect', by creating a 'better story', in which she will be 'the hero, flawless and adored'.[42]

One of the things that makes the novel particularly interesting is that it also becomes obvious that, in his own way, Nick is as constrained by appearances and public expectation as his scheming wife. He is, after all, a writer too, and as we later discover, his account of Amy's disappearance – and of his realisation that she has framed him – represents his own spin on the story. Though Nick initially presents himself to us as a baffled and concerned spouse, his behaviour becomes increasingly suspicious, something he that first acknowledges in one of the novel's most self-consciously 'meta' moments: 'Now is the part where I have to tell you I have a mistress and you stop liking me'.[43] Not only is Nick having an affair, but it also soon becomes clear that he has a repressed, though very real, streak of misogyny. As the evidence mounts up, even his unfailingly supportive twin sister Margot briefly wonders if he has done something terrible to his wife.

It is precisely because Nick is not the uncomplicated 'nice guy' that he tries so hard to be that he also, ultimately, comes to understand the 'real' or 'Actual' Amy. As a result, his canny manipulation of the media circus that has already convicted him of murder slowly brings the couple back together. Impressed by Nick's unexpected capacity to rise to her level, Amy discards her original plan and engineers a triumphant, blood-soaked return in which she can present herself as the abused but triumphant 'Final Girl' of her own twist-strewn narrative. She is no longer to be the dead but adored perfect victim, but the heroic, inspirational survivor. The finishing touch: a moving reconciliation with her seemingly contrite husband. By the final pages of the novel, then, the Dunne marriage has entered a seemingly permanent stalemate, a domestic Cold War in which Nick is perpetually outgunned by the terrifying but publicly adored wife, who chillingly declares to the reader: 'We will have a happy marriage if it kills him'.[44] What else is left, in Amy's eyes, but for them to procreate, and become, 'the world's best, brightest nuclear family'?[45]

However, although Flynn grants Amy the last word, importantly, her account ends not on a note of triumph, but doubt:

> This morning he was stroking my hair and asking what else he could do for me, and I said, 'My gosh, Nick, why are you so wonderful to me?'
>
> He was supposed to say: *You deserve it. I love you.*
>
> But he said, 'Because I feel sorry for you.'
>
> 'Why?'
>
> 'Because every morning you have to wake up and be you.'
>
> I really, truly wish he hadn't said that. I keep thinking about it. I can't stop.[46]

While some have accused Flynn of perpetuating harmful stereotypes of vengeful, 'crazy' women in *Gone Girl* (something that the author herself seems aware of: in one of Flynn's many sardonically meta moments, we find out late in the novel that Nick's tell-all exposé is entitled *Psycho Bitch*), it's this melancholy, gnawing instance of self-awareness that nevertheless underlines her nuanced but essentially feminist worldview. For Flynn's women, internal and external pressures are intrinsically related. If they are their own worst enemies, it is in part because they inhabit a world in which women are so frequently objectified, abused and patronised that they cannot help but fall into self-harming and self-defeating behaviours, despite their obvious intelligence and obsessive self-scrutiny. Amy Elliott Dunne takes this idea to the next level by demonstrating that the mantle of female victimhood can also be effectively weaponised. Crucially though, the closing lines of *Gone Girl* suggest that this is a Pyrrhic victory at best. Unlike Camille Preaker and Libby Day, Amy has no obvious external traumas to confront in addition to her inner demons. Her unhappiness is a more nebulous, more insidious entity, revolving around the compulsive need to conform to media-friendly ideals of female 'perfection' which she knows are essentially phony but is still, nonetheless, unable to resist or escape. As a result, while both *Sharp Objects* and *Dark Places* conclude with the suggestion that the protagonists are finally achieving a measure of control over their lives, the opposite is true in *Gone Girl*. The fact that Amy ends the novel in a trap that she has constructed for herself gives it all the more of a claustrophobic feel.

At the time of writing, the only Flynn publication to have appeared since 2012 is her Edgar Award-winning short story 'What Do You Do?' (2014), which was, in an indication of the public appetite for her work, published a year later as a stand-alone text, *The Grownup*. *The Grownup* begins by wryly evoking classic tales of the supernatural, but ultimately veers into more characteristically Flynn-like territory. As well as being darkly funny, the story's effective engagement with the uncanny suggests that Flynn would make an excellent horror novelist. However, although she is currently said to be working on another novel, 'a big, folkloric tale of murder in the middle of the country and how various families are affected by it',[47] her most high-profile post-2012 work has been as a screenwriter, rather than a novelist. She wrote the screenplay for David Fincher's acclaimed 2014 adaptation of *Gone Girl*, and has more recently collaborated with the British director Steve McQueen, as well as contributing to the much-anticipated television adaptation of *Sharp Objects*. The wait for Flynn's next book has only fuelled opportunities for authors operating in broadly similar thematic territory: *Gone Girl* was a key instigator of the post-2012 craze for psychological thrillers about grown women with the word 'Girl' in the title (a trend which also owes much to the mammoth success of the 2008 English-language version of Stieg Larsson's *The Girl with the Dragon Tattoo*).[48] Whatever the focus of her eagerly awaited fourth novel, Flynn's thematic consistency and obvious talent suggests that she will remain an astute and provocative creator of scenarios that relentlessly challenge conventional notions of female identity, media representation and victimhood.

NOTES

1. 'Gone Girl Finally Hits Paperback', *Publishers Weekly*, 2 December 2012<http://www.publishersweekly.com/pw/by-topic/industry-news/publisher-news/article/60220-gone-girl-finally-hits-paperback.html> (last accessed 23 May 2016).
2. This chapter has been helpfully informed by my discussions with Danielle Daly and Eva Burke, both of whom wrote on Flynn during their time as students on the MPhil in Popular Literature at Trinity College Dublin.
3. The other popular fiction phenomenon of 2012 was of course E. L. James's *Fifty Shades of Grey*, which arguably received even more media coverage than *Gone Girl*, but was generally discussed in relation to the appeal it presented to its assumed audience rather than considered as a text in its own right.
4. Maslin, 'The Lies That Buoy, Then Break a Marriage'.
5. Ibid.
6. Flynn, *Gone Girl*, p. 208.
7. Brockes, 'The *Gone Girl* Phenomenon: Gillian Flynn Speaks Out'.
8. Flynn, '*Gone Girl*' in 'Eureka'.
9. Anolik, 'Inside the Dangerous Mind of *Gone Girl*'s Gillian Flynn'.
10. See <http://gillian-flynn.com/about-gillian/> (last accessed 23 May 2016).
11. Ibid.
12. Harris, 'Gillian Flynn'.
13. Schmich, 'Author Finds the True Midwest – In All Its Darkness'.
14. Flynn, 'I Was Not a Nice Little Girl'.
15. Flynn's belief that the freedom to create villainous and/or 'unsympathetic' female characters is necessary if women are to be treated as complex, authentic individuals in both literature and the wider culture arguably aligns her in this respect with more conventionally 'literary' authors such as Margaret Atwood, Claire Messud and Ottessa Moshfegh.
16. As suggested by Becca Rothfield, Imogen Sarah Smith and Devin O'Neill, to name but a few

of the online commentators who have also made this connection . See, respectively, <https://newrepublic.com/article/119743/gone-girl-has-offered-feminism-new-hero>, <http://filmnoirfoundation.org/noircitymag/Gone-Girl.pdf>, <http://therumpus.net/2014/12/the-saturday-rumpus-essay-falling-for-the-femme-fatale> (all last accessed 20 June 2016).

17. Burkeman, 'Gillian Flynn on Her Bestseller *Gone Girl* and Accusations of Misogyny'.

18. See, for instance, Thomas C. Renzi's use of the term in *Screwball Comedy and Film Noir* (p. 81) or Paula Rabinowicz's deployment of it in *Black and White and Noir* (p. 52).

19. Crouch, 'Genre Bender'.

20. Weinman, *Troubled Daughters, Twisted Wives*, p. XXV.

21. As argued by novelist Mary Rizza in 'Bygone Girl: How Jane Eyre was the Original Domestic Noir Novel'. Available at <http://maryrizza.com/bygone-girl-how-jane-eyre-was-the-original-domestic-noir-novel/> (last accessed 26 May 2016)

22. Dugdale, 'Ten Things You Didn't Know About Domestic Noir'.

23. Flynn, *Sharp Objects*, p. 1.

24. Ibid., p. 29.

25. Ibid., p. 89.

26. Ibid., p. 85.

27. Ibid., p. 320.

28. Flynn, *Dark Places*, p. 1.

29. Ibid., p. 3.

30. There have been a number of interesting critical explorations of this era, among them *Satanic Panic: The Creation of a Contemporary Legend*, by Jeffery S, Victor (1993), W. Scott Poole's *Satan in America: The Devil We Know* (2009) and *We Believe the Children: A Moral Panic in the 1980s*, by Richard Beck (2015).

31. Kean, 'Gillian Flynn'.

32. Flynn, *Gone Girl*, p. 213.

33. Although he is certainly an important character, Ben in *Dark Places* is not the prime narrative focus in the way that Nick is here.

34. Flynn, *Gone Girl*, p. 223.

35. Ibid., p. 207.

36. Ibid., p. 213.

37. Ibid., p. 209.

38. Ibid., p. 212.

39. Ibid., p. 210.

40. Amy mentions this lifelong donning of different personas in order to fit in, as well as her childhood inability to understand 'normal' social behavior on pp. 210–11. Though I do not have room to discuss the comparison, she often resembles a grown-up version of William March's precocious psychopath Rhoda Penmark in *The Bad Seed* (1954). Amma in *Sharp Objects* also has some very 'Rhoda-like' qualities – her murderous jealousy of other youngsters in particular.

41. Flynn, *Gone Girl*, p. 225.

42. Ibid., p. 222.

43. Ibid., p. 135.

44. Ibid., p. 378.

45. Ibid., p. 394.

46. Ibid., pp. 394–5.

47. Graham, '*Gone Girl* Author Gillian Flynn on a Possible Sequel and Her Chilling New Book'.

48. Available at <http://www.npr.org/2016/02/22/467392750/the-girl-in-the-title-more-than-a-marketing-trend> (last accessed 28 June 2016). See also: 'The Girl in the Title: More Than a Marketing Trend' in *NPR Books*, 22 February 2016, Available at: <http://www.

npr.org/2016/02/22/467392750/the-girl-in-the-title-more-than-a-marketing-trend> (last accessed 28 June 2016) and 'Book Publishing Goes Wild for Girls' in USA Today, 15 June 2016. Available at: <http://www.usatoday.com/story/life/books/2016/06/14/books-girls-girl-in-the-title/85830278/> (last accessed 28 June 2016)

KEY WORKS

Sharp Objects (2006). Flynn's debut novel is arguably still her most disturbing: a haunting depiction of small-town murder and child abuse.

Dark Places (2009). Combines the story of a typically damaged and sardonic young woman with real-life episodes such as the Kansas farmhouse slaying that inspired Truman Capote's In Cold Blood (1966) and the 1980s 'Satanic Panic'.

Gone Girl (2012). Flynn's breakout hit is an enthralling, deceptive and ultimately bleak portrait of a seemingly perfect marriage founded on deception. Amy Elliott Dunne is one of the most charismatic and controversial pop culture villains of the twenty-first century so far.

Gone Girl, film, directed by David Fincher and with screenplay by Flynn (Twentieth Century Fox, 2014). Flynn's screenplay effectively streamlines the novel while playing up its morbidly funny side (particularly once the luridly spiteful machinations of 'Actual' Amy begin to take centre stage in the second half).

FURTHER CRITICAL READING

Galioto, Erica D., 'One Long Frightening Climax: Gillian Flynn's Gone Girl and Lacan's The Other Side of Psychoanalysis', Revue électronique d'études sur le monde Anglophone, 12 January 2014 <http://erea.revues.org/4057> (last accessed 14 June 2016). An interesting reading of Gone Girl which suggests that Nick and Amy ultimately prefer a manufactured 'false reality' in preference to the one imposed upon them by society.

Johansen, Emily, 'The Neoliberal Gothic: Gone Girl, Broken Harbour, and the Terror of Everyday Life', Contemporary Literature, 1 (spring 2016), pp. 30–55. Discussion of Gone Girl as a prime example the so-called 'neoliberal Gothic', in which the haunted castles of the classical Gothic are replaced by empty subdivisions and post-industrial ruins.

Weinman, Sarah, 'Introduction', in Weinman (ed.), Troubled Daughters, Twisted Wives, pp. XV–XXV. Provides a valuable introduction to the work of the 'forgotten generation' of female suspense writers whom Weinman sees as anticipating contemporary 'Domestic Noir'.

BIBLIOGRAPHY

Anolik, Lili, 'Inside the Dangerous Mind of Gone Girl's Gillian Flynn', Elle, 10 October 2014 <http://www.elle.com/culture/movies-tv/a14563/inside-gone-girls-gillian-flynn> (last accessed 23 May 2016).

Brockes, Emma, 'The Gone Girl Phenomenon: Gillian Flynn Speaks Out', The Guardian, 3 October 2014 <https://www.theguardian.com/books/2014/oct/03/gone-girl-phenomenon-gillian-flynn> (last accessed 26 May 2016).

Burkeman, Oliver, 'Gillian Flynn on Her Bestseller Gone Girl and Accusations of Misogyny', The Guardian, 1 May 2013 <http://www.theguardian.com/books/2013/may/01/gillian-flynn-bestseller-gone-girl-misogyny> (last accessed 23 May 2016).

Clarke, Nick, 'Women's Prize for Fiction: Can Gone Girl by Gillian Flynn Rob Hilary Mantel of the Hat-Trick?', The Independent, 13 March 2012 <http://www.independent.co.uk/arts-entertainment/books/news/womens-prize-for-fiction-can-gone-girl-by-gillian-flynn-rob-hilary-mantel-of-the-hat-trick-8531501.html> (last accessed 23 May 2016).

Crouch, Julia, 'Genre Bender', 25 August 2013 <http://juliacrouch.co.uk/blog/genre-bender> (last accessed 23 May 2016).

Dugdale, Ruth, 'Ten Things You Didn't Know About Domestic Noir', 31 October 2015 <http://www.femalefirst.co.uk/books/nowhere-girl-ruth-dugdall-889157.html> (last accessed 23 May 2016).

Flynn, Gillian, *Dark Places* (London: Phoenix Fiction, 2009).

Flynn, Gillian, '*Gone Girl*', in 'Eureka: From *Gone Girl* to the Selfie Stick: How One Great Idea Can Change Your Life', *The Guardian*, 6 November 2015 <http://www.theguardian.com/lifeandstyle/2015/nov/06/great-idea-gone-girl-selfie-stick-cronut-tinder-emoji-gogglebox> (last accessed 23 May 2016).

Flynn, Gillian, *Gone Girl* (London: Weidenfeld and Nicolson, 2012).

Flynn, Gillian, 'I Was Not a Nice Little Girl' (n.d.) <http://gillian-flynn.com/for-readers> (last accessed 23 May 2016).

Flynn, Gillian, *Sharp Objects* (London: Phoenix Fiction, 2006).

Flynn, Gillian, *The Grownup* (London: Weidenfeld and Nicolson, 2015).

Graham, Caroline, '*Gone Girl* Author Gillian Flynn on a Possible Sequel and Her Chilling New Book', *Daily Mail*, 24 October 2015 <http://www.dailymail.co.uk/home/event/article-3284683/Gone-Girl-author-Gillian-Flynn-possible-sequel-chilling-new-book.html> (last accessed 14 June 2016).

Harris, Paul, 'Gillian Flynn: Chronicler of the Midwest's Dark Side', *The Guardian*, 24 March 2013 <http://www.theguardian.com/theobserver/2013/mar/24/gillian-flynn-gone-girl-profile> (last accessed 23 May 2016).

Kean, Danuta, 'Gillian Flynn: An Interview' (n.d.), Orion Books <https://www.orionbooks.co.uk/Articles/Interviews/Gillian+Flynn+Interview.page> (last accessed 27 May 2016).

Maslin, Janet, 'The Lies That Buoy, Then Break a Marriage', *New York Times*, 29 May 2012 <http://www.nytimes.com/2012/05/30/books/gone-girl-by-gillian-flynn.html> (last accessed 23 May 2016).

Rabinowicz, Paula, *Black and White and Noir: America's Pulp Modernism* (New York: Columbia University Press, 2002).

Renzi, Thomas C., *Screwball Comedy and Film Noir: Unexpected Connections* (Jefferson, NC: McFarland, 2012).

Schmich, Mary, 'Author Finds the True Midwest – In All Its Darkness', *Chicago Tribune*, 29 July 2012 <http://articles.chicagotribune.com/2012-07-29/news/ct-met-schmich-0729-20120729_1_novels-gillian-flynn-flynn-lives> (last accessed 15 June 2016).

Weinman, Sarah (ed.), *Troubled Daughters, Twisted Wives: Stories from the Trailblazers of Domestic Suspense* (New York: Penguin, 2013).

CHAPTER 15

'The Bastard Zone': China Miéville, *Perdido Street Station* and the New Weird

Kirsten Tranter

China Miéville is one of the UK's most prolific and original authors, and one of the more successful of the writers associated with the 'British boom' in science fiction and fantasy in the late 1990s and early 2000s. *Perdido Street Station* (2000), the first of Miéville's three novels set in the world of Bas-Lag, won the Arthur C. Clarke Award for science fiction and consolidated his reputation as one of the most exciting authors working at the intersection of fantasy, sci-fi and horror, a genre now known as 'the New Weird'. *Perdido Street Station* gleefully overturned clichés of the fantasy genre and reimagined the political possibilities it offered, while appealing beyond the typical genre readership. It migrated across the bookshop from the 'genre' shelves to the general fiction section, garnering attention in mainstream literary circles, and its impressive sales awakened publishers to the potential market for such genre-crossing work. Miéville's reputation grew with the publication of the next two novels set in Bas-Lag, *The Scar* (2002) and *Iron Council* (2004), and his work attracted increasing attention from critics interested in the narrative complexity, political nuance and formally inventive properties of his fiction.

A playful, irreverent, yet deeply respectful engagement with genre protocols informs much of Miéville's fiction. Critics have insisted that it 'transcends' genre, but he disputes this:

> I would never disavow my generic tradition . . . Occasionally people say, 'but you're not really science fiction, you're escaping the genre'. Not really! I know it's meant nicely, but I would much rather operate as a conduit than an outlier.[1]

Born in 1972 in Norwich, Miéville grew up in London, where he still lives. He read social anthropology at Cambridge, and spent a year at Harvard before returning to the UK, where he completed a PhD on Marxism and international law at the London School of Economics. A committed socialist, Miéville was until recently a member of the Socialist Workers Party and continues to be politically active. While his politics inform his writing, he disavows any attempt to be prescriptive in his fiction. Many of his novels feature attempts to work through political problems and explicitly stage conflicts between oppressor and oppressed, yet they refuse easy resolution or sense of moral certainty. Miéville publishes literary criticism as well as journalism, and co-edits the leftist magazine *Salvage*. He has also written comics and illustrated several of his own books, including *Un Lun Dun* (2007). Miéville has won every major award in science fiction and fantasy, including the Arthur C. Clarke, Locus, Hugo, Nebula and British Fantasy Awards, and his admirers argue that his work should contend for prestigious mainstream literary prizes, such as the Man Booker.

No author is more central to the New Weird than China Miéville. He coined the term, according to fellow New Weird author M. John Harrison,[2] and much of the discussion of the genre as it evolved was concerned with trying to account for the particular combination of elements of fantasy, horror and science fiction in Miéville's work, its unique formal, stylistic and political dimensions, and its remarkable ability to connect with readers beyond genre fiction. Jeff VanderMeer argues that while authors on the margins had been writing New Weird fiction throughout the 1990s, 'the publication of *Perdido Street Station* in 2000 represented what might be termed the first commercially acceptable version of New Weird'.[3]

Most genealogies of the New Weird locate the genesis of the term in an exchange in 2003 on the Internet bulletin board of the fiction magazine *The Third Alternative*, beginning as a set of provocative queries from M. John Harrison and burgeoning into a lengthy, argumentative conversation stretching over several months and involving around fifty authors, critics, editors and others involved in the genre fiction world. 'The New Weird. Who does it?' Harrison asked. 'What is it? Is it even anything? Is it even New? . . . Should we just call it Pick'n'Mix instead?'[4] The resulting exchange hammered out the parameters that have come to define the genre. Steph Swainston, author of the important New Weird novel *The Year of Our War* (2004), notes the genre's energetically oppositional character:

> The New Weird is a kickback against jaded heroic fantasy which has been the only staple for far too long. Instead of stemming from Tolkien, it is influenced by Gormenghast[5] and Viriconium.[6] It is incredibly eclectic, and takes ideas from any source.[7]

Descriptive detail is key: 'The details are jewel-bright, hallucinatory, carefully described', as opposed to the 'lazy . . . broad brush' of 'today's Tolkienesque fantasy'.[8]

VanderMeer points to two significant points of 'stimulus' for the New Weird. The first is the formally experimental, politically progressive fiction of the 1960s New Wave movement, including authors such as M. John Harrison, Michael Moorcock, Samuel R. Delany, Jack Vance and J. G. Ballard, which often blended science fiction and fantasy. The second trend is towards grotesque horror in the 1980s, exemplified by Clive Barker.[9] These are the most contemporary antecedents for the genre, and the name 'New Weird' self-consciously evokes the New Wave and its signature journal *New Worlds*. But the name also points further back, to older points of inspiration: Weird fiction.

For Sherryl Vint, the New Weird 'reinvigorates fantastic writing as a blend of science fiction, Surrealism, fantasy, magical realism, and Lovecraftian horror that is attentive to both its pulp and its high culture influences and roots'.[10] She alludes to perhaps the most distinctive characteristic of the New Weird: the eclectic combination of recognisable elements from distinct genres (encoded in Harrison's term 'Pick'n'Mix'). The New Weird respects all these genres, and opportunistically uses bits of each. In doing so, it harks back to late-nineteenth-century and early-twentieth-century authors such as M. R. James, and others who published in the pulp magazine *Weird Tales*, including H. P. Lovecraft, author of the classic Weird tale 'The Call of Cthulhu' (1928), William Hope Hodgson and Clark Ashton Smith, whose work refuses easy categorisation. One key feature of those stories 'was that they had no respect for any supposed internal generic distinctions', Miéville writes in his manifesto/essay 'The New Weird':

> Lovecraft's writing can equally be considered SF, fantasy or horror, and he problematises these subdivisions – as does the New Weird – as he gets on with his main consideration, the abject surrender to the weird itself, in all its forms.[11]

The specific kind of weirdness that Miéville identifies in these writers is distinct from earlier forms of the fantastic; it is stranger, more alien, less amenable to meaning. The Weird's 'break with previous fantastics' manifests in its distinctive monsters, he argues, which are 'without mythic resonance', and 'renounce all folkloric or traditional antecedents'; their emblem is the tentacle, 'a limb-type with no Gothic or traditional precedents'.[12] Lovecraft's Cthulhu, a huge alien creature with a face full of tentacles and a terrifyingly incoherent voice, is the iconic weird beast.

Although most authors affiliated with the New Weird share some form of progressive politics, they remain divided over the role of political consciousness in the genre, with VanderMeer downplaying its significance.[13] But Miéville insists on a political dimension that sets it apart from conventional, conservative fantasy, arguing that it reflects a particular moment, a shift in consciousness following the mass demonstrations at the 1999 World Trade Organization meetings in Seattle. Politics is represented on a thematic level, in narrative elements such as the striking dockworkers in *Perdido Street Station*, the liberation of enslaved Remade criminals in *The Scar*, or the ongoing revolution of the railway workers in *Iron Council*; it is also implied in the particular consciousness of this writing, a scepticism about the way social relations, moral structures and literature itself are shaped by ideology and power relations. Miéville contends that:

> It is literature which knows that the world, and the literature embedded in it, are politically constructed. For the New Weird, morality is a problem, not a solution or a given, and politics is inescapable. And that makes this a fiction born out of possibilities, its freeing-up mirroring the freeing-up, the radicalisation in the world. This is post-Seattle fiction.[14]

As a Marxist, Miéville has defended fantasy as a genre that is 'good to think with' because of its engagement with the radical possibilities of imagination, and its potential to be 'a critical art'.[15] Introducing a special issue of the journal *Historical Materialism* dedicated to Marxism and fantasy, he argues that '"reality" is a grotesque "fantastic form"' under capitalism; 'we need fantasy to think the world, and to change it'.[16]

As part of its political dimension, the New Weird explicitly rejects tropes associated with J. R. R. Tolkien and their reiteration in conventional fantasy fiction. In writing *Perdido Street Station*, Miéville says:

> I was quite consciously trying to do a non-Tolkienesque fantasy . . . I kind of made a checklist: Tolkien is rural and bucolic, so let's make it urban and shitty; Tolkien is feudalism lite, so let's make it capitalism dark, and you go through like that.[17]

He has been a vocal critic of Tolkien's dependence on 'moralist, abstract logic' designed to evacuate political complexity, and is fiercely critical of Tolkien's conservative commitment to the idea of fiction as 'consolation'.[18] But despite this, Miéville acknowledges a sincere debt to Tolkien for his groundbreaking 'construction of a systematic secondary world'.[19] Such elaborately detailed worlds invite the total absorption which is peculiar to fantasy, Miéville argues, enabling a 'uniquely engaged kind of reading. Readers can inhabit these worlds, and become collaborators in the process of constantly creating them.'[20] This serious absorption in the fantastic is one that Miéville claims as central to the project of the New Weird. He celebrates suspension of disbelief taken to its extreme, imagined as absolute submission to the fantastic and akin to Lovecraft's 'abject surrender to the Weird'.

Miéville was the New Weird's most successful, well-known, polemical and influential standard bearer; he was also relatively quick to disavow the term as he began to perceive its impending dilution and commercialisation. In a 2005 symposium on the state of fantasy fiction, Miéville predicted the imminent collapse of the genre, or at least its co-option by de-radicalising market forces, and started to distance himself from it. 'That's the trouble with trying to counter clichés', Miéville observed: 'the counter-clichés cliché quicker than shit off a shovel, and with that comes domestication'.[21]

Miéville's fiction has taken different directions since the three Bas-Lag novels that form the cornerstone of New Weird fiction of the 2000s, although his most recent work signals a return to Weird themes in its preoccupation with horror-infused urban fantasy. But the genre remains alive in the work of authors such as short-story author Kelly Link, whose work is distinguished by settings where familiar, realistic situations are disturbed by dark, fantastic elements, and VanderMeer, best known for his series of novels set in the fantastic city of Ambergris. The New Weird has maintained a position at the intersection of genre and literary fiction, although critics remain divided over whether it constitutes a discrete genre at all, or could more productively be folded into affiliated categories such as Slipstream (a term that incorporates literary authors such as George Saunders and David Mitchell as well as more genre-oriented writers like Neal Stephenson and Neil Gaiman), New Fabulism, or Interstitial fiction (although the genre-crossing work associated with the last term generally lacks the distinguishing element of horror that defines the old and New Weird). The impact of the New Weird's rejection of Tolkienesque tropes of consolation can be seen in other strands of genre fiction, such as Grimdark, a form of fantasy characterised by ambiguous morality, pervasive violence and brutal politics exemplified by the novels of George R. R. Martin.

While still perhaps best known as a New Weird author, Miéville's work encompasses a variety of genres. *Iron Council* is built around the traditional narrative framework of a Western, and also contains a romance plot. *The City and the City* introduces fantastic elements into a dream-like Noir crime story. *Kraken* is a crime caper and a contribution to the genre of 'weird London', like Miéville's first novel, *King Rat*, *Un Lun Dun*, and his short story 'Reports of Certain Events in London', where a hidden, magical world lies just beneath the awareness and literal surface of the city streets. *Embassytown* is a classic science fiction novel, set on a distant planet in the far future. Miéville has written two novels for younger readers: *Un Lun Dun* and *Railsea*, a version of Herman Melville's *Moby-Dick* where the hunted monster is a giant mole and dirt takes the place of water on a planet traversed by a multitude of intersecting rail lines. Miéville's recent work, the short-fiction collection *Three Moments of an Explosion* and the novella *This Census-Taker*, returns to the blend of horror and fantasy that distinguishes his Bas-Lag novels. His latest novel, *The Last Days of New Paris*, also plays with the genre of alternative historical fiction, imagining the impact of a 'surrealist bomb' on the city in 1941.

Miéville's three novels set in the secondary fantasy world of Bas-Lag do not comprise a trilogy in any conventional sense, in that each has a self-contained plot with only a tangential relation to the others. *Perdido Street Station* is set entirely in the city of New Crobuzon, and provides an intimate, obsessively detailed rendering of the city with its complex political, cultural, architectural, geographical and social structures. The second Bas-Lag novel, *The Scar*, combines espionage and adventure plots in following the travels and travails of Bellis Coldwine, a linguist and former lover of Isaac Dan der Grimnebulin, *Perdido Street Station*'s protagonist. *The Scar* begins shortly after the events of the earlier novel, which concludes with Isaac's departure from New Crobuzon, hunted by the city's authorities. Knowing that his associates also face harassment, Bellis sails away into voluntary exile. Eventually she is press-ganged, along with the crew and enslaved Remade passengers of the ship she sails on, into life with the pirate city of Armada, an ever-growing agglomeration of ships lashed together to form a floating metropolis. *Iron Council* is set still later in time and moves between New Crobuzon and distant territory, as the protagonists search for the legendary Iron Council of the title, a group of railway workers who rebelled against their masters, stole a train and formed an autonomous social collective outside the political and geographical boundaries of the city. As Christopher Palmer notes, these three novels all explore tropes of 'saving the city' in one form or another, and celebrate forms of collective action and solidarity across lines of class and species, yet the plots are driven by types of 'difficult, uncooperative, isolated, and exiled or secretive loner'.[22]

The map that prefaces *Perdido Street Station* is the first indication that we are about to enter a fantasy world that upends Tolkien-style convention. Tolkien's *The Hobbit* inaugurated the ubiquitous device of the illustrated map that prefaces every fantasy novel, and curlicued dragons decorate his whimsical, archaic-styled drawings of Middle Earth's mountains and plains. There is a whole world here in Miéville's map, but it is contained in a single city: complex and dense and bizarre, undeniably modern, New Crobuzon is criss-crossed with train lines and skyrails and bridges, some of them broken. Not only the snaking river but also the place-names echo London, Miéville's home and deep inspiration, with an uncanny twist: Salacus Fields, Howl Barrow, Gross Coil, Raven's Gate, Nigh Sump. The prologue opens with an approach to the city along the river, narrated by a character encountering it for the first time. Through his eyes, it appears alive, predatory, abject, obscene and mysterious. Later we come to know this narrator as Yagharek, a bird-man hybrid Garuda, and although this description is provided from a barge on the water, it seems taken from the way he would more normally see the world, from the air:

> It is a vast pollutant, a stench, a klaxon sounding. Fat chimneys retch dirt into the sky even now in the deep night. It is not the current which pulls us in but the city itself, its weight sucks us in. Faint shouts, here and there the calls of beasts, the obscene clash and pounding from the factories as huge machines rut. Railways trace urban anatomy like protruding veins. Red brick and dark walls, squat churches like troglodytic things, ragged awnings flickering, cobbled mazes in the old town, culs-de-sac, sewers riddling the earth like secular sepulchres, a new landscape of wasteground, crushed stone, libraries fat with forgotten volumes, old hospitals, towerblocks, ships and metal claws that lift cargoes from the water.[23]

In a novel filled with a wild variety of actual monsters, the city itself is a metaphorical sprawling monster dwarfing and mirroring them all, generative of copious figures and comparisons. The chapter that follows takes the reader deep into the smelly streets of the neighbourhood of Aspic Hole on market day, and still further into rogue scientist Isaac Dan der Grimnebulin's apartment. In a scene by turns intimate, domestic, affectionate, wistful, erotic and shocking, Lin, a red-skinned woman artist with a head shaped like a beetle, eats her breakfast of fruit, and has enthusiastic sex with Isaac. Chapter 1 seems to lay down a challenge: if cross-species sex with bug-headed women is too much for you, you should probably go no further into this world.

Plots and subplots quickly multiply. Isaac sees an opportunity to pursue some of his scientific obsessions into new territory in response to Yagharek's request to restore his powers of flight; Lin undertakes a secret commission that puts her in terrible danger; a smuggling operation gone wrong lets loose a terrifying band of slake moths from another dimension, who feed on human minds, whose excrement is sold as a drug known as Dreamshit, and Isaac makes unlikely alliances in order to destroy the existential threat they pose to the city. This takes place against a backdrop of political and social unrest, as the dockworkers' strike is brutally suppressed and the city authorities crack down on oppositional political groups. *Perdido Street Station* offers a richly imagined, gritty urban world peopled with a vast array of monsters and hybrid creatures: the human citizens of New Crobuzon share the city with water-dwelling Vodyanoi, cactus people with sap for blood, winged Garuda, bug-headed Khepri and still stranger things. Magic coexists with technology in a fantasy-infused, gas-lit urban vision. Sentences burgeon with adjectives and lush descriptive flourishes. A motley crew of renegade scientists, criminals, artists and leftists plot how to save the world from destruction, but this is not the kind of clear-cut good-against-evil struggle that typifies much commercial fantasy fiction.

Perdido Street Station repeatedly figures and thematises the ideas of assemblage, hybridity, bricolage and 'remaking' that inform the novel on a formal level, with its conscious, deliberate mix of fantasy, horror, surrealism and science fiction in what Alexander C. Irvine describes as a 'hybridised apotheosis of hybridised genre heteroglossia'.[24] The hybrid creatures that people the city are just one example. New Crobuzon itself, with its mysterious, ancient monuments and structures, layered with ever-evolving architecture and industry, is another figure of assemblage, a 'mongrel city', as Yagharek perceives it.[25] It suggests a figure for the literary foundations of the novel, a phantasmagoric aggregate of genres and texts, both exhausted and alive. The novel performs its own mongrel mix of disparate elements, but the forms that hybridity takes in the story do not suggest an uncritical celebration of the idea.

The villainous, aptly named gangster Motley embodies this figure of hybridity and assemblage. He commissions Lin to produce a sculptural portrait of himself, the body that he regards as itself an ever-evolving work of art. Motley presents a grotesque collection of mismatched parts from a multiplicity of creatures, grafted together in a disturbing configuration of scales, fur, skin, wings, claws, feelers and fins, with multiple mouths and limbs. He looks at Lin with a tiger's eyes, waves a monkey's paw, stamps a cloven hoof. Motley's extremely modified body expresses his passionate interest in what he calls 'the hybrid zone', the dynamic of transition from one thing to another that he perceives in the hybrid creatures of New Crobuzon and the city itself.[26] It is impossible to tell what kind of thing he originally was. When Lin asks 'what *were* you?' he is disappointed and deflects her question with disgust, rejecting the query's very basis. What matters is the evolving process of agglomeration; he rejects the idea that his body represents 'pathology', as he imagines Lin perceives it. 'This is not error or absence or mutancy: this is image and essence', he angrily insists, relenting, however, impressed by her sympathetic rendering of his body: 'You too are the bastard zone, Ms Lin!' he tells her admiringly. Lin is unimpressed with 'his philosophical ramblings, his ruminations on mongrel theory'. To her, he is a 'spoilt child' with 'crackpot theories'.[27] Motley offers nothing like an idealised figure of aesthetic achievement, and presents an ambivalent point of identification for any concept of hybrid artistic creation. He has a kind of mechanical double in the Construct Council, a machine intelligence that can animate and inhabit the detritus of the city dump, improvising a body from random cast-off broken things; 'the rubbish was a body', Isaac observes, horrified, watching it assemble itself from bits of old cars, robots, umbrellas.[28]

Motley engages in his own deliberate remaking, in contrast with the unsettling figures of the Remade, people who have been physically modified, often in grotesque ways, by a form of magical surgery, mostly as punishment for a crime. Many Remakings involve organic and technological hybrids with machinery attachments or animal limbs. The Remade are social outcasts, ostracised and exploited. Isaac's local bar (The Dying Child) is unusual for the way it welcomes Remade alongside others; when we first see him visit the place, he shares the space with a man with a fox's muzzle grafted on to his face and a woman who holds a glass in a steam-powered mechanical claw.

Jonah, the man at the door of the bar, has been subject to a Remaking that was 'very small and very cruel'. A failed burglar, he refused to testify against his gang of fellow thieves and as punishment had his mouth removed, leaving smooth flesh in its place (Jonah has since cut a makeshift mouth for himself, but has done a bad job of it, leaving a 'flaccid wound'). Isaac's colleague David visits a brothel staffed by Remade prostitutes; doorways reveal women with dogs' legs, second vaginas in the place of their mouths, multiple breasts and other grotesque alterations.[29]

In *The Scar* and *Iron Council*, Remade characters and their relationships with unmodified humans are at the narrative's centre. Tanner Sack is one of the main characters in *The Scar*, a criminal whose remaking has been simple but devastating: he has had octopus tentacles grafted onto his chest in a painful procedure producing lasting discomfort, and a sense of being never at home, in or out of the water. Tanner has been Remade by the authoritarian powers of New Crobuzon, but he eventually decides to remake himself even further, this time in a way that he chooses, in a plot that reconfigures Remaking as an act of radical agency and recasts punishment as self-empowerment. Tanner has his body modified so that he is more authentically amphibian, with gills, translucent eyelids, webbed fingers and toes, and undergoes alterations to his body chemistry that make him more at home in the water. Tanner's second Remaking signals his embrace of Armada as a city offering him a new kind of freedom. In New Crobuzon, as a Remade human he was reduced to the status of a slave; as a newly Remade amphibian, he is a valued worker in the water-borne city of Armada.

In *Iron Council*, the decision of the exploited human railway workers to ally with the enslaved Remade who work alongside them is a key turning point in their political struggle, and Remaking becomes a powerful figure for the perpetual work of political revolution as well as a figure for the formal and stylistic ambitions of the novel, and by extension all Miéville's work, to remake genre fiction. *Iron Council* is the most formally experimental of Miéville's novels, and plays with syntax as it explores the possibilities of remaking language, crafting a form of fiction capable of representing radical political possibilities. The image at the end of the novel, the revolutionary train frozen in time by a magical spell to protect it from the New Crobuzon authorities that want to destroy it, refuses resolution in favour of an infinite suspension of possibility. 'The perpetual train' has become 'truly perpetual now perhaps poised always poised forever just about its wheels just about to finish turning. It waits', writes the narrator of the final section.[30] For some characters, the frozen train represents a tragic evasion of history; for others, it serves as an inspiration. It functions as something akin to an icon of 'the defiantly fantastic'[31] that Miéville locates in fantasy or science fiction itself: as it reshapes time, space and matter, 'with the dumb arrogance of its existence it paid the outrage of ontology no mind'.[32] The 'perpetual train' is an image combining possibility with impossibility, a 'monument' inviting all kinds of imaginative, emotional, political and philosophical engagement from a wide variety of people, uniting and equalising as the Council did while it existed in time: 'Old women, young, men, human cactus khepri hotchi vodyanoi and Remade, even Remade', who are 'for those yards around this moment made equals', and 'scores of children' all come to visit – to play, to pray, to wonder and to wait.[33] The train invites narration, listening, reading, and the novel closes with an image of its own future as well as a figure of political possibility, the train's promise of return and remaking: 'we will tell the story of the Iron Council and how it was made', the narrator insists, 'how . . . it is still coming'.[34]

NOTES

1. Jordan, 'A Life in Writing'.
2. Harrison, 'Remarks on the New Weird'.
3. VanderMeer, 'Introduction', p. xi.
4. Harrison, 'Remarks on the New Weird'.
5. Mervyn Peake's trilogy set in the fantastic earldom of Gormenghast, focused on the huge, grotesquely rendered castle at the centre: *Titus Groan* (1946), *Gormenghast* (1950), *Titus Alone* (1959).
6. M. John Harrison's cycle of stories and novels set in the fictional city of Viriconium on a future Earth.
7. Swainston, 'Remarks on "The New Weird"'.
8. Ibid.
9. VanderMeer, 'Introduction', p. x.
10. Vint, 'Introduction', p. 197.
11. Miéville, 'The New Weird', p. 8.
12. Miéville, 'M. R. James and the Quantum Vampire', p. 105.
13. VanderMeer, 'Introduction', p. xiii.
14. Miéville, 'The New Weird', p. 8.
15. Miéville, 'Editorial Introduction', p. 42.
16. Ibid., p. 48.
17. Miéville, 'Messing with Fantasy', p. 5.
18. Miéville, 'Tolkien'.
19. Ibid.
20. Ibid.
21. Miéville, 'Movements in Science Fiction and Fantasy', pp. 50–1.
22. Palmer, 'Saving the City in China Miéville's Bas-Lag', p. 237.
23. Miéville, *Perdido Street Station*, pp. 1–2.
24. Irvine, 'Urban Fantasy', p. 211.
25. Miéville, *Perdido Street Station*, p. 441.
26. Ibid., p. 37.
27. Ibid., pp. 99, 100.
28. Ibid., p. 391.
29. Ibid., pp. 23, 296–7.
30. Miéville, *Iron Council*, p. 562.
31. Miéville, 'Editorial Introduction', p. 45.
32. Miéville, *Iron Council*, p. 541.
33. Ibid., p. 562.
34. Ibid., p. 564.
35. Davies, 'New Weird 101', p. 6.

KEY WORKS

'Reveling in Genre: An Interview with China Miéville', *Science Fiction Studies*, 30:3 (2003), pp. 355–73. Miéville discusses his literary and cultural influences, including Mervyn Peake, Weird fiction, the role-playing game Dungeons and Dragons and more, and also talks about the evolution of his Marxist politics and its relation to his fiction.

Un Lun Dun (2007). Miéville's first novel for younger readers playfully challenges the conven-tion of 'the chosen one' in fantasy fiction and, like his first novel, *King Rat* (1998), and crime caper *Kraken* (2010), explores a magical and surreal vision of London. Two young friends discover Un Lun Dun, a hidden world beneath the city's streets, and find they have a vital role to play in the salvation of the underground city from the pernicious Smog that threatens to destroy it.

The City and the City (2009). Winner of the Arthur C. Clarke, World Fantasy, Hugo and British Science Fiction Awards, Miéville's first novel for adults after *Iron Council* is a Noir police procedural story, with reality tweaked just enough to make it fantastic. The title refers to the cities Beszel and Ul Qoma, which coexist in the same geographical location through a surreal glitch in space: in some 'cross-hatched' parts of the city they overlap; in others they are distinct. Their citizens deal with this bifurcated reality by consciously refusing to acknowledge the existence of the other place and its inhabitants when they come into view, in a practice referred to as 'unseeing'. The discovery of a dead body that crosses the city's strict boundaries leads Inspector Tyador Borlú to uncover a vast conspiracy involving a third, secret city. While in many ways this novel represents a change in style and direction, it also extends consistent themes and preoccupations of Miéville's work in its exploration of 'interstitial' zones and its central figure of a city distinguished both by strict divisions and stratification, and by zones of interpenetration or crossing.

Embassytown (2011). Set on the distant planet of Arieka, this uses the framework of a classic science fiction novel to explore problems of representation and meaning within language and narrative. The native Ariekei have a unique physiology and correspondingly unique language, voiced with their two mouths. Words are continuous with the things and concepts they represent in some fundamental way, with the result that the Ariekei are incapable of falsehood. Their encounter with humankind introduces this concept, along with the allied idea of metaphor, and the novel explores the devastating consequences.

FURTHER CRITICAL READING

Remarks on the New Weird on *The Third Alternative* Internet bulletin board, 2003. The discussion on the bulletin board of fiction magazine *The Third Alternative*, prompted by author M. John Harrison's provocation to discuss what he called 'New Weird' fiction, involved major authors and critics of the genre in a wide-ranging, contentious debate that has become 'legendary' in science fiction and fantasy circles.[35] Over the course of eighty-six days, authors, including those whose work fell under the emerging rubric of the genre, such as Cory Doctorow, Alastair Reynolds, Justina Robson, Charlie Stross, Steph Swainson, Jeff VanderMeer and Miéville himself, discussed the major features of the genre, the question of whether it even constituted a genre, and the politics of naming genres, in conversation with editor/critics Farah Mendelsohn, Jonathan Strahan and others. Miéville's own contribu-tions to the thread were later refined and formalised into the manifesto/essay 'Long Live the New Weird' in *Locus Magazine* in 2003. Although the original site has disappeared, Kathryn Cramer has archived the exchange on her own website <http://www.kathryncramer. com/kathryn_cramer/2007/07/the-new-weird-a.html> (last accessed 17 August 2017). A condensed version of the exchange appears in the VanderMeers' collection *The New Weird* (see below), although Miéville's contributions, which appear relatively late in the life of the conversation, are not included.

Edwards and Venezia (eds), *China Miéville: Critical Essays*. These critical essays cover a wide range of issues in Miéville's fiction, including formal and political questions, as well as the significance of maps in *Perdido Street Station*, Miéville's approach to language and social change, ideas of collectivity and community, and generic expectations. Caroline Edwards and Tony Venezia's 'UnIntroduction' provides a detailed account of Miéville's 'Weird Universe' and career, with a special interest in what they call his 'liquefaction of conventional genre categories' (p. 4) and an overview of scholarship on his work to date.

Freedman, *Art and Idea in the Novels of China Miéville*. Freedman approaches Miéville as a Marxist novelist, offering close readings of the Bas-Lag novels, *King Rat* and *Embassytown* and reflecting on theoretical and political concepts in Miéville's fiction, including international law, dialectics and questions of estrangement.

VanderMeer, Jeff and Anne Vandermeer (eds), *The New Weird* (San Francisco: Tachyon Publications, 2008). This anthology collects short fiction from contemporary authors associated with the New Weird alongside antecedents of the genre by authors such as Clive Barker and Kathy Koja, while Jeff VanderMeer's introduction is a useful overview of the genre. The anthology also includes a redacted version of the seminal 2003 discussion of the New Weird on *The Third Alternative* bulletin board and short reflections on the genre by European publishers, providing a snapshot of the status of the New Weird as a phenomenon beyond the UK and US.

Vint, Sherryl (ed.), *Extrapolation*, 50 (2009), special issue on China Miéville. This special issue features close readings of Miéville's Bas-Lag novels and reflections on the philosophical and political underpinnings of Miéville's work. Vint's short introduction offers a valuable consideration of Miéville's contribution to the New Weird as an author and critic.

BIBLIOGRAPHY

Davies, Alice, 'New Weird 101', *SFRA Review*, 291 (winter 2010), pp. 6–9.

Edwards, Caroline and Tony Venezia (eds), *China Miéville: Critical Essays* (Canterbury: Gylphi, 2015).

Freedman, Carl, *Art and Idea in the Novels of China Miéville* (Canterbury: Gylphi, 2015).

Harrison, M. John, 'Remarks on the New Weird', 29 April 2003 <http://www.kathryncramer. com/kathryn_cramer/the-new-weird-p-1.html> (last accessed 31 March 2016).

Irvine, Alexander C., 'Urban Fantasy', in Edward James and Farah Mendelsohn (eds), *The Cambridge Companion to Fantasy Literature* (Cambridge: Cambridge University Press, 2012), pp. 200–13.

Jordan, Justine, 'A Life in Writing: China Miéville', *The Guardian*, 14 November 2011 <http:// www.theguardian.com/books/2011/may/14/china-Miéville-life-writing-genre> (last accessed 31 March 2016).

Miéville, China, 'Editorial Introduction', *Historical Materialism*, 10:4 (2002), Symposium on Marxism and Fantasy, pp. 39–49.

Miéville, China, *Embassytown* (London: Macmillan, 2011).

Miéville, China, *Iron Council* (London: Macmillan, 2004).

Miéville, China, *King Rat* (London: Macmillan, 1998).

Miéville, China, *Kraken* (London: Macmillan, 2010).

Miéville, China, 'M. R. James and the Quantum Vampire', *Collapse*, 4 (2008), pp. 105–28.

Miéville, China, 'Messing with Fantasy', *Locus Magazine* (March 2002), pp. 4–5, 74–6.

Miéville, China, 'Movements in Science Fiction and Fantasy: A Symposium', in Jack Dann (ed.), *Nebula Awards Showcase 2005* (Rochester, NY: Roc, 2005), pp. 49–51.

Miéville, China, *Perdido Street Station* (London: Macmillan, 2000).

Miéville, China, *Railsea* (London: Macmillan, 2012).

Miéville, China, 'Reports of Certain Events in London', in *Looking for Jake* (New York: Del Rey/Ballantine, 2005); first published in Michael Chabon (ed.), *McSweeney's Enchanted Chamber of Astonishing Stories* (New York: Vintage, 2004).

Miéville, China, 'Reveling in Genre: An Interview with China Miéville', *Science Fiction Studies*, 30:3 (2003), pp. 355–73.

Miéville, China, *The City and the City* (London: Macmillan, 2009).

Miéville, China, *The Last Days of New Paris* (London: Macmillan, 2016).

Miéville, China, 'The New Weird', *Locus Magazine* (December 2003), pp. 8, 70.

Miéville, China, *This Census-Taker* (London: Macmillan, 2016).

Miéville, China, *Three Moments of an Explosion* (London: Macmillan, 2015).

Miéville, China, 'Tolkien: Middle Earth Meets Middle England', *Socialist Review*, 259 (January 2002) <http://socialistreview.org.uk/259/tolkien-middle-earth-meets-middle-england> (last accessed 31 March 2016).

Miéville, China, *Un Lun Dun* (London: Macmillan, 2007).

Palmer, Christopher, 'Saving the City in China Miéville's Bas-Lag Novels', *Extrapolation*, 50 (2009), pp. 234–8.

Swainston, Steph, 'Remarks on "The New Weird"', 29 April 2003 <http://www.kathryncramer.com/kathryn_cramer/the-new-weird-p-1.html> (last accessed 31 March 2016).

VanderMeer, Jeff, 'Introduction: The New Weird: "It's Alive!"', in Jeff VanderMeer and Anne VanderMeer (eds), *The New Weird* (San Francisco: Tachyon Publications, 2008).

Vint, Sherryl, 'Introduction: Special Issue on China Miéville', *Extrapolation*, 50 (2009), pp. 197–9.

CHAPTER 16

Sparkly Vampires and Shimmering Aliens: The Paranormal Romance of Stephenie Meyer

Hannah Priest

Stephenie Meyer was born in Hartford, Connecticut, and educated at Brigham Young University, where she studied English literature. Her debut novel, *Twilight*, a vampire novel aimed at a teenage readership, was published in 2005. Meyer has since written three sequels to *Twilight* (*New Moon*, *Eclipse* and *Breaking Dawn*), an illustrated guide to the series and a novella told from the perspective of a minor character in *Eclipse* (*The Short Second Life of Bree Tanner*); in 2008, she published *The Host*, a science fiction novel unrelated to the Twilight series, and in 2009 her short story 'Hell on Earth' was included in the *Prom Nights from Hell* anthology. In 2013, Meyer gave an interview to *Variety* magazine, in which she stated that she would not be writing any further works relating to *Twilight*.[1] Nevertheless, in sharp contradiction to this, an alternative version of the *Twilight* story (*Life and Death: Twilight Reimagined*) – in which, among other changes, the genders of characters were altered – was published in 2015 to mark the tenth anniversary of the original novel.

Meyer's personal life and background have received little journalistic or critical attention, with one significant exception. She is a practising Mormon, and her religion is frequently invoked in reviews, commentary and criticism of her work. The extent to which Meyer's religious beliefs can be seen in her novels is the subject of debate, leading to (positive and negative) evaluations of the ways in which her characters and plots are inflected by Mormon theology.[2] Elsewhere, there is a clear trend towards categorising Meyer's creative output as 'Mormon vampires'.[3]

Although Meyer's ouevre is relatively small and, with the exception of *The Host*, 'Hell on Earth' and her 2016 thriller *The Chemist*, limited to works relating to her 2005 novel, the commercial success, reception and influence of the Twilight novels and their film adaptations have resulted in her becoming one of the most significant popular authors of the early twenty-first century, as sales of the Twilight series attest. Between them, the books have sold over 120 million copies and have been translated into at least thirty-seven languages. However, the widespread dissemination of the novels in languages other than English is not necessarily just evidence of organic popularity and impact, but is also the result of a very careful marketing strategy. The translation rights to *Twilight* were bought by thirteen publishers before Meyer's novel was previewed at the Bologna Children's Book Fair.[4] When *Twilight* was published in English in October 2005, it was simultaneously published in a number of other languages as well, allowing for the possibility of unprecedented international success.

Apart from *Bree Tanner*, all of Meyer's work adheres to accepted formal and narrative conventions of popular romance fiction; however, this requires some qualification. The Twilight series, *The Host* and 'Hell on Earth' all feature a central plot concerned with the fulfilment of a heterosexual romantic relationship, and with the various obstacles that must be overcome in order for this to occur.[5] In the Twilight series the fulfilment of the relationship takes place over the course of four novels, with the 'happily ever after' ending coming at the end of *Breaking Dawn*; nevertheless, the heterosexual couple is established in the early chapters of the first book and their relationship remains the central focus of the series.

There are readily evident literary influences that make this generic classification clear. Charlotte Brontë's *Jane Eyre* (1847) has been cited, and Emily Brontë's *Wuthering Heights* (1847) has a significant intertextual relationship with *Twilight*, appearing both within the text itself and in marketing campaigns.[6] Glennis Byron posits *Romeo and Juliet* as a major influence, and the idea of 'star-crossed lovers' is something that recurs throughout Meyer's work, being a notable theme in both 'Hell on Earth' and *The Host*.[7] Other influences on *Twilight* are Jane Austen's *Pride and Prejudice* (1813) and Margaret Mitchell's *Gone with the Wind* (1936), the legacies of which are also visible in the formal and narrative conventions of the contemporary popular romance genre as a whole.

It is harder to discern in the Twilight series any influence from earlier vampire literature. The vampire tropes employed in Meyer's work – preternatural beauty, superior strength, heightened senses, acquisition of great wealth – are not the result of a particular literary influence, but rather a more general awareness of conventional tropes in popular culture. This point is underlined by a consideration of *The Host*, which is ostensibly a story of alien invasion and 'body-snatching'. Nevertheless, its narrative arc concerns the resolution of two heterosexual romantic relationships (Melanie/Jared and Wanda/Ian) in the face of seemingly insurmountable obstacles. Although these obstacles include Wanda's existence as a parasitic alien implanted in Melanie's body, the novel's trajectory – two closely-related female characters negotiate romantic relationships, and the more level-headed one ultimately intends to sacrifice her own happiness for that of her 'sister' – bears more fruitful comparison with Jane Austen's *Sense and Sensibility* (1811) than, say, Don Siegel's film *Invasion of the Body Snatchers* (1956).

Nevertheless, the presence of vampires, werewolves and aliens in Meyer's novels is important, and these narrative elements have an impact on how her works are understood in terms of genre. A more nuanced approach, qualifying categorisation through an understanding of sub-genre, associates Meyer's work with the sub-genre of 'paranormal romance'. Explicated by Joseph Crawford as the product of 'the long, interwoven histories of Gothic and romantic fictions', 'paranormal romance' is a sub-genre of fiction that emerged in the 1990s.[8] As is clear from the name, it is a form of romance (the noun) that features elements of the paranormal (the qualifying adjective). As well as the Twilight series, *The Host* (which features aliens) and 'Hell on Earth' (which features demons and angels) can also be classified as paranormal romance, and *The Chemist* as a thriller. *Bree Tanner*, where there are no romantic elements, sits outside the romance classification: it exists more as a 'paranormal adventure' story. However, as this novella is a supplementary chapter to the narrative arc of the Twilight series, it does not represent a significant deviation from the overall generic coherence of Meyer's work, at least before the recent appearance of *The Chemist*.

Another complication to the generic classification of Meyer's ouevre is offered by the marketing and reception of the Twilight series. *Twilight* focuses on characters in their late teens (albeit permanently so, in some cases) and, despite undoubted popularity with adults, its assumed readership is teenaged. When the book was first published, 'teenage' novels were most frequently grouped as a subsection of children's fiction. However, the book's marketing undermines its status as a children's book, in particular its iconic cover design, featuring a hand proffering an apple that evokes both the 'childlike' temptation of Snow White and the 'adult' temptation of Eve. While *Twilight* was far from being the first book to be marketed to teenaged readers (nor even the first vampire romance aimed at teenagers, as L. J. Smith's Vampire Diaries series precedes it by over a decade), its commercial success led to transformations in publishing, marketing and bookselling categorisation. Prior to *Twilight*'s publication, various terms had been used to designate the subset of children's fiction aimed at older readers, including' juvenile fiction' and 'young adult fiction' ('YA').[9] YA quickly became attached to *Twilight* as an apt classification of its intended readership, and it became the dominant industry term for books ostensibly aimed at teenagers. Booksellers followed suit, introducing separate YA sections in both physical and online stores that were distinct from earlier subsections of children's literature.[10]

Although young adult fiction includes texts as diverse as J. D. Salinger's *The Catcher in the Rye* (1951) and the 1980s series Sweet Valley High created by Francine Pascal, twenty-first-century YA has been dominated by a number of bestselling series, all of which feature supernatural or fantasy elements: J. K. Rowling's Harry Potter novels (initially marketed as children's fiction, but subsequently rebranded and repackaged), Suzanne Collins's Hunger Games series and Meyer's Twilight novels. In addition to this, the large number of YA paranormal romances that have followed Meyer's Twilight series has resulted in a loose association of YA with paranormal/fantasy romance. While more recent publications, such as John Green's *The Fault in Our Stars* (2012), challenge this association, use of the term 'YA' (rather than 'juvenile' or 'young adult') functions in some ways as a marker of generic expectation, rather than simply of intended readership.

The significance of *Twilight* to the creation of the YA categorisation is undeniable. In addition to changes in bookselling and marketing strategies, its popularity led to the 'rebranding' of several earlier novels, most notably *Wuthering Heights*, as 'tie-in' works to Meyer's successful series.[11] However, the Twilight series also influenced broader trends in vampire literature, film and television. Although both Smith's early Vampire Diaries novels (1991–2) and Charlaine Harris's Southern Vampire Mysteries

(2001–13) predate the publication of *Twilight*, the television adaptations of these series appeared after the publication of *Breaking Dawn* and near-concurrently with the release of the film adaptation of *Twilight*.[12] The success of the Twilight series undoubtedly informed the decision to adapt Smith's and Harris's novels; however, Meyer's vampire novels have also inspired more direct responses, in the form of fan art and parody. Of the latter, the most notable example is the *Harvard Lampoon*'s 2009 novel, *Nightlight*; Meyer is only the second novelist to get a full-length parody by the long-running US university magazine, the first being J. R. R. Tolkien, whose *Lord of the Rings* was lampooned in the 1969 *Bored of the Rings*. Of the former, the most significant example is the fan fiction 'Master of the Universe' by Snowqueens [sic] Icedragon, which was later revised and published as *Fifty Shades of Grey* by E. L. James.[13]

   In addition to the 'unofficial' responses to Meyer's work by satirists and fans, the Twilight series and *The Host* have had 'official' treatment in the form of film adaptations. *Twilight*, starring Robert Pattinson and Kristen Stewart, was released in 2008, and was followed by *New Moon* (2009), *Eclipse* (2010), *Breaking Dawn: Part 1* (2011) and *Breaking Dawn: Part 2* (2012). The Twilight films have been consistently successful at the box office, with the final instalment taking over \$340 million in its opening weekend.[14] The film adaptations have also received parody treatment, with *Vampires Suck* (2010) and *Breaking Wind* (2012) both satirising the series.

   The proximity of the first film's release to the publication of the novel series means that it is often difficult to differentiate the fandoms of the books and the films (and anyway there is obviously a very substantial crossover between these). Several journalists have highlighted reactions of Twilight fans, using examples of extreme behaviour, such as a 'mob' attacking a waxwork figure of Edward Cullen or a woman 'marrying' a cardboard replica of the character, to illustrate a narrative of 'madness' or 'mania'; nevertheless, these examples frequently involve the portrayal of Edward by Robert Pattinson, rather than serve as a direct response to Meyer's novels.[15] Similarly, the merchandise and tourism surrounding the series – including clothing, stationery, cosmetics, visitor attractions at Forks (the setting of the series), vampire cruises and sex toys – are part of the film's marketing as much as a response to Meyer's books.

   Outside of adaptation and fan response, the Twilight series has received a great deal of critical and academic attention, with journal articles, edited collections, monographs and conferences devoted to it. Again, there is frequently a crossover between analyses of the books and of the film adaptations, with the term 'Twilight franchise' being employed to cover the entire body of work. Approaches range from textual analysis to cultural history and theory, with critics examining both the franchise's content and its impact, popularity and reception. It cannot be denied that there is an undercurrent of distaste and discomfort in much of the academic discourse surrounding Meyer's work; issues of race, gender, abuse and morality have come under particular scrutiny.[16] Moreover, the relationship between the novels' 'message' and the apparent 'vulnerability' of their readership/fandom has provoked a number of articles, including several ascribing didactic or manipulative intentions to Meyer.[17] Significantly, the critical trend in Twilight scholarship towards suspicion and negativity has itself become the focus of some academic attention, with writers both noting and analysing critical inclinations towards denigrating or disavowing Meyer's work.[18]

This critical discomfort both informs and is informed by the broader popular discourse surrounding the Twilight novels, and is best exemplified by the visceral reaction to their idiosyncratic representation of vampiric physicality. In Chapter 13 of *Twilight*, the narrator (Bella) sees Edward in the sunlight for the first time and describes his skin as sparkling as though studded with precious stones.[19] Although this description can be read alongside a long tradition of presenting the vampire as preternaturally beautiful, the inclusion of 'sparkly vampires' in Meyer's work has gained a notoriety transcending its importance as a plot device. Negative responses to the idea of 'sparkly vampires' proliferate in online discussions, memes and parodies, with some recent published fiction including disclaimers to distance itself from this putative 'trend'.[20] Increasingly, the idea of 'sparkly vampires' has been detached from direct critiques of the series, becoming something of a catch-all term to characterise a perceived 'watering-down' of teen or popular culture, usually offered in comparison to some 'true' version that existed in the past.

Meyer's sparkly vampires appear in the story of Bella Swan, a seventeen-year-old who moves to Forks, Washington, to live with her father, Charlie. In *Twilight*, Bella meets Edward Cullen (a vampire) and begins a friendship with Jacob Black (a Native American living on a nearby reservation). Bella begins a relationship with Edward, despite having discovered that he is a vampire, and begins to form friendships with Edward's 'siblings' and 'parents' (the other vampires in the Cullen 'coven'). The Cullens describe themselves as 'vegetarian' vampires, as they do not feed on human blood, and they live peacefully under the terms of a treaty with the Quileute tribe (of which Jacob is a member), which determines both the territory and the behaviour of the vampires. Indications in *Twilight* that the Quileute tribe are werewolves are developed in *New Moon* and *Eclipse*, and the 'world' of the vampires is also developed in the subsequent books, with a series of antagonists threatening the Cullen coven.

However, the relationship between Edward and Bella is the main focus of the novels. Although they declare their love in *Twilight*, various obstacles impede the relationship's progress. In *New Moon*, Edward ends the relationship, citing Bella's safety as his motivation, and a new love interest – the now-lycanthropic Jacob – is introduced. Although Bella and Edward are reunited at the end of the second book, their human–vampire union becomes an obstacle in itself in *Eclipse* and *Breaking Dawn*, as other characters intervene repeatedly to obstruct and prohibit the relationship. In the final book of the series, Bella and Edward marry, and Bella becomes pregnant. She gives birth to a human–vampire hybrid, whose existence threatens to start a war between the various vampires and werewolves. This war is eventually averted through the fortuitous revelation of another human–-vampire hybrid, and the Cullens are allowed to continue their abstemious existence in peace. Bella is transformed into a vampire following the birth of her child, and thus the romance plot of the series is resolved with a 'happily ever after' ending that truly promises to last for eternity.

Central to the Twilight series are the characters of Bella, Edward and Jacob, who form a 'love triangle' of sorts after Jacob's transformation in *New Moon*. Edward's characterisation in particular is conventional to the romance genre, influenced as it is by Brontë's Rochester, Austen's Darcy and, to a lesser extent, Mitchell's Rhett Butler. Bella, too, has been read as a stock romantic character, with much of the criticism of the book centring on her apparent lack of agency and the subsuming of her autonomy into a patriarchal heterosexual union.[21] The character of Jacob complicates the romance storyline, as he is neither a villain threatening to lead the heroine away from her 'good' partner (like Austen's Wickham) nor a safe alternative to the dangerous hero (like Brontë's St John Rivers). Instead, the character of Jacob offers contrast to Edward in terms of both (supernatural) species and (human) race. As both a Native American and a werewolf, Jacob is placed at the nexus of discourses of savagery, nobility, exclusion and invasion, and his lycanthropic identity is an example of the association of the native and the animal that pervades colonial writing.[22] However, his identity as a werewolf and his confrontation with the vampiric Edward also draws on (and furthers) the increasingly popular trope of vampire-versus-werewolf animosity that can be found in fantasy literature, film and television.[23] Since the publication of New Moon, fans of the series have frequently characterised themselves as 'Team Edward' or 'Team Jacob', but this distinction evokes much more than simply a choice between rival suitors.

Meyer revisits the theme of rival males competing for the love of a female in her post-Twilight novel The Host (2008), which is set in the aftermath of the invasion of earth by a race of parasitic aliens who call themselves 'Souls' and who live multiple lifetimes implanted in various 'hosts'. The book begins with the implantation of a Soul (known as Wanderer, later nicknamed Wanda) into a host body (Melanie Stryder) in order to begin its ninth life cycle. The procedure is not fully successful, as Melanie's consciousness survives the implantation and her 'mind' remains within her body, competing with that of Wanda. Melanie attempts to regain control of her body, leading Wanda to track down a band of desert-dwelling human rebels, as she wishes to be reunited with her brother Jamie and lover Jared. The first 'love triangle' appears when Wanda also experiences feelings of desire and love towards Jared; however, a more complicated competition appears in the second half of the novel, when Wanda (independent of Melanie) becomes attracted to another man, Ian. Jared and Ian compete for the attention of the female (who is both Melanie and Wanda), while Wanda and Melanie are placed in a seemingly impossible competition over a single body and, by extension, the ability to select a lover.

Similarities in thematic and narrative concerns allow The Host to be read easily alongside Meyer's more well-known and influential work. Aside from the paranormal and romance elements that characterise the works, ideas of identity, (in)appropriate desire, self-sacrifice and reproduction proliferate. The Host's conclusion sees Wanda sacrifice herself in order for Melanie to regain her body and her relationship with Jared; however, although Wanda asks to be killed after her removal, in a narrative episode reminiscent of the male characters' attempts to abort Bella's pregnancy in Breaking Dawn, a group of men ignores her wishes and implants her into a new host. When Wanda wakes up in her new body, she is able to resume her relationship with Ian, deciding to live one final lifetime (as a human), before finally reproducing, which, for her species, results in both death and a million clone parasites who will remember and venerate their 'mother' for millennia. This, like Bella's death in childbirth followed by ascension to the role of vampiric 'super-mother' in Breaking Dawn,[24] is presented as a happy ending for the characters and a satisfactory narrative resolution for the readers.

In addition to the thematic parallels between *The Host* and the Twilight series, Meyer's work is characterised by a tendency to offer multiple (and often conflicting) narrative perspectives, and by an idiosyncratic interest in minor characters and digressive exegesis. In *Eclipse* (2007), Bella, the first-person narrator, is given 'backstories', narrated by a series of characters, which occasionally conflict with the dominant narrative of the series' 'good' vampires.[25] These stories hint at the possibility of a counter-narrative, even if only by implication and suggestion. *Breaking Dawn* (2008) develops this technique further, as sections of the novel are told from the first-person perspective of Jacob, which, again, offers some sense of a potential alternative narrative that runs against the story told by Bella. This use of multiple first-person narrators is developed even further in *The Host*, where the narrative is presented from the simultaneous but separate viewpoints of the two female protagonists. While Wanda is the 'dominant' voice, her narration often uses first-person plural pronouns or focuses on the narrators' internal conflict, undermining any sense of a singular voice.

This persistent multiplicity of narrative is perhaps most clearly seen in the supplementary material to Meyer's Twilight novels. In *Bree Tanner* (2010), Meyer takes a very minor character from *Eclipse*, a young vampire (Bree) who is captured by the Cullens and killed shortly afterwards, and narrates events from Bree's perspective. Additionally, an abortive supplementary text to the series, *Midnight Sun*, retells the events of *Twilight* from Edward's perspective.[26] However, it is in the tenth anniversary edition of *Twilight* that Meyer's fascination with alternative and counter-narratives reaches its zenith; the 2015 'dual' volume includes both a new edition of the original novel and a text entitled *Life and Death: Twilight Reimagined*. This latter novel generally follows the plot of the 2005 novel, but with some significant changes. While the 'hook' is that it is a 'gender-switched' version of the story (Edward becomes Edythe, Bella becomes Beau, and so on), Meyer makes it clear in the novel's foreword that she has revised other parts of the storyline, including some aspects of characterisation and storytelling. On reaching the final chapters, the reader discovers that Meyer has substantially revised the novel's ending, creating a narrative resolution differing significantly from that of *Twilight*. The story is followed by an afterword, in which Meyer confesses to having 'cheated' but says she is 'not sorry' for doing so.[27] *Life and Death* alters a small detail in the timing of the climactic scenes, which results in a resolution that is not only different to that of *Twilight*, but also renders any potential sequels redundant. Thus, it can be read as the most sustained counter-narrative offered within the Twilight series.

Although Meyer has said little publicly in response to criticism of her work, her use of alternative narratives allows for some subtle interactions. This can be seen most notably in the case of her 'sparkly vampires'. While the vampires' reaction to sunlight is used as a descriptive and plot device throughout the main Twilight novels, the supplementary texts reveal a discomfort with this now-notorious trait. In *Bree Tanner*, a group of 'newborn' vampires discover that their 'maker' has lied to them about the effects of sunlight. As they step into the light for the first time and discover that it makes their skin sparkle, the narrator comments on how ridiculous this is; Bree describes her newly sparkling peers as 'shining, disco-ball vampires', in a phrase that echoes some of the more critical commentary on Meyer's earlier work.[28]

More tellingly, Meyer removes the 'disco-ball vampires' entirely from her revised version of *Twilight*. While Chapter 13 of *Life and Death* broadly follows the plot of its earlier analogue, the description of Edward's female counterpart is quite different. In the much shorter description in the 2015 novel, the vampire steps into the sunlight, and her human lover simply sees light reflecting on her skin as 'prism-like rainbows': though she might be reflective, Edythe Cullen doesn't sparkle.

As noted above, Stephenie Meyer is not a prolific writer, and her output is almost exclusively sequels and supplementary material to her 2005 debut novel. However, the 'phenomenal' popularity of that material, as well as of the film adaptations and associated merchandise, means that the Twilight series can be read as one of the most significant works of early twenty-first-century popular fiction. Moreover, the influence of Meyer's work on trends in popular culture, as well as the intertextual relationship in which the Twilight series stands to both *Fifty Shades of Grey* and *Wuthering Heights*, suggests that the novels' significance transcends their characters and plots. This is a product of a highly successful admixture of classic romance tropes, idiosyncratic motifs, visible international fandoms and canny marketing strategies. While *The Host*, *Life and Death* and *The Chemist* have not attracted the same levels of attention as the Twilight novels, Meyer's work continues be the subject of academic, journalistic and popular commentary a decade after the publication of *Twilight*. It is likely that this commentary will decrease as the twenty-first century progresses; however, the (romanticised or derisory) concept of 'sparkly vampires' and the dramatic expansion and solidification of the paranormal romance genre remain a tangible and enduring legacy of the books' success and influence.

NOTES

1. McNary, 'Q&A Stephenie Meyer'.
2. See, for example, Riess, 'Book of Mormon Stories That Steph Meyer Tells to Me'; Toscano, 'Mormon Morality and Immortality in Stephenie Meyer's Twilight Series'; Babu, 'Stephenie Meyer's *Twilight*'.
3. See, for example, Sutton and Benshoff, '"Forever Family" Values'.
4. See Brown, 'Twilight in Translation'; Gleed, '*Twilight*, Translated'.
5. On the formal and narrative conventions of the popular romance novel, see Regis, *A Natural History of the Romance Novel*.
6. See Morey, '"Famine for Food, Expectation for Content"'; Glennis Byron, '©Branding and Gothic in Contemporary Popular Culture'.
7. Byron, '"As One Dead"'.
8. Crawford, *Twilight of the Gothic?*, p. 8.
9. The term 'young adult' was first used formally in relation to fiction publishing in 1957, with the creation of the Young Adult Services Division, a subsection of the American Library Association.
10. On its initial publication, prior to the creation of 'YA' departments, some booksellers expressed confusion as to where *Twilight* should be shelved in store. See Brown, 'Twilight in Translation'.
11. See Byron, '©Branding and Gothic in Contemporary Popular Culture'.
12. The film adaptation of *Twilight* premiered on 3 December 2008; the first episode of *True Blood* (the TV series based on Harris's novels) aired on 7 September 2008, and the first episode of *The Vampire Diaries* was broadcast on 10 September 2009.

13. Dara Downey discusses the work of E. L. James in detail in Chapter 10 of the present volume.
14. McClintock, 'Box Office Report'.
15. Aldridge, 'Twilight Fan Marries Cardboard Cut-out of Robert Pattinson in £2,000 Las Vegas Wedding'; Smith, 'Thrilled Fans Mob Robert Pattinson'.
16. See, for example, Wilson, 'Civilized Vampires Versus Savage Werewolves'; Michael J. Goebel, 'Embraced by Consumption'; Bealer, 'Of Monsters and Men'; Sutton and Benshoff, 'Twilight and the Modern Mormon Vampire'.
17. See, for example, Babu, 'Stephenie Meyer's Twilight'.
18. See, for example, Crawford, Twilight of the Gothic?; Sheffield and Merlo, 'Biting Back'.
19. Meyer, Twilight, p. 228.
20. See, for example, Thomas and Helgadóttir, European Monsters, back cover.
21. See, for example, Nicol, 'When You Kiss Me, I Want to Die'; Priest, '"Hell! Was I Becoming a Vampyre Slut?"'
22. See Wilson, 'Civilized Vampires Versus Savage Werewolves'; Scott, 'Female Werewolf as Monstrous Other in Honoré Beaugrand's "The Werewolves"'.
23. See Priest, 'Pack Versus Coven'.
24. I use the term 'super-mother' here, as Bella's special power as a vampire is the ability to supernaturally shield her husband and child from the paranormal abilities of other vampires.
25. The most notable examples of these are Rosalie Cullen's backstory and the story of 'The Third Wife's Sacrifice'.
26. Meyer originally expressed a desire to publish Midnight Sun, but a 'leaked' chapter delayed her plans. After the publication of E. L. James's Fifty Shades of Grey (a novel based on a Twilight fan fiction), and later Grey (a retelling of James's first novel from the perspective of the male protagonist), Meyer announced that she would not be pursuing publication of Midnight Sun. A partial draft of the story is available on Meyer's own website <http://stepheniemeyer.com/pdf/midnightsun_partial_draft4.pdf> (last accessed 1 May 2016).
27. Meyer, Life and Death, afterword.
28. Meyer, Bree Tanner, p. 48.

KEY WORKS

Twilight (2005). Meyer's debut novel, introducing the characters of Bella Swan, Edward Cullen and Jacob Black. Adapted as a film starring Kristen Stewart, Robert Pattinson and Taylor Lautner in 2008.
New Moon (2006). The first sequel to Twilight, where Jacob Black is first transformed into a werewolf and the 'love triangle' between the three main characters begins. Adapted as a film starring Kristen Stewart, Robert Pattinson and Taylor Lautner in 2009.
Eclipse (2007). The third novel in the Twilight series, in which the 'world' of vampires and werewolves is expanded, further threats are introduced, and Bella and Edward become engaged. Adapted as a film starring Kristen Stewart, Robert Pattinson and Taylor Lautner in 2010.
Breaking Dawn (2008). In the fourth novel in the series, Bella and Edward marry, Bella gives birth to a human–vampire hybrid child and then finally becomes a vampire herself. Adapted as two films starring Kristen Stewart, Robert Pattinson and Taylor Lautner in 2011 and 2012.
The Host (2008). A science fiction romance novel told (mainly) from the perspective an invading parasitic creature who has been implanted in the body of a teenaged human. Adapted as a film starring Saoirse Ronan, Max Irons and Jake Abel in 2013.
The Short Second Life of Bree Tanner (2010). A supplementary Twilight novella told from the perspective of a very minor character in Eclipse.
Life and Death: Twilight Reimagined (2015). Part of the tenth anniversary 'dual edition' publication

of *Twilight*, where the genders of characters from the original novel are altered, giving the story of Beau Swan, Edythe Cullen and (to a lesser extent) Jules Black.

FURTHER CRITICAL READING

Anatol, Giselle Liza (ed.), *Bringing Light to Twilight: Perspectives on the Pop Culture Phenomenon* (New York: Palgrave Macmillan, 2011). Essays exploring the Twilight books and films, covering literary contexts, gender, sexuality and race.
Clarke, Amy M. and Marijane Osborn (eds), *The Twilight Mystique: Critical Essays on the Novels and Films* (Jefferson, NC: McFarland, 2010). Collection of essays exploring the Twilight books and films, including chapters on abstinence, religion, adaptation and contexts.
Click, Melissa A., Jennifer Stevens Aubrey and Elizabeth Behm-Morawitz (eds), *Bitten by Twilight: Youth Culture, Media, and the Vampire Franchise* (New York: Peter Lang, 2010). Collection of essays exploring the Twilight books and films, including topics such as race, gender, fan response and commodification.
Crawford, *The Twilight of the Gothic?* Monograph examining the cultural history of the paranormal romance genre, with particular focus on Meyer's Twilight novels.
Parke, Maggie and Natalie Wilson (eds), *Theorizing Twilight: Critical Essays on What's at Stake in a Post-Vampire World* (Jefferson, NC: McFarland, 2011). Essays exploring the Twilight books and films, with an emphasis on fan culture, genre, intertextuality and gender.

BIBLIOGRAPHY

Aldridge, Gemma, 'Twilight Fan Marries Cardboard Cut-Out of Robert Pattinson in £2,000 Las Vegas Wedding', *Daily Mirror*, 10 September 2014 <http://www.mirror.co.uk/news/real-life-stories/twilight-fan-marries-cardboard-cut-out-4193568> (last accessed 1 May 2016).
Babu, Aiswarya S., 'Stephenie Meyer's *Twilight*: A Vampire Tale?', *IUP Journal of American Literature*, 4:2 (May 2011), p. 37.
Bealer, Tracy L., 'Of Monsters and Men: Toxic Masculinity and the Twenty-First-Century Vampire in the *Twilight Saga*', in Giselle Liza Anatol (ed.), *Bringing Light to Twilight: Perspectives on the Pop Culture Phenomenon* (New York: Palgrave Macmillan, 2011), pp. 139–52.
Brown, Jennifer M., 'Twilight in Translation: How Can a Cover Convey That It's More Than a Vampire Book?', *Publishers Weekly*, 252:43 (28 October 2005) <http://www.publishersweekly.com/pw/print/20051031/19710-twilight-in-translation.html> (last accessed 19 November 2015).
Byron, Glennis, '"As One Dead": *Romeo and Juliet* in the "Twilight" Zone', in John Drakakis and Dale Townshend (eds), *Gothic Shakespeares* (Abingdon and New York: Routledge, 2009), pp. 167–85.
Byron, Glennis, '©Branding and Gothic in Contemporary Popular Culture: The Case of Twilight', *The Gothic Imagination*, 31 December 2010 <http://www.gothic.stir.ac.uk/blog/branding-and-gothic-in-contemporary-popular-culture-the-case-of-twilight/> (last accessed 1 May 2016).
Crawford, Joseph, *The Twilight of the Gothic?: Vampire Fiction and the Rise of the Paranormal Romance, 1991–2012* (Cardiff: University of Wales Press, 2014).
Gleed, Kim Allen, '*Twilight*, Translated', in Giselle Liza Anatol (ed.), *Bringing Light to Twilight: Perspectives on the Pop Culture Phenomenon* (New York: Palgrave Macmillan, 2011), pp. 59–68.
Goebel, Michael J., '"Embraced" by Consumption: *Twilight* and the Modern Construction of Gender', in Giselle Liza Anatol (ed.), *Bringing Light to Twilight: Perspectives on the Pop Culture Phenomenon* (New York: Palgrave Macmillan, 2011), pp. 168–9.
McClintock, Pamela, 'Box Office Report: "Breaking Dawn – Part 2" Bites Off $340.9 Million

Global Opening', *Hollywood Reporter*, 18 November 2012 <http://www.hollywoodreporter.com/news/box-office-report-breaking-dawn-391789> (last accessed 1 May 2016).

McNary, Dave, 'Q&A Stephenie Meyer: "Twilight" Author Trades Undead for Well-Bred in "Austenland"', *Variety*, 13 August 2013 <http://variety.com/2013/film/news/qa-stephenie-meyer-twilight-author-trades-undead-for-well-bred-in-austenland-1200577471/> (last accessed 10 December 2015).

Meyer, Stephenie, *Life and Death: Twilight Reimagined* (London: Atom Books, 2015), Kindle file.

Meyer, Stephenie, *The Short Second Life of Bree Tanner* (2009; London: Atom Books, 2010), Kindle file.

Meyer, Stephenie, *Twilight* (2005; London: Atom Books, 2007).

Morey, Anne, '"Famine for Food, Expectation for Content": *Jane Eyre* as Intertext for the "Twilight" Saga', in Anne Morey (ed.), *Genre, Reception, and Adaptation in the 'Twilight' Series* (Farnham: Ashgate, 2012), pp. 15–28.

Nicol, Rhonda, '"When You Kiss Me, I Want to Die": Arrested Feminism in *Buffy the Vampire Slayer* and the *Twilight* Series', in Giselle Liza Anatol (ed.), *Bringing Light to Twilight: Perspectives on the Pop Culture Phenomenon* (New York: Palgrave Macmillan, 2011), pp. 113–24.

Priest, Hannah, '"Hell! Was I Becoming a Vampyre Slut?" Sex, Sexuality and Morality in Young Adult Vampire Fiction', in Deborah Mutch (ed.), *The Modern Vampire and Human Identity* (Basingstoke: Palgrave Macmillan, 2013), pp. 55–75.

Priest, Hannah, 'Pack versus Coven: Guardianship of Tribal Memory in Vampire versus Werewolf Narratives', in Simon Bacon and Katarzyna Bronk (eds), *Undead Memory: Vampires and Human Memory in Popular Culture* (New York: Peter Lang, 2014), pp. 213–38.

Regis, Pamela, *A Natural History of the Romance Novel* (Philadelphia: University of Pennsylvania Press, 2003).

Riess, Jana, 'Book of Mormon Stories That Steph Meyer Tells to Me: LDS Themes in the Twilight Saga and "The Host"', *Brigham Young University Studies*, 48:3 (2009), pp. 141–7.

Scott, Shannon, 'Female Werewolf as Monstrous Other in Honoré Beaugrand's "The Werewolves"', in Hannah Priest (ed.), *She-Wolf: A Cultural History of Female Werewolves* (Manchester: Manchester University Press, 2015), pp. 96–110.

Sheffield, Jessica and Elyse Merlo, 'Biting Back: Twilight Anti-Fandom and the Rhetoric of Superiority', in Melissa A. Click, Jennifer Stevens Aubrey and Elizabeth Behm-Morawitz (eds), *Bitten by Twilight: Youth Culture, Media, and the Vampire Franchise* (New York: Peter Lang, 2010), pp. 207–24.

Smith, Lizzie, 'Thrilled Fans Mob Robert Pattinson . . . Shame He's Only a Waxwork', *Daily Mail*, 10 September 2014 <http://www.dailymail.co.uk/tvshowbiz/article-1260623/Robert-Pattinson-waxwork-Londons-Madame-Tussauds.html> (last accessed 1 May 2016).

Sutton, Travis and Harry M. Benshoff, '"Forever Family" Values: *Twilight* and the Modern Mormon Vampire', in Aviva Briefel and Sam J. Miller (eds), *Horror After 9/11: World of Fear, Cinema of Terror* (Austin: University of Texas Press, 2011), pp. 200–19.

Thomas, Jo and Margrét Helgadóttir (eds), *European Monsters* (Derby: Fox Spirit Books, 2014).

Toscano, Margaret M., 'Mormon Morality and Immortality in Stephenie Meyer's Twilight Series', in Melissa A. Click, Jennifer Stevens Aubrey and Elizabeth Behm-Morawitz (eds), *Bitten by Twilight: Youth Culture, Media, and the Vampire Franchise* (New York: Peter Lang, 2010), pp. 21–36.

Wilson, Natalie, 'Civilized Vampires Versus Savage Werewolves: Race and Ethnicity in the Twilight Series', in Melissa A. Click, Jennifer Stevens Aubrey and Elizabeth Behm-Morawitz (eds), *Bitten by Twilight: Youth Culture, Media, and the Vampire Franchise* (New York: Peter Lang, 2010), pp. 55–70.

CHAPTER 17

'We Needed to Get a Lot of White Collars Dirty': Apocalypse as Opportunity in Max Brooks's *World War Z*

Bernice M. Murphy

Since the beginning of the twenty-first century, a resonant new sub-genre of popular fiction has been elevated into the publishing mainstream. So-called 'Zombie Lit' consists of novels set during the chaotic onset and/or post-apocalyptic aftermath of a viral outbreak which has resulted in the biblically unscheduled resurrection of the recently deceased.[1] According to Xavier Aldana Reyes, 'over 70 notable zombie novels were published between 2000 and 2016, and dozens more are available to the insatiable reader via Kindle'.[2] This boom is also a truly transmedia phenomenon, in that it extends far beyond literary and filmic representations of the walking dead. As the editors of *The Zombie Renaissance in Popular Culture* (2015) observe, 'We are currently experiencing a global explosion of zombie mania, with zombie representations and zombie-related material infiltrating the media and contemporary society in multiple and changing forms'. These include cinematic, literary and televisual iterations of the zombie, as well as videogames, popular music, comic books, and fan practices such as 'zombie walks' and online forums.[3] One could also include the academic realm of 'Zombie Studies' as part of this trend: critics from a wide range of disciplines have used the zombie as a starting point for the discussion of an ever-expanding range of critical and theoretical issues, among them complex moral, political and social concerns such as biomedical ethics, globalisation and post-humanism.[4] In other words, the 'zombie apocalypse' has been elevated from the status of a fairly well known but still relatively niche cultural referent into one of the most significant and widely disseminated pop culture tropes of the current era. Unlike many of the other prominent horror icons – most notably the vampire, which has often been compared and contrasted with its non-sentient near relative – the zombie has not previously had a strong foothold in popular fiction.[5] There are few obvious pre-twenty-first-century 'Zombie Lit' ur-texts that we can point to as having played a major role in establishing the basic outlines of the concept: no real equivalent to the likes of J. S. Le Fanu's *Carmilla* (1872) or Bram Stoker's *Dracula* (1897). Although there have certainly been a few notable proto-zombie narratives, of which Richard Matheson's *I Am Legend* (1954) is by far the most significant, it is still the case that, until very recently, the *print* zombie was entirely overshadowed by its cinematic alter ego. This makes the success of American author Max Brooks's 2006 novel *World War Z: An Oral History of the Zombie War* even more significant. By 2011, the novel had already sold one million copies. The 2013 release of the critically panned but commercially successful film adaptation only further increased sales.[6] As Timothy R. Fox notes, 'not only is *World War Z* the first zombie-themed book to achieve such strong sales figures in such a short period of time, but it may well be the first contemporary zombie-themed novel in the history of horror fiction to have found its way on to the *New York Times* Top 10 Bestseller list (Deutsch 2013, online)'.[7]

It was the movie screen, and not the page, which spawned our present-day conception of the zombie and, thus, eventually gave rise to *World War Z*. George A. Romero's ground-breaking independent horror movie *Night of the Living Dead* (1968) 'Americanised' a supernatural threat which had previously almost always been located in the Caribbean and associated with black magic and the non-white 'Other'.[8] As Kim Pfaffenroth rightly states, 'When one speaks of zombie movies today, one is really speaking of movies that are either made or directly influenced by one man'.[9] Set over the course of a single afternoon and night, *Night of the Living Dead* depicts the horrific ordeal undergone by a small band of survivors who seek refuge in an isolated farmhouse when the dead begin to rise from their graves. These cannibalistic ghouls appear to be driven only a primal, mindless instinct to consume the living. By making his zombies flesh-eaters, Romero could pass explicit commentary on what he saw as the mindless consumerism and materialism of late-twentieth-century American life. As Jamie Russell notes, this 'wasn't simply a spectacular ploy to drum up controversy and boost ticket sales, but central to the film's provocative vision of individuals being consumed/subsumed into the larger group'.[10]

Despite the fact that between 1993 and 2004 Romero directed only one film (*Bruiser*, 2000), the Dead series had, by the turn of the century, worked its way into the popular consciousness. As a new generation of creative talents who had grown with up the Romero-esque zombie came of age, the walking dead were rapidly incorporated into the mainstream cultural imaginary. This surge of popular interest in all things zombie-related laid the commercial foundations for Brooks's publishing triumph. Onscreen, the success of Zack Snyder's kinetic remake of *Dawn of the Dead* (2004) meant that Romero was finally able to make his fourth Dead film, *Land of the Dead* (2005). Other notable zombie films of the period included the 2007 Spanish film *[REC]* and the Canadian films *Fido* (2006) and *Pontypool* (2008), the last of which has the distinction of being the first post-structuralist zombie movie. As *Fido* and earlier re-workings of Romero (such as the unofficial sequel *The Return of the Living Dead* [1985]) had suggested, the zombie apocalypse also has considerable comic potential: this notion was expanded upon post-2000 by the likes of *Shaun of the Dead* (2004), *Dead Meat* (2004), *Zombieland* (2009), *Dance of the Dead* (2008), *Dead Snow* (2009), *Juan of the Dead* (2011), *Cockneys Vs Zombies* (2012), *Zombeavers* (2014), *Scouts Guide to the Zombie Apocalypse* (2015) and *Attack of the Lederhosen Zombies* (2016). The fact that these films are not just American, but also hail from Canada, Cuba, Germany, Norway, the UK and Ireland, provides further evidence of the fact that, as Roger Luckhurst has noted, in the case of the zombie, 'a liminal Gothic monster' has 'travelled from the speechless subaltern world of slavery into the heart of the American empire and the networks of globalised popular culture'.[11] Little wonder, then, that *World War Z*, which presents the reader with a truly global crisis, struck a chord: the contemporary zombie was already an accomplished traveller.

Zombie-centric video games also played an important role in the boom. Most important here is the Resident Evil series (1996 –), which has spawned many instalments and imitators, as well as a long-running film franchise. The contagion infected comics and the small screen too: Robert Kirkman's *The Walking Dead* (launched in 2003 and ongoing) comic book series was adapted for TV in 2010, and the uncompromisingly downbeat show which resulted rapidly became one of the most watched in the world. This, in turn, led to the publication of a series of spin-off tie-in novels, and massively increased sales for the still ongoing comic book.[12]

Numerous TV takes on the zombie apocalypse followed. These included the low-budget, high-energy effort *Z-Nation* (2014–) as well as a number of rather more oblique, atmospheric and ambitious variations on the basic concept. The small-town dead miraculously return to their loved ones, apparently *without* a longing for human flesh, in all of the following: the French series *Les Revenants* (2012); its short-lived 2015 American remake *The Returned* (2015); another American show, *Resurrection* (2014–15); and the Australian series *Glitch* (2015–). British series *In the Flesh* (2013–15) featured former zombies attempting to come to terms with their horrific actions during the so-called 'Rising', while in *Dead Set* (2008) (the scriptwriting debut of Charlie Brooker, creator of the *Black Mirror* science fiction TV series), the stars of a reality TV show find themselves caught up in a real-life undead epidemic. More recently, there have appeared two US comedy dramas about previously unassuming women who attain newfound empowerment when they are turned into (still fairly sentient) zombies: *iZombie* (2015–) and *Santa Clarita Diet* (2017).

Brooks was therefore fortunate enough to publish his novel just as the 'zombie renaissance' was beginning to take off in a wide range of other media. While 'Zombie Lit' had yet to hit the publishing big-time in 2006, there were already promising indications of a receptive readership. David Wellington's serialised online novel *Monster Island* (2004) did well enough that sequels and a print publishing deal followed: David Moody's *Autumn* (online 2001/print 2010) had a similar trajectory. Brian Keene's *The Rising* (2003) made another important contribution to the burgeoning trend. However, although these novels were generally well received by *pre-existing* horror readers, none of these titles crossed over into a mainstream audience in the way that *World War Z* soon would.

Although *World War Z* is Brooks's most famous contribution to zombie lore, it was, crucially, not his first. In 2003, his spoof survivalist tome *The Zombie Survival Guide: Complete Protection From the Living Dead* was published. The son of Hollywood legends Mel Brooks and Anne Bancroft, Brooks was, at the time of the book's publication, a sketch writer for *Saturday Night Live*. He had written an initial draft of the guide between 1998 and 1999, and then 'stuck it in a drawer' until his agent secured a publication deal.[13] In addition to being a witty homage to Romero, Brooks had penned a meticulously researched tome that treated an outlandish premise with absolute seriousness – a technique replicated in *World War Z*. It was a considerable success: by 2011, the *Guide* had sold 1.4 million copies.[14]

The *Guide* rests on the notion that zombie outbreaks are a historically longstanding and scientifically accepted phenomenon. Like the novel that followed, the *Guide* taps into the sense of 'nihilism, despair, random violence and death'[15] that characterised many post-9/11 American horror films. Yet at the same time, it details DIY techniques that supposedly help increase one's chances of survival. What we have here, then, is empowerment and catastrophe in the same cleverly assembled package. Indeed, Brooks emphasised that the *Guide* drew upon *real-world* disaster response protocols, noting of his Southern Californian childhood that 'disaster preparedness was drilled into everyday life':

> everything you need for a zombie attack, you'd need for any large scale disaster. When I wrote in *The Zombie Survival Guide* about getting a first aid kit, a hand crank radio/flashlight, an emergency blanket, bottled water (and some means of purifying more!) I didn't have to look any farther than what's already sitting in a backpack under my bed.[16]

Aside from the nature of the zombie threat and the defensive techniques used to contain it, the *Guide* also anticipates *World War Z* by underlining that the adoption of new ways of thinking and of fighting is necessary if humanity is to survive. We are told that:

> Conventional warfare is useless against these creatures, as is conventional thought. The science of ending life, developed and perfected since the beginning of our existence, cannot protect us from an enemy that has no 'life' to end. Does this mean that the living dead are invincible? No. Can these creatures be stopped? Yes. Ignorance is the undead's strongest ally, knowledge their deadliest enemy. That is why this book was written: to provide the knowledge necessary for survival against these subhuman beasts. Survival is the key word to remember – not victory, not conquest, just survival.[17]

Part of the reason, then, why both *The Zombie Survival Guide* and, later, *World War Z* resonated so strongly with readers is that Brooks so logically expanded upon the strong survivalist component already inherent in almost all previous iterations of the zombie narrative. The *Guide* deliberately resembles real-life survival manuals such as *How to Survive the End of the World: Tactics, Techniques and Technologies for Uncertain Times* by leading survivalist 'prepper' James Wesley Rawles, which was published by Penguin in 2009.[18] Rawles begins his book by describing the effect of a hypothetical influenza pandemic so virulent that it kills more than half those infected. The scenario he conjures up strongly resembles the apocalyptic fantasies dramatised by Romero and Brooks (lack of zombies aside, obviously):

> The average suburban family only has about a week's worth of food in their pantry. Let's say the pandemic continues for weeks or months on end – what

will they do when that food is gone and there is no reasonably immediate prospect of resupply? Supermarket shelves will be stripped bare . . . millions of Joe Americans will be forced to go out and 'forage' for food . . . as the crisis deepens, not a few 'foragers' will soon transition to full scale looting, taking the little their neighbours have left. Next they'll move on to farms that are in close proximity to cities. A few looters will form gangs that will be highly mobile and well-armed, ranging deeper and deeper into farmlands, running their vehicles on surreptitiously siphoned gasoline.[19]

The upshot of all this is the necessity for vigilance, preparation and ruthlessness. 'You must be ready for a coming crisis. Your life and the lives of your loved ones depends upon it', the reader is cautioned. The book's insistence upon individual self-reliance and self-sufficiency is striking: survival here, as in *I Am Legend*, is definitely a DIY enterprise. For many fans, part of the vicarious appeal of Romero's Dead films – and of the scenario of the 'zombie apocalypse' in general – has always been exactly this kind of vicarious engagement with the 'survival at all costs' theme.[20] The topic of 'survival' – and what humans might be willing to do in order to achieve it – is also very much to the forefront of *World War Z*. Complacency and materialism have made the Western world – and the US in particular – all the more vulnerable when disaster strikes. However, crucially, this is also a book about the *global* response to calamity. Brooks has stated of his inspiration for the novel:

I realized that all the zombie books that were starting to come out, and all the zombie movies I had seen, they were all about one story. They were all about one group, or one guy, in one area. And I've always thought big-picture. I'm one of those guys who won't let you enjoy a movie, because I have to just pick it apart. So I thought, 'Well, what about the rest of the world? What about Russia, China, Africa? And forget about soldiers – how would refugees deal? How would you organize the economy? How would you feed people?' I really wanted to tell the story of the planet, and the template was *The Good War* by Studs Terkel.[21]

Like the *Guide*, then, *World War Z* is first and foremost an accomplished act of literary mimicry. Terkel's 1984 non-fiction classic was a ground-breaking oral history intended to remind readers of the heroism, the horror and the many rapidly forgotten realities of world-spanning conflict. As his introduction puts it:

The memory of the rifleman is what this book is about; and of his sudden comrades, thrown, hugger-mugger, together; and of those men, women, and children on the home front who knew or did not know what the shouting was all about; and of occasional actors from other worlds, accidentally encountered; and of lives lost and bucks found.[22]

The opening pages of *World War Z* also underline that it is a 'book of memories' intended to capture a representative and authentic sense of what *really* happened on the ground, in order to retain the 'human factor' that would otherwise have been lost in the official reports, compiled twelve years after the initial outbreak.[23]

Underlining the global nature of the crisis is the fact that outbreak begins in a remote district of China. Brooks therefore draws upon contemporary fears about the spread of potentially devastating pandemics such as SARS and bird flu, both of which are said to have originated in Asia. (Timothy R. Fox has argued that in this respect the novel rehashes stereotypical 'yellow peril' anxieties in a manner that underlines its 'subtle expression' of particularly American 'nationalistic and racial anxieties'.)[24] 'Patient Zero' was a young boy diving for treasure in the so-called 'City of Ghosts', a place previously dedicated to the underworld which was demolished to make way for a new dam. While underwater, he and his father were bitten by a zombie. Though the disease that quickly spreads across the world is clearly viral, its origins therefore could also be seen as a kind of quasi-supernatural punishment for the reckless disrespect of the sacred past, a trope which is very familiar within the horror genre more broadly.

As with real-life pandemics, the spread of the zombie outbreak is facilitated by modern connectivity. It only takes a few weeks for the virus to reach Tibet and Kyrgyzstan, and then Brazil, South Africa and the US. Many of the initial outbreaks in the West begin in inner-city ghettos, where they are disregarded by the authorities until it is too late. As Darren Reed and Ruth Penfold-Mounce observe of this familiar outbreak trajectory:

> the initial spread of the zombie 'infection' is made possible by contemporary forms of rapid and mass transportation and the globalised movement of people for work and leisure . . . As the institutional basis of country and state crumble, so any form of control of borders disappears.[25]

The initial US government response to is, catastrophically, to downplay events – it is literally only when zombies start crashing into suburban living rooms that proper action is taken. What's more, the US army is seriously underprepared. As one interviewee, a former general, says (in an aside that implicitly references the real-life 'war on terror'):

> After this last war, no amount of incentives could fill our depleted ranks, no payment bonuses or term reductions, or online recruiting tools disguised as civilian computer games. This generation had had enough, and that's why when the undead began to devour our country, we were almost too weak and vulnerable to stop them.[26]

The result of this complacency and military weakness is mass panic when the implications of what is happening finally *do* start to sink in. Even when the full might of the US military is brought to bear upon millions of zombies during the novel's major action set-piece, the so-called 'Battle of Yonkers', they are wholly ineffective.[27] Brooks's description of the battle evokes the ways in which the US defence establishment had to comprehensively rethink its strategies in the wake of 9/11, when it rapidly became clear that weapons and tactics honed during the Cold War were completely unsuited to dealing with a 'new breed' of threat. As another military interviewee says:

Perfect name, 'Shock and Awe'. But what if the enemy can't be shocked and awed? Not just won't but *biologically* can't? That's what happened that day outside New York City, that's the failure that almost lost us the whole damn war![28]

The tide begins to turn in favour of the living only when the Redecker Plan, a contentious strategy which emphasises brute pragmatism, and based on a doomsday plan for extremist Afrikaners, is implemented. The rudiments of it include the following: firstly, the recognition that there is no way to save everyone; and secondly, withdrawal to a safe zone, to which only a small proportion of the civilian population can be evacuated. The people who are saved will provide a labour pool for the eventual economic restoration and will also help preserve the legitimacy of the government. Most controversially, human bait will be left behind to distract the zombies from following those selected for evacuation.[29]

Those left behind are singularly unprepared to survive. Many of the middle-class suburbanites and city dwellers who flee to the perceived safety of the north naively believing it will 'all be over by Christmas' freeze to death, and some even resort to cannibalism.[30] As one survivor recalls:

In the beginning, everyone was friendly. We cooperated. We traded or even bought what we needed from other families. Money was still worth something. Everyone thought the banks would be reopening soon. Whenever Mom and Dad would go looking for food, they'd always leave me with a neighbour . . . But after the first month, when the food started running out and the days got colder and darker, people started getting mean. There were no more communal fires, no more cookouts or singing. The camp became a mess . . . I wasn't left with the neighbours anymore; my parents didn't trust anyone.[31]

The interviews devoted to life in these refugee camps emphasise that those who clung to the old ways were doomed by their unwillingness to face up to the ways in which the world had changed. Indeed, the apocalypse, be it zombie related or not, has often been seen as a chance to break with the old ways of doing things. As David Seed observes, utopian and apocalyptic beliefs have a long and parallel development.[32] Philip Strick has also noted that science fiction and horror writers have also frequently capitalised upon the fact that the building of a new world is most conveniently (and pleasingly) preceded by the destruction of the old one.[33] In addition, Armageddon greatly simplifies everything – as in *World War Z* and many other texts of this kind, 'questions of morality and responsibility may legitimately be set aside in favour of basic matters like survival and the perpetuation of the species'.[34] Indeed, when discussing the state of mind in which he wrote *The Stand* (1978), Stephen King admitted that a certain morbid relief accompanied his apocalyptic imaginings: 'No more Ronald McDonald! No more *Gong Show* or *Soap* on TV – just soothing snow! No more terrorists! *No more bullshit!*'[35]

Susan Sontag declared in her famous 1965 essay 'The Imagination of Disaster' that the post-nuclear era was an 'age of extremity', threatened by both 'unremitting banality' and 'inconceivable terror', in which it had become clear that from now until the end of human history, every person would 'spend his individual life under

200 BERNICE M. MURPHY

the threat not only of individual death, which is certain, but of something almost insupportable psychologically – collective incineration and extinction which could come at any time'.[36] According to Sontag, apocalyptic fantasy – she was at the time writing about 1950s science fiction and horror B-movies in particular – distracts viewers from their likely fate and helps neutralise that which would otherwise be psychologically unbearable, albeit to an extent that arguably places them 'in complicity with the abhorrent' by encouraging a 'strange apathy' in relation to terrors such nuclear devastation and radiation.[37] If we update Sontag's basic argument for a post 9/11 context, it could argued that one of the reasons why *World War Z* captured the public imagination is that the novel so efficiently synthesises both longstanding *and* specifically twenty-first-century anxieties. The novel combines fears of contagion, globalisation, predatory neoliberalism, nebulous terror threats and environmental catastrophe in one panoramic, familiar and readily graspable metaphor: the zombie apocalypse. Yet it also presents us with an ultimately reassuring portrait of resilience, global cooperation and human survival – a picture that would have had an obvious appeal to a still-traumatised US readership in particular.

Indeed, one of the most striking things about *World War Z* is that despite the horrific death toll, the novel concludes on this broadly optimistic note. In this respect, it further chimes with long-standing Judeo-Christian treatments of the apocalypse theme by suggesting that immense disruption and tragedy have had positive as well as the more obviously negative repercussions. We are in fact left with the definite impression that the war has even helped bring about a fairer, more equitable world. It forced people and nations to revise their preconceived notions about how things should be run and, as in Terkel's book, work together in a common cause that unites humans of all colours, classes and creeds. As Margo Collins and Elson Bond – who argue that this element of optimism is a characteristic of the post-millennial zombie narrative in general – also observe of *World War Z*:

> despite its often-unsettling scenes, [it] ultimately offers a basically hopeful worldview – one that departs from the utter destruction prevalent in many earlier zombie depictions . . . in Brooks's post-apocalyptic world, humanity has ultimately prevailed, and, in a Nietzschian twist, is all the stronger for it.[38]

For instance, as part of the reconstruction of US society, hundreds of thousands of highly paid professionals are retrained (often by first-generation immigrants) so that they can make useful contributions to the new society. As one of the government officials in charge of this programme puts it, 'we needed to get a lot of white collars dirty'.[39] It's a process that's not without its tensions, but Brooks makes it clear that many of these individuals have found fulfilment in their new lives. The new world is also one in which environmental concerns are finally being taken seriously. Recycling, a survival necessity during the war, has now become a vitally important part of the world economy, and massive investment in sustainable bio fuels has taken place. Above all else – and again as in Terkel – there is the understanding that the threat of extinction brought people together in a way that would otherwise have been unthinkable:

I'm not going to say the war was a good thing. I'm not that much of a sick fuck, but you've got to admit that it did bring people together. My parents never stopped talking about how much they missed the sense of community back in Pakistan. They never talked to their American neighbours, never invited them over, barely knew their names . . . Can't say that's the kind of world we live in now. And it's not just the neighbourhood, or even the country. Anywhere around the world, anyone you talk to, all of us have this powerful shared experience.[40]

In the years following the publication of the *Guide* and *World War Z*, 'Zombie Lit' has remained a growth area of popular fiction publishing. Seth Grahame-Smith's *Pride and Prejudice and Zombies* (2009) kick-started the relatively short-lived but high-profile 'mash-up' trend, during which pre-existing Victorian classics were infused with all manner of supernatural menace. The influx of zombie titles has meant that literary zombies, like their vampire cousins, have also become more varied, now even departing on occasion from some important tenets of the basic Romero blueprint.[41] There are novels told partially or wholly from the zombie's point of view, zombie romances, zombie young adult novels, zombie comic books and even zombie running apps co-created by respected authors of literary fiction.[42] At the time of writing, entering the search term 'zombie novel' in Amazon.co.uk brings up over 4,000 hits, a result which suggests that there are still a great many people reading – and writing – zombie narratives.[43]

The post-2000 zombie boom was the result of a broad constellation of economic, cultural, geopolitical and commercial imperatives, and continues to span a wide range of media formats. As such, the rise of 'Zombie Lit' cannot – and should not – be attributed to any one author. However, the fact remains that in both the *Guide* and *World War Z*, Max Brooks effectively distilled many of the zombie narrative's most attractive characteristics. In addition, as a Hollywood scion who had already established a foothold in the lower rungs of the entertainment industry, he was better placed than many other aspiring genre authors to attain reviews and coverage in the mainstream media. The bestseller status quickly attained by *World War Z*, and the commercial success of the 2013 film adaptation, further cemented the novel's status as the most high-profile zombie narrative of our time. Whatever the long-term outlook for the sub-genre, 'Zombie Lit' is certainly here to stay for the foreseeable future, and Brooks's role in helping to establish it as a viable publication category is unassailable.

NOTES

1. As Xavier Aldana Reyes notes, one of Max Brooks's most notable contributions to zombie lore is in having helped establish viral contagion as the cause. See Reyes, 'Post-Millennial Horror', p. 209.
2. Ibid.
3. Hubner et al., *The Zombie Renaissance in Popular Culture*, 'Introduction', p. 3.
4. For more on the zombie as a 'post-human' construct, see Christie and Lauro (eds), *Better Off Dead*.
5. Those interested in the relationship between vampires and zombies should consult Abbott, *Undead Apocalypse*.

6. 'Brooks's "World War Z" Hits Sales Milestone', *Publishers Weekly*, 10 November 2011 <http://www.publishersweekly.com/pw/by-topic/industry-news/publisher-news/article/49456-brooks-s-world-war-z-hits-sales-milestone.html> (last accessed 27 February 2017).

7. Fox, 'The Reanimation of Yellow-Peril Anxieties in Max Brooks's *World War Z*', p. 168.

8. For more background on the original, Haitian iteration of the zombi see Luckhurst, *Zombies*, pp. 17–74, and Russell, *Book of the Dead*, pp. 9–13. Both Luckhurst and Russell provide useful rundowns of the pre-Romero zombie narrative in pulp fiction and film.

9. Pfaffenroth, *Gospel of the Living Dead*, p. 1.

10. Russell, *Book of the Dead*, p. 69.

11. Luckhurst, *Zombies*, p. 15.

12. Calvin Reid, 'Walking Dead Graphic Novels Have Legs', *Publishers Weekly*, 18 January 2011 <http://www.publishersweekly.com/pw/by-topic/industry-news/comics/article/45812-walking-dead-graphic-novels-have-legs.html> (last accessed 27 February 2017).

13. Pierce, 'Max Brooks'.

14. 'Brooks's "World War Z" Hits Sales Milestone'.

15. Wetmore, *Post-9/11 Horror in American Cinema*, p. 3.

16. 'Q&A with Max Brooks', Public Health Matters Blog, 5 October 2011 <https://blogs.cdc.gov/publichealthmatters/2011/10/q-a-with-max-brooks/> (last accessed 3 March 2017).

17. Brooks, *The Zombie Survival Guide*, p. xiii.

18. Rawles has also published several survivalist thrillers subtitled 'A Novel of the Coming Collapse', and maintains a blog which in part outlines his belief that conservative Christian values can be maintained via a 'conscious retrenchment into safe haven states'. See <http://survivalblog.com/redoubt/> (last accessed 28 February 2017).

19. Rawles, *How to Survive the End of the World As We Know It*, p. xi.

20. Perhaps inevitably, real-life advice given by Rawles has already been cited in at least one tongue-in-cheek 'zombie survival' handbook: *Everything You Ever Wanted to Know About Zombies*, by Matt Mogk (2011), which also features a foreword written by Max Brooks.

21. Pierce, 'Max Brooks'.

22. Terkel, *'The Good War'*, p. 3.

23. Brooks, *World War Z*, p. 2.

24. Fox, 'The Reanimation of Yellow-Peril Anxieties in Max Brooks's *World War Z*', p. 169.

25. Reed and Penfold-Mounce, 'Zombies and the Sociological Imagination', p. 133.

26. Brooks, *World War Z*, p. 54.

27. Ibid., pp. 92–104.

28. Ibid., p. 104.

29. Ibid., pp. 105–11.

30. Ibid., pp. 125–6.

31. Ibid., p. 127.

32. Seed, 'Introduction', pp. 6–7.

33. Strick, *Science Fiction Movies*, p. 82.

34. Ibid., p. 84.

35. King, *Danse Macabre*, p. 449.

36. Sontag, 'The Imagination of Disaster', pp. 224–5.

37. Ibid., p. 225.

38. Collins and Bond, 'New Millennium', p. 194.

39. Brooks, *World War Z*, p. 139.

40. Ibid., p. 336.

41. Kim Pfaffenroth provides a detailed outline of Romero's zombie template in the *The Gospel of the Living Dead*, pp. 2–6.

42. The fitness app *Zombies, Run!* was co-created by British author Naomi Alderman and launched in 2011.

43. <https://www.amazon.co.uk/s/ref=sr_pg_6?rh=n%3A266239%2Ck%3Azombie+novels& page=6&keywords=zombie+novels&ie=UTF8&qid=1488476333> (last accessed 2 March 2017).

KEY WORKS

The Zombie Survival Guide: Recorded Attacks (2009; with Ibraim Roberson). Graphic novel focusing on some of the most notable 'recorded attacks' on humanity detailed in the *Guide*.
Closure, Limited and Other Zombie Tales (2012). Four short stories set in the same universe as *World War Z*. It received mixed reviews but will be of interest to those who admire Brooks's earlier work.
The Harlem Hellfighters (2014; with Canaan White). Well-received graphic novel about the first infantry unit of African-American soldiers to fight in World War I.
The Extinction Parade (2014; with Raoulo Caceres). Comic book series set during another zombie outbreak. This time, vampires become involved when their food supply (humans) rapidly diminishes.
Minecraft: The Island (2017). Brooks's first novel since *World War Z* showcases his savvy ability to capitalise on rising pop culture trends: it is essentially *Robinson Crusoe* set in the world of Minecraft, the online game which had already spawned previous multiple non-fiction bestsellers.

FURTHER CRITICAL READING

Collins and Bond, '"Off the Page and Into Your Brains!"' Among other things, this further discusses the novel's 'basically hopeful worldview' (p. 194). It also usefully situates *World War Z* alongside other major zombie novels and trends which appeared at around the same time. The collection itself features essays exploring both the historical and the cultural origins of the twenty-first-century zombie narrative, as well as the many transformations it has experienced.
Hubner, Leaning and Manning (eds), *The Zombie Renaissance in Popular Culture*. Provides an engaging overview of 'zombie cultural practices' in recent popular culture, including music, video games, online forums and other forms of fan engagement.
Luckhurst, *Zombies*. An incisive and authoritative introduction to the cultural history of the zombie, from its roots in Caribbean folklore right up to the present day. An ideal starting point.
Pfaffenroth, *The Gospel of the Living Dead*. Useful guide to Romero's original Dead trilogy, with a focus on their social and theological resonance.
Reyes, 'Post-Millennial Horror'. Reyes's overview of current trends in horror fiction features a helpful discussion of *World War Z* and other notable examples of 'Zombie Lit'.

BIBLIOGRAPHY

Abbott, Stacey, *Undead Apocalypse: Vampires and Zombies in the 21st Century* (Edinburgh: Edinburgh University Press, 2016).
Benjamin, Marina, *Living at the End of the World* (London: Picador, 1998).
Brooks, Max, *The Zombie Survival Guide: Complete Protection From the Living Dead* (London: Duckworth, 2004).
Brooks, Max, *World War Z: An Oral History of the Zombie War* (London: Duckworth, 2007).
Christie, Deborah and Sarah Lauro (eds), *Better Off Dead: The Evolution of the Zombie as Post-Human* (New York: Fordham University Press, 2011).

Collins, Margo and Bond, Elson, 'Off the Page and Into Your Brains! New Millennium Zombies and the Scourge of Hopeful Apocalypses', in Christie and Lauro (eds), *Better Off Dead*, pp. 187–204.

Fox, Timothy, 'The Reanimation of Yellow-Peril Anxieties in Max Brooks's *World War Z*', in Dorothea Fischer-Horning and Monika Mueller (eds), *Vampires and Zombies: Transcultural Migrations and Transnational Interpretations* (Jackson: University Press of Mississippi Press, 2016), pp. 168-90.

Hubner, Laura, Marcus Leaning and Paul Manning (eds), *The Zombie Renaissance in Popular Culture* (Basingstoke: Palgrave Macmillan, 2015).

King, Stephen, *Danse Macabre* (London: Warner, 1993).

Luckhurst, Roger, *Zombies: A Cultural History* (London: Reaktion Books, 2015).

Newman, Kim, *Millennium Movies: End of the World Cinema* (London: Titan Books, 1998).

Pfaffenroth, Kim *The Gospel of the Living Dead: George Romero's Visions of the Living Dead* (Waco: Baylor University Press, 2006).

Pierce, Leonard, 'Max Brooks', A.V. Club website, 9 July 2010 <http://www.avclub.com/article/max-brooks-42941> (last accessed 27 February 2017).

Rawles, James Wesley, *How to Survive the End of the World As We Know It: Tactics, Techniques and Technologies for Uncertain Times* (New York: Penguin, 2009).

Reed, Darren and Ruth Penfold-Mounce, 'Zombies and the Sociological Imagination: The Walking Dead as Social-Science Fiction', in Laura Hubner et al. (eds), *The Zombie Renaissance in Popular Culture*, pp. 124–40.

Reyes, Xavier Aldana, 'Post-Millennial Horror: 2000-2016', in Xavier Aldana Reyes (ed.), *Horror: A Literary History* (London: British Library, 2016), pp. 189–214.

Russell, Jamie, *Book of the Dead: The Complete History of Zombie Cinema* (Godalming: Titan Books, 2005).

Rutherford, Jennifer, *Zombies* (London: Routledge, 2013).

Seed, David, 'Introduction: Aspects of the Apocalypse', in David Seed (ed.), *Imagining Apocalypse: Studies in Cultural Crisis* (Basingstoke: Macmillan, 2000), pp. 6–7.

Sontag, Susan, 'The Imagination of Disaster', in *Against Interpretation and Other Essays* (New York: Farrar, Straus and Giroux, 1966), pp. 209–25.

Strick, Philip, *Science Fiction Movies* (London: Octopus, 1976).

Terkel, Studs, *'The Good War': An Oral History of World War Two* (Harmondsworth: Penguin Books, 1984).

Wetmore, Kevin J., *Post-9/11 Horror in American Cinema* (New York: Continuum, 2012).

CHAPTER 18

Genre and Uncertainty in Tana French's Dublin Murder Squad Mysteries

Brian Cliff

A mong the most international of Irish mystery writers, Tana French was born in the US but has lived in Ireland since 1990. She was, she has told one interviewer, 'an international brat, grew up in three continents, so there's nowhere I can really call "home"; but Dublin's the nearest I've got'.[1] As her official bio notes, 'She trained as a professional actress at Trinity College, Dublin, and has worked in theatre, film and voiceover'.[2] She also worked as a copy-editor for the Irish crime writer Arlene Hunt's early novels,[3] an experience that surely contributed to her own approach to the genre. Her drama training similarly leaves traces throughout her novels, which are framed largely by immersive first-person narrators, requiring strong, sustained individual voices.[4] Across her first six novels, *In the Woods* (2007), *The Likeness* (2008), *Faithful Place* (2010), *Broken Harbour* (2012), *The Secret Place* (2014) and *The Trespasser* (2016), this sense of voice shapes not only the narrators but also French's use of the police procedural sub-genre, a crucial element of her work, such as the long interrogations from *In the Woods* or the extensive forensic detail in *Broken Harbour*.

Although her novels to date are structured and marketed as part of the Dublin Murder Squad series, even the fundamental genre convention of the recurring series protagonist is evaded by French: each novel has a different protagonist-narrator, often a secondary character from the immediately preceding novel. Through this pattern, quite distinct from a conventional single-protagonist series, the novels amplify each other without making a reader's understanding of one novel entirely dependent on the others. French's emotionally and psychologically rich novels therefore proceed essentially through character, giving the lie to dismissive views of crime fiction as purely plot-driven.

French's novels have won numerous awards and have all generated significant sales, domestically and abroad, despite little attempt to adapt Irish idioms, culture or police structures for readier international comprehension. Her first novel, *In the Woods*, for example, has gone through more than twenty printings to date in its Irish/

UK edition alone, and another thirty-six printings in the US, where it has sold over one million copies, out of total worldwide sales for all of her novels exceeding five million copies.[5] While selling extraordinarily well, these novels have also regularly received prominent positive reviews in Ireland, the UK and the US (where their design and marketing have been consistent), reflecting their market status as both literary fiction and popular fiction. This position speaks to a central goal in French's work, as she makes clear when discussing Donna Tartt's *The Secret History* (1992), which

> wasn't marketed as a mystery novel at all; it was presented as literary fiction, but I think it would be ridiculous to claim that it isn't both. The book itself is one of the best arguments I've ever seen against that tired, lazy distinction ... Sure, it's about the mystery surrounding a murder; but it refuses to go along with the convention that says the real mystery is whodunnit. For this book, the true mystery is deeper, buried inside the hidden places of the human mind: why the murder happened; what consequences it has, for everyone it touches.[6]

This view of 'the true mystery' is shaped her own sense of the possible, French suggests, particularly her 'aim to write mysteries that take genre conventions as springboards, not as laws . . . books where the real murder mystery isn't whodunnit, but whydunnit and what it means'.[7] This straddling of the marketplace's dividing lines is one of the key features of her work, which generates much of its unease by shifting subtly between various genres – supernatural, Gothic and crime among them – with a consistent rejection of overly familiar distinctions.

As her essay on Tartt suggests, genre conventions rarely determine the arc of French's novels, even when her characters acknowledge those conventions with a wry self-awareness, as the narrator, Rob, does in the first book: 'I could get a fedora and a trench coat and a wisecracking sense of humor; she could sit poised at hotel bars with a slinky red dress and a camera in her lipstick, to snare cheating businessmen'.[8] Nonetheless, crime fiction, particularly in its Irish form, is the genre with which French's fiction is most readily associated. Irish crime writing has developed rapidly in recent years and has begun to attract critical attention, including a range of articles by Andrew Kincaid and others, as well as the first collection of academic essays on the topic, edited by Elizabeth Mannion.[9] Prior to this recent period, there were more scattered works in the twentieth century, by authors from Erskine Childers to Brian Moore, and many more that focused on the Northern Irish 'Troubles', as Aaron Kelly has shown.[10] Despite this deeper history, Irish crime fiction's development does not necessarily map on to the genre's wider international development; for example, Arlene Hunt and John Connolly (among others) have suggested that certain kinds of mystery plots (notably serial killers, as in US-set novels by Hunt, Connolly and Alex Barclay) are not viably set in Ireland, given its intimate geographic scale.

Ireland's particularity also shapes its crime fiction in other ways. The genre's recent growth has often been – reductively, though not untruthfully – seen as coinciding with the Celtic Tiger era, Ireland's experience of a dizzying growth in prosperity from the mid-1990s followed by an even more vertiginous crash from 2008 on, with the widespread corruption and newly urgent social pressures it both created and reflected.

Indeed, as Andrew Kincaid has argued, 'Noir proves a perfect genre to capitalize on [the Celtic Tiger's] undercurrents of melancholy, alienation, grievance, and even injustice',[11] a capacity Shirley Peterson suggests has become all the more 'concentrated' since the crash.[12] In *The Likeness*, Cassie makes this point explicitly:

> Irish homicides are still, mostly, simple things . . . We've never had the orgies of nightmare that other countries get . . . But it's only a matter of time, now. For ten years Dublin's been changing faster than our minds can handle. The economic boom has given us too many people with helicopters and too many crushed into cockroachy flats from hell . . . and we're fracturing under the weight of it.[13]

This local manifestation of wider economic crises may offer some connections to international crime fiction, particularly in Alan Glynn's *Winterland* (2009), *Bloodland* (2011) and *Graveland* (2013), but Ireland's very specificity also sets Irish crime fiction apart.

The Celtic Tiger does colour much Irish crime fiction, and many Irish crime writers, Hunt, Glynn, Declan Hughes, Gene Kerrigan and Louise Phillips among them, do engage explicitly with its contexts, including all of the consequent chaotic changes in class structures, while Stuart Neville, Brian McGilloway and others continue to engage powerfully with contemporary Northern Ireland. These contexts, however, at times seem to dominate not the novels themselves so much as their marketing and criticism, as if the genre merits consideration primarily in terms of 'its relationship to contemporary economic conditions in Ireland'.[14] In this regard, Connolly, Barclay, Jane Casey and Conor Fitzgerald are notable exceptions: none of Connolly's mystery fiction is set in Ireland, as is also largely true for Casey (whose protagonist has Irish ancestry), Barclay (whose one novel set in Ireland is driven by American characters) and Fitzgerald (whose novels are set in Rome, with an expatriate American protagonist). The relative paucity of critical work on their fiction speaks to the persistent difficulty Irish literary studies has with materials that cannot be construed in terms of national identity, and to the consequent interpretative strain placed on both the novels and the critical discussion that surrounds them.

A full account of Irish crime fiction should consider not only such familiar questions of national identity, but also the shaping influence of genres like Gothic and the supernatural, an influence to which Ian Campbell Ross has called attention.[15] In the Dublin Murder Squad series, French's crossing of Gothic and other genres with Irish literary traditions – from pookas and fairy lore (*In the Woods*) to Big House novels (*The Likeness*), from the Celtic Tiger to Irish Gothic novels and Irish theatre's family traumas (*Faithful Place* and *Broken Harbour*) – deftly unsettles readers' expectations. The fundamental uncertainty this creates is at times explicit, as when *Faithful Place*'s narrator, Frank Mackey, feels

> the earth rippling and flexing underneath me like a great muscle, sending us all flying, showing me all over again who was boss and who was a million miles out of his depth . . . The tricky shiver in the air was a reminder: everything you believe is up for grabs, every ground rule can change on a moment's whim.[16]

Virtually French's only Irish counterpart on such unstable ground is John Connolly, whose work, particularly the Charlie Parker series, is (as Connolly himself says) 'fascinated by the possibility of combining the rationalist traditions of the mystery novel with the anti-rationalist underpinnings of supernatural fiction'.[17] Like Connolly, French's importance lies not just in her popularity but also in the unsettling power she generates by blurring genre boundaries.

The Celtic Tiger clearly matters in French's writing, particularly for her first four novels, with their depiction of the wider society and their protagonists' recurring eye for subtle class distinctions, which they readily manipulate in working their cases. The Celtic Tiger's direct impact on lives is most overt in *Broken Harbour*, which centres on a family that has murderously imploded under the strains of the economic collapse. Here, the economy is an essential plot engine, even as the desperately positive narrator, Michael 'Scorcher' Kennedy, the lead investigator, defends the developers of half-finished ghost estates (like the titular one): 'if it wasn't for them thinking big, we'd never have got out of the last' (recession).[18] However, despite this prominent contemporary context, French's novels also insistently ground themselves in deeper histories, whether those are of 1980s working-class Dublin poverty and economic emigration (*Faithful Place*), the post-1960s aspirational but abortive growth of Dublin's suburbs (*In the Woods*) or the colonial legacy of aristocratic estates (*The Likeness*). Even when the present looms large, the past is at the heart of the matter, magnifying the uncertainty in the series.

This uncertainty is often illustrated in French's use of what should be the most stable elements of our lives: our homes. The Celtic Tiger centred in many ways on property, and her first four novels revolve around private homes.[19] These homes have at best a fragile role in the lives of the protagonists: a desire to belong haunts most of French's narrators amidst their regrets, missed chances and turning points. Along with this fragile hold on being at home, other patterns sharpen the sense of instability across the series. One is a kind of retrospective foreshadowing that highlights, without mediating, the gap between what the narrator regrets and the reader does not yet know. Halfway through *Broken Harbour*, for example, without fully elaborating on what exactly went wrong, Kennedy remarks:

> When I think about the Spain case, from deep inside endless nights, this is the moment I remember. Everything else, every other slip and stumble along the way, could have been redeemed. This is the one I clench tight because of how sharp it slices.[20]

He is not alone in being haunted by such regrets, for French's narrator-detectives are frequently wrong, their mysteries solved almost in spite of their blind spots, their mistakes, their intimate and at times dysfunctional attachment to the cases. During *In the Woods*, Rob makes the case virtually un-prosecutable by hiding his connections to it and by woefully misreading a key character, while detectives Antoinette Conway and Stephen Moran draw critically mistaken conclusions even at the end of *The Secret Place*, as pointedly underlined in the final chapter,[21] and as they do again at key points in *The Trespasser*. This pattern is so clear as to suggest that something in the world fundamentally exceeds the grasp of reason and stands outside of rational comprehension; 'Caught the edge of understanding', as Stephen puts it, 'swung by my fingertips, before I lost hold and it soared up and away again'.[22] Indeed, as critics have noted,[23] French's are rarely, if at all, logical mysteries in which everything is explained, everything understood, neither by the detectives nor by the other characters. Kennedy's 'Positive Mental Attitude', for example, leaves him bereft before the possibility that *'There isn't any why'*.[24] His urgent need to believe in order is part of what makes the particular case so destabilising for him: 'This case was different. It was running backwards, dragging us with it on some ferocious ebb tide. Every step washed us deeper in black chaos, wrapped us tighter in tendrils of crazy and pulled us downwards.'[25] Here, only the barest outlines are grasped, and those only tenuously.

The key means of fostering this pervasive narrative instability, however, is the weight French gives to Gothic and supernatural elements. These elements can be sensory, like the 'atavistic prickle' that 'went up [Rob's] spine', or the visceral 'presence of evil . . . strong and rancid-sweet in the air, curling invisible tendrils up the table legs, nosing with obscene delicacy at sleeves and throats',[26] but they also take the less impressionistic form of the actual magic seemingly forged by Holly and her friends in *The Secret Place*. Building on such elements, French articulates her own particular version of crime fiction, characterised by the series' fundamental uncertainty, which is in turn magnified by the play between the tropes, genres and contexts.

A closer look at *Faithful Place* illustrates this. Continuing the pattern set in preceding novels, this third book is narrated by Frank Mackey, who was Cassie's undercover supervisor in *The Likeness*, where, despite limited space on the page, French established him as a dramatically strong voice. In *Faithful Place*, however, the performativity of that voice is pared back, and the reader encounters a more nuanced character. Seeking to escape his brutally dysfunctional family some decades earlier, Frank tried to emigrate with his girlfriend Rosie. When she did not make their rendezvous, he simply moved across Dublin and never went home again, returning only when Rosie's suitcase, with its poignant, spare collection of the few belongings she planned to take to London, is discovered moldering in the chimney of a long-vacant house being gutted by developers, a discovery quickly made still more grim when her body is found under the basement floor. The rest of the novel centres on Frank's efforts to determine what happened, and to untangle the ramifications of her death.

Although *Faithful Place* embodies the potential of French's fiction to distil heterogeneous influences, including the rationalist and anti-rationalist traditions John Connolly has identified, this third novel is also distinct from the rest of the series.[27] The conclusion, for example, is comparatively upbeat (in fairness, crime fiction does set a low bar for what constitutes 'upbeat'), while the central mystery is, as Rachel Schaffer has argued,[28] much more intimately connected to the narrator's past than elsewhere in the series, a tighter focus that enriches rather than simplifies the text. Similarly, the entire series draws from the deep well of Irish Gothic and supernatural fiction, but it does so most overtly in *The Likeness*, *In the Woods*, *Broken Harbour* and *The Secret Place*. Though no less 'sunk in local history', *Faithful Place* 'isn't as eccentric as French's previous novels', one reviewer aptly observed.[29] Nonetheless, the novel taps into that same well in its own way, evincing Ross Macdonald's comparatively concrete post-war California Gothic of tainted, twisted familial legacies as much as the Irish nineteenth-century writer Sheridan LeFanu's more ornate work: 'Blood tells, sonny boy. Blood tells', we hear from Frank's abusive father Jimmy.[30] As these examples suggest, this third novel is a key bridge in French's work, one that connects the series' different genres and narrative strands.

Demonstrating this same centrality, *Faithful Place* is the novel through which most of the Dublin Murder Squad series' threads intersect. Much more so than other series entries, it draws on the preceding novels while echoing in ways both overt and delicately implicit throughout the subsequent novels. Of its secondary characters, two (Michael 'Scorcher' Kennedy and Stephen Moran) serve as narrators in later books, while a third (Holly Mackey) is a key catalyst in *The Secret Place*, where she occupies almost as much space as the narrator, Stephen, who appears a third time in *The Trespasser* (2016), as that novel's protagonist-narrator Antoinette Conway's partner.

A key continuity amidst these intersecting threads is the series' use of turning points and hinge moments, often colouring the novels with a sense of glowing, immanent potential, particularly with adolescence's 'too-tender-to-touch gold' aura.[31] This aura is tinged by an acute awareness of layers of alternate, unrealised possibilities, and frequently by a stunning loss like Rob's: 'it almost knocked me over: all the things we should have had . . . I had been robbed blind'.[32] Drawing on this sense of loss, *Faithful Place* presents itself as centred on Frank Mackey's experience of 'that riptide change . . . much too strong to fight'.[33] As he elaborates later,

> All my signposts had gone up in one blinding, dizzying explosion: my second chances, my revenge, my nice thick anti-family Maginot line. Rosie Daly dumping my sorry ass had been my landmark, huge and solid as a mountain. Now it was flickering like a mirage and the landscape kept shifting around it, turning itself inside out and backwards; none of the scenery looked familiar any more.[34]

French has described this kind of experience as:

> what I'm interested in writing about – those enormous turning points that you only get a couple times in your life . . . These moments strip people down to their essentials: You get to find out what you're really made of and what is really important to you.[35]

Indeed, every French novel includes such 'enormous turning points', and she is adept at depicting their pained and often remorseful qualities, as when Kennedy contemplates the thoughts 'that slice like razors forever . . . the ghosts of things that never got the chance to happen'.[36] More insistently and immediately than the books before or after it, *Faithful Place*, overflowing with near misses, with brass rings that someone *almost* caught, pivots on this pain.

With this capacity for sweeping pathos, the hinge moments at the heart of French's novels, characterised as they are by the past's persistent haunting of the present, are most central in *Faithful Place*, with the series' closest integration of turning points, narrator and plot. Frank's early life is marked by two related turning points, one of his own making and one not. The former is his choice to escape from his family in

Dublin for an adventurous life in London with Rosie; the latter is Rosie's disappearance, which eclipsed the future he had envisioned. *Faithful Place* amplifies the weight of these turning points by having the key events ripple through not just Frank's life but the lives of his entire family, indeed of his entire street. His father, for example, crippled by his own grievances, tells Frank that 'There's things went wrong fifty years ago, and they just kept going. It's time they stopped. If I'd've had the sense to let them go a long time back, there's a lot would've been different. Better.'[37] The novel also gives Frank's turning points a less heavily determined inflection by allowing him to revise his understanding of his past. With the qualified exception of Antoinette Conway in *The Trespasser*, the other narrators never quite get enough information about their own pasts to enable such a recalibration, one that would allow them, like Frank, to shed at least some of the distorting weight of those pasts. Where Rosie had been Frank's 'own secret magnetic north' long after her disappearance,[38] he learns that she did not abandon him just before emigrating alone; on the contrary, she was murdered, as Maureen Reddy notes, '*because* she was faithful to him and *because* she was helping him get away'.[39] This revelation allows him to see his life anew and to reorient himself around tragedy rather than betrayal. Near its conclusion, *Faithful Place* suggests (as *The Secret Place* later confirms) that he will reunite with Olivia, the wife from whom he had separated but who is cast as his saving beacon, his new 'magnetic north':

> I let myself out; maybe I said good night, I don't remember. All the way out to the car I could feel her behind me, the heat of her, like a clear white light burning steadily in the dark conservatory. It was the only thing that got me home.[40]

Such openness at the conclusion, where Frank has direction but not a definite destination, jars with crime fiction's traditional expectations of resolution, but this ending is fully in keeping with the series, which paints cynicism and certainty as costumes no character wears gracefully, adopted as defensive poses, but never really integral to the book or the character in quite the way that hard-boiled conventions would sometimes have it.

It would be wrong to suggest that *Faithful Place* provides anything like full 'closure', and not only because Frank dismisses the word as 'a steaming load of middle-class horseshite invented to pay for shrinks' Jags'.[41] Even approaching the conclusion, the novel introduces further notes of grey without resolving them: the guilty party in Rosie's death had done awful, unforgivable things, but is presented with empathy, even intimacy, in a way that complicates Frank's credibility. A clearly flawed narrator, he had neglected to mention telling events in his past, events that, as the reader learns in the climactic scene, qualify the self-image he projects. These late revelations demonstrate the novel's commitment to preserving an essential ambiguity in keeping with the series' blurring of genres. As fantasy and Gothic's anti-rational elements and mystery's rational impulses cross each other's orbits, Frank makes his way through the narrative, reaching little more certainty than the bittersweet rhapsody of the novel's closing line, in which he hopes 'to God that somehow or other, before it was too late, we would all find our way back home'.[42]

Because Irish crime fiction is still emerging as an area of study, critics can seem torn between emphasising either the Irish contexts of that fiction, or specific theoretical approaches, without necessarily reconciling the two. French's novels, however, require a less divided approach. Her work most insistently demonstrates the ways in which Irish crime fiction can be intensely local while still drawing in wider strands of genre and international literature. Her unapologetically and non-stereotypically Irish contexts, particulars and details in turn suggest that international crime fiction can encompass such particular, local texts without assimilating them into homogenised genre literature.

French's novels stretch habitual assumptions about what counts as 'Irish', about the genre's boundaries, and about flexible ways of engaging varying contexts. Her particular contributions to the Irish forms of the genre include her use of uncertainty. Like the pathos in *Faithful Place*, this usage exceeds the bare requirements of the plot: rather than serving as mere ornamentation, it rises to the level of a world view, one in which characters intimately 'know how memory can turn rogue and feral, becoming a force of its own and one to be reckoned with'.[43] Mystery fiction, after all, requires at least a temporary lack of certainty, however qualified, but French's work renders this lack in a more fundamental, even existential way. A key means of achieving this for the series has been the characteristically deft blurring of genre distinctions, which, as well as facilitating the thematic uncertainty of the series, plays effectively with the potent expectations that come with different genres, and which challenges readers' confidence about how the cues of various genres should direct their attention.

The Dublin Murder Squad series continues to develop and may well take dramatically new directions. *The Secret Place* has already shifted some of the patterns by moving from a Gothic that straddles the line between psychological and supernatural forms of unease to a Gothic that partakes of actual magic, for example, while her most recent novel, *The Trespasser*, circles back to the less overtly supernatural tone of *Faithful Place*. By shaping her own relationship to the genre and by calling attention to the work of her peers, Tana French is helping define Irish crime fiction as a thriving and actively evolving enterprise.

NOTES

1. Walters, 'An Interview with Tana French'.
2. 'About the Author' <http://www.tanafrench.com/about.html> (last accessed 5 February 2016).
3. Personal conversation with Arlene Hunt.
4. French has commented on this in several interviews, including Coughlan, 'Paper Tiger', p. 343.
5. Darley Anderson Literary, TV and Film Agency, 'Tana French' <http://www.darleyanderson. com/authors/tana-french> (last accessed 10 March 2016).
6. French, '*The Secret History* by Donna Tartt (1992)' pp. 568–9.
7. Ibid., p. 572.
8. French, *In the Woods*, p. 274.
9. Mannion (ed.), *The Contemporary Irish Detective Novel*; Kincaid, '"Down These Mean Streets"'.

10. Kelly, *The Thriller and Northern Ireland Since 1969*. For a broader bibliography of Irish crime fiction, see Ross and Mawe, 'Irish Crime Writing 1829–2011'.
11. Kincaid, '"Down These Mean Streets"', p. 45.
12. Peterson, 'Murder in the Ghost Estate', p. 80n5.
13. French, *The Likeness*, pp. 11–12.
14. Casey, '"Built on Nothing but Bullshit and Good PR"', p. 92.
15. Ross, 'Introduction'.
16. French, *Faithful Place*, p. 247.
17. Connolly, *I Live Here*, p. 422. I detail this aspect of Connolly's work more fully in 'A "Honeycomb World": John Connolly's Charlie Parker Series', in Mannion (ed.), *The Contemporary Irish Detective Novel*, pp. 31–44.
18. French, *Broken Harbour*, p. 13.
19. In 'Crime Fiction's Dublin', Rosemary Erickson Johnsen has suggested that French's first four novels comprise an 'alternate . . . tour' of Dublin, with 'different levels of the housing market explored one book at a time' (p. 132). Shirley Peterson elaborates on this theme in 'Homicide and Home-icide'.
20. French, *Broken Harbour*, p. 267.
21. French, *Secret Place*, pp. 432, 450–2.
22. Ibid., p. 424.
23. See, for example, Johnsen, 'Crime Fiction's Dublin', p. 133.
24. French, *Broken Harbour*, p. 351.
25. Ibid., p. 363.
26. French, *In the Woods*, pp. 77, 374.
27. Connolly, 'Joining the Criminal Fraternity'.
28. Schaffer, 'Tana French', p. 36.
29. Stasio, 'The Old Neighborhood'.
30. French, *Faithful Place*, p. 328.
31. French, *The Secret Place*, p. 206.
32. French, *In the Woods*, p. 185.
33. French, *Faithful Place*, p. 2.
34. Ibid., p. 109.
35. 'Interview with Tana French', Goodreads.com, July 2010, <http://www.goodreads.com/interviews/show/536.Tana_French> (last accessed 5 March 2016).
36. French, *Broken Harbour*, p. 187.
37. French, *Faithful Place*, p. 331.
38. Ibid., p. 395.
39. Reddy, 'Authority and Irish Cultural Memory in *Faithful Place* and *Broken Harbor*', p. 86.
40. French, *Faithful Place*, p. 385.
41. Ibid., pp. 133–4.
42. Ibid., p. 400.
43. French, *In the Woods*, p. 211.

KEY WORKS

In the Woods (2007). This first novel establishes many of the series' patterns, including a narrator with a mysterious past trauma that connects to the main case.

The Likeness (2008). Cassie, Rob's partner from *In the Woods*, investigates the murder of a doppelgänger who had assumed Cassie's own discarded undercover identity.

Faithful Place (2010). This third novel focuses on family and city-centre Dublin, with less Gothic ambiguity, and with the Murder Squad relegated to a secondary role.

Broken Harbour (2012). This novel extends the series' supernatural Gothic to depict an unemployed father's mental decay amidst the Celtic Tiger's crash.

'*The Secret History* by Donna Tartt (1992)' (2012). One of French's few non-fiction works, this speaks directly to her ambitions for her writing.

The Secret Place (2014). Divided between first- and third-person narratives, this revolves around four teenagers who generate a collective magic that the novel does not explain away.

The Trespasser (2016). Returning to the immersive first-person narration of French's initial novels, and to the relative realism of *Faithful Place*, this sixth novel – narrated by Antoinette Conway, whose tone is closer to Frank Mackey's in *Faithful Place* than to other narrators' – tightens the focus still further by concentrating most of the narrative within the Squad itself.

FURTHER CRITICAL READING

Burke (ed.), *Down These Green Streets*. The first anthology of its kind, this includes interviews and otherwise unavailable non-fiction from most of Ireland's leading crime writers.

Gregorek, 'Fables of Foreclosure'. Gregorek links Celtic Tiger themes to considerations of genre, particularly the police procedural.

Mannion (ed.). *The Contemporary Irish Detective Novel*. The first edited scholarly book on Irish crime fiction, this covers French's work and that of eight other Irish crime writers.

Meier and Ross (eds), *Éire–Ireland*, 49:1–2 (2014), special issue, 'Irish Crime Since 1921'. This interdisciplinary special issue addresses not just crime fiction but also various historical and sociological considerations of crime itself.

Schaffer (guest ed.), *Clues: A Journal of Detection*, 32:1 (2014). A special issue devoted to Tana French, this gathers essays with thematic emphases on mothers, the Celtic Tiger, crime writing by women, and archaeology.

BIBLIOGRAPHY

Burke, Declan (ed.), *Down These Green Streets: Irish Crime Writing in the Twenty-First Century* (Dublin: Liberties, 2011). Casey, Moira E., '"Built on Nothing but Bullshit and Good PR": Crime, Class Mobility, and the Irish Economy in the Novels of Tana French', *Clues: A Journal of Detection*, 32:1 (2014), pp. 92–102.

Cliff, Brian, 'A "Honeycomb World": John Connolly's Charlie Parker Series', in Mannion (ed.), *The Contemporary Irish Detective Novel*, pp. 31–44.

Connolly, John, *I Live Here* (Dublin: Bad Dog Books, 2013), expanded and reprinted in *Night Music: Nocturnes 2* (New York: Atria), pp. 399–443.

Connolly, John, 'Joining the Criminal Fraternity', *Irish Times*, 30 September 2006 <https://www.irishtimes.com/news/joining-the-criminal-fraternity-1.1009802> (last accessed 25 August 2017).

Coughlan, Clare, 'Paper Tiger: An Interview with Tana French', in Burke (ed.), *Down These Green Streets*, pp. 335–44.

Darley Anderson Agency, 'Tana French' <http://www.darleyanderson.com/authors/tana-french> (last accessed 10 March 2016).

French, Tana, *Broken Harbour* (Dublin: Hachette, 2012).

French, Tana, *Faithful Place* (New York: Penguin, 2010).

French, Tana, *In the Woods* (New York: Penguin, 2007).

French, Tana, *The Likeness* (New York: Penguin, 2008).

French, Tana, '*The Secret History* by Donna Tartt (1992)', in John Connolly and Declan Burke (eds), *Books to Die For: The World's Greatest Mystery Writers on the World's Greatest Mystery Novels* (London: Hodder, 2012), pp. 567–72.

French, Tana, *The Secret Place* (New York: Viking, 2014).

French, Tana, *The Trespasser* (New York: Viking, 2016).

Gregorek, Jean, 'Fables of Foreclosure: Tana French's Police Procedurals of Recessionary Ireland', in Julie H. Kim (ed.), *Class and Culture in Crime Fiction: Essays on Works in English Since the 1970s* (Jefferson, NC: McFarland, 2014), pp. 149–74.

Johnsen, Rosemary Erickson, 'Crime Fiction's Dublin: Reconstructing Reality in Novels by Dermot Bolger, Gene Kerrigan, and Tana French', *Éire–Ireland*, 49:1–2 (2014), pp. 121–41.

Kelly, Aaron, *The Thriller and Northern Ireland Since 1969: Utterly Resigned Terror* (Aldershot: Ashgate, 2005).

Kincaid, Andrew, '"Down These Mean Streets": The City and Critique in Contemporary Irish Noir', *Éire–Ireland*, 45:1–2 (2010), pp. 39–55.

Mannion, Elizabeth (ed.), *The Contemporary Irish Detective Novel* (London: Palgrave, 2016).

Meier, William and Ian Campbell Ross (eds), *Éire–Ireland*, 49:1–2 (2014), special issue, 'Irish Crime Since 1921'.

Peterson, Shirley, 'Murder in the Ghost Estate: Crimes of the Celtic Tiger in Tana French's *Broken Harbor*', *Clues: A Journal of Detection*, 32:1 (2014), pp. 71–80.

Peterson, Shirley, 'Homicide and Home-icide: Exhuming Ireland's Past in the Detective Novels of Tana French', *Clues: A Journal of Detection*, 30:2 (2012), pp. 97–108.

Reddy, Maureen T. 'Authority and Irish Cultural Memory in *Faithful Place* and *Broken Harbor*', *Clues: A Journal of Detection*, 32:1 (2014), pp. 81–91.

Ross, Ian Campbell, 'Introduction', in Burke (ed.), *Down These Green Streets*, pp. 14–35.

Ross, Ian Campbell and Shane Mawe, 'Irish Crime Writing 1829–2011: Further Reading', in Burke (ed.), *Down These Green Streets*, pp. 362–8.

Schaffer, Rachel, 'Tana French: Archaeologist of Crime', *Clues: A Journal of Detection*, 32:1 (2014), pp. 31–9.

Stasio, Marilyn, 'The Old Neighborhood', *New York Times*, 16 July 2010 <http://www.nytimes.com/2010/07/18/books/review/Crime-t.html?_r=0> (last accessed 5 March 2016).

Walters, Helen M., 'An Interview with Tana French', 11 July 2011 <http://fictionisstrangerthanfact.blogspot.com/2011/07/interview-with-tana-french.html> (last accessed 10 March 2016).

CHAPTER 19

'You Get What You Ask For': Hugh Howey, Science Fiction and Authorial Agency

Stephen Kenneally

Hugh Howey began his writing career relatively recently, publishing his first works of young adult science fiction in 2009. Following in the footsteps of an increasing number of twenty-first-century genre authors, Howey chose to publish and sell his work online. Although his early young adult work, a space-opera series featuring teenage starship pilot Molly Fyde, was well received, the online publication of *Wool* in 2011 'made his career take off'.[1] Intended for adult readers rather than his previous young adult audience, *Wool* was initially published online as a series of short fictions that collectively made up a novel-length narrative, and was later re-released in novel form. Howey, like other prominent initially self-published authors such as Andy Weir and E. L. James, made a move into print publication with a book contract for *Wool* (2013). Unlike most of the authors preceding him, however, Howey made a point of retaining the online publication rights for his work and contracted only for the print publication rights, an arrangement described by *Publishers Weekly* at the time as 'unheard of in today's market'.[2] The print publication of *Wool* and its sequels (*Shift* and *Dust*, with *Shift* also being released online in three short-fiction pieces before its print publication) greatly increased Howey's profile.

Howey is one of the most prominent authors to make a transition from publishing independently online to significant mainstream print success, and he did so on his own terms. He is seen as an exemplar of such success and as a guru for authors aspiring to the same; he frequently writes blog posts about self-publication. One online guide to moving from self-publishing to traditional publishing notes: 'When Hugh Howey is asked by self-published authors how they can effectively approach agents and editors, he has advised: Wait for them to come to you'.[3] As such, his career is not only an example of the changes in publishing media and popular-fiction consumption that have occurred in the early twenty-first century, but it also touches on the related themes of power, information and control: themes that are also easily identifiable in his fiction.

Wool, *Shift* and *Dust* are known collectively as the Silo trilogy, series or saga, after the underground bunkers inhabited by their characters. They are not solely of interest due to their still-unusual history of publication and reception, although that will be discussed in more detail below: Howey's Silo trilogy is also commercially popular, interesting and well written. Very aware of their genre position as works of science fiction, these novels manage simultaneously to embrace the traditional elements and perspectives of that genre while also exploring science fiction's complex philosophical aspirations, and they do so in a nuanced and engaging fashion. While clearly reflecting a general post-2000 trend towards post-apocalyptic and dystopian writing, the Silo series draws from and comments on science fiction more generally. To consider Howey's impact on the genre of science fiction, it is useful to consider how the Silo series adheres to and works within the conventions of the science fiction genre.

The definition of science fiction is a changing and contested one (John Rieder notes that 'so many books on sf begin with a more or less extended discussion of the problem of definition'[4]) but it is generally considered to exhibit several characteristics that distinguish and define it as a genre. Firstly, science fiction is a literature of *possibility* (often contrasted with fantasy, which explores and examines the impossible).[5] As a general rule, science fiction deals with events that are either entirely possible (even if they have not actually happened) or that are plausible within a modern technological understanding. For example, while interstellar travel by humans is not possible at the time of writing, it could readily be envisioned within a modern technological worldview. While the specific innovations required might not yet exist (or even, technically, be possible), the plausibility of the concept to the reader renders it science fictional. Magical teleportation cannot be conceived of without a significant shift in paradigm: it is not believable within a modern context in the same way that spaceships and wormholes are.

Howey's work adheres admirably to this standard: *Wool* contains no technology unavailable at the time of initial publication. Even by the end of the Silo trilogy, where the advances in future technology that made the silos possible are revealed, the only 'new' technological elements introduced are nanobots, cryofreezing and memory suppression medication. All these advances could be (and are being) imagined today, contradict no established scientific tenets and are in some cases disturbingly close to existing in reality. Howey uses the epigraph of *Shift* to make it clear exactly how close and plausible his future is. We are expecting the epigraph to describe an engaging piece of alternative history, but instead it describes two technological advances that actually did happen in 2007:

> In 2007, the Center for Automation in Nanobiotech (CAN) outlined the hardware and software platforms that would one day allow robots smaller than human cells to make medical diagnoses, conduct repairs and even self-propagate.
>
> That same year, CBS re-aired a programme about the effects of propranolol on sufferers of extreme trauma. A simple pill, it had been discovered, could wipe out the memory of any traumatic event.
>
> At almost the same moment in humanity's broad history, mankind had

discovered the means for bringing about its utter downfall. And the ability to forget [that] it ever happened.[6]

This leads to a second important element of science fiction: its technological/scientific orientation. Fantasy author David Eddings once wrote, rather cruelly, that a science fiction author will 'get all bogged down in telling you how the watch works; we [fantasy authors] just tell you what time it is and go on with the story'.[7] Genre rivalries aside, technology often has an important place in works of science fiction, and not for its own sake. Rather, the technological underpinnings maintain the plausibility of the narrative as well as giving it internal consistency. An example of this consistency can be found in Howey's *Dust*: the deep underground silos were dug from the top down with powerful mechanical diggers. Since they were never retrieved, they must still be at the bottom of each silo: as, indeed, they are, and this becomes an important plot point. While it would certainly have been possible to write a science fiction novel about life in an underground silo where the specifics of exactly how the silo was dug out were not explored in depth, such details reward readers' attention and understanding with later payoffs in the form of plot development.

Howey's work, in this way, is very much classic science fiction: even the multiple revelations about how people are misled with false computer-generated images in *Wool* are supplemented with full technical details, down to exact pixel resolutions being listed in the text. A drawback to this approach, and a common stereotype of science fiction, is the implicit (or sometimes explicit) assumption that the only meaningful elements of a plot are the technological ones and that solving practical problems will lead to the resolution of all other problems, including interpersonal and psychological ones. This assumption is both present and examined in Howey's work: Juliette, one of the leading characters of the Silo trilogy, who, not coincidentally, is a mechanic and engineer, generally takes this approach. She survives her exile mostly through technical competence, and her triumphs include refitting environmental suits, repairing a generator, fixing a drainage system and arranging an underground dig. However, her lack of attention to interpersonal and political elements leads to danger and tragedy at several points. Howey, therefore, is clearly unafraid to follow science fictional clichés to their appropriate conclusions: the stereotypical technically minded main character who solves seemingly insoluble problems but has little time for human interaction finds it difficult to gain popular support or to present her ideas convincingly. Howey is also unafraid to subvert genre clichés and expectations by placing a female character in this role: this tension of working both with and against the traditional genre is a potent element of the series.

Science fiction, finally, is a literature of the future. Appropriately for a genre focused on technology and possibility, works of science fiction are often not only set in the future (relative to when they are written) but are also *about* the future in a very literal sense: they discuss possible (or at least plausible) futures for science and humanity, how their pitfalls can be negotiated, and what possibilities such futures can offer. Once again, Howey's work lives up to this standard by presenting a future whose characters are attempting to rewrite possible futures for humanity through the silos, allowing a complex examination of historical inevitability and human potential to emerge.

Howey's work is of particular note, therefore, because it exemplifies the core elements of what is considered science fiction: possibility, a technological orientation and a focus on the future. It also deliberately portrays and engages with several of the flaws of this perspective, such as a lack of focus on the interpersonal and the risk of abandoning the past altogether in a desire for the future. In this way it both encapsulates and engages with science fiction's complexities. The Silo trilogy also demonstrates Howey's ability to draw from multiple genres and sub-genres: while unambiguously science fictional in scope, it is also, as noted earlier, part of the recent trend for dystopian or post-apocalyptic fiction. The structured and controlled societies of the silos are classic dystopias, carefully engineered to manipulate their residents as much as possible to fit an external agenda; meanwhile, the entire frame of the narrative is post-apocalyptic, with the silos preserving humanity after the destruction of everyone outside them. This inclusion of both classic and more recently popularised genre elements shows Howey's versatility as an author: while very clearly working within a specific genre, he is capable of versatility in how he approaches that genre. His ability not merely to include but to engage with genre expectations and limitations suggests that Howey is deserving of consideration as an author who is both popular *and* influential within twenty-first-century science fiction.

Although Howey's work is of academic interest both as a science fictional text and in its own right, its major cultural impact has undoubtedly been due to its transition from being self-published online to mainstream popular print publication. In fact, the word 'transition' is not quite correct, as Howey has continued to self-publish his writing online: as noted, his arrangement with his US publisher Simon and Schuster granted them exclusive print rights, while Howey retained online publication rights.[8] While obviously beneficial for Howey himself, from both a self-promotion standpoint and a financial one, this arrangement also has wider implications for genre fiction publishing as a whole. These transitions from online publication and the shift in how rights are managed are particularly important characteristics of post-2000 popular fiction publishing, and Howey exemplifies them especially well.

Authors of ebooks moving to traditional publishing is a relatively recent phenomenon in itself: M. J. Rose is generally credited as the first author of an ebook to obtain a mainstream publishing contract after self-publishing online, in 1998.[9] However, Howey's retention of his identity as a self-publishing author with a professional output based primarily online challenges the dominance of traditional publishers as the only avenue of 'respectable' or 'legitimate' authorship: while the popularity of online self-publishing had already started this trend, an author's receiving an offer of print publication from a mainstream publisher is still seen as a validation of their talent and a path to legitimacy. Judy Mandel reflects this in a 2012 article on her own publication history: 'In the end, I believed there was still a measure of credibility in having a traditional publisher. Reviews come more easily and you are taken more seriously. That is changing, but I believe it is still widely the case.'[10] Even in 2009, a list of tips for self-published writers hoping to gain a traditional publishing deal included the advice:

Don't mess with the system. Some writers have asked us if it's possible to sell some rights to a publisher, but keep others for themselves. This is probably not going to happen. Publishers develop rigorous plans about how they want to market, and for that reason, they generally want control over all (or nearly all) rights. If you hold some rights and the publisher holds some rights, you will set yourself up as a competitor against your traditional publisher.[11]

The bargain Howey made, however, turns this accepted wisdom on its head: he gained the broader reach and traditional legitimacy of print through a well-known publisher, but was perceived as doing it very much on his own terms and with the publisher serving his needs rather than vice versa. Even if this is an exaggeration of the facts of the matter, the public perception of this narrative suggests that in the future, with Howey as a trailblazer, there will be more options for self-published online authors (especially authors of genre fiction, which seems uniquely suited to an online publishing model)[12] to engage with other publishing avenues to the degree that suits them. With Howey's example (and indeed encouragement through his online articles in support of self-publication) authors are likely to reconsider their default approaches, and this potential paradigm shift in how rights are managed may force publishers to do so as well.

One example that lends support to this theory is the publication history of fantasy author Michael J. Sullivan, who obtained a traditional contract for his Riyria Revelations series in 2011 after it had been self-published from 2008 onwards. When, in 2014, his publisher was uninterested in his new book, Hollow World, Sullivan used the online crowdfunding platform Kickstarter to raise funds to self-publish. After a successful campaign, Sullivan was approached by several publishers and ultimately decided to negotiate a print-only contract for Hollow World.[13] Clearly what was unachievable in 2011 was possible in 2014: Sullivan's previous successful history certainly played a factor, but it is noteworthy that he was still unable to obtain a contract for Hollow World without re-demonstrating his work's appeal and the market it had available. It seems most likely that the ongoing paradigm shift in the publishing industry, encouraged by trailblazers such as Howey, gave Sullivan scope to consider a 'radical' idea like a print-only contract.

Howey's publication route also raises broader questions about textual canonicity and authorial control: if Howey's online work is the original text, which he retains the exclusive rights to sell, and his print publisher merely has a licence to print copies of it, then arguably Wool is better understood as 'an online novel with a print version' rather than 'a novel originally published online'. It is that shift in thinking, coupled with a greater cultural acceptance of electronic formats in general, that suggests authors of genre fiction may in the not-too-distant future have not only better options but also a greater degree of control, not just over their own texts but over their own genres, than publishers customarily permit.

In Howey's Silo trilogy the titular underground silos are worlds unto themselves, inhabited by residents who never leave and are forbidden even from entertaining the idea. Created worlds of one kind or another are a common presence in science fiction; however, Howey's work focuses not only on the created worlds of the silos but also (in Shift and Dust) the processes and philosophies of their creation. When the characters comment on this, then, it can be simultaneously read as an authorial commentary on and exploration of the science fiction genre as a whole. As the characters explore the nature of the silo, Howey explores how fictional and future worlds are created within science fiction. Within the series, the near-perfectly controlled dystopian underground worlds of the silos are created and controlled by flawed human beings with the ultimate goal of 'creating' or shaping a future world for humanity by breeding and acculturating ideal future survivors/colonists. Of course, both the creators and the worlds are ultimately Howey's creations, allowing him to comment on the process of creating a science fictional world by having his characters do just that. The inhabitants of Silo 1, the creators and controllers of the silos, can functionally read people's minds, manipulate their thoughts and actions, and ultimately kill or spare them. They possess critical information unavailable to the other characters. They are the ultimate arbiters of meaning because they are the only ones who remember both the history of the world and the purpose of the silos. These powers and advantages (insight, information, control and meaning) are also those that authors have over their characters. In this way, the 'authors' of the silos echo Howey's role as author of the text. In other words, Howey's Silo trilogy is a science fiction series that not just includes but *exemplifies* several of the fundamental concepts of the genre: indeed, due to its structure, it is particularly suited to engage with and comment upon them.

A central concept to understanding the trilogy, and its role as a science fiction narrative, is that of limitation. Everyone in the silos, including their rulers (both the 'heads of IT' overseeing each silo and the real rulers in Silo 1), is profoundly limited in a variety of ways, and these limitations repeatedly influence their behaviour and perspective. While day-to-day life for normal residents of a silo is depicted as fairly mundane and reasonably content, the psychological impact of their enforced limitations is explored in some depth. The primary taboo in any silo, and punishable by 'cleaning' (a death sentence), is to want to enter the outside world: 'Expressing any desire to leave. Yes. The great offence. . . . You get what you ask for.'[14] Despite this, the top level of each silo has wall-screens showing camera views of the barren outside world, which blur and accumulate grit, leading to the need for 'cleaning', where a person is sent on a one-way trip in a temporary environmental suit to do so before the atmospheric poisons kill them. Residents of a silo, therefore, are continually shown a landscape it is forbidden for them to desire or to discuss in detail. In addition to the psychological harm this causes, it intentionally shapes and restricts their perspective on the outside world. If there were no visions of the outside world, it would be easier to imagine it as an unspoiled paradise: however, since they can see a destroyed outside world, their aspirations are limited to keeping a clear view of it through regular cleaning. Similarly, their understanding of technology and the sciences, other than what is required to maintain the silo, is limited through denial of information:

> 'I can't get over what they were able to do hundreds of years ago. People weren't as dumb back then as you'd like to believe.'
> Juliette wanted to tell him about the books she'd seen, how the people back then seemed as if they were from the future, not the past.[15]

Limiting people's understanding of the world around them cripples their ability to comprehend, imagine or create other worlds, which is exactly the goal of the controllers of the silos. This also makes a strong argument for the value of science fiction as a genre: with improved understanding of the world and the potential of the future comes the capacity firstly to imagine new worlds and then to make them real. Each silo is a world unto itself that cannot imagine other silos: within that context, no silo resident can truly imagine an external world. And beyond that, other planets are entirely unimaginable.

> He had told her once, with his star chart spread across that bed in which they made love, that each of those stars could possibly hold worlds of their own, and Juliette remembered being unable to grasp the thought. It was audacious. Impossible. Even having seen another silo, even having seen dozens of depressions in the earth that stretched to the horizon, she could not imagine entire other worlds existing. And yet, she had returned from her cleaning and had expected others to believe her claims, equally bold.[16]

This control and limitation of the silo residents is not restricted to information. Over the course of the Silo trilogy, it is revealed that the ultimate goal of the creators of the silos was to manipulate the development of each silo in every possible way, through psychological manipulation, determining which couples had the right to have children, through memory control, and even mass murder if necessary, with the ultimate goal being to free the occupants of the 'best' silo after 500 years to rebuild the world . . . and to destroy every *other* silo, including the controlling one.

Unsurprisingly, then, the series has an ambivalent relationship with power and authority, as shown in *Dust*:

> Lukas used to think he understood what it meant to be in charge. You did what you wanted. Decisions were arbitrary. You were cruel for the sake of being cruel. And now he found himself agreeing to worse horrors than he had ever imagined. Now he knew about a world of such horrors, that maybe men of his ilk weren't suited to lead.[17]

While one side's position is inherently more monstrous than the other, the perspective of both is shown, especially in *Shift*, which focuses on Silo 1 and its residents. From the perspective of the creators of the silos, they are saving humanity from itself and creating a better future using extreme measures: these including destroying human civilisation outright. However, this ostensibly noble goal leads to the residents (and even the rulers) of the silos being subject to a constant variety of dystopian pressures and cruelties. If possible, the life of the 'rulers' in Silo 1 is even more nightmarish than that experienced in the other silos: the majority of the residents are kept frozen and unageing, occasionally woken for six-month shifts before refreezing, so they can survive for the project's expected five-century duration. They are heavily medicated, monitored at all times, and subject to unquestioned and unquestionable rules. In this way the majority of residents, except for the few 'executive' members of the organisation, are discouraged from thinking about their ultimate goals and procedures: even their names and memories are taken from them to prevent the guilt of the global genocide they enacted destroying them.

The characters' need to understand their limiting and dystopian environments, and the associated need to transcend them, is fundamental to the Silo trilogy. Without understanding certain essential facts about the silos (the poison gas, the drugs in the water, the fact that the physical structure is rigged to be collapsed), the characters cannot survive a rebellion against their controllers; without understanding the context of their world (a bubble of ravaged badlands outside of which is an untouched and empty world), the characters cannot escape it. A purely practical orientation, however, is insufficient for characters to reimagine the paradigm of their existence: even under the best possible circumstances, life in the silos is a life subordinate to the vision of others and lived within the context they created. It is 'those who dare to hope', who can imagine a life outside the silo and can inspire others with this idea, who are the greatest threat of all. This is amply demonstrated by the otherwise non-threatening elderly disabled schoolteacher Mrs Crowe, who must be killed in order to stop the spread of her seditious ideas to the children she teaches. The fact that *Wool* is dedicated to 'those who dare to hope' reinforces the validity of this message outside the text.

Conversely, pure understanding of the nature of the world is also insufficient to change it: in this series, information is power but it is not the *only* power. When the reclusive Walker accidentally discovers he can tune a radio to reach other silos, it is during a running gun battle: his discovery is treated with disdain and barely concealed contempt by characters fighting for their lives, who have other priorities. When practical competence and imaginative understanding come together, as they do in Juliette and Charlotte, the characters change their world and cast off its limitations.

Continuing the idea of the Silo trilogy both exemplifying and commenting upon the science fiction genre, the positive ending to the series, where the survivors escape the silo to create their own future beyond anyone's control or limitations, is in the best tradition of aspirational science fiction, encouraging an embrace of the practicalities of technology along with the possibilities of the future. 'She imagined the world they might build with time and resources, with no rules but what's best and no one to pin down their dreams.'[18] However, in the series' darker moments it does not shy away from examining the genre's less positive legacies and assumptions: and if it is accurately to represent and reflect the genre, it must. For example, while the novels themselves contain highly positive portrayals of female characters, science fiction has a history of marginalising, eliminating or negatively depicting women: Lisa Tuttle writes that 'the absence of realistic female characters remains a glaring fault of the genre'.[19] Howey does not gloss over the ways dystopian societies can harm women in particular. When social order breaks down in a silo, which happens several times across the series, it is clear that while both men and women suffer in the ensuing violence, women are very likely to be subjected to sexual violence and rape: this is not just a common consequence of societal breakdown but is also linked to the rigorous control maintained over fertility in the silos. Relationships must be publicly registered with the state (ensuring only 'appropriate' matches are encouraged), women must have contraceptive implants fitted at puberty (controlling not just the population generally but the agency of these women in particular) and only couples who win a (rigged) lottery are permitted to have children. Even then, women are permitted only a year in which to become pregnant: pregnancies outside this window must be terminated or, if concealed, lead to the woman's execution after the child's birth. The seven-year-old Elise, who grew up outside these restrictions in a fallen silo, imagines the contraceptive implant as a poison pill growing inside women.

While the characters of the silos are in no way stereotyped or defined by their gender, and there are many prominent female characters in active roles (such as Juliette, arguably the trilogy's main character), the controlling Silo 1 is exclusively male. The women and children were cryofrozen for a number of frankly unconvincing reasons: for their own protection, to 'inspire' the men to stay performing their tasks, and to prevent arguments and fighting over women. This shows, more than anything, the patriarchal and paternalistic assumptions at the heart of the Silo project: the silo residents, and the women of Silo 1, are all children to be protected from the troubles of the world, even if that requires lying to them, and controlling and imprisoning them. It also evokes what Tuttle called 'genre SF [that was] developed in a patriarchal culture as something written chiefly by men for men (or boys)'.[20] In short, Silo 1 not only carries humanity's dark legacy but can also be read as showing the darkest implicit assumptions and historical baggage of science fiction writing: an 'ideal' world inhabited entirely by zombified men paying lip service to ideals but enslaved to a process they cannot control, spouting values their actions contradict, who see women as precious commodified treasures, rewards or breeding stock. The scenes of violent social disorder, then, show women's sexual and reproductive agency passing from the government to violent men, rather than to themselves: a woman's implant is forcibly removed, with a knife, in a ceremony that is clearly a form of rape rather than a liberation. Conversely, the final scenes in which Juliette and Courtnee drink tea by a fire in the outside world and discuss the survivors' future suggest the potential for the survivors to create a new world that is not deformed or limited by external restrictions. For the genre, it suggests the potential to create new forms and new narratives unbound by the shackles of the past. Juliette's final line echoes far beyond the text, carrying a clear message to readers and writers of science fiction: 'I think we'll make it . . . I think we can make any damn thing we like'.[21]

Howey's trailblazing path to publication and the new perspectives on self-publishing and print-only rights that he popularises encourage authors of both science fiction in particular and popular fiction in general to create, digitally publish and profit from their works in their own ways and on their own terms. Just as his work exemplifies and engages with the fundamentals of science fiction literature, re-presenting and challenging accepted orthodoxies of the genre, Howey's career challenges the status quos of popular fiction authorship and publication. His career and his novels thus combine to support and encourage texts and authors that focus on changing expectations, opening new perspectives and reclaiming agency: ultimately, this influence may be Howey's most significant impact on twenty-first-century popular fiction.

NOTES

1. Howey, *Wool* omnibus, unpaginated back matter.
2. Ermelino, 'Wool- Gathering'.
3. Friedman, 'How to Secure a Traditional Book Deal by Self-Publishing'.

4. Rieder, 'On Defining SF, Or Not', p. 191.
5. Franklin, 'Preface', pp. vii–ix.
6. Howey, *Shift*, p. 1.
7. Eddings, *The Rivan Codex*, p. 24.
8. Ermelino, 'Wool-Gathering'.
9. Friedman, 'Commodity Publishing, Self-Publishing, and The Future of Fiction'.
10. Mandel, 'Getting a Traditional Book Deal After Self-Publishing'.
11. 'After Self-Publishing: How To Find An Agent And A Publisher For Your Self-Published Book', Writer's Relief website, 9 December 2009 <http://writersrelief.com/blog/2009/12/after-self-publishing-how-to-find-an-agent-and-a-publisher-for-your-self-published-book> (last accessed 24 April 2017).
12. Grabianowski, 'The Best Way To Break Into Science Fiction Writing Is Online Publishing'.
13. Sullivan, 'About'.
14. Howey, *Wool*, p. 30.
15. Howey, *Dust*, p. 41.
16. Ibid., p. 399.
17. Ibid., p. 79.
18. Ibid., p. 399.
19. Tuttle, 'Women in SF'.
20. Ibid.
21. Howey, *Dust*, p. 401.

KEY WORKS

Wool omnibus (2013). Print collection of the five short-fiction pieces that comprise *Wool*. Multiple characters inhabiting an underground silo have their stories weave together as they explore the mysteries of their world.

Shift omnibus (2013). Print collection of the three short-fiction pieces that comprise *Shift*. This prequel to *Wool* set in a recognisable near-future US explores the establishment of the silos.

Dust (2013). Print publication of the third novel of the Silo trilogy. The characters of *Wool* and *Shift* attempt to outwit the controllers of the silos and to escape them.

The electronic versions of all three texts can be obtained directly from the author's website <http://www.hughhowey.com> or via <http://www.amazon.com>.

FURTHER CRITICAL READING

Bould, Mark and Sherryl Vint (eds), *The Routledge Concise History of Science Fiction* (London: Routledge, 2011). A good overview of the development of science fiction as a modern genre, with discussions of a wide variety of sub-genres.

Clute, John, David Langford, Peter Nicholls and Graham Sleight (eds), online *Encyclopedia of Science Fiction* <http://www.sf-encyclopedia.com>. This continually updated electronic text (previous editions were available in print, but the *Encyclopedia* has been published online by Gollancz since 2011) is composed of in-depth articles on an incredible variety of science fictional topics, sub-genres, authors and texts, and is written by experts in the field. A highly authoritative source.

Friedman, Jane. A leading authority on online publishing, her articles on <https://janefriedman.com/> give great insight into this relatively new field.

BIBLIOGRAPHY

Eddings, David, *The Rivan Codex* (New York: Del Rey Books, 1998).
Ermelino, Louisa, 'Wool- Gathering', *Publishers Weekly*, 22 March 2013, p. 16.
Franklin, H. Bruce, 'Preface', in J. Peterson (ed.), *St James Guide to Science Fiction Writers* (Detroit: St James Press, 1996), pp. vii–ix.
Friedman, Jane, 'Commodity Publishing, Self-Publishing, and The Future of Fiction', Jane Friedman website, 8 January 2014 <https://janefriedman.com/self-publishing-future-of-fiction> (last accessed 24 April 2017).
Friedman, Jane, 'How to Secure a Traditional Book Deal by Self-Publishing', Writer Unboxed website, 25 May 2015 <http://writerunboxed.com/2015/05/25/secure-a-traditional-book-deal-through-self-publishing> (last accessed 24 April 2017).
Grabianowski, Ed, 'The Best Way To Break Into Science Fiction Writing Is Online Publishing', io9 website, 6 July 2009 <http://io9.gizmodo.com/5308518/the-best-way-to-break-into-science-fiction-writing-is-online-publishing> (last accessed 24 April 2017).
Howey, Hugh, *Wool* omnibus (London: Century, 2013).
Howey, Hugh, *Shift* omnibus (London: Century, 2013).
Howey, Hugh, *Dust* (2013).
Mandel, Judy, 'Getting a Traditional Book Deal After Self-Publishing', Jane Friedman website, 12 December 2012 <https://janefriedman.com/getting-a-traditional-book-deal-after-self-publishing> (last accessed 24 April 2017).
Rieder, John, 'On Defining SF, Or Not: Genre Theory, SF, and History', *Science Fiction Studies*, 37:2 (2010), pp. 191–209.
Sullivan, Michael J., 'About', Welcome to the Worlds of Michael J. Sullivan website <http://riyria.blogspot.ie/p/about.html> (last accessed 24 April 2017).
Tuttle, Lisa, 'Women in SF', in J. Clute, D. Langford, P. Nicholls and G. Sleight (eds), *The Encyclopedia of Science Fiction* (2015) <http://www.sf-encyclopedia.com/entry/women_in_sf> (last accessed 24 April 2017).

Cherie Priest: At the Intersection of History and Technology

Catherine Siemann

Cherie Priest was born in Tampa, Florida, in 1975, and grew up in various locations in the American South. As an adult, she moved to Chattanooga, Tennessee, earning an MA in Rhetoric/Professional Writing from the University of Tennessee at Chattanooga. From 2006 to 2012, she lived in Seattle, Washington, a significant location in her Clockwork Century novels, before returning with her husband, Aric Annear, to Chattanooga. She is the author of nineteen full-length works to date, starting with the Eden Moore series of Southern Gothic ghost stories, the first of which was *Four and Twenty Blackbirds* (2005). More recent works include the Borden Dispatches series, *Maplecroft* (2014) and *Chapelwood* (2015), which pit the notoriously acquitted late-nineteenth-century alleged axe murderer Lizzie Borden against Lovecraftian eldritch horrors. *The Family Plot* (2016) is a contemporary haunted house novel, set in Chattanooga, while *Brimstone* (2017) is a dark historical fantasy set during World War I.

I Am Princess X (2015), aimed at a young adult readership, combines traditional narrative with graphic novel elements. It tells the story of a young girl who, through a webcomic, finds evidence that her childhood best friend, supposedly killed in a car accident, might have survived after all. Priest has also written a number of standalone novels and a pair of urban fantasies, Cheshire Red Reports. Significantly, Priest is one of the most prominent second-generation authors of steampunk, a genre usually set either in the nineteenth century or in a culture evolving from it, where advanced steam-powered technology has opened up new problems and possibilities. It has also become an aesthetic, favoured by makers and tinkerers, alternative fashion designers and filmmakers. While the original steampunk novels were set in Victorian Britain, Priest has successfully translated the steampunk genre to American settings.

In this respect Priest is best known for her Clockwork Century steampunk series (2009–13, with a coda in 2015). Spanning the nation from Seattle to New Orleans, to Richmond, Virginia and Washington, DC, the series explores a world in which the American Civil War did not end in 1865. 'Stonewall Jackson survived Chancellorsville. England broke the Union's naval blockade, and formally recognized the Confederate States of America. Atlanta never burned.'[1] Consequently, the Civil War continued on into the 1880s. While the Clockwork Century novels contain a network of recurring characters, each has one or two distinct protagonists, who cover the spectrum of race, class and gender. They include a Union inventor and a Southern spy, a Seattle widow and her son's juvenile delinquent friend, a Confederate nurse and a couple of air pirates, one of them white and the other a former slave. The trappings of the steampunk subculture, goggles and airships included, are presented here with practical reasons behind them, while the extended war has led to the invention of new and deadly steam-powered war machines. Into this mix, Priest also manages successfully to juggle an environmental catastrophe that has caused the creation of 'rotters': zombies resulting from a massive toxic event. In the Clockwork Century, she has brought these elements together to create a full and satisfying extended narrative.

As noted, steampunk is simultaneously a genre, an aesthetic and a subculture, incorporating technology and aesthetics which extrapolate from the steam-powered technologies of the nineteenth century. It originated as the brainchild of a trio of Californian science fiction writers, and had a brief first flowering in the 1980s and early 1990s. Drawing on the aesthetic and imagination of Jules Verne and H. G. Wells, authors K. W. Jeter, James Blaylock and Tim Powers created romps set in an alternative nineteenth-century Britain filled with evil mad scientists and the clever inventor heroes who opposed them, in a world filled with high tea and just a taste of Dickensian squalor. In a letter to the editor of *Locus* magazine, Jeter suggested that Victorian fantasies such as these might well be the next big thing, and suggested the descriptive term 'steampunk' as a play on the then-cutting edge science fiction sub-genre cyberpunk. Perhaps inevitably, cyberpunk pioneers William Gibson and Bruce Sterling contributed to the new genre with *The Difference Engine*, published in 1990. Gibson and Sterling's work, positing a Victorian London in which Charles Babbage's mechanical computers had been successfully constructed in the 1830s, combined well-researched alternative history with dystopic speculation. But although *The Difference Engine* brought mainstream attention to steampunk, it did not immediately give rise to a host of imitators; steampunk's heyday came much later, starting in 2008. While a number of significant works after *The Difference Engine* contained steampunk elements or aesthetics, including Neal Stephenson's *The Diamond Age* (1995), Philip Pullman's *The Golden Compass* (1995) and China Miéville's *Perdido Street Station* (2000), it was not until the late 2000s that steampunk rose to prominence as a genre, or rather a sub-genre of science fiction.

But while steampunk fiction was relatively quiet, steampunk itself was shifting arenas. Makers and tinkerers, like Jake von Slatt and Datamancer, began exploring the aesthetics and creating artefacts from an imagined high-tech steam-powered world. Steampunk became a part of the Maker Faire and the Burning Man exhibitions, and *Steampunk Magazine* explored the genre from an anarchist perspective. Whether subculture, cosplay or alternative fashion, steampunk clothing, ranging from top hats and goggles to full Victorian dress, became an increasingly common sight at nightclubs and science fiction conventions alike. Movies like *The Wild Wild*

West (1999, a reimagining of the 1960s genre-crossing television series) and *The League of Extraordinary Gentlemen* (2003), as well as the French film *The City of Lost Children* (1995) and the Japanese anime *Steamboy* (2004) brought steampunk to the screen. Dedicated steampunk events like TeslaCon and the Steampunk World's Fair were launched, featuring bands, burlesque performers and performance artists self-identifying as steampunk.

The second wave of steampunk fiction was launched by the publication of Ann and Jeff VanderMeer's *Steampunk* anthology, in 2008. This collected short stories and excerpts from novels sharing the elements of steampunk, and in its wake a new group of steampunk authors came into their own. Many of them admitted they were unfamiliar with Jeter, Blaylock or Gibson and Sterling, but came to steampunk through the costumes, artwork and gadgets they had come across at Maker Faire or at science fiction conventions. Cherie Priest, Gail Carriger, George Mann, Scott Westerfeld, Pip Ballantine and Tee Morris have been among the most prominent of these second-wave steampunk authors. Steampunk has expanded its boundaries, from its early associations with science fiction and alternative technology, to include elements of the supernatural, mysteries and a sub-sub-genre of steampunk romance novels.

Second-wave steampunk was notable for its heroines, who were rarely constrained by the limits of Victorian society for more than a few introductory chapters. This is in contrast to the first wave; in a 1992 interview, Bruce Sterling had commented on the dearth of female roles in his text by saying, 'What the hell could you do when you were a woman in Victorian England?'[2] Now they were adventurous, inventive and unconventional, creating steam-driven technology and charting their own courses. However, other forms of diversity were often lacking; characters tended to be upper or middle class, and no matter their own countries of origin, many of these authors set their novels in Victorian England. One notable exception was Scott Westerfeld's young adult Leviathan trilogy. In an alternative World War I, the British have genetically engineered bioweapons and the Germans an equally impressive, but entirely mechanical, array of machineries of war, and the novels move across Europe, through the Middle East and Asia, and finally to the Americas. Cherie Priest has been the most successful at integrating a steampunk aesthetic with a North American setting, primarily the Pacific Northwest and the South.

Perhaps in keeping with its nineteenth-century setting, steampunk has been critiqued as being too often filled with an uncritical attitude towards the British Empire.[3] That has begun to change, both with social engagement within traditional steampunk, which I have called elsewhere the steampunk social problem novel,[4] and with the publication of anthologies like *Steampunk World* (2014), opening up steampunk to its global possibilities. *The SEA Is Ours: Tales from Steampunk Southeast Asia* (2015) focuses specifically on Southeast Asian locales and writers, while *Steamfunk* (2013) does the same with African-American authors and subjects. By the mid-2010s, steampunk had hit the mainstream. Costumes and props were now mass-manufactured, for those unable or unmotivated to craft and construct for themselves. Network television shows like *Castle* had incorporated steampunk into plots, and the aesthetic was no longer the property simply of a subculture or a fandom. The publishing industry may have overcommitted to steampunk; in 2013, the same year that Priest's final full-scale Clockwork Century novel was published, Mike Perschon remarked that 'the market was flooded with too much poorly-written steampunk', so that the genre itself began to fall into disfavour, a feeling that was widely held. However, in January 2016, Perschon said that more recent works had restored his faith in steampunk as a genre.[5] Its move into a broader global scale may provide steampunk with new life; if the second wave has crested, the third wave is still to come.

While Cherie Priest may not have had as much broad cultural impact as some authors discussed in this collection, she is significant as one of the most popular and prolific of the second-generation steampunk authors, and one whose work has served as an introduction to the genre for many readers. She is perhaps the first steampunk author to have an extended series set entirely in North America, with James H. Carrott calling 2009's *Boneshaker* 'the popular fiction poster-child for contemporary steampunk'.[6] Her impact has been tracked by John M. McKenzie in his examination of steampunk on Google Trends, where he notes that for the years 2009–12, there was a notable spike in steampunk popularity in the month of October, concurrent with the release of the first four books in the Clockwork Century series.[7] As noted, Priest is best known for this series. Beginning with *Boneshaker*, the series consists of *Clementine* (2010), *Dreadnought* (2010), *Ganymede* (2011), *The Inexplicables* (2012) and *Fiddlehead* (2013). Although the larger series arc concluded with *Fiddlehead*, in 2015 the novella *Jacaranda* provided a coda to the Clockwork Century.

Priest has said that when she first discovered steampunk, she was fascinated by the aesthetic and the subject matter. However, she was puzzled by the attitude she found among many participants in the Internet posting boards where steampunk was discussed, that is, the absolute determination that the setting should necessarily be Victorian Britain. In considering what were, to her, the primary characteristics of that period – colonialism, the Industrial Revolution, socioeconomic disparity and so on – she noted that all of these could also be found in the nineteenth-century US.[8] An interest in technology and an optimistic view of its potential were not confined to one side of the Atlantic, either. Thus, the Clockwork Century was conceived. The Civil War setting was new to steampunk (but had already become popular as a setting for alternative history novels like Harry Turtledove's *The Guns of the South* [1992]). In Priest's series the Union and the Confederacy share the space between Canada and Mexico with the Republic of Texas, with Western settlements awaiting the conclusion of the war in order to become part of the Union. (The map provided in Gibson and Sterling's *The Difference Engine* shows a very similar North America to Priest's, divided between the US, the Confederacy, the Republic of Texas and North-West Territories.) Priest stated, in an afterword to *Boneshaker*, that she has, at times, played fast and loose with timelines and other historical facts. 'I get so much hate mail from people complaining about how badly I've mangled history . . . I'm like, "really, you just went right past the zombies. And you were OK with that?"'[9]

Boneshaker, as the first of the series, carries the burden of defining this new world, both for those readers already familiar with steampunk as well as for others. Priest begins by showing us a world in the aftermath of disaster. The American Civil War is ongoing in 1880, and both Union and Confederates are suffering. While neither side shows signs of surrender, both are running short of manpower, armaments and food supplies, as well as the wherewithal to acquire them. Seattle, which had been a growing trading centre at the time of the Yukon Gold Rush, has been largely destroyed in a catastrophic accident, thanks to the invention of a drilling machine to be used in mining the frozen North. The inventor, Dr Leviticus Blue, called it the Incredible Bone-Shaking Drill Engine, but during its first demonstration the engine went amok and destroyed half the city, either by accident or in an attempt to raid the vaults of Seattle's banking district. In addition to undermining the city's structure, the Bone-shaker has released a subterranean gas that kills all who breathe it, and causes many to rise again as zombie-like 'rotters'. This wholesale environmental devastation 'serves as an amplification of the increasingly toxic environments created by the unregulated wastes of the Industrial Revolution' as well as paralleling the steampunk audience's fears of our looming twenty-first-century environmental catastrophe.[10]

In an attempt to contain the Blight gas released in the Boneshaker incident, Seattle has become a walled city, condemned as unsafe for human habitation. A small number of survivors, fugitives and ne'er-do-wells and Chinese immigrant labourers who have nowhere else to go have learned to adapt to the contaminated environment, wearing gas masks to keep from breathing in the toxins. Underground vaults and a nearly completed railway station have been adapted to become living quarters, sealed off from the Blight and made habitable by clean air pumped in from the outside. *Boneshaker* centres on Briar Wilkes, daughter of Sheriff Maynard Wilkes, hero to this underground Seattle population, and widow of Leviticus Blue, who was of course the perpetrator of the catastrophe. Briar has gone from being a wealthy society wife to a social outcast barely scratching out a living for herself and her son Ezekiel (Zeke), at the water purification plant on the still-inhabited Outskirts. When Zeke finds his way into the condemned city, hoping to find proof of his father's innocence, Briar follows him into this strangely transformed and rotter-infested underground city. The mysterious inventor and drug kingpin Minnericht, who moves to control Seattle, may or may not be Leviticus Blue in disguise; Briar must face him and uncover his secrets in order to rescue her son. At the novel's end, Briar is contemplating the future for herself and Zeke, but in subsequent novels we learn that they have settled in the underground city and that she has inherited her father's mantle, as Seattle's new sheriff.

The underground economy of Seattle depends largely on its one natural resource, the poisonous Blight gas, which is transformed into a drug called yellow sap. This drug is prized by soldiers on both sides of the ongoing Civil War for its euphoric effects, but it gradually accumulates in users' systems, ultimately transforming them into rotters. The realisation of the deadly risks involved with Blight gas, which both Union and Confederates are interested in weaponising, and with yellow sap, is the central preoccupation of the remainder of the series. *Dreadnought*, the third novel in the series, opens up the world of the Clockwork Century to encompass much of the North American continent, as nurse Mercy Lynch journeys from a Confederate hospital in Virginia to Seattle, via airship, riverboat and an armoured Union steam engine of gargantuan size and power, called the Dreadnought. Journeying through the Rockies, the Dreadnought encounters a superhorde of rotters created when Mexican troops marching on the Republic of Texas were involved in an accident with an airship carrying a cargo of Blight gas. Mercy, who has treated sap addicts, and seen their transformation, begins to make the connection between the symptoms. On her arrival in Seattle (where she has gone to be reunited with her long-lost father), she studies the effects of both Blight gas and yellow sap. In *The Inexplicables* we learn that Mercy has been sending the results of her studies to Captain Sally Louisa Tompkins, commander of the Robertson Hospital in Virginia, and in *Fiddlehead* Captain Sally attempts to warn the Confederate higher-ups of the risks, to no avail. Meanwhile, in *Ganymede* we learn that the rotters, locally termed *zombis*, have begun to appear in New Orleans.

The Inexplicables returns the narrative to Seattle, where Zeke Wilkes's erstwhile juvenile delinquent companion, the sap-dealer and addict Rector Sherman, has made his way into the walled city, seeking his fortune. He finds himself caught between the criminal empire of Yaozu, Minnericht's successor as yellow sap drug kingpin, and the more lawful underground dwellers known as Doornails, at a time when outside drug dealers are seeking to muscle in on Seattle's resources. Rector is the least sympathetic of the Clockwork Century's viewpoint characters, but gives the reader insight into the mind of a sap user, as well as providing an outsider's perspective on the now-familiar communities of the Seattle Underground. But while Seattle is facing a crisis from the outside, we have also seen the establishment of an airship dock within the city's walls, and the promise that postal and telegraph services will be returning to the abandoned city, now a frontier within the frontier. Briar Wilkes represents the return of law and order, while Mercy Lynch and Huojin, a young engineering genius, adapt medicine and technology to their environment.

The final full-length entry in the series, *Fiddlehead*, moves away from the Northwest, and back first to the Confederate capital in Danville, Virginia, and ultimately to Washington, DC, itself, where African-American genius inventor Gideon Bardsley has invented a Babbage-style proto-computer, the Fiddlehead, which is capable of complicated long-range calculations. The Fiddlehead has projected that the combination of Blight gas and yellow sap is going to lead to the inexorable defeat of both Union and Confederacy alike, unless something is done quickly. Just as Captain Sally is unable to convince the Confederate leadership that the threat is real, President Ulysses Grant finds himself equally unable to steer his own War Cabinet away from the use of weaponised Blight gas. Former Confederate spy turned Pinkerton agent Maria Boyd is hired by former President Abraham Lincoln (kept alive after the assassination attempt by a steampunk mechanical chair) to recover Mercy Lynch's letters to Captain Sally, from across Confederate lines, in order to convince the Union government to take the necessary steps. Interestingly, *Fiddlehead* differs from the other entries in the series not only because of its east coast setting, but also because it pulls largely away from the intertwined storylines that draw the protagonists of the other novels together. 'Belle' Boyd and airship captain Croggon Hainey, who also appears here, were the primary characters of the earlier novella, *Clementine*, and other characters make brief appearances or are referenced, but historical figures, particularly Grant and Lincoln, and also Frederick Douglass, Mary Todd Lincoln and others, inhabit the forefront of the narrative.

The Clockwork Century narrative is left somewhat uncertain at its end. Rogue capitalist Katherine Haymes, who has attempted to sell the weaponised Blight gas first to the Confederacy, and now to the Union, is defeated in the end, but the zombie apocalypse has not been deferred entirely. In the final scene, dated December 1880, Grant looks out at the electrified fence beyond the White House lawn, as 'a bright burst of sparks announced the demise of something human-shaped, but no longer human'.[11] Adaptation, rather than victory, seems to be the order of the day. In 2015's *Jacaranda*, a horror novella set in 1895 and mostly tangential to the Clockwork Century central narrative, we learn that the 'sap-plague' has run its course, with only a few remaining undead victims still wandering the wilderness.

This refusal to provide neat and tidy happy endings is one of the strengths of the series. Seattle is in the process of being rebuilt, but facing both established and new perils; although law has reappeared in the form of Briar Wilkes, Yaozu's drug trade continues, with the grudging acknowledgement that he, too, is good for Seattle. Rector Sherman may or may not fall back into the use of illicit drugs; he may choose Yaozu or the Doornails for his ultimate allegiance. And while *Jacaranda* lets us know the zombie plague is past, the main narrative leaves us with its resolution far from accomplished. The series, which is highly cinematic, both in its visual descriptions as well as its action-adventure storylines, also leaves space for more profound reflections on the margins of its somewhat frenetic plots.

Priest's series is exceptional for its thoughtful use of steampunk signifiers. As Priest told James Carrott:

> When it came to steampunk, it just didn't seem to have a mythology to account for all the minor tropes of it. It was a collection of things that people wore, or a collection of things that people watched or listened to. Like goggles, a gas mask . . . There's so much that's borrowed from fetish culture as well as Goth culture and the maker movement and the rest. And I wanted to give it a unifying mythology.[12]

While other second-wave steampunk authors simply dressed protagonists up in goggles and top hats, without much thought beyond conforming to the aesthetic, or assumed airship travel was present because it was a steampunk thing to have, Priest specifies reasons for the trappings. In *Boneshaker* alone, we learn that gas masks are used to survive in Seattle's contaminated air, that goggles are used to detect the poison gas outside the city's walls, and that protagonist Briar Wilkes wears an external leather corset as a back support for manual labour. The novel is full of various steampunked contraptions, from Jeremiah Swakhammer's noise-making disruptor gun, the Doozy Dazer (good for temporarily disabling rotters, long enough to make one's escape) to saloonkeeper Lucy O'Gunning's mechanical arm.

Airships, a steampunk constant, are everywhere here because they are practical in the wide-open landscape, and in particular for breaching the walls surrounding Seattle. Abraham Lincoln's mechanical chair, in *Fiddlehead*, keeps him alive after the encounter in Ford's Theater. Priest talks about researching patent archives in Chattanooga for 'crazy war machines . . . they were the most steampunk things I had ever seen . . . except they never happened, because they ran out of war'.[13] By creating an alternative history in which they do not run out of war, Priest is able to incorporate armoured steam engines, prototype submarines, Union and Confederate 'walkers' and many similar gadgets.

The Clockwork Century is also notable for representing the complexity of the times and places in which it is set. Priest's characters live in a diverse world but, unlike many steampunk characters, they share the prejudices and preconceptions of their time. In Seattle's underground, the otherwise likable Jeremiah Swakhammer is distrustful of the Chinese community; even the more accepting 'Doornails' refer to them as 'Chinamen' and regard them as Other, though many of them come around both to Chinese medicine and to Chinese cuisine over the course of the series. The Chinese community holds itself somewhat apart from both the Doornails and the drug traffickers, but two of the most significant figures, the drug kingpin, Yaozu, and the budding engineering genius, the teenaged Huojin, are Chinese. Native Americans are represented by the cross-dressing princess Angeline Sealth, daughter of the Duwamish chief after whom the city was named; Angeline points out that the other Natives are far too sensible to linger in the poisoned environs. As the Civil War has lingered on, most Southern states, with the exceptions of Mississippi and Alabama, have freed their slaves in order to recruit them as troops. African-Americans are represented by three major characters. Two are former slaves: the air pirate Croggon Hainey (in *Boneshaker*, *Clementine* and *Fiddlehead*) and the scientific genius Gideon Bardsley, inventor of the Fiddlehead computer. The third, the madam Josephine Early, in *Ganymede*, is one of the *gens de couleur libres* who live in the stratified society of New Orleans.

Mike Perschon, in writing about the 'steampunk new woman' in Priest's novels, has said: 'Unlike many steampunk writers, Priest doesn't cut corners laying the tracks for her alternate history: while her heroines are strong women, they don't live in a world of egalitarian emancipation'.[14] There are no girl geniuses or unreflectingly liberated women. When Briar Wilkes and Angeline Sealth wear men's trousers, it is for a reason, and it does not go unremarked upon by others. Belle Boyd must remove some of her voluminous petticoats to fit into an airship's ball turret. Josephine Early takes good care of her girls, but her position as a free woman of colour in New Orleans has set her life path on its inevitable course. Briar Wilkes evolves from wife of a wealthy, much older man, to struggling outcast, to sheriff of Seattle. Nurse Mercy Lynch, whose scientific acumen first pinpoints the connection between Blight, yellow sap and zombification, struggles to write the reports of her findings because of her limited formal education. Maria 'Belle' Boyd, former spy and current Pinkerton agent, transmits important information at crucial moments, despite her checkered history and shifting loyalties. And while drug kingpins Minnericht and Yaozu at least have their uses in Seattle's economy, industrialist Katherine Haymes, trying to capitalise on the company her father has left to her, is willing to rain destruction down on Atlanta and other major cities with the Blight gas her company plans to produce. The ultimate battle of the series is between Boyd and Haymes, suggesting the importance of women even in a society that restricts them.

Although the Clockwork Century is set outside the boundaries of Victorian Britain, it reflects much of what is most interesting about second-wave steampunk fiction. With its acknowledgement of social issues, combined with its action-packed storylines and its plentiful steampunked technology, but perhaps most crucially, its celebration of imperfection, Cherie Priest's steampunk series redefines the genre for the twenty-first century.

NOTES

1. According to the publicity outline for Priest's short story 'Tanglefoot' (2009), published online, which was the first work in the Clockwork Century universe.
2. Fischlin, Hollinger and Taylor (1992), 'The Charisma Leak', p. 12.
3. Carrott and Johnson, *Vintage Tomorrows*, pp. 184–5; VanderMeer, with Chambers, *The Steampunk Bible*, p. 213.
4. Siemann, 'The Steampunk Social Problem Novel'.
5. Perschon, 'Top Steampunk Reads of 2013'; Perschon, 'Top Steampunk Reads of 2016'.
6. Carrott and Johnson, *Vintage Tomorrows*, p. 72.
7. McKenzie, 'Clockwork Counterfactuals', pp. 138–9.
8. Carrott and Johnson, *Vintage Tomorrows*, p. 73.
9. Ibid., p. 77.
10. Siemann, 'The Steampunk Social Problem Novel', p. 12.
11. Priest, *Fiddlehead*, p. 366.
12. Carrott and Johnson, *Vintage Tomorrows*, p. 73.
13. Ibid., p. 75.
14. Perschon, 'Useful Troublemakers', p. 32.

KEY WORKS

Four and Twenty Blackbirds (2005). The first in Priest's three-book Eden Moore series of Southern ghost stories.

Boneshaker (2009). Briar Wilkes follows her teenaged son into abandoned Seattle, which has been walled off since a catastrophic event has filled the city with deadly gas; there she finds zombies, a surprising underground culture, and the answer to mysteries in her own past. Winner of the Locus Award for Best Science Fiction Novel.

Clementine (2010). Ex-Southern spy Belle Boyd, now a Pinkerton agent, teams up with former slave turned air pirate Croggon Haney in pursuit of a stolen dirigible and some dangerous technological secrets.

Dreadnought (2010). Nurse Mercy Lynch travels across the North American continent from Virginia to Seattle via airship, riverboat and steam engine in order to reunite with her estranged father; along the way, she encounters a deadly outbreak which may be related to a strange new drug popular on the battlefields of the American Civil War, now in its second decade.

Ganymede (2011). Madame Josephine Early calls upon an old lover, airship pirate Andan Cly, to help the Union by rescuing a submersible boat which could turn the tide of the war.

The Inexplicables (2012). Orphan and drug addict Rector Sherman finds his way into the walled city of Seattle and finds that the seemingly abandoned city is not what he expected.

Fiddlehead (2013). Genius and former slave Gideon Bardsley has invented a proto-computer called the Fiddlehead, which is predicting catastrophe; President Grant and former President Lincoln join forces with a former Confederate spy to save the world.

Maplecroft (2014). Acquitted alleged axe murderess Lizzie Borden versus unspeakable Lovecraftian horrors.

Jacaranda (2015). A mechanised, haunted hotel on an island off the Texas coast draws a group of people there in the wake of a deadly storm; set some years after the Clockwork Century series proper, it gives us glimpses into how things concluded.

I Am Princess X (2015). Priest's first young adult fiction is a hybrid of graphic novel and traditional text, about a teenaged girl who suddenly discovers that her dead friend's online comics are everywhere; and that her friend may still be alive.

FURTHER CRITICAL READING

Bowser, Rachel A. and Brian Croxall (eds), *Like Clockwork: Steampunk Pasts, Presents and Futures* (Minneapolis: University of Minnesota Press, 2016).
Brummett, Barry (ed.), *Clockwork Rhetoric: The Language and Style of Steampunk* (Jackson: University of Mississippi Press, 2014).
Carrott and Johnson, *Vintage Tomorrows*.
Taddeo, Julie Anne and Cynthia J. Miller (eds), *Steaming into a Victorian Future* (Lanham, MD: Scarecrow Press, 2013).
VanderMeer with Chambers, *The Steampunk Bible*.

BIBLIOGRAPHY

Carrott, James H. and Brian David Johnson, *Vintage Tomorrows: A Historian and a Futurist Journey Through Steampunk into the Future of Technology* (Sebastopol, CA: O'Reilly Media, 2013).
Fischlin, Daniel, Veronica Hollinger and Andrew Taylor, 'The Charisma Leak: A Conversation with William Gibson and Bruce Sterling', *Science Fiction Studies*, 19 (1992), pp. 1–16.
McKenzie, John M., 'Clockwork Counterfactuals: Allohistory and the Steampunk Rhetoric of Inquiry', in Barry Brummett (ed.), *Clockwork Rhetoric: The Language and Style of Steampunk* (Jackson: University of Mississippi Press, 2014), pp. 135–58.
Perschon, Mike, 'Top Steampunk Reads of 2013', *The Steampunk Scholar*, 27 December 2013 <steampunkscholar.blogspot.com> (last accessed 21 August 2017).
Perschon, Mike, 'Top Steampunk Reads of 2016', *The Steampunk Scholar*, 31 January 2016 <steampunkscholar.blogspot.com> (last accessed 21 August 2017).
Perschon, Mike, 'Useful Troublemakers: Social Retrofuturism in the Steampunk Novels of Gail Carrier and Cherie Priest', in Julie Anne Taddeo and Cynthia J. Miller (eds), *Steaming into a Victorian Future* (Lanham, MD: Scarecrow Press, 2013), pp. 21–41.
Priest, Cherie, *Boneshaker* (New York: Tor Books, 2009).
Priest, Cherie, *Clementine* (Burton, MI: Subterranean Press, 2010).
Priest, Cherie, *Dreadnought* (New York: Tor Books, 2010).
Priest, Cherie, *Fiddlehead* (New York: Tor Books, 2013).
Priest, Cherie, *Four and Twenty Blackbirds* (New York: Tor Books, 2005).
Priest, Cherie, *Ganymede* (New York: Tor Books, 2011).
Priest, Cherie, *I Am Princess X* (New York: Arthur A. Levine Books, 2015).
Priest, Cherie, *Jacaranda* (Burton, MI: Subterranean Press, 2015).
Priest, Cherie, *Maplecroft* (New York: Roc Books, 2014).
Priest, Cherie, *The Inexplicables* (New York: Tor Books, 2012).
Siemann, Catherine (2013), 'The Steampunk Social Problem Novel', in Julie Anne Taddeo and Cynthia J. Miller (eds), *Steaming into a Victorian Future* (Lanham, MD: Scarecrow Press, 2013), pp. 3–19.
VanderMeer, Ann and Jeff VanderMeer (eds), *Steampunk* (San Francisco: Tachyon, 2008).
VanderMeer, Jeff with S. J. Chambers, *The Steampunk Bible* (New York: Abrams Image, 2011).

About the Contributors

Clare Clarke is Assistant Professor of Nineteenth-Century Literature at Trinity College Dublin. She has published widely on crime and detective fiction. Her first book, *Late Victorian Crime Fiction in the Shadows of Sherlock* (Palgrave Macmillan, 2014), was winner of the HRF Keating Prize. Her second book, *The Rivals of Sherlock Holmes*, will be published by Palgrave in 2018.

Brian Cliff is Assistant Professor in the School of English at Trinity College Dublin, where he has also directed the Irish Studies degree. His recent publications include essays on John Connolly and on Deirdre Madden; *Synge and Edwardian Ireland* (Oxford University Press, 2012), co-edited with Nicholas Grene; and a reprint of Emma Donoghue's *Hood* (Harper, 2011), co-edited with Emilie Pine. He co-organised 'Irish Crime Fiction: A Festival' in November 2013 with eighteen leading Irish and Irish-American crime novelists. He is currently working on a survey of Irish crime fiction for Palgrave, and a monograph about community and contemporary Irish writing.

Dara Downey has been a lecturer in English at Maynooth University, and University College Dublin, and currently lectures in the School of English, Trinity College Dublin. She is the author of *American Women's Ghost Stories in the Gilded Age* (Palgrave, 2014) and co-editor of *Landscapes of Liminality: Between Space and Place* (Rowman and Littlefield, 2016). She is editor of the *Irish Journal of Gothic and Horror Studies* (online) and Vice-Chair of the Irish Association for American Studies, as well as a founding member of the Irish Network for Gothic Studies. She is currently working on a monograph on servants and slaves in American uncanny fiction.

Kate Harvey is a postdoctoral teaching and research fellow in Children's Studies at the National University of Ireland, Galway, where she teaches courses on children's literature and film, and children and the creative arts. Her research interests include adaptation for children, Shakespeare in children's media, and theatre for young audiences. She is also a regular reviewer of children's books for Children's Books Ireland and iBbY Ireland.

Clare Hayes-Brady is a lecturer in American Literature at University College Dublin and the author of *The Unspeakable Failures of David Foster Wallace* (Bloomsbury Academic, 2016; paperback 2017). Her PhD focused on communication in the work of David Foster Wallace. Other research interests include: the interaction of literature with film; transatlantic cultural heritage; performative sexuality (both normative and queer), resistant gender modes and the history of burlesque; digital humanities and modes of transmission; adolescence in contemporary fiction; and dystopian narrative.

Gerard Hynes has taught on the MPhil in Popular Literature and MPhil in Children's Literature at Trinity College Dublin. He is co-editor of *Tolkien: The Forest and the City* (Four Courts Press, 2013) and has published on fantasy and the theory and practice of world-building, especially in the works of J. R. R. Tolkien and China Miéville. He has recently contributed to *Revisiting Imaginary Worlds: A Subcreation Studies Anthology* (Routledge, 2017) and *The Routledge Companion to Imaginary Worlds* (forthcoming).

Rebecca Janicker is Senior Lecturer in Film and Media Studies at the University of Portsmouth. She is the author of *The Literary Haunted House: Lovecraft, Matheson, King and the Horror in Between* (McFarland, 2015) and the editor of *Reading 'American Horror Story': Essays on the Television Franchise* (McFarland, 2017). Other publications have focused on the Gothic fictions of Robert Bloch, Stephen King, Richard Matheson and H. P. Lovecraft, as well as on adaptations of horror for film and comics.

Stephen Kenneally received his PhD from Trinity College Dublin in 2016 for a thesis exploring the emergence and changing representation of LGBT characters in fantasy novels in the period 1987–2000, entitled 'Queer Be Dragons'. His research interests include queer theory, fantasy, genre theory, LGBT history and immersive performance. He is currently working on articles about constructed fictional terms for homosexuality in fantasy and about AIDS representation in fantasy novels, and has recently published a chapter in *Gender and Sexuality in Contemporary Popular Fantasy* edited by Jude Roberts, Esther MacCallum-Stewart (Routledge, 2016) on the difficulties of locating texts in non-evident or hidden literatures.

Jarlath Killeen is a lecturer in Victorian literature in the School of English, Trinity College Dublin. His most recent monograph is *The Emergence of Irish Gothic Fiction* (Edinburgh University Press, 2014).

Ian Kinane is Lecturer in English Literature at the University of Roehampton. He is the author of *Theorising Literary Islands* (Rowman and Littlefield, 2016) and co-editor (with Dara Downey and Elizabeth Parker) of *Landscapes of Liminality: Between Space and Place* (Rowman and Littlefield, 2016). He is currently preparing an edited collection on didactics and the modern Robinsonade for young readers, as well as a manuscript on Ian Fleming, James Bond and British-Jamaican cultural relations. He is also the editor of the *International Journal of James Bond Studies*.

Stephen Matterson is Professor of American Literature in the School of English at Trinity College Dublin, and a Fellow of the College. He has published widely on US literature, with emphasis on twentieth-century poetry and literature of the mid-nineteenth century. In addition to a series of co-edited collections of essays, his book publications include *American Literature: The Essential Glossary* (Edward Arnold and Oxford, 2003), and *Melville: Fashioning in Modernity* (Bloomsbury Academic, 2015).

Bernice M. Murphy is Assistant Professor in Popular Literature in the School of English, Trinity College Dublin, and a Fellow of the College. She is also director of the MPhil in Popular Literature. She has published extensively on topics related to popular literature and popular culture. Her books include *The Suburban Gothic in American Popular Culture* (AIAA, 2009), *The Rural Gothic: Backwoods Horror and Terror in the Wilderness* (Palgrave Macmillan, 2013), *The Highway Horror Film* (Palgrave Pivot, 2014) and the textbook *Key Concepts in Contemporary Popular Fiction* (Edinburgh University Press, 2017). She is the co-founder of the online *Irish Journal of Gothic and Horror Studies* and is a founding member of the Irish Network for Gothic Studies (INGS).

Keith O'Sullivan is Senior Lecturer in the School of English, Dublin City University, prior to which he was head of English at the Church of Ireland College of Education. He has co-edited (with Padraic Whyte) *Children's Literature and New York City* (Routledge, 2014) and (with Valerie Coghlan) *Irish Children's Literature and Culture: New Perspectives on Contemporary Writing* (Routledge, 2011). In 2013 he was co-recipient of a major Government of Ireland/Irish Research Council award to establish the foundations of a national collection of children's books.

Tara Prescott is Lecturer in Writing Programs and Faculty in Residence at the University of California, Los Angeles. She is the author of *Poetic Salvage: Reading Mina Loy* (Bucknell University Press, 2016), editor of *Neil Gaiman in the 21st Century* (McFarland, 2015), co-editor (with Aaron Drucker) of *Feminism in the Worlds of Neil Gaiman* (McFarland, 2012) and co-editor (with Michael Goodrum and Philip Smith) of *Gender and the Superhero Narrative* (University Press of Mississippi, 2015). Her TEDxUCLA talk, 'Hike Your Own Hike', is available on YouTube.

Hannah Priest is Associate Lecturer at Manchester Metropolitan University. Her research focuses on the intersections of sex, violence and monstrosity in medieval and contemporary popular culture. She has published a number of articles on the Twilight series and YA paranormal romance, including chapters in *The Gothic World*, edited by Glennis Byron and Dale Townshend (Routledge, 2013) and *The Modern Vampire and Humanity*, edited by Deborah Mutch (Palgrave Macmillan, 2013). She is the editor of *The Female of the Species: Cultural Constructions of Evil, Women and the Feminine* (Inter-Disciplinary Press, 2013) and *She-Wolf: A Cultural History of Female Werewolves* (Manchester University Press, 2015).

Kate Roddy is an occasional lecturer, tutor and seminar leader at Trinity College Dublin and Open Education, Dublin City University. Her research interests include sixteenth-century literature and comic book studies. She has published on: heresy and martyrdom; Marian literature; gender and sexuality within comic book fandom; and authorship and metafiction in the works of Grant Morrison.

Jim Shanahan is a lecturer in the School of English, Dublin City University. His main interest is in eighteenth- and nineteenth-century Irish fiction. He reads Terry Pratchett for pleasure and enlightenment.

Catherine Siemann directs the Writing Centre at the New Jersey Institute of Technology and has a PhD in Victorian literature from Columbia University. The combination of studying nineteenth-century literature and teaching STEM students has led to an interest in steampunk, which she has published on in *Steaming into a Victorian Future*, edited by Julie Anne Taddeo and Cynthia Miller (Rowman and Littlefield, 2013), *Ada's Legacy*, edited by Robn Hammerman and Andrew Russell (ACM Press, 2016) and *Like Clockwork: Steampunk Pasts, Presents, and Futures*, edited by Rachel Bowser and Brian Croxall (University of Minnesota Press, 2016). Current research interests also include Mary Shelley, Ada Lovelace and writing centre studies.

Kirsten Tranter publishes fiction and criticism and is the author of three novels, most recently *Hold* (HarperCollins, 2017). She completed a PhD at Rutgers University on English Renaissance poetry, and has taught literary studies and creative writing with a special interest in questions of genre and the boundaries of the literary at the University of California, Berkeley, the University of Technology, Sydney, and other institutions. She is a co-founder of the Stella Prize for Australian women's writing.

Index